Social States

PRINCETON STUDIES IN
INTERNATIONAL HISTORY AND POLITICS

SERIES EDITORS

G. John Ikenberry and Marc Trachtenberg

A list of titles in this series appears at the back of the book.

Social States

CHINA IN INTERNATIONAL INSTITUTIONS, 1980–2000

Alastair Iain Johnston

PRINCETON UNIVERSITY PRESS

PRINCETON AND OXFORD

Library of Congress Cataloging-in-Publication Data

Johnston, Alastair I.
Social states : China in international institutions, 1980–2000 / Alastair Iain Johnston.
    p.   cm.   (Princeton studies in international history and politics)
Includes bibliographical references and index.
ISBN 978-0-691-05042-3 (hardcover : alk. paper)
ISBN 978-0-691-13453-6 (pbk. : alk. paper)
1. International relations—Sociological aspects. 2. China—Foreign relations—1976-.
3. Socialization—China. 4. Social interaction—Political aspects—China. 5. International
cooperation. 6. Security, International. I. Title.
JZ1251.J64 2008
355′.0310951—dc22   2007023205

British Library Cataloging-in-Publication Data is available

This book has been composed in Sabon

Printed on acid-free paper. ∞

press.princeton.edu

Printed in the United States of America

10 9 8 7 6 5 4 3 2 1

Contents

Acronyms

ACD	arms control and disarmament
ACDA	Arms Control and Disarmament Agency
AMS	Academy of Military Sciences
APEC	Asia Pacific Economic Cooperation
APL	anti-personnel landmine
ARF	ASEAN Regional Forum
ASEAN	Association of Southeast Asian Nations
ASEM	Asia-Europe Meetings
BAS	Beijing Area Study
BMD	ballistic missile defense
BJP	Bharatiya Janata Party
BWC	Biological Weapons Convention
CAEP	China Academy of Engineering Physics
CASS	Chinese Academy of Social Sciences
CBM	confidence building measures
CCCW	Convention on Certain Conventional Weapons
CCP	Chinese Communist Party
CD	Conference on Disarmament
CDSTIC	China Defense Science and Technology Information Center
CFCs	chlorofluorocarbons
CIA	Central Intelligence Agency
CICIR	China Institute of Contemporary International Relations
CITES	Convention on International Trade in Endangered Species
CMC	Central Military Commission
CNP	comprehensive national power
COS	Conference of the States
COSTIND	Commission on Science, Technology, and Industry for National Defense
CSBM	confidence and security building measures
CSCAP	Council on Security Cooperation in the Asia Pacific
CSCE	Commission on Security and Cooperation in Europe
CTB	comprehensive test ban
CTBT	Comprehensive Test Ban Treaty
CW	chemical weapons

CWC   Chemical Weapons Convention
DOD   Department of Defense
DPRK   Democratic People's Republic of Korea
ECJ   European Court of Justice
EEP   experts/eminent persons
EIF   entry into force
EMP   electromagnetic pulse
EU   European Union
FAO   Foreign Affairs Office
FCCC   Framework Convention on Climate Change
FPPC   Five Principles of Peaceful Coexistence
GAD   General Armaments Department
GDP   gross domestic product
GSD   General Staff Department
IAPCM   Institute of Applied Physics and Computational
           Mathematics
ICBL   International Coalition to Ban Landmines
ICRC   International Committee of the Red Cross
IDSS   Institute of Defence and Strategic Studies
IGO   inter-governmental organization
IIS   Institute of International Studies
IMF   International Monetary Fund
IO   international organization
IR   international relations
ISG   intersessional support group
ISIS   Institutes of Strategic and International Studies
ISM   intersessional meeting
IUCN   International Union for the Conservation of Nature
IWEP   Institute of World Economics and Politics
KMT   *Kuomintang*
MIRV   multiple independently targetable reentry vehicles
MOFA   Ministry of Foreign Affairs
NATO   North Atlantic Treaty Organization
NDU   National Defense University
NFU   no first use declaration
NGO   non-governmental organization
NPT   Non-proliferation Treaty
NTM   national technical means
ODA   overseas development assistance
OLS   ordinary least squares
OSCE   Organization for Security and Cooperation in Europe
OSI   on-site inspection
P-5   Perm-Five

PD	prisoners' dilemma
PII	Protocol II (landmines protocol)
PKO	peacekeeping operations
PLA	People's Liberation Army
PNE	peaceful nuclear explosion
POW	prisoner of war
PRC	People's Republic of China
PSNSS	Program on Science and National Security Studies
PTBT	Partial Nuclear Test Ban Treaty
RMB	renminbi
ROK	Republic of Korea
SCS	South China Sea
SDI	Strategic Defense Initiative
SEA	Southeast Asia
SIT	social identity theory
SLBM	submarine launched ballistic missiles
SOM	Senior Official Meeting
START	Strategic Arms Reduction Talks
TAC	Treaty of Amity and Cooperation
TMD	Theater Missile Defense
UN	United Nations
UNCHR	United Nations Commission on Human Rights
UNDP	United Nations Development Programme
UNGA	United Nations General Assembly
UNSSOD	United Nations Special Session on Disarmament
USSR	Union of Soviet Socialist Republics
WTO	World Trade Organization

Acknowledgments

IN THE MANY (too many!) years during which I have been working on this project, I have become indebted to a great number of people. First, Felicity Lufkin, who is really quite fine for any number of reasons, helped me through a second book and through much, much more. Second, I am thankful to the 120-plus interviewees from the Chinese, US, Canadian, Singaporean, and Japanese governments who graciously allowed me to ask them about Chinese diplomacy in security institutions. Most of them requested that I not use their names due to the sensitivity of the subject. I am also grateful to Anastasia Angelova, James Perry, Jeff Panton, Laura Dodge, Matt Stephenson, Michael Griesdorf, Theresa McNiel, Victor Shih, and Jennie Johnson for the terrific research assistance they supplied over the years. I would also like to thank the following individuals for comments, criticisms, and help along the way: Allen Whiting, Amitav Acharya, Banning Garrett, Bates Gill, Bonnie Glaser, Brad Roberts, Brian Knapp, Chen Zhiya, Chris Chyba, Chris Wing, David Sedney, David Wright, Donica Pottie, Dunbar Lockwood, Evan Medeiros, Frank Von Hippel, George Bunn, George Lewis, Gwen Kutz, Harlan Jencks, Hiro Katsumata, Jean-Marc Blanchard, Jeff Checkel, Jeff Legro, Jim Fearon, Josh Handler, Julia Bentley, Karen Brookes, Karl Eikenberry, Lisbeth Gronlund, Marty Finnemore, Mary Tighe, Mark Moher, Michael Nacht, Michael Pillsbury, Paul Evans, Paul Godwin, Peter Almquist, Peter Katzenstein, Ralf Emmers, Robert Ross, Ron Montaperto, Samuel Kim, Scott Sagan, Ted Postol, Todd Rosenblum, Tom Christensen, Wang Yizhou, Wendy Frieman, Will Lowe, Wu Baiyi, Yuan Ming, and Zhang Tuosheng. I received very useful feedback on various ideas in this book from participants at the MIT Security Studies seminar, the security seminar at Stanford's Center for International Security and Cooperation (CISAC), Harvard's Weatherhead Center for International Affairs ethics seminar, the Sociological Institutionalism seminar at Stanford, the Summer Symposium on Science and World Affairs, the China Defense Science and Technology Industry Information Center, the Institute of Applied Physics and Computational Mathematics, the China Foundation for International and Strategic Studies, UPENN Dartmouth project on East Asian International Relations, and the ARENA project on socialization in European institutions. Special thanks go to Professor Yuan Ming at Peking University for inviting me to be a visiting scholar at Peking University in 1996. Much of the initial interviewing about China's arms control foreign policy process was done during my time at her institute. I am also very grateful to Scott Sagan for inviting me to spend time at CISAC in 1998 and 1999, where I learned a great deal about my topic and other topics from interacting with its collection of first-rate scholars. My deep thanks as well to Barry Desker, Amitav Acharya, Kwa Chong Guan, and other colleagues at the Institute of Defence and Strategic Studies in Singapore for providing an excellent environment within which to work on this manuscript in 2003.

This book is dedicated to the memory of my fine father, Antony Miles Johnston, and to my dear mother, Margot Lampman Johnston, for gamely tolerating my interest in China. It is also dedicated to my teachers, Harold Jacobson and Michel Oksenberg, whose work on China's participation in international institutions was pioneering in both the IR and the China fields. Their passing is a huge loss to both fields. But more important it is a loss of two really fine people. Finally, the book is dedicated to my two loves, Felicity and Kali.

Preface

THIS BOOK starts from a very simple and unoriginal premise: actors who enter into a social interaction rarely emerge the same. More specifically, actors' behavior that prior to social interaction tended to diverge may converge as a result of this social interaction.[1] It tests the implications of this premise for cooperation in international relations by looking at an empirical puzzle: why would Chinese foreign policy decision makers—for the most part socialized in a relatively hard realpolitik strategic ideology, operating in an era of overwhelming and potentially threatening US power after the end of the cold war, and not offered obvious positive or negative material incentives—agree to cooperate in security institutions that did little to enhance China's relative power, and indeed had potential to do damage to its relative power interests?[2]

For mainstream international relations theories, this starting premise is at one and the same time an uncontroversial statement and a rather radical one. It is uncontroversial because mainstream IR accepts that social interaction can change behavior through the imposition of exogenous constraints created by this interaction. Thus, for instance, structural realists claim that the imperatives of maximizing security in an anarchical environment tend to compel most states most of the time to balance against rising power. Contractual institutionalists also accept that social interaction inside institutions can change the behavior of diverse actors in cooperative directions (e.g., changed strategies) by altering cost-benefit analyses as different institutional rules act on fixed preferences.

It is a radical starting point (at least for mainstream IR theory, but not for political science in general) if one claims that the behavior of actors

---

[1] By "convergence" I do not mean cooperation. I mean "increasing similarities" in basic characteristics of action. Actors' behavior can become increasingly similar and increasingly conflictual (as neorealists argue happens through "selection" in an anarchical environment). Nor do I use the term, as Botcheva and Martin do, to mean the isomorphism of state public policies as a function of participation in international institutions (Botcheva and Martin 2001).

[2] Of course, this is a puzzle only if one starts with standard realist assumptions that realpolitik actors operating under conditions of anarchy and facing more powerful states should be worried above all about preserving and enhancing their relative military power. It is not a puzzle if one does not start with this assumption. There should be, by now, plenty of skepticism in IR about the empirical and theoretical validity of this starting assumption, but the fact is that these assumptions still tend to define what the field considers "normal" and thus what the field considers puzzling. So this is where I start.

converges because of endogenous change in the normative characteristics and identities of the actors, or because of social identity–based, nonmaterial desires to conform. Put differently, convergence in the behavior of the participants in a social interaction may often have little to do with exogenous constraints and a lot to do with socialization (Wendt 1994: 384). This is, essentially, the claim made by those promoting the "sociological turn" in IR theory.

This book, then, is about socialization, and it is about whether socialization helps explain China's cooperation in major security institutions in the 1990s that had a potentially constraining effect on its relative power. More to the point, it proceeds from the constructivist claim that social interaction in international relations can affect actor interests in such a way as to then change the fundamental characteristics of the normative structures that constitute the world political system. Even more to the point, it looks at a critical but understudied link in this claim, namely the link between the presence of particular normative structures at the international level and the constraining effect of these norms on the behavior by the actor/agent at the unit level (whether the state or non-state actor level). Specifically, the book explores three microprocesses—mimicking, persuasion, and social influence—and examines how these work in cases of China's participation in a selection of international security institutions such as the United Nations' Conference on Disarmament in Geneva, the ASEAN Regional Forum and associated regional multilateral security dialogues, the Comprehensive Test Ban Treaty, and the anti-personnel landmine regimes.

The conclusion of the book is, in brief, that there is considerable, if subtle, evidence of the socialization of Chinese diplomats, strategists, and analysts in certain counter-realpolitik norms and practices as a result of participation in these institutions. Together with my earlier arguments about the origins of realpolitik norms and practices in Chinese history (Johnston 1995, 1996), I believe that this evidence casts doubt on a materialist explanation for realpolitik norms and practices rooted in the effects of international anarchy.

Constructivism, as Jeff Checkel has rightly point out, has been enamored by the sociological institutionalists' claim about the isomorphism in the norms and practices in world, regional, and local politics, but has not been very successful in explaining the microprocesses (Checkel 1998; Finnemore 1996a). For an approach whose central causal process is socialization, constructivist research thus far has been relatively quiet about how precisely actors are exposed to, receive, process, and then act upon the normative arguments that predominate in particular social environments. Yet, the ontology of social constructivism should point researchers squarely in the direction of these microprocesses: the susceptibility of structures to minor perturbations, contingencies, nonlinearity, and path dependence set in motion by the conscious reflection and action of agents of change (e.g., ideas or norms entrepreneurs) all mean that it may indeed matter a lot, when explaining state behavior, how small groups, even individuals, are socialized through social interaction with other small groups and individuals in other states (and non-state entities).[3] Put simply, the value-added of the sociological turn in the international relations subfield rests heavily on showing what socialization microprocesses look like, how they are supposed to work, and whether they matter in a very common-sense way: whether they produce behavior—cooperative or conflictual— that would have been different had the actor not been exposed to the socialization processes in the first place.

To date, constructivism has only just begun to focus on socialization processes from the perspective of the "socializee." To be sure, this situation is changing with the emergence of some excellent detailed research on socialization processes in various European institutions. But it is still generally accurate to say that constructivist-oriented or -influenced research has not said much about how socialization works and why there are variations in the degree or completeness of socialization. And, of course, the new research that has looked at these questions in some detail has been limited to European institutions (and mostly not security institutions) where the empirical evidence needed for such detailed microprocess analysis is abundant relative to most other regions of the world.

Is there space for socialization arguments in IR theory? And if so, what would socialization arguments might have to look like to fill this space, that is, to ask questions central to the discipline that are unasked or badly or simplistically asked? Put differently, is there, implicitly or explicitly, a "demand" for socialization arguments? There is certainly empirical space created by other social sciences. There are healthy and robust research programs and cumulative empirical findings in social psychology, sociology, and political socialization on socialization processes of individuals and groups. But little of this has made it into IR theory.

There is also plenty of theoretical space in IR for socialization arguments. Realist theories say that socialization in the anarchical international environment is a key explanation for realpolitik practice. But realist socialization, in fact, is not socialization either in any standard social science definition or in any common use language sense; it is selection. It cannot account for the fact that many key actors are socialized into non-realpolitik practices and yet survive quite well under so-called anarchy. The democratic peace and democratic security community arguments are cases in point.

---

[3] For an excellent discussion of this ontology, see Cederman 1997.

Contractual institutionalism is right to point out that so much of state behavior goes on inside international institutions, which as Keohane even suggested, can serve as social environments (Keohane 1984). He comes to this conclusion from the observation that so much of a state's behavior can change through long-term involvement in institutions. But as contractual institutionalism has evolved, it primarily sees institutions as exogenous rule-based, sanction-based constraints on non-changing agents.

Socialization is central for constructivists, of course. Indeed it is, in a sense, the one process concept in IR that is uniquely constructivist.[4] But, as I will argue in chapter 1, constructivists have mainly focused on correlational analysis that suggests how ideas and identity "matter." In this respect, constructivism has been in a stage of development similar to contractual institutionalism a few years ago, keen to show theoretical plausibility, but less worried about how or why or to what degree ideational variables matter.

Finally, there is also a great deal of policy space for socialization arguments. After all, governmental and non-governmental diplomacy is often an effort to persuade, shame, cajole, and socially "pressure" states to change their collective minds and behavior. The concept of engagement, as assessed historically by Schweller, is at base one of a number of strategies toward rising major powers, in addition to balancing/containing, bandwagoning, and accommodating, but one aimed at changing the non–status quo elements of a rising power's strategy through the use of cooperative diplomatic measures (Schweller 1999). Certainly one can find this implied socialization assumption in the diplomacy of various states aimed at "engaging" China. One element of ASEAN engagement policy toward China has been an effort to "socialize" China into the rules of regional normative order (the so-called ASEAN way and its codes of conduct). One of the goals of Japan's ODA to China has been to turn China into a "responsible major power," "with self-awareness to contribute to the security and prosperity of the new international community after the end of the Cold War as well as of the East Asian region" (Kojima 2001).

---

[4] I do not want to leave the impression from this discussion that I believe various forms of realism, contractual institutionalism, and constructivism are alternative theories of cooperation. I do not consider constructivism a theory. Rather, like Wendt, I view it as an approach that can bundle a distinctive ideational ontology together with a wide range of extant "middle-range theories" about human and group behavior. Most fundamentally, like game theory, it lacks a basic foundational assumption about what motivates action. So this book is not about realism versus institutionalism versus constructivism as though these were three roughly equivalent theories of international relations. Rather it tests the plausibility of a set of explanations about cooperation, under the rubric of socialization, that are fundamentally different from arguments that derive from various versions of realism and contractual institutionalism.

The Clinton administration's strategy of constructive engagement was, for some, aimed at pulling China into the "international community," and exposing it to new norms of the market and domestic governance.[5] The policy was challenged by skeptics of engagement in Washington precisely because, in their view, it has failed to socialize China; that is, it failed to bring China into this putative "international community."[6]

But how precisely socialization is supposed to work through a diplomacy of engagement has never been all that clear, whether practiced by ASEAN, Japan, or the United States. It would seem worthwhile, then, to take seriously as a topic for academic inquiry a process that actual practitioners of international relations have believed is a reality in their world.

There is, then, lots of space to treat institutions as social environments. This means viewing microprocesses unique to social interaction that endogenously affect actor interest, preferences, and/or identities.

One useful way of exploring the phenomenon of socialization is through the study of China's participation in international institutions. Let me explain. The genesis of this study is, in part, my previous work on strategic culture (Johnston 1995, 1996b). It, too, reflected an effort to wrestle with the basic claim at the heart of mainstream IR theory, namely that anarchy and material power distributions are fundamentally determinative of the frequency and type of conflictual behavior in IR. My first book, then, was an effort to contribute to this debate, to see if indeed strategic cultures existed, if they did how would one know it, and if one could observe them, did they affect strategic behavior independently of anarchical material distributions of power under anarchy?

What I found, contrary to my initial expectations,[7] was that Chinese strategic culture in the Ming dynasty, as embodied in classical texts on

---

[5] See, for instance, the statements by various members of the Clinton administration: William Perry, "U.S. Strategy: Engage China, Not Contain," *Defense Issues* 10:109 at http://www.defenselink.mil/speeches/1995/s19951030-kaminski.html; Samuel Berger, "A Foreign Policy Agenda for the Second Term," Center for Strategic and International Studies, Washington, DC, March 27, 1997, at http://www.whitehouse.gov/WH/EOP/NSC/html/speeches/032797speech.html; Assistant Secretary of State Stanley O. Roth, "U.S.-China Relations on the Eve of the Summit," World Economic Forum, Hong Kong, October 14, 1997, at http://www.state.gov/www/policy_remarks/971014_roth_china.html; and Secretary of State Albright in "The U.S. and China," for *Diario Las Americas*, Miami, Florida, July 5, 1998, at http://secretary.state.gov/www/statements/1998/980705.html. Moderates in the Bush administration essentially endorsed a similar language about socializing China into a putative international community.

[6] For a representative example of the socialization discourse used even by critics of engagement, see Waldron 2001.

[7] The long-standing conventional wisdom is that China possessed a unique strategic culture that stressed defensiveness, anti-militarism, pacifism, and an official ideology of security based on magnanimity toward adversaries at peak points in relative power. The roots of

strategy and as manifested in strategy toward Mongol "threats," was a hard realpolitik one. In that period of history, Chinese strategic culture demonstrated a number of traits: the environment was considered to be highly conflictual; potential adversaries were described in zero-sum terms; offensive uses of force were considered highly efficacious, especially when relative power was favorable. And, there was an explicit axiom that strategy should flexibly respond to changing power circumstances free of political or moral restraints. There was indeed a strategic culture but a realpolitik one. Moreover, Ming strategy toward the Mongols reflected this realpolitik strategic culture. Ming strategists basically stressed that conflict with the Mongols was inevitable, that offensive strategies were best, and defensive or accommodationist strategies were useful only when relative power prevented the Ming from going on the offensive. Not surprisingly, then, the Ming rulers were more offensive strategically in the first seventy-five or so years of the dynasty. As power waned after this, strategies shifted to defensive and accommodationist ones. In short, as it turned out, the Ming read realpolitik texts, thought like realpoliticians, and acted like realpoliticians.[8]

Contrary to many readings of the book, it did not make an essentializing argument about a *Chinese* strategic culture across time. Nor was it an argument about the relationship between big C culture on the one hand and strategy on the other. It was emphatically not an argument about an inherent collective personality of the Chinese people. Rather it made an argument about the socialization of Chinese decision makers in particular periods of time (in this case, in the Ming dynasty) into a hard realpolitik strategic culture, a strategic culture that was and is not necessarily ethnoterritorially bounded. As a socialization argument it held out the possibility that decision makers exposed to other strategic cultures could be socialized in alternative understandings of how to achieve security. In other words, it was an argument about strategic culture, not an argument about Culture and strategy.

Colleagues and critics who contended that material structures or material incentives and disincentives fundamentally structure the strategic choices of states read the book and said, in essence, "Thanks. You've developed procedures for extracting strategic culture from texts, analyzing effects on decision makers, and then analyzing effects on behavior, and in a society where the claims about the content of strategic culture

---

this were in early Chinese political philosophy, associated mainly with Confucian-Mencian thought: security was best achieved through beneficence, moral government, and enculturation, not force.

   [8] In retrospect, given how the word "culture" tends to conjure up essentialized visions of groups, perhaps strategic ideology would have been a better term.

should lead to behaviors very different from dominant neorealist arguments, you come up with details about the ideational constructs that realpoliticians develop. All you've done is to show in more detail how strategic culture is epiphenomenal to power realities of anarchy. End of story." And, some would add, "even if strategic culture is not epiphenomenal, when two hypotheses make the same predication, parsimony is the tiebreaker. And on these grounds, material structural explanations clearly are more parsimonious."

Needless to say, I am not yet willing to make these concessions. I have three reasons. First, there is no a priori reason to believe an ideational account of realpolitik is epiphenomenal to a material structural account. This has been a standard materialist realist assumption—that ideational variables may help explain deviant cases, but they cannot explain non-deviant cases. Yet logically, one does not follow from the other. There is no reason why ideational variables cannot also explain so-called normal or expected international behavior. To make this standard materialist realist claim, one would have to believe that there are arenas of human political and social activity that are "idea-less," or where perceptions/worldviews do not matter. This would require, then, a theory of why these are turned off when exogenous conditions are consistent with realist theory and turned on when they are not. I do not believe any version of realism has successfully developed such a theory.

Second, constructivists should be especially interested in making the ideational case for realpolitik. To this point, they have staked their claim to relevance by focusing mostly on what mainstream realist theories would call deviant cases or irrelevant cases (humanitarian intervention; weapons taboos; democratic norms in alliance cooperation; the development of European identity; norms of democratization or human rights; among others). But to question material realism and its variants requires reexamining cases and phenomena that materialist realism claims to explain. So there is no reason yet, until ideational arguments for realpolitik go nowhere,[9] for ceding realpolitik explanations to standard realist theories.

Finally, when two explanations make the same prediction, parsimony should not automatically be a tiebreaker. The parsimonious explanation may still be wrong. Rather the first response should be a critical test—spin out additional empirical implications that are competitive and see which set holds up.

---

[9] That is, arguments that treat realpolitik as a learned norm. See, for instance, Vasquez's (1993) claim along these lines. See also Rousseau's (2002 and 2006) very important work on the belief systems that underpin realpolitik preferences.

The present book, then, is broadly speaking a critical test: If realpolitik axioms embodied in realpolitik strategic cultures are epiphenomenal to anarchical structures, then they should not change as long as an anarchical material structure and its conflictual effects persists. If, on the other hand, realpolitik strategic cultures *are* independent of the anarchical materials structure, and are learned, absorbed for instance through exposure to key discourses and reinforced by experience, then they are, in principle, mutable or changeable. So, do realpolitik ideational structures change? How and under what conditions? And how would one test for this?

Here contemporary China provides a useful set of cases for exploring the plausibility of socialization arguments. Constructivists have posited that international institutions in particular are often agents of counter-realpolitik socialization. They suggest that there is a causal link between the presence of particular normative structures embodied in institutions and the incorporation of these norms in behavior by the actor/agent at the unit level. For one thing, the interaction with activists, so-called norms entrepreneurs, is most likely inside institutions. For another, social conformity pressures are more concentrated inside institutions. Third, inside institutions, interaction among agents on specialized issues and exchanges of specialized information are sustained and intense. Finally, institutions often have corporate identities, traits, missions, normative cores, and official discourses at odds with realpolitik axioms. So, for example, some arms control institutions expose actors to an ideology where interalia: multilateral transparency is better than unilateral non-transparency; disarming is better than arming as a basis of security; cooperative security is better than unilateral relative power strategies for achieving state security; and evidence of cooperative potential is greater than evidence of fixed conflictual environment. All of these axioms challenge aspects of realpolitik ideology.

So, if there is any counter-realpolitik socialization going on, it ought to be happening in international institutions. But to test this, ideally, one needs a state where the predominant security ideology prior to involvement in institutions is at a maximum distance from that of the institutions (e.g., hard realpolitik, unilateralist). One also needs a "novice" state (socialization, after all, often refers to the process of inducting newcomers such as youths, immigrants, recruits, new states) into the membership norms and practices of a social group. In particular, one needs a tabula rasa state that then becomes rapidly involved in international institutional life. China is such a state.[10] Its strategic elites since 1949 have been social-

---

[10] It is important to note that I usually use "China" as a shorthand for China's foreign policy decision makers or policy officials and representatives. As is clear from the main chapters, the unit of analysis is individuals and small groups. "China" is often more convenient than "Chinese officials with the most influence on foreign policy decision X."

ized in the hard realpolitik of Marxism-Leninism, modern Chinese nationalism, and, for Mao at least, elements of classical strategic thought. It has been one of the most dispute-prone major powers from 1949 to the 1980s (after the United States). Until 1980, it was essentially uninvolved in international institutions, arms control or otherwise. But by the late 1990s, its participation rates were not significantly different from other major powers, and, in comparison to its level of development, it was overinvolved.

The notion of using China's participation in international institutions in the late twentieth century as a critical test of my arguments developed from a study of Ming strategic culture was not, of course, the only inspiration for this project. Another was a dissatisfaction with the absence of details about how precisely one could actually observe the socialization processes that constructivism claims are continuously at work in world politics. I am not an international relations theory architect. I see myself as an engineer. I need to understand how one applies the theories and claims and arguments produced by constructivism's architects (Wendt, Ruggie, Finnemore, Katzenstein, Kratochwil, Meyer, Onuf, and Hopf, among others). How does one do empirical work if one is hoping to test constructivist arguments? When I began this project, there were not many engineers around.

I am relieved to find out just how many people shared my concerns about empirical processes.[11] In the past handful of years, a small number of detailed, process-oriented, richly descriptive, and inferential research on the conditions of socialization in international institutions have been published.[12] Some of this work has discovered processes and effects of social interaction inside institutions that accord with my findings in the Chinese case, as I will discuss in more detail later. However, almost all of this work has focused on European institutions. Scholars have focused either on the processes of socialization experienced by bureaucrats, managers inside various EU institutions, or on those experienced by novices to European institutions—the new entrants from various Eastern European countries, for example—as they are exposed to deliberate efforts by extant European institutions and their norms entrepreneurs to inculcate Eu-

---

[11] Jeff Checkel and Thomas Risse have been the most persistent and insightful in calling for greater attention to the empirical microprocesses of socialization.

[12] See, for instance, the special issue of *International Organization* (Fall 2005) on socialization in European institutions; the special issue of *Comparative Political Studies* (February–March 2003) on rationalist and constructivist approaches to understanding how the EU functions, especially Checkel 2003 and Lewis 2003; Hooghe's test of rationalist and constructivist explanations for EU officials' images of Europe (2002); Kelley's (2004) test of institutional conditionality and socialization explanations for change in minority policies in Eastern Europe; Schimmelfennig 2002; and Gheciu 2005.

ropean values and identity. Not that these are exactly easy cases or most likely cases, but for the most part, the objects of socialization—say, the bureaucrats moving from national socialization environments to international or supranational ones—express lower levels of resistance, and their material interests at stake are less frequently in the realm of "high" security politics than the China cases I examine in this book. On case selection grounds, then, testing hypotheses about socialization on Chinese participation in international security institutions predominantly in an era of unipolarity and on issues where material power interests are at stake can help strengthen the conclusions about socialization in this burgeoning literature on Europe.

This focus on China's behavior inside international (security) institutions is work built on the shoulders of many expert scholars in the field. Participation in international institutions has not been a major focus of Chinese foreign policy studies, despite the fact that some of the richest behavioral data about Chinese foreign security, economic, and cultural policy is found in the statements, votes, and behind-the-scenes interactions by Chinese diplomats inside these institutions. But there is a small and growing collection of very rich empirical research that is implicitly, sometimes explicitly, sensitive to socialization processes that can occur inside institutions.

Samuel Kim's pathbreaking body of work shows how from the 1970s to the present, China has moved from "system-transforming" to "system-reforming" to "system-maintaining" preferences inside the United Nations system. The persistence of free-riding behavior into the 1990s does not imply a fundamental desire to dismantle or radically overhaul the UN more to China's advantage. Not all of this shift in China's basic approach to UN institutions is a function of participation alone. As in much of China's diplomacy of the 1980s and 1990s, the driver has been domestically generated, a desire for rapid economic growth that benefits the legitimacy of Communist Party rule. But the system-maintaining preferences have also been anchored by multilayered material and ideational incentives and constraints, including diffuse image, that create new indifference curves linking interests that, in the past, were not connected (e.g., Kim 1999).

Harold Jacobson and Michel Oksenberg's pioneering study of China's participation in international economic institutions in the early 1980s showed how this led to organizational, ideational, and material responses in the Chinese foreign policy process that encouraged a deepening of China's engagement with the rest of the world. In some ways, their book anticipated some of the concepts of interest to constructivists. They described processes of change in Chinese diplomacy that are variants of mimicking, persuasion, and social influence. They note that participation in institutions can lead to greater cooperation as new domestic policy institutions are created to mediate interaction with the international institution (this has some similarities with mimicking). Or it can lead to cooperation because of the intensive interaction, often inside the international institution itself, between agents of the state and agents of the institution. This interaction, in turn, can lead to learning and internalizing the institution's norms (this resonates with propositions about persuasion).[13] Or it can lead to cooperation because of the rewards and penalties offered by the institution (Jacobson and Oksenberg 1990:6).[14]

Likewise, Pearson shows that those in the Chinese policy process most extensively interacting with officials from the World Bank and IMF are those who are most committed to transparency in policy making and to exchange rate predictability (Pearson 1999:224). Cooperation has been elicited by a range of foreign policy goals: from concerns about maintaining an image as a "team player" to heading off the use of economic coercion against China to using international commitments as a lever against opponents to more fundamental domestic economic reform (Pearson 1999b).

Elizabeth Economy's work on China's participation in environmental institutions such as the Framework Convention on Climate Change process shows that, while overall conservative pro-development organizational interests eventually came to dominate the policy process, the repository of more proactive views on China's role in reducing greenhouse gases was among scientists in environmental research institutes who interacted most intensively with Western climate change specialists (Economy 1994).

Ann Kent's study of China's approach to international human rights regimes shows how, within the broad goal of minimizing threats to the rule of the Communist Party, China's diplomacy in this realm has been constrained in part by an acceptance of procedural norms of participation inside institutions, and by a sensitivity to multilateral praise and blame (Kent 1999).

The common thread in much of this work is that the persistence of realpolitik-derived concerns about preserving sovereignty and autonomy has been moderated in certain instances either by changes in definitions

[13] They show, for instance, how Chinese participation in the IMF and World Bank helped to spread Ricardian economic concepts inside the Chinese policy process (Jacobson and Oksenberg 1990:143–44).

[14] They did not differentiate between material and social incentives. For another excellent, more recent, study of how precisely participation in less high-profile institutions (educational, for instance), mediated by the nature of China's local bureaucratic political structures, created positive incentives for greater participation in global economic and cultural processes, see Zweig 2002.

of interest or by linking realpolitik interests to other values, such as image and status, in new policy trade-offs. There appears to be a common recognition across these works that China's socialization inside these institutions is a "work in progress"—fragile, and susceptible to the deeply ingrained hyper-sovereigntist crisis response mechanisms of a regime with shaky legitimacy.

As a general rule, however, the work on China's multilateral diplomacy has only just begun to tap into theories and methods offered by the international relations field. The concept of socialization tends to remain undefined, the separate microprocesses through which social processes can constrain behavior left unclear. There is, at times, an implicit assumption that socialization is teleological, that progress toward acceptance of an institution's pro-social norms is socialization, while regression is evidence for the absence of socialization.[15]

This book does not radically challenge the flavor of the arguments of this burgeoning literature on China's participation in institutions. Indeed, it is not surprising that a literature rooted in the rich analyses of one country—local knowledge, so to speak—has a more constructivist feel to it than more general IR treatments of cooperation in institutions. Area

---

[15] Often the causal arguments explaining variation in the quantity and quality of China's cooperation are not clearly differentiated, and the implications for broader disciplinary and even policy questions about the conditions for conflict and cooperation are left underaddressed. Moore and Yang suggest, for instance, that a hybrid concept of "adaptive learning" best accounts for evidence of both minimax cooperation and genuine preference change (Moore and Yang 2001:228). Admittedly, learning is a slippery term in IR theory. But it is also clear that, conceptually, adaptation and learning are fundamentally different microprocesses. To put it metaphorically, adaptation refers to tactical shifts in cooperation, say, by a player with prisoners' dilemma preferences, as the exogenously imposed relative costs of defection increase (say, through the offer of side payments or the threat of sanctions). Learning, however, is most usefully viewed as a change in the basic preferences of the player, a shift away from one type of preferences through intensive socialization processes (which could shift preferences in either more cooperative or more conflictual directions). Although in practice these causal processes may be sequenced, they need not be, and they need to be kept analytically separate because they have very different explanations for cooperation and for its durability. Adaptation in the context of a prisoners' dilemma game suggests that once exogenous incentives change, players will move back to the old pattern of opportunistic defection. Learning suggests that cooperation can be sustained even as the material incentives dissipate. Though I do not use the learning versus adaptation framework in this book, it roughly maps onto the differences between persuasion and social influence. As I point out in the book, the institutional designs conducive to these different processes are not the same. Thus, whether an actor's cooperation is a function of learning (persuasion) or adaptation (social influence) implies very different policy prescriptions about institutional design. For more details on my distinction between learning and adaptation, see Johnston 1996b:31–33. For a summary of the learning theory literature, see Levy 1994. For a discussion of the sequencing of strategic and nonstrategic causes of behavioral change, see Jupille, Caporaso, and Checkel 2003:22–23.

specialists can be more attuned to the important nuanced changes in policy discourses and outputs that are not easily coded into the typologies typical in the discipline. Many are predisposed to be sympathetic, if only implicitly, with a theoretical approach that ontologically leans toward historical contingency and intensive endogeneity in social and political processes.[16] Rather this book tries to refine, clarify, and test more systematically the social processes that might lie behind changing levels of cooperation, and to show how IR theory both illuminates and benefits from the intensive study of China's international relations, in particular China's policy toward international security institutions.[17]

The book begins with a review of the status of socialization in various clusters of theory in the international relations subfield today. It then outlines three microprocesses of socialization—mimicking, social influence, and persuasion.

Mimicking explains pro-group behavior as a function of borrowing the language, habits, and ways of acting as a safe, first reaction to a novel environment: "I will do X because everyone seems to be doing X and surviving. So, until I know better, X is what I will do." But by doing X, the actor can fall into habits of discourse and practice that constrict its options down the road. It is not the same thing as a rational search for successful exemplars (what can be called emulation).

Social influence explains pro-group behavior as a function of an actor's sensitivity to status markers bestowed by a social group, and requires some common understanding in the social value the group places on largely symbolic backpatting and opprobrium signals: "I should do X because others believe X is the appropriate thing to do and I will be rewarded socially for doing so." The chapter then develops some simple hypotheses about how different institutional designs should be conducive to different kinds of socialization processes, and then justifies the research design choices I have made, noting why China's participation in international security institutions in the 1990s, primarily, is a good initial test of these three microprocesses.

Persuasion explains pro-group behavior as an effect of the internalization of fundamentally new causal understandings of an actor's environment, such that these new understandings are considered normal, given,

---

[16] But not all. There is a tradition in area studies of sweeping cross-temporal, primordialist generalizations about an area as well. Some of the most vigorous "orientalizing" has been done by area specialists. For a nice statement of the argument that good theory testing and development rests on good local or area knowledge, see Christensen 1998.

[17] Thus far, the vast majority of work on China in multilateral institutions has focused on economic and environmental institutions, not security institutions. For exceptions, see Johnston 1986, 1996b; Medeiros and Gill 2000; and Medeiros 2006.

and normatively correct: "I should do X because it is good and normal for me (us) to do so."

Chapters 2 through 4 then look separately at each of these microprocesses and some least likely cases that appear to offer some initial confirmation of the plausibility of various forms of socialization. They then outline some additional empirical implications that one might expect to see if the causal claims in the main cases are correct. The chapters move from most to least "rationalist" of these microprocesses.

Chapter 2 looks at mimicking and how the mere fact of having to participate in some of the first major international arms control institutions, such as the Conference on Disarmament in which Chinese diplomats participated, led the PRC to adopt in limited fashion the habits, language, and even organizational models of arms controllers in these institutions. Before a clear security "interest" in participation developed, the PRC found that in order to participate in any meaningful way, it had to adopt some of the more common forms of participation.

Chapter 3 looks at social influence, the impact of social backpatting and opprobrium on cooperation. The main cases are the Chinese decision to sign the CTBT and the Protocol II of the Conventional Weapons Convention. In both instances, the military and economic costs of signing were not trivial. In both cases, signing was not induced by material incentives or disincentives. In both cases, there is considerable evidence that diffuse image—the desire to minimize opprobrium costs—weighed heavily on Chinese leaders as they calculated the costs of these agreements.

Chapter 4 looks at evidence for persuasion as a social process that helps account for the development of a limited, protomultilateralist discourse and practice, especially among those most directly involved in regional security institutions such as the ASEAN Regional Forum. It finds that although some of the multilateralist discourse has been hijacked by those who see multilateral institutions as potential anti-US tools, the original sources of this discourse came from extensive and intensive interaction in regional institutions (the ARF and related processes) whose designs were conducive to persuasion.

The tests in these chapters are eclectic ones. They are designed to explore the plausibility of these three microprocesses under fairly tough case selection conditions, and then to explore other empirical extensions. The chapters can be read mostly as stand-alone chapters, so the reader is welcome to skip one or more or read them in any particular order. The point is not to test which of the three microprocesses best explains Chinese cooperation in international institutions. Rather the goal is to show how each works.

Before getting to the substantial part of the book, I want to note at the start what this book does not claim. First, it does not claim that through socialization in international institutions *all* Chinese leaders and officials have fundamentally changed their strategic culture(s) or ideologies, and have abandoned realpolitik for notions, say, of cooperative security. As will be evident, I am making more limited claims—albeit within the context of hard or least likely cases—about how under certain conditions certain parts of the decision-making process have been weaned away from realpolitik calculations of maximizing relative power. Put differently, there is now greater tension within the PRC's overall diplomatic thinking and practice between harder realpolitik and softer idealpolitik than ever before. But I am not arguing that multilateralism, say, has supplanted realpolitik as the predominant ideational construct behind China's foreign policy.

Second, this is not a book about constructivism versus rationalism, where the "logics of appropriateness" trump the "logics of consequences" in all cases. As is evident, at least two of the socialization microprocesses I will discuss could fall within the "rationalist" paradigm (mimicking and social influence)—an actor is, roughly speaking, maximizing some utility by choosing alternatives that appear to increase the probability of meeting some goal. In the case of mimicking, survival is being maximized by copying the group. In the case of social influence, self-perceptions of status are being maximized through interaction with other humans. Where I part from most versions of rationalism, however, is that these rationalisms are social, not material. Only persuasion entails a process that might fall clearly within the rubric of the logics of appropriateness, where socialization leaves actors with new definitions of self that provide self-evident and normal notions of expected behavior. The reality is that socialization, broken down this way, does not fit neatly into either a constructivist or a rationalist approach.

Social States

CHAPTER 1

Socialization in International Relations Theory

THE STATUS OF SOCIALIZATION IN INTERNATIONAL RELATIONS THEORY

Socialization is quite a vibrant area of inquiry in a range of social sciences. It is a core concept in studies in linguistics and the acquisition of language (Schieffelin and Ochs 1986), sociology and social psychology and theories of in-group identity formation and compliance with group norms (Turner 1987; Napier and Gershenfeld 1987; Cialdini 1987; Nisbett and Cohen 1996), political science and the acquisition of basic political orientations among young people or explanations of social movements (Beck and Jennings 1991), international law and the role of shaming and social opprobrium in eliciting treaty compliance (Chayes and Chayes 1996; Young 1992, Susskind 1994; Moravcsik 1995), and anthropology and the diffusion of cultural practices, among other fields and topics. It is gradually becoming a more vibrant area in world politics as well, since socialization would seem to be central to some of the major topics in international relations theory today: preference formation and change;[1] national identity formation; the creation and diffusion of, and compliance with, international norms; the effects of international institutions, among other topics.

It is curious, though, how undertheorized socialization has been in much of IR, despite the fact that most noncoercive diplomatic influence attempts by most actors most of the time are aimed at "changing the minds" of others, at persuading, cajoling, or shaming them to accept, and hopefully internalize, new facts, figures, arguments, norms, and causal understandings about particular issues. That is, the goal of diplomacy is often the socialization of others to accept in an axiomatic way certain novel understandings about world politics.[2] Especially in the second half

---

[1] This is particularly relevant when trying to explain how new states, "novices," decide on the content and institutional structure of their foreign policies, not an unimportant topic when looking at the effects of decolonization or the collapse of the Soviet empire.

[2] As Nadelmann remarks in the context of prohibition regimes, "The compulsion to convert others to one's own beliefs and to remake the world in one's own image has long played an important role in international politics—witness the proselytizing efforts of states on behalf of religious faiths or secular faiths such as communism, fascism, capitalism, and democracy (1990:481).

of the Clinton administration, for example, the engagement of China was seen as a way of teaching Beijing about allegedly predominant norms and rules of international relations (free trade; nonuse of force in the resolution of disputes; nonproliferation; multilateralism, etc.). The engagers spoke of bringing China into the "international community" (defined normatively), an enculturation discourse if ever there was one. So even if, in the end, many attempts to use diplomacy to effect the internalization of new ways of thinking and behaving fail, it still makes sense to try to explain why actors (state and non-state) engage in this kind of activity in the first place. But of course, we do not really know how many of these attempts do fail because we have not really tried to define, isolate, and measure the effects of socialization processes in IR.

This is not to say that predominant IR theories ignore the concept of socialization entirely. Classical realism seems torn between its impulse to essentialize the drive for power in a self-help world on the one hand and its sensitivity to historical contingency on the other. Morgenthau, for example, does not rule out the possibility that actors internalize group norms of behavior such that action takes on a "taken-for-grantedness." Indeed, he laments the disappearance of a time in European interstate relations when individual kings and absolute rulers heeded certain norms of behavior for fear of the social punishments from violation (e.g., shame, shunning, loss of prestige and status) (Morgenthau 1978:251–52). He even leaves open the possibility that definitions of power and interest are culturally contingent, implying at least that there is variation in how actors are socialized to conceptualize legitimate ways of pursuing legitimate interests. But if so, it is not clear how actors are socialized into or out of perceptions of the world as competition for power and influence in an anarchical system. In other words, by accepting the cultural contingency of power and interests, logic would suggest that Morgenthau would have to accept that the realpolitik impulses that characterize world politics are in fact not given, but learned. Yet for classical realists there is no obvious theory of socialization to explain radical variations in interpretations in the meaning of power and interest.

This is true as well for so-called neoclassical realism (Rose 1997). Rejecting the structural realist critique of reductionism, this scholarship has (re)discovered that subjective and intersubjective interpretations of power and interest matter in explaining the behavior of states and thus international outcomes. Yet it also persists in arguing that there are unchanging universal facts about international life that constrain state behavior, namely that international relations are a realpolitik struggle among self-interested, security-seeking, relative power-sensitive states operating in anarchy. I am not clear how you can have it both ways: once you allow for independent causal importance of subjective or intersubjective interpretations of the external world, you open the door to the possibility that there can be vast disjunctures between estimates of this world and the "real" world of material power distribution and realpolitik pursuits of interest. That is, you open the door to the possibility that subjective and intersubjective interpretations of the world can change even as the realities of material power distribution remain constant. If this possibility can exist, then, in principle, the real world has a less independent, predictable effect on actor behavior. As such, the "realities" of anarchy and relative material power imbalances are no longer so determinative. If so, these realities are not likely to be important independent sources of actor preferences or beliefs about the external world. This is clearly not where the neoclassical realists want to end up. Moreover, this conclusion then begs the question of where these preferences and beliefs come from. Neoclassical realism has no answer, or at least none that flows logically from realist theor(ies). Thus, it has no theory of socialization.

Neorealism uses socialization to describe the homogenization of self-help balancing behavior among security-seeking states interacting under conditions of anarchy (Waltz 1979:127–28). But the use of the term is problematic. First, the process of homogenization is not really socialization in commonsense usage. While Waltz uses an example from crowd psychology to argue that interaction in groups can create a "collective mind" across individual members (1979:75), his discussion of interaction in IR essentially drops the collective mind image and replaces it with a "selection and competition" image. It is emulation and selection that leads to similarities in behavior of actors through interaction: states that do not emulate the self-help balancing behavior of the most successful actors in the system will be selected out of the system such that those remaining (assuming there are no new entrants into the system) will tend to share realpolitik behavioral traits.[3] It is unclear as to whether the theory assumes states will also share epiphenomenal realpolitik foreign policy ideologies, because the theory is unclear as to whether states are conscious agents pursuing balancing outcomes or simply unconscious participants in the creation of unintended systemic balances. That is, it is not clear whether social interaction in anarchy leads to emulation or mimicking.[4]

[3] For a sophisticated discussion of the neorealist concept of emulation, see Resende-Santos 1996. For an acknowledgment of structural realism's tendency to describe competition, rather than socialization, see Thies 2001:2.

[4] I differentiate between emulation and mimicking in the following way: emulation involves the conscious, careful search for exemplars and success stories, a dissection of the reasons for their success, and the application of these lessons to the maximization of some specific expected utility. Thus, it involves internalizing, as well, the causal models of the way the world works that exemplars themselves use to maximize their utility. Thus, to emulate a successful balancer in an anarchical environment means also to share its realpolitik "worldview," its cause-effect understandings. Mimicking involves copying what most other

In any event, it is simply not empirically obvious that this kind of selection even occurs. It is hard to pick exemplars in world politics due to the uncertainty about what constitutes success under the security dilemma. It seems odd to claim that uncertainty about relative power drives states to look for successful balancers, but that apparent uncertainty does not make it difficult to identify who in fact are the appropriate exemplars out there.[5] What lessons should a state draw from the collapse of the Soviet Union? That deterrence and containment work against threatening or rising power? Or that transnational arms control coalitions successfully socialized a group of influentials in the Soviet Union to adopt cooperative security strategies under the rubric of "new thinking," despite US military pressure? Both the United States and the Soviet Union balanced against each other. One failed, one succeeded. How, then, do state actors decide whether or not balancing is a successful strategy in IR worthy of emulation? As Dan Reiter has argued, historical experience in alliances, rather than some search for obvious transhistorical exemplars, is often the criteria states use when deciding when and what type of balancing is appropriate (Reiter 1996).

Neorealism, then, exaggerates the structural pressures toward homogenization. Often different states do not sit in competition with each other over scarce resources; rather, some find "niches" where the requirements for survival are different, hence, their different traits can survive side by side without some selection pressures toward homogenization.[6]

For another, the death rates of states have declined dramatically in the twentieth century. Unsuccessful actors—those that eschew self-help, that fail to balance internally or externally—tend not to disappear anymore (Fazal 2001). New states have emerged in the latter half of the twentieth century in an era when failed or unsuccessful states are not routinely eliminated. These new states presumably retain heterogeneous traits and characteristics, supported in some respects by institutions and rules analogous to those that support socially weak and failed individuals in many domestic societies. That is, it is not obvious that the "fitness" of states has in-

---

actors in a social environment do in the absence of a conscious, calculated search for any one exemplar utility maximizer. Rather copying is done by a novice seeking a relatively efficient way of surviving in an uncertain and new environment prior to a sophisticated search for information about the most successful, exemplar utility maximizer.

[5] Farkas makes a similar point (1998:34).

[6] This is an important feature of evolution that neorealism's rendition misses. As a somewhat useful comparison here, Darwin's finches showed that two species can develop sufficiently different survival needs (e.g., the food for especially small finches is not substitutable for the food for especially large ones) and that these needs do not leave them in competition over similar resources. Thus, there is less competition over who is fittest, and hence one species does not tend to eliminate or crowd out the other. See Weiner 1994.

creased over time, given a constant anarchical environment—at least not fitness defined in terms of an ability to balance successfully. Somehow the international system has allowed "unfit" states to develop a range of strategies for surviving without self-help balancing—norms against aggression, arms control agreements, a concept of sovereignty that "equalizes" unequal actors, among others.[7] This being the case, the characteristics of the system structure must, by definition, be much more varied and complex than the simple tending-toward-balances anarchy of a neorealist world. Thus, the social environment in which these new states are socialized must be not only one that rewards or selects states that copy "successful" self-help balancers, but one that may also reward or support "deviant" heterodox behavior. If so, then so much for the homogenizing effects of social interaction—socialization—in anarchy (see Kocs 1994).

Second, most uses of socialization refer to a process of preference formation and/or change. Child socialization involves a child developing tastes, likes, dislikes—social and material—through social interaction first with the family and then broader social groups. Political socialization usually refers to the acquisition by young people of political orientations and preferences from parents or peers. For neorealism, however, socialization appears to have little to do with preferences and interests. Perhaps this stems from the microeconomic language and analogizing that Waltz uses—economics generally models preferences as stable, while different environments (institutions, price, supply, productivity, etc.) constrain the ability of actors to achieve preferred outcomes. In any event, for neorealism, material structure (what passes for a social environment for neorealism) is the key constraint on state behavior. Socialization simply results in a greater awareness by actors of the costs of pursuing preferences that neglect the structural imperative of balancing. That is, socialization means that states acquire a greater sensitivity to signals emanating from the material structure about who succeeds and who fails and why. The interpretation of this information should be relatively unproblematic for rational unitary actors—successful states balance, unsuccessful states do not. But the process by which an actor comes to read these signals correctly does not involve change in the nature of the actor—its identity or preferences or understandings of the nature of the international system. So it is hard to see why it should be called socialization.[8]

---

[7] History matters here. Many of these norms and practices that protect the survival of "unfit" states evolved in the twentieth century out of movements for self-determination and the diffusion of the principle of sovereign equality into the postcolonial world. My thinking here has been informed by Brenner's helpful discussion of the distinction between evolutionary algorithms and learning processes in explaining social evolution (1998).

[8] As Wendt puts it, Waltz's use of the term "socialization" is surprising, given there is no social content to neorealism's concept of structure—it is the product of material power factors, *not* the product of the nonmaterial traits and characteristics (identities and prefer-

Finally, for neorealism socialization can go in only one direction—toward the convergence of behavior around realpolitik norms of behavior. This rules out the possibility of system-level socialization in non-realpolitik directions. Yet there are sufficient and substantively interesting deviations from neorealist claims—cases of norm-conforming behavior in the absence of obvious material threats or promises—to suggest that there are domestic and systemic normative structures that socialize actors (Kier 1997; Finnemore 1996b; Price and Tannenwald 1996; Price 1998). Indeed, one could legitimately question whether material structure plus anarchy does any socializing at all, given the empirical frequency of non-balancing behavior (Reiter 1996; Schweller 1994; Schroeder 1994; Johnston 1998b). Moreover, whatever realpolitik socializing that does go on is, arguably, not dependent on structural anarchy, but on prior realpolitik norms, the sources of which may reside at both the system and unit levels (Johnston 1996a, 1998a).

Contractual institutionalism generally does not focus on socialization processes per se in IR. For many contractual institutionalists, true to their microeconomic and game theoretic styles of analysis, the notion that social interaction can change preferences and interests or fundamental security philosophies and ideologies is not a central concern. Modeling is usually done assuming these things are fixed. Social interaction inside institutions is assumed to have little or no effect on the identities or interests of actors (or institutionalists are divided as to whether there are any effects).[9] That is, actors generally emerge from interaction inside institutions with the same attributes, traits, and characteristics with which they entered. These characteristics have no effect on the attributes, traits, or characteristics of the institution itself—an efficient institution in principle should reflect the nature of the cooperation problem, not the nature of the actors themselves—and these characteristics, in turn, have no impact

---

ences) of the interacting units. Thus, socialization becomes convergence of behavior around balancing and relative gains concerns, not the convergence of actor attributes (e.g., identities, preferences, and interests) (Wendt 1999). Although socialization in common usage does include the convergence of behavior around socially preferred models or exemplars, the process usually involves some degree of internalization of these exemplars such that they become normatively taken for granted, and thus elicit pro-social behavior in the absence of material constraints (rewards and punishments).

[9] I am grateful to Celeste Wallander for pointing out to me some of the divisions over institutions and preferences in the contractualist camp. Wallander allows for variation in interests but argues that institutions do not cause this variation (see Wallander 1999). Other contractualists claim to the contrary that interests can be changed through involvement in institutions, mainly via complex learning. Explicating this learning process ought to be high on the institutionalist research agenda (see Keohane 1984:132). But it not clear what the causal mechanisms would be, nor whether the process would be endogenous to the institution itself or a function of shifting domestic coalitions.

on actor identities. Iteration, the intensity of interaction, the provision of new information about the beliefs of other actors, and so on, do not seem to have any effect on the basic preferences of actors. Being enmeshed in an iterated but potentially finite PD does not make the D,C payoff less desirable, in principle. Whether social interaction is short run or long term, it has no effect on underlying preferences. All it does is change the costs and benefits of pursuing these preferences. The quality or quantity of prior social interaction among players should be irrelevant to the calculus of whether or not to defect (Frank 1988:143).

The undersocialized nature of institutions in contractualist arguments is highlighted by the motivations contractualists *do* focus on when explaining pro-group behavior. Cooperation is elicited in institutions in basically three major ways.

One is issue linkage. Take, for example, a suasion game, where one player has a dominant cooperation (C) strategy, leaving the other player to defect (D). The Nash equilibrium (C,D) is one that leaves the player with a dominant C strategy somewhat dissatisfied, while giving the player playing D its best payoffs. The dissatisfied player therefore has an incentive to use threats or promises (e.g., tactical issue linkage) to move the outcome to a more advantageous set of payoffs (Martin 1993). Persuasion here is nothing more and nothing less than an effort to change the cost-benefit calculations of the defecting player with exogenous positive or negative incentives so as to secure cooperation. Persuasion does not change that player's underlying desire to defect in a suasion game, nor does it change basic beliefs—or common knowledge—about what kind of game is being played.

A second way that institutions can elicit norm-conforming behavior is by providing reasons for actors to worry about their reputations. A prior reputation as a cooperator brought to a stag hunt game, for example, can reassure others that the actor genuinely prefers a C,C outcome. This can stabilize the Nash equilibrium. Thus, it is in the interest of actors with common interests to first acquire a cooperative reputation, particularly from situations in which cooperation can be quite costly. The desire to establish a trustworthy reputation thus can be an incentive to engage in norm-conforming, pro-social behavior (Kreps 1992).

The reputation argument has at least one major problem. As Frank (1988) points out, this kind of reputation should never be a reliable or credible one to a rational observer. Being able to observe reputation-building behavior means that such behavior is probably undertaken with the likelihood that it will be observed. Indeed, there is no point engaging in it for reputational purposes unless it is observable to others. But if a behavior or an action is designed to be observed, and both the observer and actor know this, then the observer should have doubts that it is indeed high-cost behavior. The only way to reduce these doubts is for the actor to behave in such a way that an observer is convinced the behavior cannot be calculated. Thus, the paradox: the most credible reputation is one that is based on behavior that is automatic, emotional, and uncontrolled, not calculated (Frank 1988). This implies that in order to minimize in-group defection, distrust, and conflict, groups have an interest in instilling in their members deeply rooted, credible, "taken-for-granted" responses to social interaction. So, in the end, normative socialization becomes the basis for credible reputations.

A third feature of institutions that helps elicit cooperative behavior— perhaps the most important one for contractualists—is information. Interaction in institutions can provide new information that can affect beliefs about causality, about means-ends relationships, and/or about the preferences of others (Martin 1999:84). This information can reduce uncertainty about the credibility of others' commitments, and thus help actors' expectations converge around some cooperative outcome. Thus, information only affects beliefs about the strategic environment in which the actor is pursuing fixed preferences. It does not appear to feed back to a reassessment of the desirability of these preferences in the first place. The usual way that information affects preferences is through its effect on elite change (assuming the actor is an aggregate political entity such as a state). Information about the failure of some strategy, for instance, could lead to a loss of support for one set of elites pursuing their definitions of interests and their replacement by another set with different definitions of interests. There is a sort of infinite regress problem that much of the work on information runs into, however. That is, what makes this information about failure conclusive, unless there is prior agreement on the criteria for success and failure? What leads to prior agreement on these criteria? Information about the validity of these criteria that all actors find credible? What leads to this kind of agreement on the credibility of the criteria about credibility? Information about the credibility of the credibility of the credibility of these criteria, and so on? At any stage one could simply state, unproblematically, that actors received credible information about a phenomenon and leave it at that for the purposes of modeling interaction from that point on. But this does not escape the problem that at any given point, the criteria for establishing the credibility of new information are problematic.

Thus, there is something vaguely mystical about how contractualists treat information inside institutions. Information is rarely contested; it has an obviousness about it that unproblematically reduces uncertainty. The meaning of new information often seems to need no interpretation. Why do institutions reduce uncertainty? Because of new information about preferences, beliefs, and strategies. What makes such information credible? Usually, contractualists point to the costliness to the provider of the information (costliness in terms of some loss of material welfare or power). But contractual institutionalists have no theoretical advantage here, no theory of the conditions under which new information will influence preferences, beliefs, or strategies and by how much. Moreover, the social context of information appears to be irrelevant, or at least the origins of common definitions of costliness, essential for information to be credible, are unexamined. The Bayesian updating of beliefs, as a practical empirical research matter, says nothing about how to determine how a myriad historical social relationships that constitute one subset of beliefs filters this new information.[10]

Yet empirically we know that the same information will be interpreted differently depending on whether it comes from "people like us" (the information is more authoritative and persuasive) or comes from a devalued "other" (Kuklinski and Hurley 1996:127). Economic transactions, for instance, bargaining over price where people exchange information relating to their preferences and their bottom line, vary dramatically depending on whether or not the parties are friends—friends offer higher payments and accept lower prices than strangers (Halpern 1997:835–68). Face-to-face bargaining is more likely to lead to mutually beneficial exchanges even under conditions of asymmetric information (e.g., where the seller, for instance, has private information about the value of the product) because it elicits norms of honesty that increase trust and information sharing (Valley, Moag, and Bazerman 1998).[11] Even in prisoners' dilemma (PD) relationships, information about the other as an opportunist is not static. Hayward Alker reports on lab experiments involving two individuals playing an iterated PD: the two could not communicate directly with each other, but transcripts were made of their comments about

---

[10] I do not include here a review of the literature on signaling games and information in IR. I will discuss this in more detail in the context of persuasion. Suffice it to say, the more interesting work on how information is interpreted in the context of signaling games between players with asymmetrical private information overlaps considerably with the constructivist interest in the social context of information, since the credibility of signals in conveying information depends in many instances on prior social relationships and the identities and interests formed from these. Nonetheless, much of the signaling literature focuses on how the context of information alters actors' beliefs about the credibility of information (mostly about the credibility of threats and promises in IR or about the policy attitudes of politicians in American politics), not the basic identities or interests of actors per se.

[11] As Valley, Moag, and Bazerman put it, face-to-face negotiations "nearly always involve a significant proportion of the early bargaining time taken up in getting to know more about one another . . . setting a positive tone for the entire negotiation" (Valley, Moag, and Bazerman 1998:230). That is, social interaction helps actors come to conclusions about the identity of the other, and hence how information from the other should be sent and interpreted.

what they thought the other was trying to do in their game. Judging from the transcripts, at the start of the interaction both assumed the other was defecting because it was in his nature, it was dispositional, and there were initially a lot of mutual efforts to punish. Once the interaction became more or less locked into a string of mutual cooperation, the occasional defection was dismissed as situational, or chalked up to random misperceptions (Alker 1996). That is, a string of mutual cooperative moves changed the actors' assessments of who exactly they were playing, such that noncooperative behavior was no longer seen as dispositional but was instead situational. In other words, descriptively similar information about a move, defection, was interpreted differently before and after actors entered into a social relationship. Social identity theorists have also noted that individuals playing a PD are more likely to cooperate than individuals representing groups. Group affiliation—the tendency for in-group identification to require extreme demonstrations of devaluing the out-group—becomes a critical contextual variable for understanding variation in cooperative behavior (Dawes, van der Kragt, and Orbell 1988). Thus, social context is an important variable in how well information reduces uncertainty in a transaction, and in which direction this uncertainty is reduced (e.g., clarifying the other as a friend or an adversary).

For contractualists, then, information rarely changes basic preferences or interests, and there is, as far as I know, no effort to see how it changes common knowledge such that actors jointly reevaluate the nature of the game being played.[12] Yet the significance of the iterated PD games that Alker reports on lies precisely in this point: a string of cooperative interactions led the players to take the same information—a defection by the other—and reinterpret it as a mistake or as a consequence of the situation rather than of the other player's disposition. In effect, the game was redefined, shifting from a PD where both players believed they and the other held a preference for the D,C outcome to an assurance game where both players believed they and the other held a preference for C,C.

To be fair, contractualist arguments do not a priori reject the possibility that information changes preferences instead of strategic environments. The advice is to test for both, but in practice the tendency is to discount the possibility of the former. There appear to be two reasons for this. First, modeling with fixed preferences is easier for contractualists influenced by choice-constraint, or choice-theoretic (game-theoretic) epistemology and

---

[12] Yet, it is plausible to argue that new causal information can lead to the creation of new interests: scientific information about the process of global warming, for example, has created an interest in stemming increases in greenhouse gas emissions where such an interest never existed before. On contractualism's neglect of explanations for common knowledge, see Risse 1997:1.

methodology.[13] Second, preferences are difficult to observe, as are changes in them. What often may appear to be a change in preferences is, instead, a change in strategies. Any likely source one might turn to to observe preferences (e.g., from statements through to actions) could well be itself a product of strategic interaction, hence unrepresentative of true preferences (e.g., a deceptive move, a second best action, a document that itself is a product of bargaining among actors in an interagency process). Thus, it is safer and easier to either assume preferences or to deduce them from some prior theoretical assumption about the nature of the actor.[14]

This seems to be a reasonable, cautionary argument for a sound methodological choice. It does reveal, however, an implicit disciplining move that constrains efforts to think about changing preferences through new information acquired via social interaction inside an institution. There are a number of possible responses. First, theoretically deduced or assumed preferences are not so easily juxtaposed with observed preferences. Theories do not appear deus ex machina. They are almost invariably based on some initial inductive observation about a phenomenon. It is often not logically obvious what the preferences of actors ought to be from observing their position in society or their organizational constitution as actors. Thus, for instance, it is unlikely there is an obvious a priori theory of the preferences of religious groups in the United States about humanitarian intervention without some information about the political ideologies of these groups. Nor can a useful theory about the preferences of militaries (e.g., that they organizationally favor offensive doctrines and capabilities) be easily derived from some deductive assumptions about the universal characteristics of militaries (as Kier [1997] shows). Theoretical assumptions about preferences can only come from moving back and forth between initial empirical observations and theoretical hunches. But for many choice-theoretic approaches, empirical observation of preferences is ruled out as too risky and the measurement error is considered too high. But from empirical observation it is clear too that the theoretical deduction of preferences is itself fraught with risks and uncertainties. It should not be a priori privileged as a "better" way of figuring out what actor preferences are. Why not pit hypotheses based on theoretically deduced preferences against inductively analyzed preferences to see which set predicts behavior that is more consistent with empirical evidence?

[13] As Keohane implied in his seminal work, *After Hegemony*, institutionalists use a structural-functional analysis of the constraints institutions place on actors, and it is to these exogenously given constraints that actors respond in ways influenced by their subjective or cognitive characteristics (1984:132).

[14] See Frieden 1999 for a sophisticated statement of these arguments.

Second, the bias against observing preferences seems to exaggerate the difficulty of observing them. To be sure, validity and reliability of measures for accessing the preferences of actors are problematic, since the only way to observe is to look at some phenomenon external to their cognition, e.g., a speech act, a gesture, a decision.[15] There is always the possibility that these external manifestations are in some sense strategic, and not direct representations of preferences. But given the theoretical importance of the question—whether preferences change through social interaction, and how stable the preferences are—it seems premature to give up trying to observe change. As Herrmann notes, human cognitions are the "input variables that make a human problem-solving paradigm go. They are essential whether the paradigm assumes rational maximizing behavior or not. It is surprising how little effort we have made to figure out ways to infer them" (Herrmann 1988:180). The response should be, how do we reduce the measurement error to the lowest possible level and maximize the internal validity and reliability of indicators of preferences and desires?

All of this is not to say that contractualists rule out the possibility of preference change. Some recognize that institutional life can change what people desire. As Shepsle and Bonchek note, "While debate and deliberation may often seem like window dressing, it is entirely possible that, from time to time, some persuasion, reconsideration, conceivably even coercion takes place, the result of which is that someone changes preferences" (Shepsle and Bonchek 1997:44). Contractual institutionalists just do not think it happens that often, or that it involves messy empirical work showing that it has happened. Game theorists, therefore, admit that they do not know how to model change in the likelihood function in Bayesian updating.[16]

Therefore, when behavior changes, persuasion is generally not the first answer for contractual institutionalists. When preference change *is* detected, the first impulse is to ask a liberal/pluralist question: how has the institution affected the distribution of power resources across domestic actors leading to new interests reflecting new political coalitions? Martin rightly notes that institutional theory no longer needs to show that institutions matter: that case has been made. Rather it needs to show how they matter: "[We] require a finer-grained understanding of the mechanisms through which institutions might exert their effects" (Martin 1999:86). But socialization is, apparently, not one of the mechanisms that interests contractual institutionalists.

---

[15] Developments in the theory and technology of brain imaging may change this, however.
[16] I thank Ken Shepsle for clarifying game theorists' arguments about likelihood functions.

This disinterest in socialization is somewhat surprising, though. First of all, given the prominence of coordination games and focal points in institutionalist theorizing about social norms, habits, customs, and conventions that constrain rationally optimizing behavior, one might expect more curiosity about the social and historical origins of focal points. Institutionalists are ready to admit that focal points can be products of shared culture and experience.[17] Martin notes that bargaining inside institutions may allow states to establish focal points in a coordination game (Martin 1993:101). But the origins of these focal points in IR are not of central concern, and institutionalists do not explicate the microprocesses by which bargaining reveals or creates (or convinces actors to accept) a focal point inside an institution.[18] In essence, shared culture and social experience may help actors choose among equilibria, but institutionalist theory per se does not endogenize this choice. This is acceptable if one assumes stability in focal points and conventions. But this is an assumption, not an empirical claim. Moreover, a different ontology leads to a different assumption about focal point stability, and hence to greater interest in explaining the social origins of focal points. That is, a constructivist or complex adaptive systems ontology holds that continuous interaction between multiple agents over time leads to changing social structural contexts (emergent properties) that, in turn, affect how agents define their interests. In macro historical terms, this means that social conventions and focal points can evolve and change rather dramatically, nonlinearly, and in path-dependent ways. Indeed, this ontological difference between contractual institutionalists and constructivists is a major reason why the former are often not analytically interested in how or if preferences change. A constructivist ontology opens the door to relatively unstable preferences, giving more weight to preferences as determinative of behavior (and to normative social contexts), thus requiring researchers to pay special attention to observing rather than deducing preference change.

Second, contractualists, at least those who claim neorealist pedigrees, would have to admit that there are retardants in neorealist socialization

[17] The "conspicuousness" or "prominence" of some equilibrium outcome in a coordination game that turns it into a focal point can be a function of socialization in a shared "culture" (Morrow 1994:96).

[18] In more sociological terms, bargaining can entail a process of empathetic discovery of shared notions of prominence and conspicuousness about particular outcomes. Or it can lead actors to "discovering" shared focal points, in effect by creating feelings of group solidarity. In some cases, this could lead to discovering that the group shares a priori interests. More interesting, however, is the process by which this discovery is in fact the *creation* of new interests that actors believe are shared because they believe members of an in-group *should* share interests. In other words, the social and psychological rewards of membership precede the "discovery" of shared interests.

processes; hence, they would have to admit that there is at least a crude neorealist socialization process at work to begin with. The logic is as follows: given that some contractualists accept neorealist assumptions of anarchy and security maximizing, in order to explain why actors might develop absolute gains concerns and recognize common interests that might necessitate setting up institutions, they would have to admit the possibility that neorealist socialization can be imperfect, incomplete, obstructed. Yet, instead of asking whether incomplete socialization might be attributable to counter-socialization processes inside institutions, they would rather look to domestic political change, exogenous technological change, or the emergence of multiple issues areas to explain absolute gains concerns and common interests.

Finally, and most interesting perhaps, contractualists use a definition of institutions that seems to be very sociological: the intent and effect of an institution—if it operates efficiently—seems almost to be to socialize states. Martin, for example (following Mearsheimer, following Keohane), defines an institution as "a set of rules that stipulate ways in which states *should* cooperate and compete with one another. . . . [Institutions] prescribe *acceptable* forms of state behavior, and proscribe *unacceptable* kinds of behavior" (Martin 1999, emphasis added). This language implies that the most effective institutions are those that get actors to internalize or at least take for granted that which is prescribed and proscribed. States would over time drop calculations according to consequences, and replace them with invocations of appropriateness. Otherwise, so-called prescribed and proscribed behavior would simply be behavior that was rewarding or unrewarding rather than what was acceptable or unacceptable.[19]

Recent liberal theorizing in IR also seems to dance around the concept of socialization without incorporating it clearly into its ontology or epistemology. On the one hand, a leading liberal theorist,[20] Andrew Moravcsik, seems open to the possibility that social interaction changes interests and

[19] Abbott and Snidal (1998) try to meld rationalist and constructivist perspectives on the role and effect of formal international organizations, and touch on the possibility that IOs can help states "change their mutually constituted environment and, thus, themselves" (25). But the bulk of the article focuses on the uses of IOs by states or on the roles IO play in mediation, enforcement, and the provision of information. Despite the promising claim at the start to look at IOs as agents which "influence the interests, intersubjective understandings, and environments of states" (9), in the end the issue is essentially dropped.

[20] There is a more mainstream materialist branch of liberal theorizing about how domestic preferences interact with domestic political institutions to create national-level responses to external economic and political change. But scholars in this tradition—exemplified by IPE scholars such as Ron Rogowski and Jeffry Frieden, among others—start from the assumption of fixed material preferences, and thus have nothing to say about socialization.

preferences through identity construction: he critiques constructivists, and rightly so, for neglecting agency at the state and substate levels when looking at the diffusion of norms. In particular, he takes them to task for neglecting how the formation and distribution of preferences at the domestic level mediates the diffusion of norms from the system structure (1997:539). This suggests that he accepts the possibility that this diffusion occurs, that it can lead to internalization (e.g., socialization), but that variation in internalization across states will be a function of prior state and substate identities. On this point he is, I think, essentially right.

Elsewhere he uses the language of sociology in a way that seems to keep the door open for theorizing about socialization. "Liberal theory seeks to generalize about the social conditions under which the behavior of self-interested actors converges toward cooperation or conflict" (1997:517). One social condition is the degree of convergence or divergence over values and beliefs. But it is not clear where this convergence comes from. He remarks that "for liberals, the form, substance and depth of cooperation depends directly on the nature of these patterns of preferences" (1997:521), that is, on the distribution of preferences created by social interaction among multiple actors. It is not clear, however, how particular distributions of preferences feed back to affect the degree of convergence or divergence over values that is predictive of cooperation or conflict. He then suggests that preferences may indeed vary in "response to a changing transnational social context," and as an example, "the position of particular values in a transnational cultural discourse may help define their meaning in each society" (1997:522–23). This suggests another feedback loop, linking the degree of convergence or divergence of values to changes in preferences. Yet, he also appears agnostic as to whether social preferences or social identities inside states are socially constructed at the state or interstate level: "Liberals take no distinctive position on the origins of social identities, which may result from historical accretion or be constructed through conscious collective or state action, nor on the question of whether they ultimately reflect ideational or material factors" (1997:525). In the end, it seems that all liberal theory adds to the issue of socialization in IR is an awareness that the diffusion of norms will be filtered by domestic institutions that aggregate preferences and produce policy outcomes. The explanation for the social origins, content, and construction of these preferences is left outside of the theory. That is, liberal theory is agnostic about where preferences come from (Moravcsik 1997:525).

Needless to say, for social constructivists, socialization is a central concept. As Onuf puts it, "social relations *make* or *construct* people—*ourselves*—into the kinds of beings we are" (Onuf 1998:59). In their accounts of the creation and diffusion of international norms, constructivists mostly focus on the "logics of appropriateness"—pro-norm behavior that is so deeply internalized as to be unquestioned, automatic, and taken for granted. This naturally raises questions about which norms are internalized by agents, how, and to what degree. Kratochwil and Ruggie imply that by treating institutions as social institutions "around which actor expectations converge," the interesting question becomes the processes by which this intersubjective convergence takes place. The term "social institution" certainly implies that the degree of convergence before and after entering into an institution should be different for reasons that primarily have to do with interaction among agents inside the institution (Kratochwil and Ruggie 1986). So some process of socialization must be going on. Yet the empirical work in this regard has tended to follow the sociological institutionalists' focus on macro historical diffusion of values and practices (such as rationalism, bureaucracy, and market economics), measured by correlations between the presence of a global norm and the presence of corresponding local practices (Eyre and Suchman 1996; Price 1998; Finnemore 1996b). Finnemore has gone beyond correlation to causation by focusing on how international agents (e.g., international organizations and ideas entrepreneurs) have actually gone about "teaching" values and constructing domestic institutions and procedures inside states that reflect emergent international norms and practices. States then adhere to these norms and practices even when these seem inconsistent with their material welfare or security interests.

The problems with constructivist approaches to socialization, however, are fairly basic. First, inheriting much of the epistemology of sociological institutionalism, constructivism has tended to leave the microprocesses of socialization underexplained.[21] It tends to assume that agents at the systemic level have relatively unobstructed access to states and substate actors from which to diffuse new normative understandings. That is, once actors are interacting inside institutions, the diffusion and homogenization of values in the "world polity" seem virtually automatic, even, and predictable. This leaves variation in the degree of socialization across units—the degree of contestation, normative "retardation," and so on—unexplained. And it leaves the causal processes unexplicated.[22] Even Fin-

---

[21] For a similar critique, see Checkel 1998:335 and Risse 1997:2. As Wendt puts it: "In social (and IR) theory . . . it is thought to be enough to point to the existence of cultural norms and corresponding behavior without showing how norms get inside actors' heads to motivate actions" (Wendt 1999:134).

[22] See for example, Meyer et al. 1997 and Haas 1998:26. Haas posits that "interpersonal persuasion, communication, exchange and reflection"—socialization—occurs in thick institutional environments where epistemic communities are active, but there is no discussion of microprocesses of persuasion nor conditions under which variation in the effectiveness of persuasion—hence the completeness of socialization—might be observed. Nadelmann identifies normative persuasion as a central process by which prohibition regimes emerge—for

nemore's detailed story of teaching often stops at the point where agents at the international level deliver norm-based lessons to rather passive students. There is less attention paid to the processes by which units or unit-level actors understand, process, interpret, resist, and/or act upon these "lessons." That is, it is unclear how exactly pro-normative behavior is elicited once the models of "appropriate behavior" are displayed or communicated to agents at the unit level. This neglect is surprising,[23] given constructivists' focus on reflective action by multiple agents: if this kind of agency exists in the diffusion of norms, what happens when it runs into reflective action by multiple agents at the receiving end of these "teaching" efforts? This question is left unexplored.[24] The result is, however, that causal processes by which systemic normative structures (constitutive, regulatory, and prescriptive) affect behavior are mostly assumed, rather than shown.[25]

Put visually, suppose for the moment one could conceive of the relationship between structures and agents as is done in figure 1.1.[26] At its simplest, social (normative) structures require institutional environments where the institution itself or actors within it try to transmit to new members the predominant norms of the structure. The agent processes these norms, filtered by prior features of identity, and they then mediate the development of foreign policies and practices that govern interaction with other agents and with the institution. The interaction of these policies and practices reproduces, while also perhaps modifying, the original social structures and institutional environments. Much of the constructivist empirical work focuses on the first step in this process and skips over the second, drawing correlations between the norms being taught by agent-

---

instance, antislavery norms in British diplomacy—but it is unclear why political leaders and government officials were persuaded by moral arguments (1990:494). Keck and Sikkink (1998) go a long way in looking at the microprocesses by which transnational activist networks "persuade," but international institutions as social environments per se are not the focus of their research. Adler (1998:133) also notes that the OSCE has an explicit mission to socialize members by trying to persuade them that they are, or ought to be, like "us"— liberal, cooperative, and sharing a European identity. But it is not clear why this persuasion ought to work on initial members who are somewhat illiberal and noncooperative. Finnemore and Sikkink (1998) address this general problem in their survey of constructivist work on norm diffusion, however.

[23] But this neglect is beginning to change with new studies on socialization in European institutions (see note 53), and on how normative localization or hybridization occurs when local agents with prior identities respond to norm diffusion (Acharya 2004).

[24] For similar critiques see Checkel 1998:332 and Moravcsik 1997:539.

[25] This may change as scholars pick up on Finnemore and Sikkink's summary of some plausible causal processes (1998).

[26] The figure describes the interaction with only one agent. The relationships described here would apply to all other agents involved in the interaction as well.

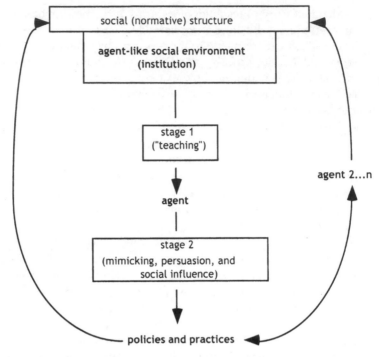

Figure 1.1. Structures and agents in a notional socialization process

like institutions on the one hand and the content of state practices on the other. Yet it is precisely the second stage that determines how effectively socialization takes place, if at all, and therefore how one might find variation in interests and behavior across actors who are nonetheless exposed to the same institutional social environment. In short, it is at this second stage where one needs to look in order to understand if, and how, socialization microprocesses are at work in world politics.

Second, when constructivists do begin to look at these microprocesses of socialization and the constitutive effects of social interaction, the focus is almost exclusively on persuasion. By usage, it usually means something akin to the noncoercive communication of new normative understandings that are internalized by actors such that new courses of action are viewed as entirely reasonable and appropriate. Here they tend to borrow in some form or another from Habermas's theory of communicative action. The argument is that social interaction is not all strategic bargaining. Rather, prior to strategic bargaining, actors have to arrive at "common knowledge"; that is, they must first come to share basic assumptions about the deep structure of their interaction: who are legitimate players and what is a legitimate value to be bargained over? Even more important, this agreement needs to be narrow enough so that a vast range of potential equilibria that could arise in their strategic interaction becomes off-limits, beyond the pale. In other words, for them to even interact strategically, they need to establish focal points that are so deeply accepted as to be stable.[27] Thus, right from the start, bargaining is not simply a process of manipulating exogenous incentives to elicit desired behavior from the other side. Rather it involves argument and deliberation all in an effort to change the minds of others.[28] As Hasenclever, Mayer, and Rittberger put it, "[T]he parties to a conflict enter a discourse where they try first to bring about agreement concerning the relevant features of a social situation and then advance reasons why a certain behavior has to be avoided. These reasons—as far as they are *convincing*—internally motivate the parties to behave in accordance with the previously elaborated interpretation and the justified expectations of others" (Hasenclever, Mayer, and Rittberger 1997:176–77, emphasis mine; see also Knoke 1994:3 and James 1998:7).[29]

There are a couple of questions here. First, it is not obvious why, from the perspective of actually doing empirical research on socialization in IR, one should focus on Habermas to the neglect of a very rich research tradition on persuasion in communications theory, social psychology, and political socialization. It is certainly not a novel argument from the perspective of these traditions, and it is not clear how the application of the communicative theory of action would go about showing whether persuasion or coercion explained behavior that was increasingly pro-social over time. That communicative action has to be "convincing" is a huge requirement, and thus far constructivists have not really shown how debates over common knowledge, for example, "convince" actors to agree to a "mutually arrived at interpretation" of social facts. Under what social or material conditions is "communicative action" more likely to be successful? How would one know? The conditions seem to be quite demanding, involving a high degree of prior trust, empathy, honesty, and power equality.[30] Constructivists seem to rely on an identity argument here: that is, persuasion is more likely to occur when two actors trust one another such that each accepts the "veracity of an enormous range of evidence, concepts and conclusions drawn by others" (Williams 1997:291). Put simply,

---

[27] See Johnson 1993:81 on this point.

[28] For an excellent exegesis of Habermas's theory of communicative action, see Risse 1997.

[29] Sometimes persuasion can mean both something akin to communicative action *and* something more normatively coercive, entailing shaming or opprobrium. Here compliance with a norm need not be a function of internalization but is, rather, a function of state elites' aversion to public criticism (Risse and Sikkink 1999:13–14; Keck and Sikkink 1998:16). This confuses persuasion with social influence, in my view.

[30] See the conditions explicated by James (1998:7–11, 15–17).

identification leads to affect and affect leads to a greater probability that the arguments and interpretations of the other will be accepted as valid, and internalized. How the initial level of identification necessary for communicative action comes to be is unclear.

But the more important problem is a second one. While it is understandable why constructivists would want to focus on persuasion—this is their trump card in disputes with neorealists and contractualists over whether social interaction can change actor preferences and interests in pro-social ways, and it is the purest type of socialization—at least two other effects of social interaction can lead to pro-normative behavior in the absence of exogenous material threats or promises. These are social influence and mimicking. The first is a term that encompasses a number of sub-processes—backpatting, opprobrium or shaming, social liking, status maximization, and so on—where pro-normative behavior is rewarded with social and psychological markers from a reference group with which the actor believes it shares some level of identification. The latter refers to copying pro-normative behavior as satisficing means of adapting to an uncertain environment prior to any detailed ends-means calculation of the benefits of doing so. With their almost exclusive focus on persuasion—or communicative action—constructivists have a hard time distinguishing between the range of microprocesses that help explain pro-normative behavior.

Socialization is too important to ignore in world politics. It is what actors in world politics often try to do to each other. It already appears to varying degrees and with varying importance in the main clusters of international relations theory. Treating international institutional life as an environment where social interaction, independent of material rewards and punishments, may change everything from actor preferences, to beliefs, to behavior could provide new insights into the conditions of international cooperation.

Given the fact that much human behavior is inherently overdetermined, that one act of cooperation is often the product of the simultaneous considerations of multiple interests, testing for the effects of socialization depends on careful research designs that create conditions helpful for observing the effects of socialization and for determining its substantive importance. It is to this issue that I now turn.

DEFINITIONS, MICROPROCESSES, AND METHODS

There is general agreement across the social sciences that socialization is a process by which social interaction leads novices to endorse "expected ways of thinking, feeling, and acting." As Ochs puts it in relation to childhood socialization: "[T]hrough their participation in social interactions children come to internalize and gain performance competence in . . . sociocultural defined contexts" (Ochs 1986:2). In Stryker and Statham's words, "Socialization is the generic term used to refer to the processes by which the newcomer—the infant, rookie, trainee for example—becomes incorporated into organized patterns of interaction" (Stryker and Statham 1985:325). Berger and Luckman define the term as "the comprehensive and consistent induction of an individual into the objective world of a society or sector of it." It gives people identities; they are "assigned a specific place in the world." Socialization, then, involves internalization: "the immediate apprehension or interpretation of an event as expressing meaning, that is, as a manifestation of another's subjective processes, which thereby becomes subjectively meaningful to myself." And internalization means the development of shared identification such that people come to believe "[w]e not only live in the same world, we participate in each other's being" (Berger and Luckman 1966:129–30). Thus, socialization is aimed at creating membership in a society where the intersubjective understandings of the society become "objective facticities" that are taken for granted (Berger and Luckman 1966:44).

Political scientists have not wandered far from these basic themes in their definitions of socialization. Ichilov refers to political socialization as "the universal processes of induction into any type of regime." These processes focus on "how citizenship orientations emerge" (Ichilov 1990:1). Sigel refers to political socialization as the "process by which people learn to adopt the norms, values, attitudes and behaviors accepted and practiced by the ongoing system" (cited in Freedman and Freedman 1981:258). Beck and Jennings essentially see political socialization as a process by which adolescents acquire political orientations from their families and from major sociopolitical forces and events in formative periods (Beck and Jennings 1991:743). IR theorists have generally simplified socialization to processes "resulting in the internalization of norms so that they assume their "taken for granted" nature" (Risse 1997:16). Ikenberry and Kupchan borrow from Sigel and define socialization as "a process of learning in which norms and ideals are transmitted by one party to another." In IR they limit this to a Gramscian-like process whereby state elites "internalize the norms and value orientations espoused by the hegemon and, as a consequence, become socialized into the community formed by the hegemon and other nations accepting its leadership position." This hegemonic order "comes to possess a 'quality of oughtness' " (Ikenberry and Kupchan 1990:289–90).

There are a couple of common themes here: the first is that socialization is most evidently directed at, or experienced by, novices, newcomers, whether they be children, inductees into a military, immigrants, or "new" states.

The second theme is the internalization of the values, roles, and understandings held by a group that constitutes the society of which the actor becomes a member. Internalization implies, further, that these values, roles, and understandings take on a character of "taken-for-grantedness" such that they are not only hard to change, but that the benefits of behavior are calculated in abstract social terms rather than concrete consequentialist terms. Why should one do X? "Because . . . ," or "Because X is the right thing to do," or "Because X is consistent with who I am," rather than "Because it will lead to Y, and Y benefits me."

One should assume, however, that there can be degrees of internalization, given that not all actors are always exposed to exactly the same configuration of social pressures, nor do they enter into a social interaction with exactly the same prior identifications. Thus, while pro-social behavior because of its "appropriateness" may be the ideal, at the opposite end of the spectrum should be pro-social behavior because of its material consequences (positive and negative). At this point, pro-social behavior cannot be attributed to internalization or socialization in pro-social norms of the group.

But if internalization of pro-social values is the hallmark of socialization, and if the other end of the spectrum is behavior motivated by the calculation of material costs and benefits,[31] this leaves a vast amount of pro-social behavior produced by neither process.

This leads to a final and important point. The focus on internalization tends to lead constructivists to focus on persuasion. This is, as noted, what really distinguishes them from neorealists and contractual institutionalists: the internalization of group norms and values is largely a cognitive process of argumentation, reflection, and acceptance of the oughtness of particular norms. But beyond persuasion, the literature on socialization (outside of IR theory) identifies a range of reasons for why one might see pro-normative behavior in the absence of exogenous (dis)-incentives. Axelrod, for instance, lists identification (the degree to which an actor identifies with a group), authority (the degree to which "the norm and its sponsor are seen as legitimate"), social proof (essentially mimicking of a valued in-group's behavior), and voluntary membership (where defection from group norms carries costs in self-esteem) as critical mechanisms for reinforcing pro-normative behavior (Axelrod 1997a:58–59). All of these depend on the acquisition of some kind of

---

[31] Putting aside, for the moment, the fact that constructivists would have to argue that at a certain level, the rational and conscious maximization of individual material benefit is due to the internalization of socialized values placed on material benefits, and is mediated by socially determined processes of rational calculation (e.g., long term versus short term; relative weight of trade-offs, etc.).

identification with or affective attachment to a group—that is, socialization. Ikenberry and Kupchan list three: exogenous shocks that lead to elite transformation in a state; exogenous material inducements that lead, over time (and somewhat mysteriously) to the internalization of norms that were once adopted for instrumental reasons; and normative persuasion or transnational learning through direct inter-elite contact (Ikenberry and Kupchan 1990:290–92). Beck and Jennings refer to three possible, somewhat overlapping, socialization processes whereby adolescents acquire the political orientations of their parents: parents provide social identities that bring with them political interests; power and affect relationships establish certain communication patterns in the family such that parents influence the political personalities of younger members; or the political traits of parents are transmitted through a process of inheritance or mimicking (Beck and Jennings 1991:744). Constructivism has tended to neglect many of these microprocesses.

Arguably, these multiple processes boil down to three: mimicking, social influence, and persuasion. A critical question, then, is when and to what degree do these separate processes help explain why actors change their behavior in pro-normative or pro-social ways? In practice, these processes are likely to be interactive. But separating out their key differences is important because this will help us examine how durable pro-social conformity is over time and what kinds of institutional designs are most conducive to this durability. Thus, broadly speaking, the speed, uniformity, and effectiveness of norm diffusion ought to depend a great deal on what kind of institutional social environment leads to what kind of socialization microprocess.

Mimicking

Mimicking is a microprocess whereby a novice initially copies the behavioral norms of the group in order to navigate through an uncertain environment. It is an efficient means of adapting to uncertainty prior to any detailed ends-means calculation of the benefits of doing so. To be sure, this microprocess stretches the concept of socialization somewhat, since pro-group behavior is only indirectly an effect generated by the nature of the social environment. Rather, pro-group behavior is a function of the desire to survive in a novel social environment. That is, while mimicking is distinct from exogenously induced threats or punishments, and is not characterized by individual efforts to optimize long-run material well-being, it is not the same class of causes as persuasion and social influence. The former two are mechanisms that motivate. In mimicking, the mechanism that motivates copying can be survival under uncertainty. But mimicking can also stem from persuasion, or from social incentives to accept another actor as a behavioral exemplar, in which case the motivation is covered by the other two microprocesses. So mimicking could be one behavioral outcome of persuasion and social influence, a microprocess that shows how these two other microprocesses can lock actors into path-dependent behavior.

On the other hand, choosing which groups to mimic involves a degree of prior identification. Moreover, mimicking pro-social behavior can lead to internalization of norms through repetition. Or, alternatively, by mimicking an actor goes on record as behaving in some particular way. It may then be loathe to deviate from this precedent for status and image reasons. Many of the procedural constraints and work habits and standard operating procedures that actors develop in order to minimally function inside an institution come from mimicking the behavior of others in the group. These can then limit the legitimate forms of participation in the institution (Frank 1985:18; Biddle 1985:162; Ochs 1986:2–3; Cialdini, Kallgren, and Reno 1991:203–4). Mimicking can also lead to acceptance of the intersubjective norms of the group governing basic communication. In other words, mimicking can achieve basic agreement on legitimate ways to resolve conflicts even though no Habermasian communicative action has taken place.[32] In short, mimicking can be both a condition for and effect of more direct forms of socialization such as social influence and persuasion.

Social influence

Social influence is a microprocess whereby a novice's behavior is judged by the in-group and rewarded with backpatting or status markers or punished by opprobrium and status devaluation. The appropriate reference in-group and the degree to which certain backpatting and opprobrium signals are valued depend on prior identity construction. Social rewards and punishments can elicit pro-normative/social behavior in the absence of persuasion or direct internalization. Rewards might include psychological well-being, a sense of belonging, a sense of well-being derived from

---

[32] James notes that communicative action involves agreement on the medium through which discussion of conflict takes place. This agreement—like learning a common foreign language—comes prior to all other communication (James 1998:7–11); hence, socialization, whether via persuasion or social influence, requires a basic level of communicative cooperation to begin with. I have no problem with this argument. But there is no reason why this basic agreement need be achieved through discussion and argumentation that two or more equal, empathetic actors eventually find convincing. Mimicking the language, procedures, and habits—the parameters of this medium of communication—can lock an actor seeking to survive in uncertainty into such agreement as well.

conformity with role expectation, status, and so on. Punishments might include shaming, shunning, exclusion and demeaning, or dissonance derived from actions inconsistent with role and identity. The effect of (successful) social influence is an actor's conformity with the position advocated by a group as a result of "real or imagined group pressure" (Nemeth 1987:237). Conformity can be either with the descriptively normative behavior of a group (e.g., what most people in the group do) or with its prescriptively normative behavior (what most people in the group believe should be done). The difference between social influence processes and persuasion is neatly summarized by the phrase Festinger used to describe compliance due to social pressure: "public conformity without private acceptance" (Booster 1995:96). Persuasion would entail public conformity with private acceptance. Persuasion, at least of the kind where the authoritativeness of the persuader is what convinces, has been called "mediated informational influence, e.g., "I thought the answer was X . . . but everybody else said Y, so it really must be Y." Social influence, instead, comes in the form of "mediated normative influence," e.g., "I believe the answer is X, but others said Y, and I don't want to rock the boat, so I'll say Y."[33] The rewards and punishments are social because only groups can provide them, and only groups whose approval an actor values will have this influence. Thus, social influence rests on the "influenced" actor having at least some prior identification with a relevant reference group. Social influence involves connecting extant interests, attitudes, and beliefs in one "attitude system" to those in some other attitude system, e.g., attitudes toward cooperation get connected to seemingly separate attitudes toward social standing, status, and self-esteem in ways that had not previously occurred to the actor (Zimbardo and Leippe 1991:34). Thus, one could call this a second-order socialization microprocess—while actors' preferences and interests may not change, these interests are linked together in ways in which they were not in the past. For instance, preferences in the security field become linked to preferences in social status and prestige.

Persuasion

Persuasion is a microprocess whereby novices are convinced through a process of cognition that particular norms, values, and causal understandings are correct and ought to be operative in their own behavior. Persuasion has to do with cognition and the active assessment of the content of a particular message. As a microprocess of socialization, it involves

[33] M. Deutsch and B. Gerrard, cited in Betz, Skowronski, and Ostrom 1996:116.

changing minds, opinions, and attitudes about causality and affect in the absence of overtly material or mental coercion.[34] It can lead to common knowledge, or "epistemic conventions" (that may or may not be cooperative), or it can lead to a homogenization of interests. That is, actors can be persuaded that they are indeed in competition with each other, or conversely that they in fact share an interest in cooperation. The point is, however, that the gap or distance between actors' basic causal understandings closes as a result of successful persuasion.

Persuasion can itself result from one or all of the three microprocesses. The first pertains to the nature of the message. Persuasion involves a process of cognition where counter-attitudinal messages are compared with preexisting arguments. The latter change because of the superiority of new evidence weighed by a priori internalized truth standards. The second pertains to characteristics of the persuader, in particular the affective relationship created by the social or intellectual attractiveness of the persuader. This attractiveness heightens the persuader's authoritativeness, and hence the persuasiveness of his/her message. The third has to do with the cognitive and social characteristics of the persuadee that mediate the evaluation of the content of the message and/or the authoritativeness of the messenger. Since persuasion involves the internalization of new attitudes, values, and norms, this type of microprocess ought to lead to the most durable and self-reinforcing pro-social behavior.[35]

RESEARCH DESIGN ISSUES: WHY INSTITUTIONS?

We need to know at least three things in order to test for the presence and effects of socialization. First, what are the characteristics of the social environment in which agents are interacting at time t? If this environment has agent-like or "teaching" properties, what are the norms and associ-

---

[34] I just want to underscore that I am talking about changes in fairly fundamental beliefs, not relatively shallow, transient, or low-level attitudes about the efficacy of certain political choices and strategies. The difference is not always obvious, but as I will argue in chapter 4, persuasion as it pertains to socialization is interesting precisely because it involves basic reevaluations of collective "thought styles" (Farkas 1998:43) that can include preferences or strategies, as long as these strategies pertain to basic methods for achieving basic goals (e.g., multilateralism versus unilateralism as a "cause" of security). Much of the work on persuasion in political science has focused on what are, at root, rather minor changes in positions on public policy, not major changes in entire thought systems (see, for instance, Lupia and McCubbins 1998).

[35] Since one should expect variation in the durability of norms depending on the type of socialization microprocess, it does matter, then, whether one can observe internalization or not. Holding preferences constant for the purposes of modeling prevents one from exploring this important issue.

ated behaviors that actors in the environment are supposed to adopt and, ideally, internalize? In other words, what is the predominant ideology of the social environment? Second, what are the characteristics of individual agents involved in the social environment at time t? How do these characteristics retard or propel the socialization process? Third, how do these agents then interact with this environment at time $t + 1$? What are the policy processes through which newly socialized agents act upon the broader social environment?

The net effect of socialization, therefore, will be a function of the characteristics of the environment interacting with the characteristics of the agent in an ongoing tight feedback relationship, mediated by a foreign policy process. In IR one way of testing for socialization, then, is to use international institutions on the one hand and individuals and small groups involved in state policy processes on the other as, respectively, the social environment and individual agents of interest—the units of analysis, if you will. My reasoning is as follows.[36]

For the most part, when IR specialists or sociological institutionalists look for the effects of socialization, the unit of analysis has tended to be the state (or state elites in a fairly aggregated way) (Eyre and Suchman 1996; Meyer et al. 1997; Finnemore 1996a, 1996b; Waltz 1979). This presents problems when examining particular institutions as social environments since states as unitary actors do not participate in institutions; rather, state agents do, e.g., diplomats, decision makers, analysts, policy specialists, non-governmental agents of state principals, and so on. Moreover, treating the unitary state as actor presents problems when applying the most well-developed literature on socialization found typically in social psychology, sociology, communications theory, and even in political socialization theory. Most of this literature examines the effects of socialization on individuals or small groups.

A constructivist ontology allows (even demands) that the unit of socialization be the individual or small group. As Cederman points out, constructivism's ontology can best be captured by the notion of complex adaptive systems whereby social structures and agent characteristics are mutually constitutive, or locked in tight feedback loops, where small perturbations in the characteristics of agents interacting with each other can have large, nonlinear effects on social structures (Cederman 1997; Axelrod 1997b, 1997c; Hamman 1998). Thus, it matters how individual agents or small groups are socialized because their impacts on larger emer-

---

[36] I use a fairly loose definition of international institutions. Institutions are more or less formal organizations with identifiable names and with more or less obvious criteria for membership or participation. This allows one to differentiate among specific social environments with specific ideologies or normative "messages."

gent properties of the social environment can be quite dramatic.[37] This focus on individuals and small groups also enables constructivists to deal with the legitimate critique from proponents of choice-theoretic approaches that what is observed as the normatively motivated behavior of a group at one level may be the aggregation of the strategic behavior of many subactors at a lower level (Lake and Powell 1999:33).

There are good reasons, then, for studies of socialization to focus on the socialization of individuals, small groups, and, in turn, the effects of these agents on the foreign policy processes of states.[38]

But if these are appropriate units of analysis, why choose international institutions as the environments of socialization? After all, state actors experience a myriad of socializing environments from bilateral interactions at the state level, to intra-bureaucratic environments at the policy level, to training and work environments inside bureaucratic organizations themselves. Let me try to make the case. One of the critical claims constructivists make is that "anarchy is what states make of it" (Wendt 1992). In other words, material power structures do not determine state interests or practices, and thus realpolitik practice by unitary rational actors is not an immutable "fact" of international politics. In order to make this case, constructivists or their fellow travelers have, for the most part, underscored the empirical "deviations" from realist or material power interests theories: altruistic foreign aid (Lumsdaine 1993); weapons taboos (Price and Tannenwald 1996); "autistic" force postures in developing states (Eyre and Suchman 1996); "autistic" military doctrines (Kier 1997); and limits on the conduct of war (Legro 1995; Finnemore 1996c). These have been important cases that have gone far in undermining the mainstream realist edifice. But at some point the critique needs to go beyond so-called deviant cases to look at cases and phenomena that materialist realist theories claim they can explain; that is, constructivism is going to have to make the argument that realpolitik practice is a reflection of realpolitik ideology and norms.[39] To explore this claim against

---

[37] This is, after all, the point of much of the work on how transnational networks affect state behavior (Keck and Sikkink 1998; Evangelista 1999; Adler 1998), "teaching" and the diffusion of norms, and the creation of national interests (Finnemore 1996b). The roots of this complex adaptive systems approach, as it relates to normative structures in IR, go back to Durkheim's work on the creation and re-creation of "social facts" through the interaction of individual normative agents. See Ruggie 1998:29.

[38] Ruggie calls this a focus on "innovative micro-practices," a hallmark of constructivist research (Ruggie 1998:27).

[39] I define realpolitik ideology, or strategic culture, fairly specifically to mean a worldview where the external environment is considered to be highly conflictual, where conflicts with other actors tend toward zero-sum, and where, given these conditions, the use of military force is likely to be quite efficacious in the resolution of conflicts. Vasquez calls this a power politics paradigm. I do not define realpolitik simply as the "prudent" pursuit of the power

realism's structural materialist argument requires setting up a critical test where both approaches spin out alternative but *competitive* propositions, predictions, expectations, and so on, to see which additional set of empirical observations is confirmed or disconfirmed.[40]

But there is an additional empirical implication that could provide an important test of constructivist versus material realist accounts of realpolitik: that is, if constructivists are right, realpolitik ideology and practice ought to be changeable—independent of material power distributions and "anarchy"—when actors are exposed to or socialized in counter-realpolitik ideologies. If materialist realist theories are right, realpolitik discourse is epiphenomenal to realpolitik practice, and neither should change in the presence of counter-realpolitik ideology.[41]

This is where international institutions come in. Constructivists suggest that international institutions in particular are often agents of counter-realpolitik socialization. They posit a link between the presence of partic-

---

interests of nation-states, as some realists do. This, it seems to me, is too vague and thus its presence or absence is empirically hard to falsify. Moreover, it does not really describe how realist theorists themselves believe decision makers socialized in anarchy understand this environment.

[40] Elsewhere I expressed some doubts about the wisdom of this kind of critical test for traditionally materialist realism versus ideational explanations (see Johnston 1996a). The reason was that materialist and ideational ontologies could be seen as incommensurate, that one had to subsume the other, that I believed the ideationally based realpolitik came prior to realpolitik pathologies emanating from structural anarchy, and hence that a critical test between theories derived separately from each made no sense. Desch picked up on this and suggested that I eschewed critical testing, period (Desch 1998:161). My earlier conclusion rested on empirical evidence that many critics did not find convincing, and evidence that I also indicated did not establish an especially strong test of my argument. (I did not reject the value of critical tests among competing ideationally based theories, but that is a minor debating point.) So in this book, the research design is premised on what I believe is a stronger critical test of materialist and ideational explanations for realpolitik pathologies in IR. This is necessary in order to establish whether materialist or ideational ontologies stand alone as an adequate basis for exploring realpolitik ideology and practice. For a very promising research program that shows how some realpolitik values—specifically a concern about relative gains—vary in the real world, see Rousseau 2002.

[41] Note that I do not accept that an actor's sensitivity to changes in relative power confirms material realism. I have argued elsewhere that one could argue that this sensitivity is ideationally rooted: Rousseau (2002) shows this empirically. Indeed, this is the whole point of testing for socialization. Similarly, when I conclude that cooperation occurs despite relative power concerns, this does not mean that I believe "relative power concerns" is a phenomenon exclusive to, hence confirming of, material realist arguments, or that socialization arguments necessarily expect cooperative behavior and a rejection of realpolitik pathologies. Socialization can go in both directions—actors can be socialized into or out of realpolitik practices. But to deal with the important charge that realpolitik ideology and practice are both epiphenomena of material structures, the critical test necessarily involves looking for evidence of non-realpolitik socialization.

ular normative structures embodied in institutions and the incorporation of these norms in behavior by the actor/agent at the unit level. It is in institutions where the interaction of activists, so-called norms entrepreneurs, is most likely, and where social conformity pressures are most concentrated. It is in international institutions where multilateral diplomacy with its emphasis on interpersonal communication, debating, and argumentation is manifest (Muldoon 1998:3). Institutions often have corporate identities, traits, missions, normative cores, and official discourses at odds with realpolitik axioms,[42] indeed at odds with the socialization pressures that neorealists argue come with being sovereign, insecure actors operating in anarchy. For example, some arms control institutions expose actors to an ideology where, interalia, multilateral transparency is normatively better than unilateral non-transparency; disarming is better than arming as a basis of security; common security is better than unilateral security; and evidence of the potential for cooperative, joint gains in security in the international system is greater than evidence that the environment is a fixed, conflictual one. All of these axioms and assumptions challenge the core assumptions of realpolitik ideology. So, if there is any counter-realpolitik socialization going on, it ought to be happening in particular kinds of security institutions.[43] I do not mean to imply that institutions are the only fora in which socialization in IR goes on. Since the focus is on microprocesses, obviously state agents and principals in the policy process are exposed to a wide variety of socialization experiences and interactions inside their own states. I am simply interested in how broader non-realpolitik norms in international security might be diffused. Institutions are an obvious place to look.[44]

Note, however, that treating institutions as social environments means positing that different social environments vary in terms of their persuasiveness and social influence. This means asking how institutions as social environments vary in ways conducive to socialization. We need, then, a

---

[42] For a discussion of organizations and their goals, see Ness and Brechin 1988:247, 263–66. See also Muller's discussion of the ideology of the non-proliferation regime and how the causal and principled ideas of the regime relate to its norms and proscriptive regulations (Muller 1993); Barnett and Adler on the role of international institutions in the construction of security communities (Barnett and Adler 1998:418–21); Alter's discussion of the legitimacy of the European Court of Justice's legal culture and doctrine and how this constrains states from challenging the ECJ even when its rulings run against state preferences (Alter 1998:134–35); and Schimmelfennig's description of the goals of European institutions (Schimmelfennig 2002:7).

[43] Risse makes a similar point, suggesting that communicative action should be more frequent inside institutions than outside of them (Risse 1997:17).

[44] Or as Shambaugh put it: "The more provocative question is whether an actor's preference, interests and identity can be altered initially as a result of its association with an international institution and vice versa" (Shambaugh 1997:8).

typology of institutional forms or institutional social environments. Unfortunately, we do not have one. One could imagine, though, at least several dimensions for coding institutions as social environments. Here I am borrowing and expanding on the typology of domestic institutions developed by Rogowski (1999):

1. membership: e.g., small and exclusive or large and inclusive

2. franchise: e.g., where the authoritativeness of members is equally allocated, or unevenly (though legitimately) allocated

3. decision rules: e.g., unanimity, consensus, majority, supermajority

4. mandate: e.g., to provide information, to deliberate and resolve, to negotiate and legislate

5. autonomy of agents from principals: low through high

Different institutional designs (combinations of measures on these five dimensions) would thus create different kinds of social environments, leading to differences in the likelihood and degree of persuasion and social influence. For instance, to take one extreme ideal type (as I explain in chapter 3), persuasion is likely to be an especially prevalent and powerful socialization process when membership is small (social liking and in-group identity effects on the persuasiveness of the counter-attitudinal message are strongest); when the institutional franchise recognizes the special authoritativeness of a couple of actors (the authoritativeness of the messenger is likely to be high); when decision rules are based on consensus (this requires deliberation which, in turn, can trigger more flexible cognitive evaluation of new information); when the institution's mandate is deliberative (requires active cognition, and agents may be more autonomous since there is no obvious distribution of benefits at stake so there is less pressure to represent the principal); and when autonomy of agents is high, e.g., when the issue is narrow or technical or when the principal just does not care much (when the principal is less attentive or relevant).[45] All these design-dependent effects will be enhanced for novices who are exposed to the environment over long periods of time (Zimbardo and Leippe 1991, ch. 5).

---

[45] Here Risse and I are, I think, moving along parallel tracks. He notes, for instance, that nonhierarchical and network-like international institutions "characterized by a high density of mostly informal interactions should allow for discursive and argumentative processes" (Risse 1997:18). Martin and Simmons, coming at the question from a contractual institutionalist perspective, also imply that institutions where participants are reliant on "expert" sources of information should be "most influential in promoting cooperation" (Martin and Simmons 1998:742). See also MacLaren 1980 for similar hypotheses.

Conversely, given the microprocesses of social influence I outlined earlier, backpatting and opprobrium are more likely to be at work when membership is large (this maximizes the accumulation of backpatting/shaming markers); when the franchise is equally allocated (there are no obvious "authoritative" sources of information); when decision rules are majoritarian (an actor's behavior is on record, and therefore consistency effects may be stronger); and when the autonomy of agents is low (agents have to represent principals, thus reducing the effects of persuasion on agents).

But how would one know if mimicking, social influence, or persuasion had led to pro-social/pro-normative behavior in international institutions? First, as I noted earlier, one would have to show that social environments in institutions are conducive to mimicking, social influence, or persuasion. Second, one would have to show that after exposure to or involvement in a new social environment, attitudes or arguments for participation have indeed changed, converging with the normative/causal arguments that predominate in a particular social environment, or that they reflected social influence pressures emanating from that environment. Third, one would have to show that behavior had changed in ways consistent with these arguments. Finally, one would have to show that material side payments or threats were not present, or at least were not part of the decision to conform to pro-social norms. Broadly speaking, these are the tests this study sets out to conduct.

RESEARCH DESIGN ISSUES: WHY CHINA?

Given the research design requirements for analyzing the effects of socialization on cooperation, a strong case can be made for looking at China. Precisely because counter-realpolitik institutions may be critical environments for counter-realpolitik socialization, an easy case can be made for studying arms control institutions and China. In many instances, these institutions embody a non-realpolitik, even anti-realpolitik, ideology centered on the notion of common security (though, admittedly, in uneasy tensions with sovereignty-centric axioms as well). China is at one and the same time a "novice" and a hard-realpolitik state. This status is ideal for testing for socialization since this is precisely the kind of state where the effects of socialization (if there are any) should be easiest to observe given the potential contrast between a China that has not participated and a China that has participated in these institutions.[46] And it is the kind of

---

[46] I do not use socialization here in a normative sense. Nor do I believe that China prior to entry into these institutions was in some sense unsocialized. It was merely differently socialized.

state where resistances to this kind of socialization should be greatest, given the prevalence of hard-realpolitik worldviews. Together this means that China is a "least likely" case for socialization arguments, but one where the effects of exposure to international institutions should be relatively easy to observe.

Noviceness is, unfortunately, undertheorized in IR. If socialization is to have a profound impact on state or substate actors, it should be most obvious in novices. Who are novices in IR? The obvious candidates are newly liberated or created states, or recently isolated states. This suggests where to look for "most likely cases" for the purposes of theory testing: newly decolonized states from the 1950s on; newly independent states that emerged in the wake of the Soviet Union's collapse, for instance. These are states that are most likely to experience the IR equivalent to "primacy effects," where early experience and information will have out-of-proportionate effects on inferences drawn from later experiences and information.[47] New states literally have had to set up foreign policy institutions, determine what their foreign policy interests are on a range of novel issue areas, decide in which of a myriad social environments in IR they should participate (e.g., which institutions, which communities of states—middle power, major power, developed, developing), and which competitive and cooperative relations to foster.[48] It is precisely these kinds of states where one ought to expect socialization effects from involvement in international institutions to be greatest. China is not exactly a novice in the same way as the newly independent states of the former Soviet Union. But in terms of its involvement in international institutional life, it clearly went through a period of noviceness in the 1980s and into the 1990s, as it moved from virtual aloofness from international institutions to participation rates that are not all that different from those of the US and other developed states.

A few simple statistics will suffice in showing the pace of China's integration into international institutional life. Figure 1.2, for instance, shows China's shift, particularly after Mao's death in 1976, from being a "novice" in international institutional life to being a participant at levels nearing those of most major developing and developed states.[49]

---

[47] See Choi (1993:52–53).

[48] See, for instance, the argument in Chafetz, Abramson, and Grillot (1996). The authors argue that the debate in Ukraine in the 1990s over whether to sign the NPT was in large measure a debate over whether Ukraine's identity was that of a great power (hence it could legitimately keep and develop nuclear weapons) or a middle European power (in which case it should de-nuclearize and join the NPT).

[49] This figure includes all "conventional" international bodies, identified as IO types A–D in the Union of International Associations' *Yearbook of International Organizations*.

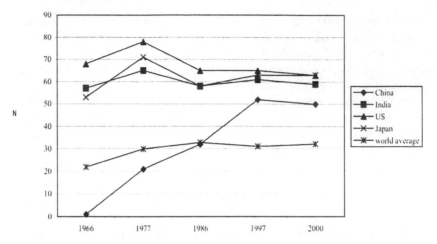

Figure 1.2. Comparative involvement of international governmental organizations. Source: Union of International Associations (2000/2001).

For another view of this change in Chinese participation rates, figure 1.3 uses level of development as a predictor of membership in international organizations for all states in the international system. The assumption here is that more resource-constrained states with fewer linkages to the global economy should be less involved in political institutions as well. High levels of development are associated with high levels of interdependence, hence with a high demand for institutions that can regulate these interactions. Thus, GDP/capita can act as a proxy indicator for a demand for institutions.[50] The figure shows that over the 1990s, China became increasingly *over*involved in international organizations given its level of development. Prior to the 1990s, China's participation rates fell below the regression line. That is, for its level of development China was under-involved in international organizations (IOs). Put differently, its demand for institutions was lower than it should have been, given its level of development. Beginning in the 1990s, however, China became overinvolved. In essence, in the 1990s China moved from well below to well above the regression line.

In security institutions, China's increasing participation rates over the 1980s and 1990s are equally impressive. Figure 1.4 indicates that China's

[50] I used GDP/capita as a predictor for the number of IGO memberships for each state for which both sets of data were available, and entered these data into an ordinary least squares (OLS) regression equation for the years listed in figure 2.4. The regression equations are as follows: *1977,* $y = .001x + 38.238$, $R^2 = .21$ $p = 0.00$; *1985,* $y = .001x + 36.437$, $R^2 = .207$ $p = 0.00$; *1989,* $y = .001x + 41.421$, $R^2 = .228$ $p = 0.00$; *1997,* $y = .001x + 38.501$, $R^2 = .163$ $p = 0.00$; *2000,* $y = .001x + 38.225$, $R^2 = .172$ $p = 0.00$.

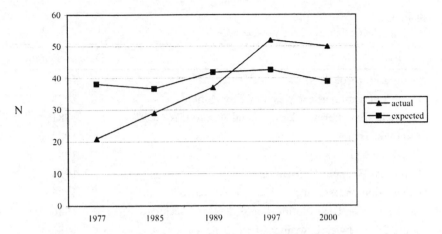

Figure. 1.3. China's actual and expected membership in international organizations, based on OLS regression of development data as a predictor of IO memberships. Sources of data: Union of International Associations (2000/2001) and World Bank.

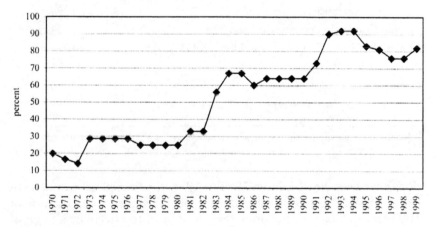

Figure 1.4. China's arms control treaty accessions as a percentage of eligible accessions.

accession to multilateral arms control agreements as a percentage of all possible agreements it was eligible to sign jumped rapidly, beginning in the early 1980s.

This has not simply been a function of an increasing number of international security institutions: the rate of increase in China's participation has been faster than the rate at which new international security institu-

TABLE 1.1
China's Arms Control Treaty Accessions

Treaty	Date of Signature
Geneva Protocols	1952
Latin American Nuclear Weapons-Free Zone	1973
Convention on Certain Conventional Weapons (CCCW)	1981
Antarctic Treaty	1983
Outer Space Treaty	1983
Biological Weapons Convention	1984
Convention on Assistance in Case of Nuclear Accident	1986
Convention on Early Notification of Nuclear Accident	1986
South Pacific Nuclear Weapons-Free Zone	1987
Convention on the Physical Protection of Nuclear Material	1989
Seabed Treaty	1991
Non-Proliferation Treaty	1992
Chemical Weapons Convention	1993
Convention on Nuclear Safety	1994
London Convention on Nuclear Dumping	1994
CCCW Protocol II (landmines) and Protocol IV (lasers)	1996
Africa Nuclear Weapons-Free Zone	1996
Comprehensive Test Ban Treaty	1996
Southeast Asia Nuclear Weapons-Free Zone	1999*

* Indicated it would be the first nuclear power to sign the treaty protocol.

tions have been created. From 1982 to 1996, for example, the total number of possible treaties increased from nine to eighteen, or an increase of 100 percent. China's accessions rose from three to fifteen, or a jump of 400 percent. By 1996, the only eligible treaties that China had not signed on to were the Partial Nuclear Test Ban Treaty (PTBT) and the Environmental Modification Treaty. In 1986 China publicly pledged to end atmospheric testing (which it had done in practice in the early 1980s), thus, in effect, unilaterally committing itself to the major provision of the PTBT. The Comprehensive Test Ban Treaty (CTBT), in any event, makes the PTBT irrelevant (see table 1.1).

These data suggest, then, that China's noviceness in the 1980s, and its increasing involvement in international institutions over the 1990s, created necessary conditions, at least, for socialization effects from international social environments. If materialist realist theories are right, however, this pattern of participation should be irrelevant to the reasons for China's cooperation. There should be no socialization effects of a non-realpolitik kind on the PRC. Indeed, Chinese decision makers' realpolitik suspicions about entrapment in multilateral security commitments should not change. To the extent that materialist realist arguments can explain increases in Chinese participation in international institutions, one should find evidence that, at best, all relevant actors in China see arms control institutions as tools for balancing against US power. There should not be much internal debate on this score. All this should be especially true after the collapse of the Soviet Union in 1991 and the emergence of the United States as the sole military-political superpower (see figure 1.5).[51] In a (nearly) unipolar world, according to neorealists, one ought to see candidate poles such as China trying to balance against the United States, eschewing arms control commitments that might place constraints on its relative power capabilities (Layne 1993; Waltz 1997).

Thus, China is a hard case for non-realpolitik socialization and, hence, an easy case for structural realism. It is a hard case as well precisely because of the fairly deeply ingrained realpolitik worldview among China's elites, reinforced by an account of modern history where China has been a victim at the hands of militarily and economically more powerful states in a highly competitive and dangerous international system (Johnston 1996a, 1998a; Christensen 1996; Deng 1998; Callahan 2004). Any evidence for socialization effects in the China case, then, would go a long way in confirming the analytic value of socialization, and in highlighting the analytic flaws of materialist realism and its claims about the epiphenomenality of realpolitik ideology.

If contractual institutionalist arguments are right, then pro-social or cooperative Chinese behavior should be a product of one of three factors: (1) exogenous material incentives or disincentives constraining a hard-realpolitik China from pursuing its prisoners' dilemma (or worse, deadlock) prefer-

---

[51] If one uses the International Institute for Strategic Studies data, the United States lead in military power increases still more. In 1987 the United States accounted for 39 percent of world military expenditures in 1985 dollars, the Soviet Union for 17 percent, and China for 2.6 percent. In 1992, these figures stood at 44 percent, 7.1 percent, and 4 percent respectively figures are about one-third of the actual expenditures. Regardless which data are used, the United States does not constitute a unipole using Modelski's categorization of polarity (a unipole controls 50 percent of world expenditures or more, in bipolarity two states combined possess more than 50 percent of the expenditures with each having 25 percent or more, and any other distribution is a multipolar one) (Modelski 1974). But neither can one call the system multipolar. Thompson calls this kind of distribution near unipolarity (Thompson 1988). From the perspective of military power distribution, then, since the early 1990s the PRC ought to have been preoccupied with balancing against US power.

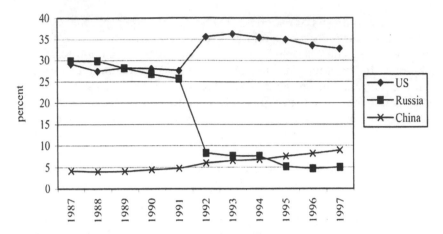

Figure 1.5. US, Russian, and Chinese shares of world military expenditures. Source: Arms Control and Disarmament Agency, *World Military Expenditures.*

ences; (2) new information that reassures a PD or "deadlock" China that it cannot be exploited or entrapped in the arms control institutions (e.g., that participation is essentially costless); (3) or changes in who makes decisions either because of policy failures or because effective involvement in the institution requires a shift in the locus of decision making.

If constructivists are right, any prosaically or cooperative behavior that emerges from China's cooperation in the arms control institutions should be a function either of mimicking the discourse and practices of counter-realpolitik institutions, or of the inherent desire to acquire status markers as a cooperator in a global system increasingly managed by international institutions, or of changes in a preference for multilateralist outcomes (in which case there should be a convergence over time in the security ideology that Chinese decision makers take to these institutions and that is promoted by the institutions themselves).

The China case is useful from a research design perspective for one other reason, namely, another prominent source of change in behavior toward international security institutions, domestic political change, is essentially held constant. As I noted earlier, contractual institutionalist and choice-theoretic work, when it does looks for changes in elite preferences and foreign policy behavior, often looks first to changes in domestic political alignments, elite transformation, and so on. One would be hard-pressed, however, to find dramatic changes in domestic political configurations, elite political ideology, or, indeed, in the composition of the top leadership over much of the period under study in this book. From 1978 through to the mid-1990s, Deng Xiaoping was China's preeminent leader, the first among equals in foreign policy strategy. The Communist Party of China retained its monopoly on power throughout this period. Deng's successors, while of a very different generation, nonetheless were politically socialized inside the party and state apparatuses. One simply does not see, therefore, the kinds of changes in governments, official ideologies, or rearrangements of political power relationships among relevant domestic interest groups that can precede rapid change in foreign policy. This is not to say that domestic institutions, particularly those organizations involved in security policy processes, are irrelevant, or that these have not changed at all. Indeed they have, and their evolution is not irrelevant to explaining the evolution in Chinese arms control policy, as I will discuss in chapter 2. But this domestic institutional development does not really constitute a major change in domestic political alignments where, as contractual institutionalist and liberal theory suggest, one should normally look for major changes in foreign policy.

CASE SELECTION AND ANALYSIS

The preceding discussion establishes why China's involvement in international security institutions is an effective general case for studying the effects of socialization.

Together, these design issues suggest three general sets of empirical expectations. Assuming an actor enters the institution and its particular social environment with realpolitik preferences and causal and principled beliefs, and assuming the institution's ideology embodies causal and principled beliefs that are generally inconsistent with realpolitik ones, the following are three sets of plausible empirical expectations.

First, if some of China's increasing cooperation in international institutions is a function of path-dependent mimicking, we should expect to see: no change in the causal arguments behind decisions to cooperate; rather one should see arguments that reflect short-term conformity because of the novelty of a situation, or a desire to acquire more information about the institution to reduce operational uncertainty. Discourse and behavior should reflect the constraints of the linguistic and organizational procedures of the institution, with little obvious cost-benefit calculus other than a short-term desire to "learn the ropes."

Second, if social influence (in this case, status concerns and desire to maximize backpatting and minimize opprobrium) is at work, one should expect to see: commitments to participate and join that take place in the absence of material side payments or threats of sanctions; arguments for joining or participating that stress backpatting and image benefits, diffuse reputation benefits, and opprobrium costs; arguments that stress the "inevitability" or lack of choice in participation; and, as a first cut, initial bargaining positions, if stuck to, that would put the state in a distinct minority, and isolate it from the reference group—commitments to pro-social behavior would be made only when it was clear that noncommitment would be highly isolating.

Finally, if persuasion is at work, one should expect to see (after exposure to this environment): arguments about participation that include declining concern about detrimental effects of participation on relative capabilities and security; heightened concern about beneficial effects for global, regional, and national security; and conformist behavior later in the process that could not be expected earlier on, given the initial causal understandings of the Chinese participants. In short, you should get increasing comfort levels even as the process encroaches more on the autonomy and unilateral security options of the state. Moreover, this more fundamental support for multilateral security institutions should become more obvious over time, especially for those who have participated directly in these processes. If persuasion is not at work, one should expect to see the prevalence of free riding and relative power arguments in discussions of participation in security institutions. The key terms in these institutions' discourses should not show up in Chinese deliberations. Indeed, one should find even harder realpolitik arguments in the policy process as China faced a unipolar, US-dominated international structure after 1991. Contractual institutionalism would also expect the prevalence of free riding and relative power arguments, but one should also see arguments about the value of side payments, or about short-term reputational gains/losses that are explicitly linked to other issue areas, or about information that indicates the costs of cooperation were lower than expected. These, then, are the general propositions that I test in this book.

The book centers on how mimicking, social influence, and persuasion effects work their way through the policy process to produce policy change. Choosing the main empirical cases, however, requires some care. I focus mainly on five institutions. In most of these cases, the level of China's ultimate cooperation was unexpected by most observers at the time, cooperation was not necessarily in China's relative power interests, and/or there were no obvious material incentives (such as side payments) to encourage participation. For the analysis of mimicking, I focus mainly on the organizational and ideational effects of China's participation in the Conference on Disarmament in Geneva from 1980 on. For the analysis of social influence, I look at the Comprehensive Test Ban Treaty (1994–1996) and the Convention on Certain Conventional Weapons landmines protocol negotiations (1995–1996). In this regard I also look at the Ottawa Treaty banning anti-personnel landmines (1996–1997), a treaty that China did not join despite overwhelming support for the treaty from other states. I look at the details of this case as a guard against selecting on the dependent variable. As for persuasion, I examine China's participation in the ASEAN Regional Forum (1994–2000) and related regional security dialogues. In addition, I develop a number of other empirical observations one might expect to see if these socialization processes are at work.

Let me explain these choices a bit more.

The universe of arms control institutions and treaties in which China could participate or has participated is not very large. Moreover, most of China's accession to or participation in arms control institutions and treaties can be classified as very low cost. For example, the Seabed Treaty and Outer Space Treaty—banning nuclear weapons deployments in the sea or in outer space—were essentially costless for the PRC since there is no evidence of any intention to deploy or actual deployment of nuclear weapons in these places. China's decision to join the NPT appears to have been affected to a large degree by the opportunities accession opened up for access to US nuclear power technology and for the export of Chinese nuclear-related technology. These sorts of cases of cooperation, while important for the substantive effect on levels of dealing with the problems at hand, are not surprising, and they are uninteresting for testing socialization arguments.[52]

There are, however, a small number of cases where China has essentially agreed to cooperate even though there are potential relative power costs to doing so, in the absence of obvious material side payments or sanctions. These are the interesting cases. China's participation in the CTBT and the Landmine Protocols of 1996, and in the ASEAN Regional Forum—the only formal multilateral security institution in East Asia—are these kinds of cases.

At the end of each chapter, I also look at additional empirical implications and cases, so as not to select wholly on the original dependent variable. Not all of these are confirming cases; in some cases the change in Chinese behavior is not in the cooperative direction. A socialization argument would hypothesize that in these cases, the socialization effects are weaker, due either to stronger resistance (more powerful relative power effects) or to weaker persuasion and social influence conditions. These short cases are worth looking at to see if socialization effects are indeed more constrained than they were in the CTBT, landmines, and ARF cases. Thus, the research design is eclectic and varies to some degree across the three main chapters.

---

[52] For a good discussion of the more or less standard explanations for China's cooperation in institutions of all kinds (territorial security, domestic stability, information gathering, management of relations with great powers, economic development, and prestige), see Lanteigne 2005.

In sum, I think a strong case can be made for looking at change in China's involvement in international security institutions over the 1980s and 1990s in order to probe the effects of socialization. China's prior realpolitik strategic culture, its noviceness, its rapid move into institutions that embody anti-realpolitik normative goals, and the ability to control or test for the effects of materialist and domestic political independent variables together create conditions for about as good a test of socialization microprocesses as one can hope for in the real world.

The one condition that is not so ideal is, of course, access to the policy process. Since much of the evidence for the effects of socialization microprocesses necessarily comes from arguments for or against pro-social behavior, the more the access to the details of policy making, the better. The Chinese cases make this difficult, and I am terribly envious of my colleagues who have looked at socialization microprocesses in European institutions. By necessity, then, the data for the case studies come from an eclectic mix of sources. Some are open-source analyses appearing in specialists' articles in journals or in papers written for a range of non-governmental and international conferences and fora. Some are open-sourced documents and information circulated in these institutions by Chinese actors. Some are internal circulation analyses and documents, not technically secret but nonetheless on average likely to reflect more authoritative views and arguments than official government statements. Just as important, however, I have relied on over 120 interviews with arms control specialists from China, the United States, Canada, and Singapore, most of whom have been involved in the policy processes or interagency discussions of their respective countries. I am obviously constrained in accessing the policy process, especially in a system that has developed a term, "asymmetric transparency" (*bu dui cheng tou ming du*) specifically to justify its lack of openness on security questions. The IR subfield has tended to slight or undervalue interviews. There are a number of reasons, but probably one of the key ones is a distrust that agents are willing or able to accurately report on their intentions behind an action. Such reporting may be deliberately deceptive, or exaggerated, or overly modest due to the personality or cognitive abilities of the interviewee. Often, instead, the researcher's preference is, in the face of this interpretive uncertainty, to deduce intentions from prior theoretical assumptions about the organizational affiliation of the actor, or about his or her material interest. As I noted earlier, this is problematic on empirical grounds. And it biases the search for the effects of socialization on interests, desires, preferences, and intentions right from the start. Yes, intentions and/or notions of appropriateness are difficult to observe. But if interviewing is done carefully with attention paid to where the interviewee fits into the decision process, with follow-ups, with careful wording of questions, with sensitivity to the interpersonal dynamics between interviewer and interviewee, and with triangulation interviews with others, one can reduce some of the measurement error that inheres in using face-to-face self-reporting of intentions behind actions.

CONCLUSION

This chapter has tried to establish the theoretical importance of testing for the effects of socialization microprocesses in world politics. Socialization infuses, sometimes explicitly, sometimes implicitly, much of the debate in international relations theory about the origins of, and changes in, actor interests in IR. It also infuses, sometimes explicitly, sometimes implicitly, policy debates in a number of states, including the United States, over how to deal with rising powers, "rogue" states, and other potentially "revisionist" actors in IR. Yet there has been a great deal of confusion or neglect in both spheres about how precisely socialization is supposed to work.

Various versions of realism hold that states are socialized by their exposure to an international anarchical environment, but only in one direction—toward realpolitik definitions of interest and practices. Those that maladapt are likely to suffer a reduction in security, or worst of all, elimination as a state. This socialization process ensures that, over time, there is a convergence in the system around realpolitik behavioral pathologies. Most realisms, however, rely more on a selection argument than a socialization argument, and they exaggerate the homogeneity of the socialization process.

Contractual institutionalism—while eschewing the term *socialization*—nonetheless holds out the possibility that extended social interaction in institutions (e.g., iterated PD games) provides new information that can change "beliefs" about the interests, intentions, and capabilities of other actors. This is, however, a socialization argument without using socialization language, and there is no reason why this new information, as Alker points out, cannot also lead to redefinitions of identity and interest (Alker 1996). Nor is there any a priori reason for contractual institutionalism to downplay social rewards and punishments as, potentially, just as important as exogenously provided material side payments and sanctions in eliciting cooperation.

Constructivists, of course, focus on socialization. It is the central dynamic process for constructivist theorizing. Socialization is the process through which identities are constituted through social interaction. With some notable exceptions,[53] however, much constructivist empirical work

[53] See the special issue on socialization in European institutions in *International Organization* 59:4 (September 2005).

has tended to focus more on correlations between the norms promoted by norms entrepreneurs (individuals or institutions) at the international level and pro-normative behavior by states as actors at the unit level. This work brackets the microprocesses of socialization, and thus downplays variations in the effectiveness of norms entrepreneurs, variations in the degree of unit-level resistance, and variations in the kinds of behavioral responses at the unit level.

This chapter, then, has gone to some lengths to establish why the individual and small group makes sense as a unit of analysis in testing for socialization. The chapter has also established the case for a new look at international institutions as critical social environments in which socialization effects are likely to be observable. And I have argued why China—a state whose leaders have traditionally been hostile to relative power-constraining institutions—provides some useful hard or least likely cases with which to examine how institutional social environments might socialize the foreign policy agents of the state. On, then, to the details.

CHAPTER 2

Mimicking

ONE WAY in which novices are *initially* inducted into the norms of a group is through requiring them to copy what all other members are doing. While the goal is that, over time, the inductee will internalize prescriptive norms that undergird behavioral routines, it is only necessary at the start that she/he follow the behavioral norms of the group.

The inductee, of course, has every reason to copy these norms, especially in new and decentralized social environments where it is not obvious initially what the prescriptive norms are, nor whether they should be followed. That is, under conditions of uncertainty, where the costs of not adapting are initially quite high (the newcomer has to sink or swim; there is no time to develop one's technique!), it is safe to simply copy what everyone else is doing (Frank 1985:18; Holland 1995:29; Cialdini 1984:117; Cialdini, Kallgren, and Reno 1991:203–4; Brown 2000:133). The rational assumption made by the inductee is that there has to be some individual benefit, since others would not be doing what they were doing if they did not believe it was individually beneficial. The benefit, however, need not be to acquire the rewards that other people appear to be acquiring. Indeed, when mimicking, it is not initially clear what these rewards might be. Rather the actor assumes there has to be some reward at some point, otherwise why would all others be acting in a more or less similar fashion? In a sense, the actor has no preference over means, and only vaguely formed preferences over ends. He or she will do anything necessary, and quickly, to survive in a new environment. The actor assumes that everyone else is reasonable, hence acting from his/her own interests and surviving. Thus, it pays, initially, to mimic. As Hirshleifer (1995:209) puts it simply: "[I]nformation is costly to acquire; it is cheaper to rely on cheap information conveyed by the decisions of others." Precisely because everyone else is acting a particular way, the information is cheap but credible, since the inductee can reason that the behavior is not likely to be deceptive. Mimicking provides a novice the modal procedures, models, norms, languages, and perhaps preferences that, immediately upon entry, seem necessary to survive, based on the guess that everyone else seems to be surviving.

Mimicking differs from emulation. Emulation involves the conscious and careful search for exemplars and success stories, a dissection of the

reasons for their success, and the application of these lessons to the maximization of some specific expected utility. It involves internalizing, as
well, the causal models of the way the world works that exemplars themselves use to maximize their utility. Thus, to emulate a successful balancer
in an allegedly anarchical environment means also to share its realpolitik
"worldview," its cause-effect understandings. Put another way, the difference would be between someone who upon seeing a political demonstration joined the movement of the crowd (mimicking), and someone who
first searched out the demonstration leaders to discuss with them the relative merits of the action for achieving their political ends (emulation).

Mimicking is also not, strictly speaking, the same as bandwagoning, at
least not in the sense of threshold models of political action (Granovetter
1978). Threshold models tend to rest on some kind of social backpatting
or shaming mechanism, such that social movements (or fads) take off or
fizzle out depending on the distribution of individual thresholds for these
kinds of incentives. That is, bandwagoning depends on how many others
have acted first, generating what kind of social pressure on those waiting
to act. Mimicking, on the other hand, is not necessarily a response to
social pressure. Rather it is, in a sense, a response to safety.

To be sure, from a perspective of mimicking, an actor joins a social
institution because it anticipates benefits. But it anticipates benefits not
because it has concrete, full, or wide-ranging information about the benefits of participation per se, nor because it has experienced benefits in
the past. Rather, it sees others anticipating benefits and assumes that it
too can hope to gain. This can be reinforced by status concerns. That is,
if one does not join, then one may not just suffer a loss of material benefits, but may also be viewed by others as out of fashion, behind the times,
and thus missing out of a status-enhancing experience. This can lead to
choosing behaviors that may not be beneficial if the actor behaved only
according to private information (since the private information is discounted in an uncertain environment) (Hirshleifer 1995:191). Or at
least, by the time the actor is certain through private information that
participation could be disadvantageous for a particular interest (e.g.,
military power), it has made commitments that make it costly to act on
the private information (e.g., status concerns, issue linkages, etc.). Thus,
by mimicking an actor can get locked into procedures, behaviors, and
languages characteristic of the social environment. The lock-in or constraint occurs on two levels—the new costs of backing out are very high;
the procedures, behaviors, and languages themselves constrain options
inside the institution.

Practically speaking, mimicking involves borrowing models of organizing and talking about issues that are central to the group. To be sure, this
microprocess stretches somewhat the concept of socialization, since pro-

group behavior is only indirectly an effect generated by the nature of the social environment. Sometimes called "anticipatory socialization" (Biddle 1985:162), mimicking is a survival strategy for a particular social environment. Mimicking is distinct from pro-group behavior elicited by exogenous discrete threats or punishments, and it is not characterized by individual efforts to optimize long-run material well-being. But it is not the same kind of cause as persuasion and social influence. The latter two are mechanisms that motivate. In mimicking the immediate mechanism that motivates is survival under uncertainty.

What does mimicking mean concretely? Novices in an institution are unlikely to be completely familiar with the procedures, routines, and language of interaction. If they continue to ignore or violate these, they may not be punished but they will not be able to have much impact on the proceedings. They may lose the opportunity to gain from mastering the main forms of social interaction. These considerations may prevent a retreat to anti-group behavior at the start of interaction. But fairly early on, once an actor mimics, certain features of this process can lead to path-dependent lock-in, such that violations of behavioral norms may become increasingly costly over time. The lock-in can occur in at least three ways.

One way is through organizational and institutional development. Participation in an international institution may functionally require the creation of specialized organizations and expertise to handle policy toward the institution. This may, in turn, create a standard organizational interest-based commitment to the international institution. Or organizations can develop missions premised in large measure on continued interaction with the international institution, and embodied in organizational culture.

It is surprising how little has been written on this effect from participation in international institutions. Abbott and Snidal note that in providing a "stable negotiating forum, enhancing interaction and reputational effects," international institutions often have to develop "elaborate organizational structures" to fulfill these functions (Abbott and Snidal 1998:10–11). But there is no mention of the effect of promoting these functions on the organization of state-level actors who, after all, populate the institution itself. There has to be some local or domestic bureaucracy or agency, first, to bargain over the development of, say, rules of coordination inside an institution, and second, to implement the coordination at the national level. This does not mean that the organizational structure at the national-level need be a functionally efficient one. As sociological institutionalists have shown (Finnemore 1996a; Eyre and Suchman 1996), often national-level agencies are set up as symbols of a broader norm or identity (e.g., identity as a "modern" state, for instance). But either way, there are local-

(or national-) level organizational consequences from participation in institutions that can enhance the state's intention and ability to cooperate.

Unfortunately, the small amount of literature on the issue is unclear as to the concrete hypothesized effects of this national-level organizational development. Karvonen and Sundelius note that theories of complex interdependence might expect that as more and more parts of the national economy are dependent on interaction with other states, often in multilateral settings, one should see a decentralization and diffusion of foreign policy from foreign ministries to a wider range of domestic policy ministries. This will increase problems of foreign policy coordination, even as the state as a whole has a greater stake in participation in international institutions. Their findings suggest that the causal arrows run the other way—that the increasingly complex domestic welfare or regulatory economy requires more interaction with other states through institutions. Thus, decentralization and coordination problems are a function, in a sense, of changes in domestic economic and political structures, not international ones (Karvonen and Sundelius 1990:213, 224–25).

But it is not altogether clear that these effects—decentralization and coordination problems—will inhere in the security field. Precisely because, for instance, increasingly complex arms control agendas at the international level require the participation of a wide range of technically specialized actors in the national policy process, there are particular benefits from tighter coordination because of the issue at stake—relative military power. This can lead to both an increasing stake for the state in the international institution—because a wider range of state actors now participate in the institution directly or indirectly—*and* increased coordination between specialized arms control bureaucracies.[1] In a sense, this can lead to the creation of a k group inside the state—a smallish, specialized, concentrated cross-bureaucratic constituency willing to act collectively behind a commitment to continued participation in the international institution. This does not mean that all these national-level agencies or groups share the same policy preferences on particular issues on the agenda in

---

[1] The effect might be similar to that of distributing subcontracting for major weapons systems through most US states and many congressional districts. A wider range of politicians have to worry about voting against funding than if the subcontracting were concentrated in a smaller number of states. As arms control issues become more complex and technical, a wider range of bureaucracies develop arms control functions and expertise (even if these experts represent still a small proportion of the agencies' personnel and mission). Or, as another example, take arms control treaty commitments. As these become more complex (in particular involving highly technical verification issues), more units/agencies may have to develop ACD expert offices, hence more agencies have interest in at least maintaining certain levels of participation in ACD (e.g., verification offices and/or export control offices in relevant ministries).

an international institution—but they may at least share an interest in participation in the institution, and a general preference for arms control solutions to security problems.

A second way in which mere participation in an institution can lead to lock-in is through the acceptance of procedures and norms of behavior of the group. The domestic organization and/or actors who actually participate in the institutions adopt certain standard operating procedures in order to articulate their interests, become accepted, or gain the benefits from prestige.[2] This may require the training of experts or people with the technical knowledge required for participating in the institution. In doing so, other kinds of procedures, routines, and modes of operation become out of bounds or irrelevant, and this may constrain action based on other kinds of interests.

A third, related, way is through the constraining effects of the discursive practices of the group.[3] There are accepted forms of argument, articulation, and interaction that exclude other forms. In particular, the linguistic practices of an institution can inhibit the articulation of arguments that run counter to the ideology of the institution. The members of the foreign policy process in a state have to use the language of the environment in which they operate at the international level. And when they do, they may internalize the socially accepted meanings of this language such that there are obvious, taken-for-granted, or appropriate ways of thinking and acting about a foreign policy issue.[4]

Whether or not this third type of lock-in actually happens depends on how discourse actually constrains actors' behavior. There are debates about the discourse-behavior link, of course. On the one hand, some

---

[2] I benefited from Michael Barnett's account of his transformation from an academic into a Rwanda expert during a stint in the United Nations bureaucracy (personal e-mail, May 26, 1999). See also Laffey and Weldes 1997:217. Joseph Nye notes that the institutionalization of regimes can "change standard operating procedures for national bureaucracies" (cited in Hasenclever, Mayer, and Rittberger 1997:148).

[3] Lock-in can occur in a fourth and fifth way: persuasion and backpatting after a novice enters an institution and mimics the behavior of others. Mimicking pro-social behavior can lead to the internalization of group norms through repetition or any of the mechanisms outlined in chapters 3 and 4. Alternatively, mimicking can establish patterns of behavior, or behavioral precedents, that actors who are sensitive to status and image may be loathe to violate, as I discuss in chapter 3. In the long run, it is likely that one or both of these socialization microprocesses becomes important for explaining long-term lock-in.

[4] Internalization of the meanings of terms may not be necessary to get pro-group behavior, according to some theorists of discourse and behavior. There is a difference between behavior because the rules of interaction simply do not allow for any other type of behavior, and behavior because it is considered normatively appropriate. This is the difference between "rules" and "interpretations," according to Wittgenstein. See Fierke 2002:338 on this point.

argue that language embodies worldviews and ideologies that limit the range of possibilities for action. Language categories delimit the articulation of alternative arguments. This can be done interalia by delegitimating alternatives and making them appear deviant or abnormal, or by making them inconceivable,[5] or by empowering individuals inside the state's policy process who accept the international institution's discursive practices,[6] or by providing individual status from appearing as a competent communicator of this language, or by tying the speaker into a finite but highly restrictive network of concepts, actions, and institutions (Ochs 1986:2– 3; Luke 1989; Waever 1990; Searle 1992; Bourdieu 1991:49; Yee 1996:94–97; Fierke 2002; Fairclough 2003:21–24).[7] If one does not accept the "official language" in some policy arena, then one is marginalized, suffering what Bourdieu refers to as "the sanctions of the linguistic market" (Bourdieu 1991:51). Language is not value free; it will reflect the culture of the social group, be it an identity group (e.g., arms controllers) or an international institution (e.g., arms control institutions).

On the other hand, the constraining effects of linguistic categories may be exaggerated, or at least contingent. Sarcasm, irony, the deceptive uses of language, and the redefinition or domestication of terms,[8] for instance, all suggest that discourse may at times be less limiting than linguistic determinists believe (Donahue and Prosser 1997:24). Some cognitive psychologists also dismiss the language-affects-thought argument as unsupportable (Bowerman and Levinson 2001:13). More recent research in anthropological linguistics suggests, in addition, that the constraining effect of a newly learned language requires that the learner accept the socially shared interpretation of language terms (Hanks 1996:175–76). In other words, one cannot assume that terminology shared by specialists (e.g., arms control language), for instance, leads to a shared understanding of these terms. It will depend on whether these terms embody indisput-

---

[5] This kind of claim falls largely under the rubric of "linguistic relativism" in both linguistics (Whorf 1956) and philosophy (Wittgenstein 1958).

[6] A particular language is required to make one qualified to communicate within the boundaries of competence established by the institution.

[7] This is called autocommunication. An actor adopts discursive practices that are regarded as socially rewardable because they imply membership in an elite group of competent practitioners (Broms and Gahmberg 1983).

[8] As one example, the term "Chinese characteristics" (*Zhongguo tese*) was most famously used by Deng in 1984 to modify the term "socialism." Socialism with Chinese characteristics became a liberating term, since it meant in practice at the time that China could experiment with capitalist modes of production and consumption. Marketization, in essence, became the Chinese characteristics of state socialism. By the 1990s, however, "Chinese characteristics" were used to limit debate on sensitive political questions. It became a disciplinary tool rather than a liberating one. Arguments could be delegitimized if they were accused of having insufficient Chinese characteristics.

able normative or causal claims. Thus, to show the constraining effects of a specialized language, one has to show not only that this language is increasingly used by a novice actor but also that the novice is also increasingly sharing the meanings of these terms.

One can imagine how these three separate lock-in processes might be combined: in order to survive as novices in a technically demanding international institution, a state's agents (say, foreign policy experts) adopt the procedures and work habits used by most other actors in the membership of an institution. These procedures require the creation of an internal policy process that develops a constituency with an institutional and/or ideological stake in participation. Moreover, the procedures and work habits of the institution limit the legitimate forms of participation (including discourses) in the institution (see Frank 1985:18; Biddle 1985:162; Ochs 1986:2–3; Cialdini, Kallgren, and Reno 1991:203–4). None of these three processes requires that the novice in the institution immediately internalize the values of the group (that is, they do not necessarily require persuasion). All can occur even though the end point of conformity may be suboptimal in terms of material well-being. But the effect of these three mimicking lock-in processes is a path-dependent development of policy toward the institution that makes it increasingly difficult to back out, ignore, or defect from the norms of the institution. When mimicking occurs, the likelihood that an actor will initially judge participation to be "successful" is high because the expectations are so low to begin with— mere survival under conditions of uncertainty. Thus, one simple expectation from mimicking is that participation breeds participation. Put simply, arms control talk can lead to arms control walk.

Of course, mimicking need not lead to especially tight lock-ins. As an actor "learns the ropes," it can innovate, even to the extent of learning to defect more efficiently (more deceptively) from group norms. Defection through "voicing" can at least reduce some of the social costs from defection through "exiting," or nonparticipation in the first place. But this will always take place within the organizational, procedural, and discursive limits established through mimicking. Thus, the effects of mimicking will usually be hybridity in these three areas. This is also likely because, in reality, the novice is not entirely tabula rasa when it begins to mimic. Even novices are socialized into views of appropriate organizational structures, appropriate languages, and appropriate behavioral norms that they bring into the environment and that mediate the effects of mimicking. These may encourage resistance to the new procedures. But the wider the gap between practices required by the new environment and those brought from the old, the less likely these older practices will be successful (either in terms of social rewards or in terms of one's ability to affect institutional outcomes).

In sum, lock-in processes will emerge from three different processes: the creation of national (or domestic) organizations to handle the development and articulation of interests in the institution; adopting the institution's primary behavior routines; and adopting the institution's primary discursive practices, with concomitant constraints on how actors talk and think about the institution. Arguably, China's initial and tentative moves into arms control institutions in the early 1980s produced these effects.

NATIONAL/DOMESTIC ORGANIZATIONAL DEVELOPMENT

As I noted in chapter 1, there is no question that China's participation rates in international security institutions increased dramatically over the 1980s and 1990s.[9] What then, were the organizational effects of participation? I will focus for the moment on the UN Conference on Disarmament (CD), since this was the first major international arms control institution in which China participated. The requirements for participation in the CD were critical in the creation of arms control institutions and expertise inside China. Not surprisingly, then, China's entry into the CD corresponded to the beginning of the period of the greatest growth in its participation rate in arms control institutions and arrangements.

China joined the CD in 1980, after sending an observer delegation in 1979. It is not clear why China's leaders specifically decided to join the CD when they did. This was a period in which China began to participate more fully in a range of international economic institutions, many within the UN system, and there seems to have been some argument made that participation in the gamut of UN-related institutions was appropriate to China's overall post-Mao policy of "opening to the outside."[10] Participation in the CD corresponded roughly with Deng Xiaoping's reevaluation of Lenin and Mao's inevitability of war thesis. This revision itself was related to the need to build a peaceful international environment for domestic economic development.[11]

Within this broad notional receptivity to staking out a higher profile in international institutions, more specifically it appears that Deng decided China should become more active in UN arms control activities. Evidently, Deng personally determined that China should send a delegation to the UN Special Session on Disarmament (UNSSOD I) in 1978. There had apparently been some internal opposition to participation, as China

---

[9] For a more detailed history of the arms control community, see Medeiros 2006.

[10] See Jacobson and Oksenberg 1990.

[11] In interviews with arms control specialists and practitioners in China in the spring and summer of 1996 in Beijing, this argument was repeatedly made.

had initially abstained from the vote to set up the UNSSOD in the first place. The Disarmament Commission had called on all nuclear weapons states to join the CD in Geneva in the wake of UNSSOD I. Some Chinese leaders initially felt they needed more time to prepare. So China did not send a delegation to the first meeting of the CD. In the second half of 1979, China began preparations for entry into the CD in 1980.[12]

It is important to note, however, that there is no good functional explanation for China joining the CD in 1980. There was nothing on the agenda of the CD at the time that Chinese leaders believed had any relevance to Chinese security. No other states were implicitly or explicitly offering side payments or sanctions to induce Chinese participation. Nor were there any reputational gains to be had from showing up; China had refrained from active support of UN disarmament activities in the 1970s and had not obviously suffered reputationally. Rather, joining seems to have been a spillover effect from participating in other UN agencies. Chinese leaders believed that as a great power China also ought to be in this kind of institution, and that possibly China might be able to observe close up how US-Soviet rivalry played out in international security institutions.

Once in the CD, there were new incentives to stay there. One was that the CD eventually took up issues that were considered to have potential benefits for Chinese security (e.g., the Chemical Weapons Convention and its potentially constraining effects on Soviet CW capabilities). More interesting, however, was the development of a habit of involvement through the development of organizations and procedures for participation. The incentives were dynamic ones, increasing over time as arms control gradually became a more central part of China's multilateral diplomacy. Participation in the CD required a level of expertise and sophistication that in turn required training arms control experts primarily in the Ministry of Foreign Affairs (MOFA). To deal with CD issues, in 1982 the MOFA set up an arms control division (the *si chu*, or "fourth division") inside the International Organizations Department. The division was quite small (fully staffed, divisions have about ten to fifteen people) and was tasked with handling all multilateral arms control issues. The primary qualification was good English skills, not technical expertise in arms control. While small compared, for instance, to the US ACDA, the fourth division was roughly the size and composition of other divisions inside the International Organizations Department. In other words, there was a prior institutional model for the ACD division.

Nonetheless, the CD was used as a training ground for a larger number of MOFA arms control experts. From 1980 through to 2000, the MOFA

[12] Interview with senior military arms control specialist, June 1996.

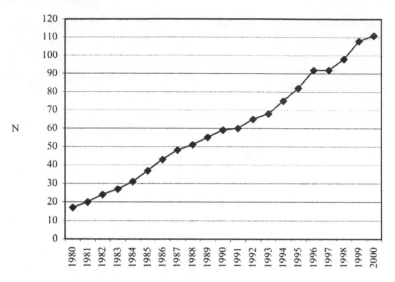

N

Figure 2.1. Cumulative sum of new members in China's delegation to the Conference on Disarmament. Source: Compiled from Conference on Disarmament delegation name lists, CD/INF (various years).

rotated sixty ministry officials through the CD delegation, providing them with firsthand experience in multilateral negotiations. All told, including personnel from the Chinese military and other specialized research institutions, by 2000 about 110 different individuals had been rotated through the CD delegation. The rate of training or experience was fairly constant across time, as figure 2.1 shows.[13]

Early on, the MOFA realized that China was handicapped without a higher bureaucratic status for its arms control community and without more efficient and regular mechanisms for drawing on scientific expertise. Thus, by 1985 Chinese leaders accepted a MOFA proposal to create a separate position for an ambassador for disarmament.[14] The MOFA also tried throughout the 1980s and into the 1990s to increase the size and authority of its arms control staff by requesting that the division (*chu*) be elevated to a department (*si*). This request was denied for at least a couple of reasons. One was that other players in arms control, such as the PLA and the nuclear weapons technical community, were worried

---

[13] These data are drawn from the delegation name lists provided for each CD session. The slightly steeper curve from 1994 to 1996 represents the increased size of the delegation during the CTBT negotiations in the CD and the requirement of including more nuclear weapons technical experts.

[14] Interview with former senior MOFA official involved in arms control, June 1996. Prior to 1985 the head of China's UN Office in Geneva was concurrently the ambassador for disarmament.

that the MOFA might then dominate the interagency process. But more critical was that the top leaders did not believe that arms control was an important enough issue for China. Into the early 1990s they viewed it as primarily a US-Soviet/Russia issue. In their view, China's status as a developing state, with a "peaceful foreign policy" and a tiny nuclear force, simply meant that arms control was mainly for other major powers. The experts disagreed.[15]

However, in 1997 the MOFA was finally given permission to turn the fourth division into the Arms Control and Disarmament Department, separate from the International Organizations Department. With the rather sudden complication of the CD workload—negotiations over the CWC, BWC verification procedures, the CTBT, a fissile material production cutoff treaty, among other issues that emerged in the mid-1990s—the fourth division was simply too small. Moreover, given the growing complexity of the issues, hence the need to coordinate with a wider range of interested agencies, there was probably a sense that one agency/organization had to be able to consistently take the lead in coordination. In principle, the creation of the new department not only meant the potential doubling or tripling of the number of people working on multilateral arms control in the MOFA, it also meant that the ministry acquired somewhat more authority in the interagency process. Prior to his elevation as the first director of the new department, the chief MOFA arms control official, Sha Zukang, was a deputy department head and division head. This made him roughly the equivalent in bureaucratic rank to Qian Shaojun, the official head of the arms control community in the Commission on Science, Technology, and Industry for National Defense (COSTIND) (later transferred to the General Armament Department), the umbrella organization under which most of China's military-industrial complex was situated. Qian had to sign off on all the negotiating positions that Sha took to the CTBT negotiations, for instance.[16] Sha's elevation to department head helped to make him the primary official voice on multilateral arms control issues.[17]

Some of the institution building was also required by new treaty obligations. For instance, under the Chemical Weapons Convention, China was required to set up a national authority that had to coordinate the regular

---

[15] Interviews with Chinese arms control specialists connected to the military and to the nuclear technical community, May and June 1996.

[16] Qian also had a military rank of major general, as well as a rank in the Communist Party, which together would have given him a composite rank that was higher than Sha's.

[17] Interview with Chinese arms control specialist from the nuclear technical community, January 1997; e-mail exchange with former Foreign Ministry official, October 2006. Reports from US arms control specialists engaged in bilateral discussions with China suggest that Sha had indeed become the primary interlocutor on arms control policy. Conversations with US arms control specialists in the Department of Defense and the Arms Control and Disarmament Agency, June 1998.

submission of information to the international implementing organization (e.g., annual declarations of chemical production facilities). It also had to develop protocols for on-site inspection and other verification-related activities. Under the CTBT China set up a national data center as part of the treaty's global international monitoring system. These activities are supposed to be highly routinized, following detailed templates, and thus require the input of scientists and technical specialists. As a result of the scientific requirements for participation in verification procedures, new agencies formerly with no responsibility for arms control developed a certain amount of expertise. For example, the Earthquake Bureau's seismologists were brought into the ACD policy process on CTBT-related verification issues. The Chemistry Industry Ministry also developed expertise on CWC verification procedures.

Thus, China's arms control diplomacy helped develop a community of experts beyond the MOFA. This process began in the mid-1980s. Although some chemical and radiological specialists were brought to Geneva from time to time in the early 1980s, it was not until the nuclear winter issue captured the attention of arms controllers around the world in the mid-1980s that interaction between the MOFA and weapons scientists became more regularized. The Chinese ambassador for disarmament at the time, Qian Jiadong, recommended in 1985 that China send nuclear weapons scientists to a major conference on nuclear winter taking place that year in Italy. This afforded Chen Xueyin, one of the key weapons scientists at CAEP/IAPCM, the opportunity to meet with other arms control scientists from the United States and Soviet Union. Chen came away feeling there was a common language with other scientists, and he was inspired to recommend that China's weapons community set up a working group to focus on arms control research that could be useful for China's arms control diplomacy.[18]

This working group evidently served as the embryonic connection that eventually brought weapons scientists from the IAPCM and the CAEP—its parent organization—into the decision-making process with the MOFA and the PLA's GSD.[19] Indeed, this consultation process evolved

---

[18] Interview with senior Chinese arms control specialist from the nuclear technical community, June 1996. This accords with the date given in IAPCM material on the start of arms control research in the institute (IAPCM 2001:1).

[19] Out of this came the Program on Science and National Security Studies (PSNSS) at the IAPCM, set up in 1989. In 1990 the CAEP and IAPCM also set up an MA and PhD program for training students in Physical Dimension of Nuclear Arms Control (Du 1996). Out of this also came a regular series of more informal academic seminars on technical and policy issues attended by ACD experts from the technical community, the GSD, and the MOFA. This series has been important in developing cross-unit contacts and in floating new ideas and proposals. The PSNSS was replaced by a new Arms Control Research Office in the IAPCM, set up in 1996. This office, in principle, has approved space for thirty to forty people, many times more than in the PSNSS. It is also providing a new home for some IAPCM

into a genuine interagency one, possibly with the CTBT's arrival on the CD agenda in 1993–1994.[20] For the CTBT negotiations, for example, the MOFA arms control division, the COSTIND testing community (represented by CAEP and IAPCM scientists), and to a lesser extent the GSD, held regular coordination meetings prior to and after each meeting of the CD in Geneva. The testing community was able to insert key positions (such as the insistence up until the end that the treaty allow peaceful nuclear explosions) into China's negotiating brief. Those in the technical community who work on BMD issues were also apparently responsible for the insertion of a lengthy discussion of the dangers of US BMD development into a major speech by Sha Zukang to the CD in October 1996.[21]

Other scientists associated with COSTIND's CDSTIC—an institution whose primary job is to collect, analyze, and disseminate new information about weapons systems and capabilities from around the world—were involved fairly early on in arms control–related research. In 1983, the CDSTIC set up an arms control small group—initially called the Geneva Talks Small Group (*Reneihua tanpan xiaozu*), later called the Arms Control and Disarmament Program—to help prepare and provide information to the CD delegation on technical issues relating to test bans and the chemical weapons convention. The size, budget, and research scope of this group grew roughly at the same pace as China's participation rates in global arms control. It began with three people, expanded to five in 1987–1988, to nine in 1994, and eleven by 1998. Later it was elevated to a division-level unit (*chu ji*).[22] In addition, as the arms control agenda became heavier, this program was assigned the responsibility for organizing most of the cross-unit exchanges on arms control in Beijing—bringing together experts from the NDU, IIS, CICIR, MOFA, the Nuclear Materials Association, CAEP, and the Aerospace Ministry, among other institutes.

With the CTBT, and then the fissile material production cutoff issue moving onto the CD agenda in the mid-1990s, one of the important tech-

---

scientists formerly connected with the testing program, and now out of work with the CTBT. The office focuses on CTBT OSI, fissile material production cutoff, verification, and nuclear non-proliferation. Interview with arms control specialist from the technical community, January 1997.

[20] As early as the mid-1980s, there were meetings between MOFA's Fourth Department, the GSD, and COSTIND specialists to discuss the drafting of documents and position papers that China took to the CD. But these meetings appear to have been less regularized and specialized than the interagency process for the CTBT negotiations. Interview with former MOFA official, May 1997.

[21] Interview with arms control specialist from the nuclear technical community, January 1997.

[22] Interviews with arms control specialists in the nuclear technical community, May 1996 and July 2000. A written Chinese source, however, claims that the program was first established in late 1979 (Liu 2000:514).

nical questions has been verification. In order to develop an authoritative voice on verification issues, and to study the implications of some of the more intrusive verification proposals in these negotiations, the CAEP set up a Center for Verification Technology Studies in 1995.

Thus, the requirements of participation in the CD and related activities led to the creation of a group of arms control experts in the MOFA, a scientific community with an interest in this activity, and a formal process of policy coordination between these two communities and the PLA.

China's participation in global arms control processes was also responsible for institutional and research development in the uniformed military. It is much harder to discern when this process began. But sometime in the early 1990s, the PLA set up an arms control leading small group in the Central Military Commission (CMC)/General Staff Department (GSD) system, headed possibly by a vice chairman of the CMC. This small group was tasked to coordinate arms control policy research across the GSD system. It was apparently not as developed bureaucratically as the COSTIND community nor, certainly, the MOFA arms control community. Although it was the third major player in the interagency process that developed over the 1990s, this group did not weigh in on every issue. It played a minor role in CTBT policy debates—the testing community in COSTIND being the key constituency in the military-industrial complex. But on the landmine protocol question, it was the key PLA actor.[23]

In order to improve the general quality and quantity of arms control research in the uniformed military, in the mid-1990s the Academy of Military Sciences (AMS) also set up an arms control group in its Strategy Department. This group focused on the history of arms control, the conceptual basis of arms control, the content and scope of current arms control processes, guiding principles in the "art of struggle" in the arms control arena, and models of decision making.[24]

In sum, the fact of participation in international arms control processes has led to the development of institutions and organizations required for interacting in these institutions and, with due regard to their hybridity, taking on similar forms as those of other states (see table 2.1 for a summary).[25]

The (sparse) literature on the effects of interdependence on foreign policy institutions has stressed the decentralization of foreign policy as more

---

[23] Interviews with Chinese arms control official, July 1996; a senior military officer in the PLA General Staff Department, July 1996; senior PLA arms control specialist, June 1996; and retired military officer, June 1996.

[24] Discussion with arms control specialists at the PLA Academy of Military Sciences, July 1996.

[25] My thanks to Evan Medeiros for help with some of the details for this chart.

and more domestic-oriented agencies and organizations develop "foreign affairs" interests and relationships. One hypothesis is that with decentralization comes increased problems of policy coordination, making on average for less coherent foreign policy strategies overall (Karvonen and Sundelius 1990). This is possible (and I will address this in more detail later). But there may be an opposite effect: as arms control interests take root in a wider array of agencies, a wider number of organizations have to at least consider their interest in arms control policy. This means that there may be a wide constituency in favor of at least some level of arms control participation at the international level. Although this might not translate into active cross-organization lobbying for similar arms control policies— indeed one should expect bureaucratic differences—it might at least translate into cross-organizational lobbying against a retreat from various arms control commitments. Thus, decentralization may help reinforce the ratchet effect from participation.[26]

To be sure, Chinese arms control policy faced problems of coordination as it became more involved in international institutions. But more fundamentally, this participation forced coordination where none had existed before. Coordination was not immediate. The first major interagency linkages did not appear until about five to six years after China entered the CD. For example, it appears that the first major internal conference on arms control was held in 1986. Organized by the China Institute of Contemporary International Relations (CICIR)—a research arm of the Ministry of State Security—the conference drew together experts from the CICIR, the Institute of World Economics and Politics (IWEP) of the Chinese Academy of Social Sciences, the Strategic Studies Institute at the National Defense University, the General Staff Department's Intelligence Sub-department, the State Council's Center for International Studies, COSTIND's Information Center, and the Academy of Military Science's Operations Research Institute, among others. A number of participants complained about the lack of horizontal linkages and coordination within the Chinese arms control community, and some even obliquely criticized the military for not being more forthcoming with information relevant to policy discussion on arms control. As two participants from CICIR put it in their paper, those engaged in "national defense construction" could better serve the arms control and disarmament "struggle" by more quickly understanding the information needs of this struggle, and they called for establishing all-China academic conferences on arms control (Huang and Song 1987:6–8). There was also a general recognition at the conference that China's arms control policy had been too simplistic,

---

[26] Similar to the effects on military programs in the United States when subcontracts are distributed around a wide number of districts and states.

Table 2.1
Selected Arms Control and Multilateral Security Policy Institutions

Institution	Approximate Functioning Year
Conference on Disarmament delegation	1979–1980
Disarmament Division (fourth division) in the International Organizations Department, Ministry of Foreign Affairs (MOFA)	1982
CDSTIC Geneva Talks Small Group, later renamed the Arms Control Program (1987)	1983
Beijing arms control seminar*	Late 1980s?
Scientists Group on Arms Control	1987?
Arms Control Research Group, China Aerospace Corporation	1987
Military Products Export Leading Small Group	1990
Program for Science and National Security Studies (PSNSS), Institute of Applied Physics and Computational Mathematics (IAPCM)	1989
Academy of Launch Vehicle Technology, arms control group	Early 1990s?
Arms Control Office, Foreign Affairs Office, COSTIND	Late 1980s?
"703" arms control group, PLA General Staff Department (GSD)	1991
Program for Verification Technology Studies, China Academy of Engineering Physics	1995
Arms Control Physics Research Office, Institute of Applied Physics and Computational Mathematics (IAPCM)	1996

Arms Control Office**, in the Foreign Affairs Office, PLA General Armaments Department	Late 1990s
"703" arms control group, PLA General Armaments Department	1998–1999 (transferred from GSD)
CWC National Implementation Office, State Economic and Trade Commission	1996
Office for the Control of Nuclear Materials, China Atomic Energy Agency	1990?
arms control group***, Strategy Department Second Research Office, PLA Academy of Military Sciences	1996
Center for Arms Control and Non-proliferation Studies in the Institute of American Studies, Chinese Academy of Social Sciences	1998
Arms Control and Disarmament Department (with separate nuclear, CWB, conventional missiles, and comprehensive divisions), Ministry of Foreign Affairs	1997
Technical Exchange and Arms Control Division (General Armaments Department, CDSTIC)	1998–2000?
Arms Control and Disarmament Association (coordination group under the Ministry of Foreign Affairs)	2001
Arms Control Division****, China Institute of Contemporary International Relations	Late 1990s
Comprehensive Bureau (regional security dialogues), PLA General Staff Department Foreign Affairs Office	mid-1990s?

* A regular cross-agency seminar on arms control issues run by CDSTIC's arms control program.

** Previously under COSTIND's CDSTIC, established in the late 1980s.

*** A less formal arms control study group was based at the AMS since the early 1990s.

**** Previously, arms control research was handled under the Comprehensive Division in the CICIR.

inflexible, and insufficiently concrete. As Pan Zhenqiang, the chief arms control expert at the National Defense University, put it, "Merely raising principles is insufficient. We must have even more concrete topics on which to express our position" (Pan 1987:27). In the words of IWEP analyst Wang Shuzhong, China's "leftist" denunciations of arms control in the past had led to poor analysis. As a result, China's policies in the 1970s had been "limited to a few basic principles and lacked initiative and flexibility" (Wang 1987:86). These policies only hindered China from developing responses to the widening array of arms control issues that it was forced to confront as a result of its engagement in multilateral institutions such as the CD (Wang 1987:86).

By the mid-1990s, however, the requirements of participation in CD treaty negotiations essentially compelled the Chinese to set up a functioning interagency process. The CTBT seems to have been the key impetus. Essentially, the MOFA Disarmament Division and the ambassador for disarmament would take the lead in establishing a negotiable agenda for the interagency process. Because the CTBT issue was considered a testing question, the nuclear testing community—represented by the CAEP and the IAPCM—was the other key actor in the interagency. As such, the Second Artillery played a minor role even though a CTBT affected its warhead modernization options. Meetings held before and after each session of the CD would hammer out bargaining positions for the next negotiation session. At key points in the CD negotiations—for example, in January 1996—senior officials from the testing community were assigned to the CD delegation to provide technical advice, to represent the interests of the testing community, and to provide for quicker decision making just in case China had to adjust to a fast-moving negotiation process.

The requirements for participation in global arms control negotiation processes, such as those in the CD, were not the only impetus for the development of an arms control constituency and cross-agency coordination, however. In some cases, this constituency building was in response to particular events or actions of other states. For example, Reagan's Strategic Defense Initiative (SDI) was a critical issue in first encouraging cross-unit research relationships that had not existed before. In reaction to Reagan's speech, CASS-IWEP organized a cross-unit meeting on SDI sometime in 1984. This brought together for the first time in a formal meeting participants from the AMS, GSD, COSTIND, MOFA, and the Aerospace Ministry, among other groups. Prior to this meeting, interunit contacts were governed by strict secrecy rules and heavily compartmentalized information flows. The SDI research programs set up in response to Reagan's speech (some were based in IWEP, some in COSTIND, some in the Aerospace Ministry, some in MOFA's China Institute of International Studies, and some in the Second Artillery) all required consultation among diplomatic, scientific, and strategy specialists because the issue was inherently cross-disciplinary.[27] Out of this rudimentary interagency process and consultations came reports that substantially established China's opposition to SDI, a position it took into international institutions such as the CD.[28]

In addition to all this institutional development and the creation of horizontal bureaucratic and personal linkages within the arms control community, new channels of information were being set up to disseminate arms control–related information and research. In addition to open journals on international relations and security issues, as of the late 1990s there were at least five additional publications specifically aimed at this community:

- *Junkong xinxi jianbao* [Short reports on arms control information], published by the China Defense Science and Technology Information Center. This reproduced Western articles, shorter opinion pieces, and news clippings on arms control without translation. It had a fairly regular publication date, coming out about once per week.

- *Selected Readings in Arms Control and Disarmament.* This, too, was published by the CDSTIC. It also provided untranslated copies of Western articles on China, arms control, and security from journals such as *Comparative Strategy, International Security, Arms Control Today.* This series began in 1991 with articles on the START treaty.

- *Junbei kongzhi yanjiu tongxun* [Bulletin on arms control research]. This was published by the Arms Control and Disarmament Program in the CDSTIC. It had separate studies by Chinese arms control specialists on current policy issues. For example, one of the IAPCM's top experts, Chen Xueyin, published a piece in this series on complete disarmament in 1992 (Chen 1992a) and another in the same year on safety and security of warheads (Chen 1992b).

- An occasional papers series on nuclear and arms control issues. This was published by the Nuclear Science and Technology Information Research Institute (*He kexue jishu qingbao yanjiu suo*). This was a document series in which arms control experts published their views on everything from international law and the legitimacy of nuclear weapons (CNIC-NMC-047), to the law of the sea and nuclear weapons (CNIC-NMC-048), to international law and no first use (CNIC-NMC-24).

- *Guowai he wuqi dongtai* [Foreign nuclear weapons trends]. This was also published by the Nuclear Science and Technology Information Re-

---

[27] Interview with senior arms control and strategic studies specialist, May 1996.
[28] For one such report, see Zhuang 1984.

search Institute, and was possibly the longest-running source of information on arms control–related questions for the technical community, as it was first published in 1975. This journal also published pieces by IAPCM specialists on nuclear questions. It provided summaries of the state of play in multilateral negotiations, and monitored foreign reactions to developments in Chinese nuclear capabilities.[29]

It is clear, then, that the mere fact of participation in the CD and other related multilateral arms control discussions required the development of bonafide arms control experts and organizational/logistical structures to support them. This was a crucial first step in surviving as an arms control novice in an unfamiliar institutional environment.

MIMICKING INSTITUTIONAL ROUTINES AND PROCEDURES

In addition to the need to develop organizations and coordination mechanisms, participation required action inside the international institutions that did not dramatically violate the behavioral and discursive practices of the institution.

Once involved, China's rates of participation inside these institutions picked up. One indicator of this was the changing frequency with which the Chinese diplomats submitted working papers and statements for consideration by other states. Figure 2.2 shows the cumulative frequency of working papers presented to the UN Disarmament Commission (First Committee) from 1980 through 1994. Working papers can typically range from general comments on a particular agenda item, to a suggestion for wording change in a sensitive passage in a negotiating document, to a detailed scientific analysis of a technical arms control issue. The data show a rather quick jump in this form of participation from the late 1980s on.

Another indicator was the changing frequency with which the emerging arms control community produced research and analysis on issues relevant to China's participation in institutions. Figure 2.3 shows the cumulative sum of arms control studies conducted by the technical arms control community based in the China Academy of Engineering Physics (CAEP), its Institute of Applied Physics and Computational Mathematics (IAPCM), and the IAPCM's Program on Science and National Security (PSNSS).[30] The frequency of these studies increased in the early 1990s as the CD began to consider the CTBT issue more seriously. These studies

[29] For instance, No. 6 of December 2, 1994, and No. 5 of September 9, 1995, had articles on foreign reactions to China's latest tests.

[30] The CAEP is principally responsible for China's nuclear weapons designs and testing.

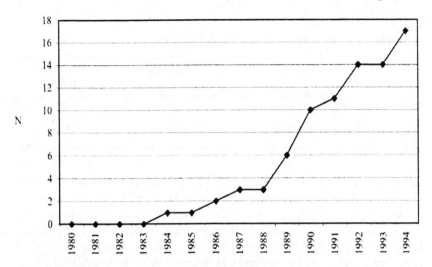

Figure 2.2. Cumulative sum of Disarmament Commission working papers produced by the PRC

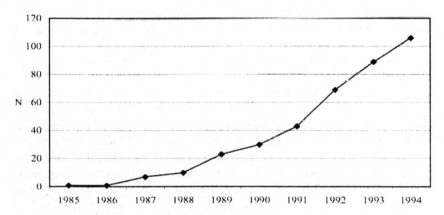

Figure 2.3. Cumulative sum of IAPCM studies. Source: Program on Science and National Security Studies (1994:136–50).

were critical in outlining the weapons community's positions on treaty bargaining, and for generating technical information essential for more active participation in international security institutions as the agendas of these institutions evolved.

Together these indicators suggest a strong relationship in the changing rates of participation in international security institutions over time. Indeed, the correlations between such disparate arms control–related activi-

TABLE 2.2
Correlation Matrix of PRC Arms Control Activities

	CD Working Papers	PSNSS Working Papers
PSNSS working papers	.96	–
Arms control treaty accession rate	.942	.947

ties as the production of CD working papers, the writing of arms control studies by China's technical community, and China's treaty accession rate are very high (see table 2.2). Put differently, increased activity in one area was accompanied by increased activity in another. If, for example, China's increased participation rates in the CD were simply "busy," though shallow, responses to the changing CD agenda, with little relationship to treaty accessions or to the mobilization of talent and resources in the policy process, one would not expect these intercorrelations to be so consistently high.

These changing rates of participation, at a pace faster than the growth in the range of possible activities China could be engaged in, suggest, then, there was some intentionality behind increasing levels of participation. That is, there was some change in Chinese decision rules such that the relatively low levels of participation prior to the 1980s were no longer acceptable or appropriate.

The most obvious explanation is a path-dependent one. Here the argument would be that China's initial involvement in international security institutions placed China's decision makers in an environment where there were incentives to become more involved. Increasing levels of involvement led to increasing returns from participation, returns that were distributed across new actors who emerged to handle the agenda of the institutions. These returns involved everything from organizational gains from increased participation, access to new information and resources of use to these organizations, to social backpatting from participation in a large, highly legitimate community, among other benefits (the costs from reduced involvement were, for the most part, the opposite of these gains).[31] The test of path dependence in arms control issues is whether lock-in led to outcomes that were inefficient for increasing relative power and security, but nonetheless too costly for other reasons to avoid. I will come back to this in the next section.

The evidence suggests, then, that activity breeds activity. The intellectual and organizational requirements of participation in international se-

[31] For a discussion of path dependence and lock-in, see Pierson (2000).

curity institutions at time t was an important variable in accounting for this participation at time $t + 1$. Involvement in the CD and accessions to treaties required that China act, speak, and negotiate. This required research, expertise, and content. In turn, this required institutional support for this behavior. What started initially as a nonfunctionalist reason for joining the CD, for instance, created a growing stake in participation, where reaction to agenda setting by others led to organizational responses that otherwise would not have occurred.

MIMICKING INSTITUTIONAL DISCOURSES

In addition to the pace of routinized activity within these institutions, participation also led to changes in discursive practices. In many instances, China's initial participation was rather anemic, as Chinese diplomats mostly observed proceedings; when they did participate, it was to make inappropriate attacks on Soviet social imperialism or US hegemonism. The Chinese delegation to the CD, for example, was criticized in the early 1980s by others in the CD for this unconstructive and rote Maoist discourse. In response, from 1983 on, Chinese statements began to place less emphasis on the responsibilities of the superpowers for arms control problems in the world and more on substantive agenda issues even though, in the early years of its participation, the PRC leaders did not view many of these agenda items as particularly relevant to China's own security. As one indicator of this shift in discursive practice, figure 2.4 shows the changing ratio of these frequencies, an indicator that in relative terms Chinese statements focused increasingly on the agenda and less on its political demands that the superpowers take the lead in arms control.[32] Moreover, relatively speaking, Chinese statements focused more and more on China's own participation in the arms control agenda. Figure 2.5 shows the declining ratio of statements about the superpowers' participation in relation to statements about China's participation in and/ or responsibility for arms control.[33] In effect, Chinese diplomats learned

[32] I coded each of the opening statements by the head of the Chinese CD delegation at the first session of the CD each year. These opening statements provide a *tour d'horizon* of Chinese views of international relations and the positions it outlined for various arms control issues on that year's agenda. Each sentence in each document was coded for references to the United States or USSR and for a particular arms control issue theme. The UN documents coded were: CD/PV 53 February 5, 1980; CD/PV105 February 12, 1981; CD/PV 192 February 8, 1982; CD/PV 242 February 16, 1984; CD/PV 292 February 19, 1985; CD/PV 339 February 13, 1986.

[33] Sentences in the opening statements to the CD (see previous note) were coded for reference to proactive actions with regard to arms control, e.g., references to positions taken, statements issued, commitments made, and concerns about arms control. Sources: CD/PV 53 February 5, 1980; CD/PV105 February 12, 1981; CD/PV 192 February 8, 1982; CD/PV 242 February 16, 1984; CD/PV 292 February 19, 1985; CD/PV 339 February 13, 1986.

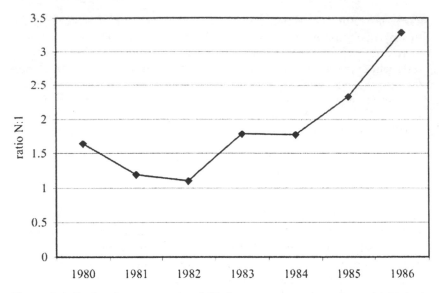

Figure 2.4. Ratio of statements on ACD issues to statements about the United States and Soviet Union in the Conference on Disarmament. Source: Conference on Disarmament plenary session statements (CD/PV), various years 1980–1986.

fairly quickly to portray China as more proactive, and they became less concerned about using the CD as a forum for bashing the superpowers on issues of less direct relevance to the CD's purposes.

This learning process appears to have moved faster in China's arms control and disarmament diplomacy than in other areas of foreign policy. For example, early on China's arms control diplomats in the CD dropped some of the more offensive politicized language that was still found in regular Chinese commentary on international relations. For example, one of the main terms used to criticize the USSR in Chinese foreign policy discourse beginning in the 1960s—social imperialism—was used as late as March 1982 in the Communist Party organ, the *People's Daily*, but did not appear at all in the official statements from the Chinese delegation made in the Conference on Disarmament.[34] Other language and concepts were simply dropped from China's arms control discourse after it was clear how inappropriate these were for the CD and for the post-NPT environment. For example, in the first Chinese statement to the CD in February 1980, nuclear proliferation was considered a right of states: "We hold that, when the Superpowers are constantly expanding their

[34] Determined by a keyword search of *People's Daily* and a review of the Chinese statements to the CD from 1980 to 1982 (CD/PV 53 February 1980; CD/PV 105, February 1981; CD/PV 152 February 1982).

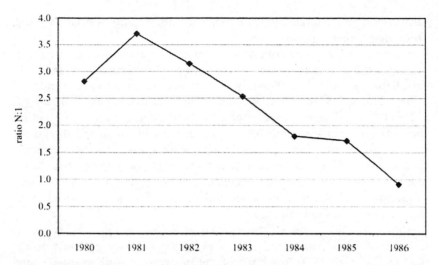

Figure 2.5. Ratio of statements about superpower and Chinese participation in and/or responsibility for arms control. Source: Conference on Disarmament plenary session statements (CD/PV), various years 1980–1986.

nuclear arsenals and carrying out nuclear threats, it is clearly not fair to ask all non-nuclear-weapons States to give up their right to acquire nuclear weapons for self-defense. . . . Of course, this does not mean in any way that we advocate or encourage nuclear proliferation."[35]This position did not appear in any subsequent statements to the CD.

Participation in multilateral arms control institutions and exchanges also gave Chinese specialists a vocabulary that allowed for more sophisticated engagement in these processes. Templates from the UN CD, for instance, were used by the Foreign Ministry to draft working papers for the CD.[36] Specialized universal ACD vocabulary became part of the Chinese discourse in appropriate fora. For example, the term "arms control" (*junbei kongzhi*) was used with increasing frequency over time within the specialist community. Previous to participation in the CD and other international fora, for instance, "disarmament" (*caijun*) was the only politically correct term in the Chinese lexicon. In this older discourse, arms control was a negative term: arms control was what the US and Soviet superpowers engaged in to consolidate their quantitative and qualitative lead in weapons and to avoid more dramatic disarmament.[37] Dis-

---

[35] CD/PV 53, February 1980, p. 26.

[36] Interview with a former senior Foreign Ministry official in charge of arms control policy, June 1996.

[37] See the discussion of the terms "arms control" and "disarmament" in Liu 2000:2.

armament, on the other hand, was what the developing world demanded, and what China supported.

Chinese research and commentary on arms control and disarmament affairs first began to use the term "arms control" on a more regular, apolitical basis around 1986.[38] Possibly the first organization to adopt the term "arms control" in its name was the Arms Control program under the CDSTIC. The Fourth Division of the MOFA's International Organizations Department—responsible, as noted, for China's multilateral arms control diplomacy from the early 1980s on—was initially informally known as the Disarmament and Arms Control Division. After that, "arms control" was increasingly an acceptable term to describe both China's diplomacy on disarmament issues and the organizations involved in research and policy development.

Other core arms control concepts entered Chinese experts' lexicon as a result of participation in the CD. In China's first-ever statement to the CD in February 1980, the head of the delegation, Ambassador Zhang Wenjin, called for "international supervision and inspection" to ensure implementation of any prohibition of chemical weapons. At the time, this was the most explicit comment about verification that the PRC had issued. A CD working paper issued shortly thereafter by the Chinese delegation on prohibiting chemical weapons also referred to the need for "measures for international control and supervision to ensure the strict implementation of the provision of the convention."[39] By 1981, however, Chinese representatives had incorporated the appropriate term "verification" into their vocabulary. In a working paper on nuclear disarmament submitted to the CD in 1981, the Chinese called for "supervision by national technical means of verification as well as effective means of international verification."[40] In other words, the Chinese delegation had accepted that arms control needed verification and that this could be done both through unilateral spying and through multilateral mechanisms. In 1982, on the chemical weapons question the Chinese delegation actually called

---

[38] The term "arms control" (*junbei kongzhi*) was used in the *People's Daily* as early as the 1970s when quoting US or Soviet governments on arms control activities. But the term was not used to describe Chinese activities until the 1980s. The term starts to be used regularly in articles on disarmament in the internal circulation journal of the Institute of World Economics and Politics, *Internal Reference Materials in World Economics and Politics* [*Shijie jingji yu zhengzhi neican*] from mid-1986 on, and in the open China Institute of International and Strategic Studies journal, *International Strategic Studies* [*Guoji zhanlue xue*] in 1987. The term "arms control talks" (*junkong tanpan*) was not used in the *People's Daily* until September 1986.

[39] CD/102 "Chinese Delegation Proposals on the Main Contents of a Convention on the Prohibition of Chemical Weapons" (June 3, 1980), p. 3.

[40] CD/CDP/WP.44 "Working Paper on the First Stage of Nuclear Disarmament Measures of the Comprehensive Programme of Disarmament" (1981), p. 2.

for the most intrusive form of verification—"on-site inspection"—to verify any CW treaty.[41] This is not to suggest that China's political leaders became instant supporters of intrusive arms control verification measures. But it did mean that for the first time, Chinese arms controls specialists had verbalized the standard arms control axiom that intrusive verification was a key to successful arms control compliance.

Along with the use of the term "arms control," arms control specialists began to accept and disseminate some of the conceptual content behind the term that had developed in the Western discourse. For example, American arms control theory focused on a threefold conceptualization of the value of arms control—preventing war, reducing the costs of war if it broke out, and reducing military spending. After Chinese specialists dropped the pejorative vision of arms control, they too endorsed this conceptualization, though in somewhat modified fashion. For example, a textbook on arms control put together to train specialists in the nuclear weapons technical program in the early 1990s noted without comment that arms control can help reduce the dangers of military conflict, reduce the probability of war, and help restrain a conflict once it has broken out.[42]

One also saw a shift in the argument structures about ACD. Initially in the 1980s China's arms control and disarmament proposals in the CD and elsewhere were fairly vague about technical details such as verification, for instance. Chinese officials argued normatively but not technically. That is, such and such measures *should* be taken, but there was little discussion of incentive structures, credibility, and compliance issues.[43] However, as a cadre of experts developed with training in, and exposure to, these concepts, and as the international agenda shifted to negotiating treaties that had real military implications for China (e.g., CTBT, PII) in the 1990s, the discourse shifted to details about compliance and implementation. This did not mean that Chinese arms controllers endorsed any and all verification procedures. But they came to accept that in principle,

[41] See CD/PV no. 53, February 1980, p. 26, and CD/PV no. 152, February 1980, p. 51. This explicit call for intrusive verification was unusual this early on in China's participation in the CD, and applied only to chemical weapons but not to its stance on nuclear weapons. This probably reflected the real concern that chemical weapons were integrated into Soviet operational plans for an attack on China.

[42] See Du 1996:15. The textbook was the product of lectures on arms control theory put together by the IAPCM's Program on Science and National Security Studies for graduate students in nuclear physics specializing in arms control. Recall that the PSNSS was inspired by contacts between Chinese nuclear weapons scientists and Western arms control technical specialists in the mid- and late-1980s. See also Liu Huaqiu's handbook on arms control and disarmament compiled for China's leaders in which the threefold purposes of arms control are discussed (Liu 2000:2).

[43] As noted above, the exception was on chemical weapons.

verification was a necessary component of a credible treaty—in contrast to China's past normative appeals for compliance with unrealistic proposals for all-around disarmament. And China's arms control specialists became capable of arguing about the technical details of verification regimes. In other words, over time China's cadre of arms control experts could engage in technical components of potential agreements more fully.

CONCLUSION

Mimicking is, perhaps, the least social of the socialization processes discussed in this book. It is also the process closest to a "logics of consequences" rationalist process. But it is not asocial, nor is it not nonrational. Obviously, mimicking requires some example of group behavior to copy. And the decision to mimic does not entail a well-thought-through calculation of the costs and benefits. Rather it involves a satisficing decision about survival in an unfamiliar environment. The more other people act uniformly, or the more obvious it is that the group is acting uniformly, then the easier it is for one to make this decision quickly. Institutions provide the group—the CD's members, for instance—and formal and informal institutional rules provide the uniformity of behavior. China's entrance into the arms control arena in the 1980s helped create policy institutions, policy activity, and policy language needed to survive in this new foreign policy issue area. Most interesting is the endogenous effect of this participation. Some of the endogeneity was determined by the development of organizational interests that increased the role of the arms control bureaucracies in the policy process. Some appears to have been determined by the required use of the language of arms control within the international institutions. The acquisition of arms control language exposed China's developing arms control community to new arms control concepts. This did not mean, of course, that due to mimicking Chinese arms controllers lined up with other players on all issues in the CD. The CD is not like the US Marines. The boundaries of appropriate behavior inside arms control institutions are wider than that. But CD participation helped delegitimize the anti-Soviet rhetoric of China's earlier arms control diplomacy; it helped Chinese arms controllers understand the importance of verification; and it helped create a community of experts in China who pushed more traditional arms control perspectives in the multilateral arms control policy process.

This mimicking process is not unique to arms control. As Jacobson and Oksenberg showed with regard to China's initial participation in keystone international economic organizations, the mere requirement simply to participate has far-reaching constraining effects on policy options (though they do not use the term "mimicking"). In the case of joining the IMF and World Bank, for instance, China had to adopt universal models of accounting systems. This in turn led Chinese economists to change their thinking about the importance of the services sector in economic development (Jacobson and Oksenberg 1990:144–45).

This suggests that "process" is important, despite the skepticism that process dilutes outcomes, allows obfuscation, and leads to lowest common denominator behavior, especially in inclusive institutions (Downs, Rocke, and Barsoom 1997). This is a critique leveled at informal and formal multilateral institutions that are insufficiently results–oriented. In retrospect, however, it is hard to imagine how the Chinese government would have been able to accept, even if reluctantly, some of the core arms control concepts behind the CTBT—e.g., intrusive verification—if Chinese arms controllers had not existed. With that long-term effect of mimicking in mind, let me turn next to the puzzle of why China's leaders accepted a relative-power-constraining institution such as the CTBT.

CHAPTER 3

Social Influence

IDENTITY is a popular term in international relations theory right now. The concept is central to arguments about the social construction of preferences, and about why actors behave according to "logics of appropriateness." But constructivists have been somewhat vague about the operationalization and observation of identity,[1] and the expected patterns of behavior that emanate from having an identity. I will come to the first question later. But with regard to the second, constructivist research has used at least two different understandings of identity, each with different behavioral implications. The first emphasizes the conflictual effects of identity, the second the cooperative effects.

First, some constructivists emphasize how identities tend to produce conflictual behavior with out-groups. Sometimes the literature refers to robust findings from social identity theory (Tajfel and Turner 2001; Turner 1987), but often it does not, borrowing instead from more humanities-derived notions of "othering" as implicit in the process of identity construction. Regardless, this approach argues that the process of in-group identity creation creates conditions conducive to the devaluation of out-groups. People acquire self-esteem from identification with a high-valued in-group. Change in the valuation of the in-group can occur only in relation to an out-group. Thus, self-esteem as a member of an in-group is directly related to perception of the high valuation of the group, which is premised on a devaluation of an out-group. In group identification, moreover, is premised on stereotyping of self (positively) and other (negatively), hence is the basis for ethnocentrism and discrimination, regardless whether there is any existing conflict of material interest.

As for cooperative effects, these derive largely from social identity theory and/or role theory, though the literature can often be unclear which. From SIT one can argue that the flip side of devaluation of an out-group is other-regarding thought and action toward the in-group. As an individual develops higher levels of identification with the group, s/he sees self and other members of the group as increasingly similar, thus eliciting empathy

---

[1] For a range of suggestions, see Chafetz 1997; Wetherell 1987:141–70; and Sellers et al. 1998:18–39. For a more detailed discussion of the problems of observing and measuring identity, see Abdelal et al. 2006.

and altruism. From role identity theory constructivists have borrowed the notion that actors take on social roles vis-à-vis others. These roles entail behavior that is considered normatively appropriate or even deeply habitual (and thus unconsciously enacted).[2] Although role theory could predict either conflictual behavior (the role of a revolutionary leader could lead to a normatively "appropriate" effort to coercive spread of an ideology or cooperative behavior) or cooperative behavior (the role of a middle power mediator could lead to normatively "appropriate" participation in peacekeeping operations), generally it has been used to explain adherence to norms that run counter to realpolitik practice in world politics (e.g., it is appropriate as a civilized state to abide by norms against the use of chemical or nuclear weapons; to eschew slavery; or to oppose apartheid).

But there is at least one more expectation with behavioral effects that comes from having an identity—or a social category with associated constitutive norms, relational norms, social purposes, and cognitive structures (Abdelal et al. 2006). This is a sensitivity to the accumulation of status markers bestowed by the group. How does the desire to acquire social rewards from the in-group affect decisions to cooperate? This question is the focus of this chapter.

Specifically, I explore the implications of the following propositions:

1. actors in world politics value image and status as ends in and of themselves along with wealth, relative power, and a range of other desires (a proposition that decision makers and historians of world politics have long recognized);[3]

2. the desire to maximize status and image and the desire to maximize wealth or relative power are not necessarily compatible, and actors often have to make trade-offs between these desires, especially in an

---

[2] On normative appropriateness, see Wendt 1994; Kowert and Legro 1996:462; Jepperson, Wendt, and Katzenstein 1996:60–61; and Knoke 1994:7. On habituation, see Hopf 2002. Although this is not the place for a more extended discussion, it is worth noting that constructivism has tended to obscure or ignore the distinction between social identity–theoretic and role-theoretic assumptions about the link between identity and behavior. For the former, the content of shared identity is less important for explaining relevant behaviors (in-group cohesion and out-group competition) than the fact of sharedness. In the latter, the opposite is true.

[3] See the examples of the diplomacy of honor and face in O'Neill 1999. The discourse surrounding the Indian nuclear weapons test of May 1998 is one of the clearest recent examples of status and self-image as a driver in security policies. There is virtually no evidence that Chinese nuclear capabilities had any substantial impact on India's decision to test its bomb (Hymans 2001). Rather discourse was either anti-Pakistani or, in international fora, replete with references to India deserving more attention from other major powers, for not being listened to, or for being slighted in various fora in the global non-proliferation regime.

era when participation in international institutions that embody sov-
ereignty-restraining norms has become one marker of status (Chayes
and Chayes 1996);

3. sometimes other desires lose out in this trade-off, meaning that
sometimes actors believe that the status rewards from behavior ex-
ceed the rewards from increases in relative power or wealth. This
behavior is, by definition, cooperative or pro-group if it sacrifices
relative power and wealth to accumulate markers for behavior that
is valued by the group.

The role that status maximization plays in eliciting cooperative behavior has been undertheorized in IR. Most of the work on status has focused
on it as a source of conflict. Status inconsistency theories and frustration-
aggression arguments suggest that the desire to maximize status can lead
states to engage in conflictual behavior (Organski and Kugler 1980; Vertzberger 1990; Lemke and Reed 1998; Oneal, de Soysa, and Park 1998).
In traditional realism, status (aka prestige) is seen as the collective recognition by others of a state's military power and wealth. Thus, states that
seek to maximize status do so by competing for power and influence. The
pursuit of status is thus often seen as contributing to zero-sum conflicts
(Gilpin 1981). Yet it is clear from a vast literature on social influence that
an actor's desire to accumulate status markers can also be a source of
within-group cooperation.[4]

The concept of identity enters the story in two ways, one purely normative and one purely instrumental. In normative terms, an actor's self-categorization may be internalized enough such that certain behaviors are
considered appropriate for its social category. When its behavior is perceived by the group to be inconsistent with this self-categorization and
runs into group opprobrium, the actor changes its behavior because of
cognitive discomfort from inconsistency with or the violation of the norms
of behavior appropriate to its identity. (This account derives more or less
from a role-theoretic concept of identity, though social identity theorists
might claim that social influence derives from an individual's desire to
be viewed as a highly valued "prototypical" member of the in-group.)
In instrumental terms, since status is bestowed by a group, an actor

---

[4] In contractual institutionalism, reputation is usually seen as a strategic tool used by an
actor to alter others' beliefs about its propensity to cooperate, thus increasing the credibility
of its contractual commitments. But this kind of reputation needs to be distinguished from
more diffuse reputations or images where the actor does not take into account specific contractual payoffs from maintaining a cooperative reputation, but where such a reputation is
valued as appropriate to the actor's identity and is recognized as such by valued social
groups. Acknowledging this image then becomes a social reward for pro-group behavior.

wishing to accumulate status must first identify with the group such that it recognizes the value attached to particular status markers. Then the actor must act in ways consistent with what the group considers to be highly valued norms of behavior. In principle, a purely instrumental calculation would lead an actor to migrate from group to group searching for that group which, in simple terms, supplies the most status markers. Or it would lead an actor to engage in hypocritical but deceptive behavior, trying to meet the social behavioral expectations of as many groups as possible so as to acquire as many status markers as possible.[5] In practice, a couple of things could prevent this migration from happening: strong group norms against hypocrisy (so as to prevent precisely this kind of liminal existence that may threaten the cohesiveness of the group); or the sufficient internalization of behavioral scripts (as constitutive norms) such that there is certain stickiness to an identity. In any case, the concept of identity (as I will expand on in a moment) is central to exploring why concerns about image or diffuse (noninstrumental) reputation may help elicit cooperative behavior.

The chapter first begins with a discussion of the theoretical microfoundations and microprocesses of social influence, drawing from work in social psychology and sociology on the effects of identification with group membership. It then goes on to look at how social rewards and punishments can change incentives for actors such that defection may no longer be the optimal strategy. It then generates some hypotheses about what to expect empirically if social influence is at work. Finally, the chapter tests these on case studies of China's behavior in negotiations toward the Comprehensive Test Ban Treaty from 1994 to 1996 and in negotiations over the landmines protocol of the Convention on Certain Conventional Weapons. Additional empirical implications are addressed at the end of the chapter, including two potentially disconfirming cases, China's lead-

---

[5] This means a fair amount of strategic behavior should go into the provision of status markers. That is, there should be incentives within in-groups to provide or withhold status markers in order, say, to entice pro-social behavior of particularly important actors. This also raises the question of whether the supply of status markers is itself a collective action problem that needs to be explained. I touch on this at the end of the chapter. I assume for the moment that there is some distribution of actors in the in-group that includes sufficient numbers of "activists" committed to providing status markers to ensure there is no collective action problem governing supply and that the status-seeking actor knows this. As I will note at the end, status markers have particularly interesting implications for the collective action problem behind the supply of side payments necessary for overcoming collective action problems. That is, status markers are relatively cheap and easy to supply even though they can have sufficiently high value to act as a side payment. Suffice it to say, one cannot do everything. In this chapter I am interested more in how the availability of a supply of status markers affects the decisions of an actor wishing to maximize them. This is a decision-theoretic question.

ers' decision not to sign the Ottawa Treaty banning the production and use of landmines, and their apparent imperviousness to criticism of human rights conditions.

As I noted in chapter 1, China is a useful case because the tension between status concerns and the desire to maximize relative material power is so clear. On the one hand, there is a general consensus among observers of China's foreign policy that China's behavior can often best be described as realpolitik. Whether rooted in traditional strategic culture, modern nationalism, or structural anarchy,[6] it is clear from Chinese foreign policy discourse and practice that maximizing relative military and economic power has mattered a great deal to China's leaders, and that this is a central explanation for free riding and defection strategies in international institutions. Good examples of this realpolitik free riding include China's efforts over the 1980s and 1990s to avoid any Perm-5 negotiations on controls on strategic nuclear forces, and China's opposition to timetables and ceilings for developing states under the Framework Convention on Climate Change. Yet there are critical cases of substantive cooperation when one would not have expected it from a state so concerned about preserving and enhancing relative power. In these cases, China has cooperated despite potential constraints on its relative power and in the absence of two standard sources of cooperation in institutions—material rewards and punishments.

There are at least two other kinds of explanations that might be at work in these cases. One is that Chinese preferences change, such that relative power is less desirable than some other good. Here the operative process would be persuasion. Another possibility is elite transformation where major political change occurs when new elites with different preferences come to control the policy process. Neither of these explanations seems to be at work in these cases. As I will note, there is no evidence that Chinese decision makers were persuaded, through intensive interaction inside the CTBT negotiation process, to change their underlying views about the negative implications of the CTBT on Chinese security. As for the second possibility, since China did not undergo any destabilizing or radical changes in leadership or leadership ideology in the 1980s, nor in the 1990s when the CTBT and landmine protocols were being negotiated, we can safely discount this factor in these cases. As I will argue, social influence seems most credible in these cases. The institutional environment—the CTBT negotiations—created conditions conducive to the efficacy of social influence (a high-profile, legitimate institution where the overwhelming number of participants were supportive of the process, and

---

[6] Different sources of Chinese realpolitik are explored in Johnston 1995, 1996a; Christensen 1996; and Nathan and Ross 1997.

where there were no credible offers of material side payments for cooperation). And Chinese leaders' sensitivity to their international image made them responsive to these conditions.

SOCIAL INFLUENCE IN THEORY

It is fair to say that the predominant approaches or schools in IR theory today—neorealism and contractual institutionalism—share a common assumption about actor motivation, namely that actors are driven at a meta-preference level by the desire to maximize individual utility, usually defined in atomistic materialist terms (power capabilities, wealth, political perks of office, etc.). This preference is held constant while theorists examine how exogenous changes in the material power distributions or in institutional rules affect the strategic choices of actors.

But it is important to note that this assumption about motivation is just that—an assumption. In fact, outside of IR theory the social sciences have long acknowledged that basic motivations can vary: Skinnerian behavioralism contended that what is desired is that which is rewarded. Mead, Durkheim, and other sociologists argued that individuals are motivated by a sense of social solidarity, the desire to belong to, cooperate in, and be reaffirmed by a social group.[7] Relatedly, sociological institutionalists and organizational theorists (and in IR, the social constructivists) have underscored the desire to do what is socially appropriate as a key motivation in human behavior (Finnemore 1996a).

Sociological and social psychological approaches, then, would ask whether there are motivations and incentives to act that are uniquely related to an actor's interaction with social groups, and that would be absent in isolation from social groups. One such set of motivations and incentives has to do with what is called social influence. Social influence refers to a class of microprocesses that elicit pro-normative behavior through the distribution of social rewards and punishments. Rewards might include psychological well-being, status, a sense of belonging, and a sense of well-being derived from conformity with role expectations, among others. Punishments might include shaming, shunning, exclusion and demeaning, or dissonance derived from actions inconsistent with role and identity. The effect of (successful) social influence is an actor's conformity with the position advocated by a group as a result of "real or imagined group pressure" (Nemeth 1987:237).[8] Conformity can be either with

---

[7] For an excellent summary of different theories of motivation, see Turner 1988.

[8] Actually, Nemeth adds that conformity can involve a change in behavior *or* belief. This, in my view, blurs the difference between social influence (the former) and persuasion (the latter).

the descriptively normative behavior of a group (e.g., what most people in the group do) or with its prescriptively normative behavior (what most people in the group believe should be done). The difference between social influence processes and persuasion is neatly summarized by the term Festinger used to describe compliance due to social pressure: "public conformity without private acceptance" (cited in Booster 1995:96). Persuasion would entail public conformity with private acceptance. Persuasion, at least of the kind where the authoritativeness of the persuader is what convinces, has been called "mediated informational influence," e.g., "I thought the answer was X . . . but everybody else said Y, so it really must be Y." Social influence can, instead, come in the form of "mediated normative influence," e.g., "I believe the answer is X, but others said Y, and I don't want to rock the boat, so I'll say Y" (cited in Betz, Skowronski, and Ostrom 1996:116). The rewards and punishments are social because only groups can provide them, and only groups whose approval an actor values will have this influence. Thus, social influence rests on the influenced actor having some prior identification with a relevant reference group. Social influence involves connecting extant interests, attitudes, and beliefs in one "attitude system" to those in some other attitude system, e.g., attitudes toward cooperation get connected to seemingly separate attitudes toward social standing, status, and self-esteem in ways that had not previously occurred to the actor (Zimbardo and Leippe 1991:34).

There is considerable evidence that identification with a group can generate a range of cognitive and social pressures to conform. But, like persuasion, the microprocesses of social influence are multiple, complex, and still the subject of much debate.[9] Generally, however, the literature on social influence has isolated the following possibilities. As will be evident, the boundaries between these microprocesses are blurry.

---

[9] Constructivist-oriented scholars have tended to blur the distinction between persuasion and pressure in IR, or at least have not paid much attention to distinguishing the very different microprocesses. Important work on the behavioral effects of international norms, for instance, has emphasized the role of international normative "pressure" but the term seems to be used to jump over or bridge crucial points in the norm diffusion process without explaining why precisely a norm violator might react in a pro-normative fashion. Keck and Sikkink, for instance, refer to human rights networks being able to embarrass norm violators such that in order to save face, they adjust their behavior (Keck and Sikkink 1998:24). But it is not clear why a norm violator would care about pressure that does not come with concrete threats of sanctions that affect wealth and relative military power. In one of their cases—for example, Argentina under military control in the 1970s—the differential effects of image per se and a desire to "restore the flow of military and economic aid" are not obvious (Keck and Sikkink 1998:107).

The first cluster of arguments comes from social identity theory but is rooted in hypotheses about the cognitive discomfort associated with perceived divergence from group norms. As noted earlier, social identity theory is founded on powerful evidence that mere self-categorization as a member of a particular group generates strong incentives to conform to the group's norms and practices. Identification with a group leads to exposure to prototypical traits of this category or identity. In one version of SIT, a so-called social comparison or social projection hypothesis, group members hang their self-esteem on appearing to be pro-group (leading to more extreme prototypical group norms over time). If a real or imagined disjuncture appears between group norms and those of any individual member (or is exposed and pointed out), the trauma to self-esteem can motivate an actor to reduce this discrepancy through greater conformity.[10]

A second possibility has to do with social liking. Liking typically means that an individual experiences a sense of comfort interacting with others with whom she/he is perceived to share traits. Thus, "[o]ne should be more willing to comply with the requests of friends or other liked individuals" (Cialdini 1984, 1987). Put differently, since liking someone is a product of reward in the presence of this person, it stands to reason that the behavior liked by the liked person or group of persons will be more prevalent in their presence. The desire to conform to behavior advocated by liked persons is strengthened if this comes in the wake of recently resolved disagreements. That is, the atmospherics of new or renewed friendship after spats will be more positively stimulating and compliance-gaining than if there had been no prior disputes (Lott and Lott 1985:127–29).

A third possibility comes from consistency theory (which can be a microfoundational argument in role theory as well). Considerable experimental and field research suggests that people are loathe to appear inconsistent with prior behavior or publicly affirmed beliefs. Cialdini found, for instance, that people were more likely to continue to conform to certain norms and behaviors after taking an on-the-record action that reflects these particular norms, than if they were simply asked to conform (Cialdini 1984, 1987:169). That is, they experience discomfort with being perceived as inconsistent or hypocritical, and, conversely, experience a positive mood with being viewed as consistent with past commitments. People are sensitive to others' judgments of their "global integrity" such that when the self-perception of this integrity is challenged by others, "people attempt to restore it" (Petty, Wegener, and Fabrigar 1997:620), typically through group-conforming behavior. This is, generally speaking, a positive evolu-

---

[10] On SIT and the psychological discomforts of nonconformity, see Turner 1987; Gerard and Orive 1987; Stryker and Statham 1985; Barnum 1997; and Axelrod 1997a.

tionary trait, since it means people will act more predictably, which can increase trust, the credibility of commitments, and the robustness of reciprocity (Cialdini 1984:69). This does not mean that fear of losing a reputation for trustworthiness is the only motivation to behave consistently. Psychological discomfort appears to be an important driver as well.

The compulsion to be consistent generates a powerful effect on individual conformity to the group. Membership in a group usually entails on-the-record statements or behaviors of commitment (e.g., pledges of loyalty, participation in group activities, commitments to fulfill a membership requirement). These behaviors, even if relatively minor, establish a baseline or threshold identity such that behaviors that diverge from these identity markers are discomforting inconsistencies. That is, a commitment can generate a reevaluation of identity, such that a cluster of behaviors related with the new identity become appropriate, and are reinforced by the desire to avoid defecting against this new identity. One experiment, for instance, cajoled subjects previously opposed to nuclear war to write an essay favoring it, while "a subsequent measure typically showed a moderation of the anti-war stand" (Jones 1985:76).[11] In addition, the more the new identity-conforming behavior is repeated, the more extreme, and tenaciously held, the actor's beliefs and attitudes become, thus reinforcing his or her commitment to the group (Petty, Wegener, and Fabrigar 1997:612).

Finally, the desire to maximize status, honor, prestige—image—can be another driver behind group-conforming behavior. So can its opposite, the desire to avoid a loss of status, to avoid shaming or humiliation and other social sanctions. Status refers to "an individual's standing in the hierarchy of a group based on criteria such as prestige, honor and deference." Typically, status is closely related to others' "expectations of ability or competent performance" (Lovaglia 1995:402). Choi offers a useful and related definition: "An individual's status is communal certification of his or her relative proficiency in conventions" (Choi 1993:113). Competency or proficiency need not mean a mechanical ability to do some task, but can mean a high ability to represent some normative ideal. A competent or proficient non-proliferator is, in the eyes of an anti-proliferation community, a responsible actor, a consistent, effective proponent of non-proliferation norms. Image is the public manifestation of status. A positive image refers to the package of favorable perceptions and impressions that one believes one creates through status-consistent behavior.

---

[11] This parallels the success that the Chinese had in getting US Korean War POWs to collaborate. Minor commitments to very mildly critical statements about the United States in essay competitions led over time to more extreme positions, even in the absence of material rewards, because each minor commitment changed the POWs' sense of identity, such that the subsequent behavior was more consistent with the new identity. See Cialdini 1984:76–77.

Numerous motivations are behind maximizing status. Often status brings with it power, wealth, and deference, and vice versa. Gilpin, for instance, refers to prestige as "a reputation for power." States are at the top of the status hierarchy because of their economic and military power (Gilpin 1981:30–33). Moreover, in Gilpin's view, status is highly coercive: status markers are forced out of subordinate states through superior power, often through military victory. This is fine as far as it goes, but often status markers and immediate material gains are not correlated.[12] For example, status markers such as citations, medals, or public recognition may have no obvious material reward. Moreover, the desire to maximize status need not entail efforts to defeat others to seize status: it can entail group-conforming behavior designed to "buy" status. The reward is psychological well-being from backpatting; the punishment is psychological anxiety from opprobrium.

A second possible motivation is to maximize reputational effects attributed to particular status markers. Here status is an instrument: a good image can encourage actors to deal with you in other arenas, can help build trust leading to reciprocity and decentralized (uninstitutionalized) cooperation (Kreps 1992). In this sense, image can also be used deceptively—one might want a positive image to convince other states to cooperate, setting them up for the sucker's payoff in some exploitative prisoners' dilemma game. This conceptualization has three problems, however. The first is, as Frank points out, if people know about this instrumentality, then an actor's image or reputation as a cooperator has no advantage (Frank 1988). So it is in the actor's interest to make cooperation automatic, deeply socialized, in order to make the reputation for cooperation credible. But then no advantages can be accrued, since deception is abandoned. The second problem is that instrumentality assumes the actor is seeking some concrete, calculable benefit from having a good image, an image that can be translated into leverage in some explicit, linked, immediate issue area. Yet often there are no obvious concrete benefits, or they are quite diffuse and vague. Indeed, there are sometimes concrete material costs. In this case, sensitivity to image may be related to identity.[13] Finally, for the most part instrumental arguments about reputation invoke external (and material) costs as the disincentive to acting in

[12] Anthropology and sociology have, for the most part, accepted that wealth *and* status, not just wealth, have been the basic drivers of social behavior. Political science and economics have tended to focus only on the former, or isomorphize the two, calling the driver "power." But as I will argue, it is worth trying to maintain the distinction because these two drivers can lead to different and contradictory predictions about social conformity.

[13] Much of the scholarship on reputational explanations for cooperation is confused about this difference between social image and a concern for contractual reputation. See, for example, Kelley 2004:428.

antisocial ways. That is, observed antisocial behavior is costly because it might lead to a loss of trust and thus a loss of exchange opportunities and payoffs (mostly calculated in streams of economic welfare or political power). But this neglects, as Ostrom points out (Ostrom 1998:12), internal costs such as anxiety or loss of self-esteem due to social opprobrium.

This, then, is the third reason for a concern about status. A particular high-status image may be considered a good in and of itself. Frank, for one, argues that the desire to maximize prestige and status has physiological and psychological benefits (Frank 1985:32). Harre attributes the drive to people's "deep sense of their own dignity, and a craving for recognition as beings of worth in the opinions of others of their kind." To be fulfilled, this craving necessarily depends on *public* affirmation of one's worth, success, and status (Harre 1979:3, 22). Hatch notes that "the underlying motivation is to achieve a sense of personal accomplishment or fulfillment, and the individual does so by engaging in activities exhibiting qualities that are defined by the society as meritorious" (Hatch 1989:349). This motivation blurs into another: the desire to compete in order to acquire the status of a winner. The value of relative gains—winning—is not the payoff from the game per se, but from the status bestowed upon victors (Hatch 1989:347). Bourdieu notes, "the goal of domination is not the control of material resources for purely material needs, but to enhance or affirm social standing through the exclusiveness of taste" (cited in Hatch 1989:344). Adam Smith, surprisingly, remarked that "it is not economic motivation that prompts men to work, but status, respect, esteem, moral mettle, qualities which would allow him to be a man of worth and dignity" (cited in Hatch 1989:345). Franck argues, in reference to the fact that most states abide by most institutional legal commitments most of the time in IR, conformist behavior is due mainly to a desire to be a member of a club and to benefit from the status of membership (Franck 1990:38).

An individual will be sensitive to arguments that his/her behavior is consistent or inconsistent with his/her self-identity as a high-status actor. This sensitivity ought to depend as well on who is making these arguments. The more the audience or reference group is legitimate, that is, the more it consists of actors whose opinions matter, the greater the effects of backpatting and opprobrium (Dittmer and Kim 1993:9,14–15). The legitimacy of the audience is a function of self-identification. Actors more easily dismiss the criticisms of enemies and adversaries than they do those of friends and allies. Thus, the strength of backpatting and opprobrium depends on two related factors: the nature of the actor's self-categorization, and which other actors, by virtue of this self-identification, become important, legitimate observers of behavior. Changes in identities mean that different audiences matter differently. These are mutually constitutive processes.

To give an example, when I was a PhD student in Ann Arbor, Michigan, in the 1980s there was a particular charity that would run a donation drive each year (perhaps it still does).[14] It would position people with signs and a donation bucket at as many street corners as possible in the downtown. If you gave to the charity, you were given a colored paper tag to wear. The tags played an extremely important socially sanctioning role. There were clear benefits from wearing a tag. Some were unrelated to social status. For instance, wearing a tag meant that you would not be hounded to give at the next street corner. But perhaps more importantly, the tags signaled to those who had not given that you had just engaged in a socially helpful activity, underscoring their stinginess, and thus providing self-backpatting, self-superiority benefits. It signaled to those who had also given that you were one of the club, one of the giving community. This provided mutual backpatting benefits. The more people whom you might bump into wearing tags, the more mutual backpatting benefits.

There were, therefore, clear costs to not wearing a tag as well. First, you could be hassled at every street corner. Second, as the community of tag wearers grew in size, as a non-wearer you stood out more and more as someone who had not participated in an act of social responsibility, thus accruing shaming costs. These shaming costs accumulated regardless of whether you were in a part of town where you might be hassled by the charity. In other words, in the downtown area it would be difficult for an outside observer to determine whether the costs to the non-wearer were "material" (e.g., the high hassle factor at street corners) or "social" (e.g., shaming and opprobrium). But away from the downtown, where the hassle factor was irrelevant (since there were no buckets or charity workers), if a non-wearer felt uncomfortable and was eventually compelled to wear a tag (even, say, going so far as to pick up one dropped on the street), this suggested there was normative coercion produced by the tags independent of the material "hassle" costs.[15]

All of the social influence effect hinged, of course, on an intersubjectively agreed upon notion of what socially valuable behavior looked like—giving to charity. I would argue, then, that the production of positive and negative normative sanctions sufficient to induce cooperation in

[14] The example and argument here are inspired by an exam question that Robert Axelrod put to his social science modeling class when I was a graduate student at Michigan.

[15] It would be rational, then, for the charity to have planted a "seed" number of tag wearers to establish a visible minority of socially aware "givers" such that the potentially genuine givers saw opportunities to acquire backpatting benefits and avoid opprobrium costs. I have no idea whether this was done.

the absence of material side payments or threats rests on two conditions. First, there must be an intersubjective normative consensus about what "good" behavior looks like, even if the status seeker does not "internalize" or sense that this behavior is obligatory.[16] Without this shared standard, then the material fact of wearing or not wearing a charity tag will have no agreed interpretation, and consequently the act of wearing or not wearing will have no meaning, generating no shaming or backpatting effects.[17] Second, even if there is a shared interpretation of the meaning of wearing or not wearing a charity tag, these actions will not generate normative pressures if they are unobserved and private.

Thus, the second condition is a forum or institution that makes wearing or not wearing a public, observable act. The forum could be something as loose as a process where voluntary reporting on some agreed commitment is scrutinized, where defectors would stand out either by not submitting a report or by submitting shoddy and incomplete ones. Or it could be something as strict as a multilateral negotiation process where actors are required to state bargaining positions, justify them, and then "vote" in some form on the outcome. Thus, constructivists and institutionalists are both right. Constructivists are right that normatively induced cooperation requires shared understandings of what appropriate behavior looks like. But this may not be enough without an institutional structure that provides information about the degree to which actors are behaving in ways consistent with this shared understanding.[18] This information takes the distance between an actor's behavior and the socially approved standard and makes it public. It is this distance that generates backpatting and shaming effects. In principle, the larger the relevant audience of cooperators, the more powerful these effects are. I say relevant because the requisite size of the audience depends on the legitimacy of the audience. Legitimacy here refers to the degree to which it is the social norms of this particular audience that matter, or that have an effect on a potential free rider. If, say, an actor completely rejected the social norms of a particular group, then no matter what the size of that group, it could not generate backpatting or shaming effects. Owners of coal-fired electricity plants cannot shame an environmentalist.

The converse of social backpatting derived from status is shaming or opprobrium derived from violating status-related norms and practices. It

[16] Franck makes a similar point about symbolic validation of participation in international institutions (Franck 1990:117).

[17] Elster makes a similar point in his discussion of argumentation (Elster 1995:248).

[18] Keohane notes, for instance, that one of the things international institutions do is provide a forum in which an actor's conformity with group standards can be evaluated. He links this to a more instrumental notion of reputation than I do here, however (Keohane 1984:94).

is widely accepted in a number of subfields that fear of opprobrium is a motivation for group conformity, even if suboptimal from a welfare perspective. As Oran Young remarks apropos international institutions, "Policy makers, like private individuals, are sensitive to the social opprobrium that accompanies violations of widely accepted behavioral prescriptions. They are, in short, motivated by a desire to avoid the sense of shame or social disgrace that commonly befalls those who break widely accepted rules" (Young 1992:176–77; see also DiMaggio and Powell 1991:4; and Price 1998:641). The specific microprocesses that compel people to avoid opprobrium are similar to those that encourage people to seek out backpatting.

One final point: different groups infuse value into different kinds of status markers. The same group may infuse different value into the same kinds of status markers over time. Thus, if an actor is solely motivated by desire to maximize the accumulation of these markers, it will have to adopt behavior deemed appropriate by the dominant or most prominent reference group at any particular time. In IR, for instance, the identity category "major power" has had different status markers over history. In the past, these were things like empire or military assertiveness. But today, in Chayes and Chayes's view, the markers of major power status can include participation in status quo institutions that regulate, more or less noncoercively, interstate relations. To so maximize status markers as a major power today may require increasingly pro-social behavior, in contrast to major powers of the past (Chayes and Chayes 1996:7, 230).[19] This makes sense in the postcolonial era. Many of the states that make up the international audience or reference groups are smaller or medium-size states that emerged from the nineteenth-century colonial international system. The foreign policy ideologies of these states are more likely to reject traditional, nineteenth-century models of major powerhood as destructive and exploitative. Moreover, given an acute sensitivity to power differentials, despite (or perhaps because of) the equalizing effects of sovereignty norms in the latter half of the twentieth century, these states are more likely to rely on international institutions as power equalizers. Thus, these states are more likely to define appropriate major power behavior as that which supports international institutions and eschews tra-

---

[19] A somewhat similar point is made by Franck in his discussion of the increasing legitimacy of international organizations. These represent a community of equal sovereignties, regardless of material power, and as a result, participation in and support for IOs has become a critical marker of appropriate, hence socially rewarded, behavior in IR. State leaders who are sensitive to the accumulation of backpatting or the avoidance of opprobrium, therefore, may be more inclined to behave in ways that at least appear to reinforce the legitimacy of IOs. See Franck 1990:101, 104.

ditional unilateralism and power political behaviors. This provides incentives for major power leaders who are particularly sensitive to diffuse image to modify state actions in ways that fit more closely with status-rewarded major power behaviors.[20]

To summarize, the desire to maximize status and image through the accumulation of backpatting benefits (symbolic status markers, praise, etc.) can generate a number of incentives for pro-social behavior. Pro-social behavior motivated by status maximization is not altruistic or pro-group. Rather it reflects an actor's egoistic pursuit of social rewards and avoidance of social sanctions (Batson 1987:35). But it cannot exist without the prior existence of a group and without a common understanding of the value or meaning that the group places on putative status markers. This much, at least, must be shared by the actor and the group.

How Social Influence Works

If these are the reasons why actors might be sensitive to backpatting and opprobrium markers, how might this sensitivity affect the decision calculus of a realpolitik actor? Here we need to look at the effects of these social rewards and punishments on a realpolitik actor's calculation of the costs and benefits of cooperation.

If indeed China's leaders have internalized a traditionally realpolitik concern about shielding China's relative power from potentially constraining commitments to international regimes, then one should be able to basically model their diplomacy using a simple N-person's prisoners' dilemma model (figure 3.1).[21] The C line represents the payoffs to the

---

[20] For a description of the process by which new status markers become accepted in social groups, see Webster and Hysom 1998.

[21] The CTBT case is not technically a pure example of a free-riding opportunity for China. That is, unlike the model in figure 3.1, China's nonparticipation in the CTBT treaty would have meant there would be no treaty, hence no opportunity to free ride off the institution. But this does not mean that free-riding benefits of some type were unavailable. Three of the five nuclear powers had committed to a voluntary testing moratorium prior to the start of treaty negotiations (the United States, Britain, and Russia). France committed to a moratorium by 1996. It is not unreasonable to assume that even in the absence of a formal CTBT, and as long as China continued to adhere to a low-key, slow testing pace, the other nuclear powers would have continued their informal moratorium. As such, China would have been offered a free-riding opportunity, and thus the general point of the model in figures 3.1–3.5 would be valid. The landmine protocol case, however, is a cleaner example of a free-riding opportunity for China, as its agreement to the protocol was not necessary for the protocol's existence. These figures suffice for showing how social influence can affect the calculus of a realpolitik opportunist, e.g., a player who sees the world essentially as multiple prisoners' dilemmas. I thank Phillip Saunders for urging me to clarify this point.

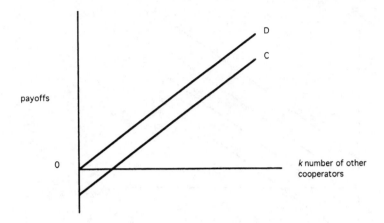

Figure 3.1. Free riding

actor from cooperation as each additional member of the group cooperates. The D line represents the payoffs to the actor from defection as
each additional member of the group cooperates. If China were the only
cooperator (e.g., if it were the only state trying to reduce some global
security "bad" while others continued to maximize their relative power),
its payoff would be negative since it would be constraining its relative
power while having little effect on stabilizing the security environment. If
it did not cooperate while others also defected, then although it could not
derive any benefits from the cooperation of others, it would not at least
lose utility. Thus, it would pay not to cooperate even if there were no
other cooperators. This payoff from defection would hold even as the
number of cooperators increased. As these players contributed to a public
good, China would benefit from the provision of this good, but by free
riding it would not incur the cost of providing its share of the good. Thus,
the payoff line from defection will always be greater than the payoff line
from cooperation. In an N-person PD, China should never have an incentive to cooperate.

Yet it is also true, as I outline early in the book, that China has participated in an increasing range of international arms control, environmental,
economic, and scientific/technical regimes. In a number of these cases,
China is participating in a regime or institution in part because it is being
offered side payments (e.g., China's accession to the Montreal Protocols
on the reduction of ozone-reducing gases was, in part, conditioned on the
creation of a financial mechanism to reduce the costs of phasing out CFC-
producing technologies; China's joining the Zangger group in 1997 was
linked to the US decision to implement the 1985 nuclear cooperation

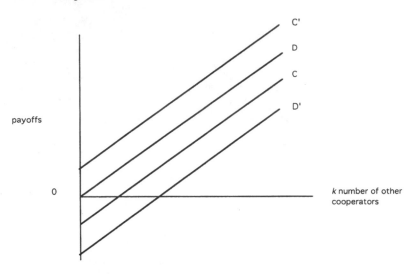

Figure 3.2. The effects of material side payments and sanctions

agreement). In these cases, the effect of side payments (see fig. 3.2) is to raise the C line to a point where it pays to cooperate regardless of the size of the number of other cooperators (from C to C') (whereas the effect of sanctions is to make it more costly to defect than cooperate, regardless of what others do, moving D to D'). Side payments and sanctions, however, need not change the slope of the C or D lines.

These are the uninteresting cases of cooperation, however. The interesting cases are those in which China's involvement has occurred in the absence of side payments or threats of material sanctions. In other words, there is some factor that is altering the costs-benefit calculus such that the payoffs from defection are not so unproblematically greater than from cooperation. One of these factors may well be social influence. After entering international institutions, particularly from the late 1970s and into the 1980s, Chinese decision makers appear to have become more sensitive as to how their behavior played publicly in front of largely status quo second and third world audiences that set the agenda in international institutions such as the Conference on Disarmament in Geneva.[22] In par-

---

[22] The origins of the Chinese leadership's sensitivity to their international image could be the topic of another book. It is possible that this sensitivity did not begin after the PRC's involvement in status quo international institutions. Arguably, in the days of the Sino-Soviet alliance and later during the period of an independent revolutionary foreign policy of the 1960s, image was also important. The audiences, however, were different. During the Maoist period, a certain positive social utility, for instance, came from appearing to be hostile to status quo institutions, and from appearing to be a leading radical voice for dramatic reconstitution of the international system.

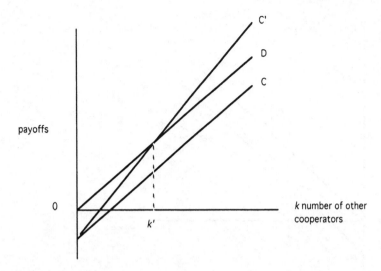

Figure 3.3. Backpatting

ticular, the leadership became more concerned to project an image of a responsible major power and to enhance its international prestige.[23] This concern induced caution in the pursuit of pure defection strategies.

Within international organizations and institutions the participating/ cooperating audience is relatively large. Although the opportunities to free ride are potentially greater—given the number of potential cooperators—the scrutiny of each player is more intense and state behavior is often more transparent than in bilateral relationships, due to the rules of these institutions. In this context, a concern about image has two very different effects on a realpolitik actor's payoff structure, corresponding to the effects of backpatting and opprobrium.

Backpatting is a benefit incurred from being seen as a cooperator or an active pro-social member of a group. An actor receives recognition, praise, and normative support for its involvement in the process. Backpatting can reaffirm an actor's self-valuation, its self-categorization as a high-status actor, with concomitant payoffs for self- and public legitimation. Ceteris paribus, as the size of the cooperating audience grows, the actor accrues more backpatting benefits. Thus, for every additional member of the institution, a potential defector receives a certain added payoff from backpatting as long as it cooperates. The benefits are cumulative. As figure 3.3 indicates, this increases the slope of the payoffs from cooperation (from C to C').

[23] See the discussion on the reasons for China's accession to the World Heritage Convention in Oksenberg and Economy 1998. See also Tang and Zhang 2004:2, 4.

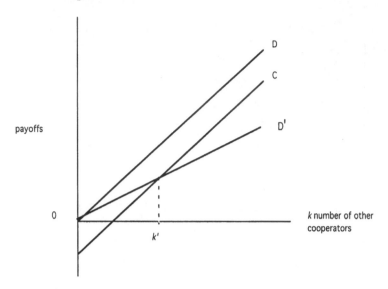

Figure 3.4. Opprobrium

Opprobrium, of course, carries social costs—a denial of the prior status and prestige of the actor—as well as psychological ones—a denial of the actor's identity as one deserving of backpatting. Opprobrium can also be modeled as an accumulation of shaming markers that diminishes the value of free riding as the number of participants/cooperators in a regime increases. A certain social cost is incurred with each additional participant/observer in the reference group. As the group increases, the criticisms accumulate, and this increases the costs of defection. The effect, as shown in figure 3.4, is to depress the slope of the payoffs from defection (from D to D'). At a certain point, an increase in the slope of the payoffs from cooperation and/or a decrease in the slope of the payoffs from defection may create a crossover point in the two lines. This is the point where the size of the audience (k) is such that the backpatting benefits and opprobrium costs change the cost-benefit analysis. It is at this point that it begins to pay to cooperate as the size of the audience increases.

When backpatting benefits and (implicit or threatened) opprobrium costs are combined, this can dramatically reduce the size of the audience needed to make it pay to cooperate (this is shown by k'' in figure 3.5). The policy objective for other players, at its simplest, is to make this k as low as possible such that it does not take a large audience of cooperators to induce a defector's cooperation.

Note that the *net* effects of social influence on the cost-benefit calculus of cooperation in a treaty are similar to the provision of material side

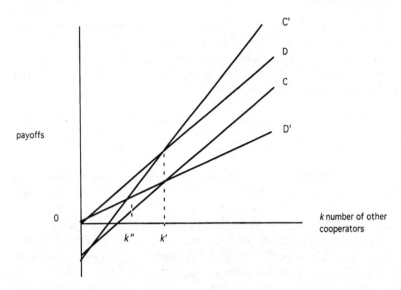

Figure 3.5. Opprobrium and backpatting

payments and sanctions. It is important to point out, however, that back-patting and shaming change this cost-benefit calculus in a very different way from side payments or sanctions. Side payments or sanctions, whether provided by the institution or by a key player or players in the institution, have a constant effect on an actor's utility regardless of how many others cooperate/participate/backpat or shame. Backpatting or shaming have cumulative effects that depend precisely on how many others cooperate/participate/backpat or shame. That is, the former is not a social effect of the institution. The latter are social effects *only*, and would not exist without the existence of, and interaction with, the group. Recall figure 3.2: the effect of the side payments and sanctions is to raise the entire C payoff line and/or depress the entire D payoff line, respectively, while not changing their slopes, such that the C' payoff line ends up above the D payoff line, or the D' payoff line ends up below the C payoff line. A sanction for defection (imposed by an enforcer or hegemon, for instance) is equally costly regardless of the size of the group cooperating. Cooperation brings higher utility regardless of what other members of the group do. Thus, the audience size and its legitimacy are irrelevant. Put another way, the institution, the forum in which the audience is active, is irrelevant. Therefore, backpatting and opprobrium are uniquely social inducements to cooperation, requiring a social interaction in a forum in which the actions of the potential free rider are judged. Backpatting and opprobrium lose their impact outside of a social group. The fact that this forum is legitimately designed to promote cooperation accentuates the legitimacy and weight of the social backpatting and opprobrium directed at potential defectors. These alternative forms of social influence would not carry this weight if unilaterally targeted by one actor at another in a bilateral, institutionless relationship.

HYPOTHESES ABOUT SOCIAL INFLUENCE

The presence or absence of a social interaction by definition matters for whether social influence elicits cooperation. But how might one fine-tune this statement further such that one can talk about variations in the strength of social influence? As I noted in chapter 1, treating institutions as social environments means positing that different social environments vary in terms of their social influence. This means asking how institutions as social environments vary in ways conducive to social influence. Different institutional designs (combinations of measures on these four dimensions) would thus create different kinds of social environments, leading to differences in the likelihood and degree of social influence. The typology I offered earlier is useful here. Again, borrowing and expanding on the typology of domestic institutions developed by Rogowski (1999), the microprocesses I outlined earlier suggest that backpatting and opprobrium will likely have more effect when membership is large (this maximizes the accumulation of backpatting/shaming markers); when decision rules are majoritarian or where reasons for supporting or opposing consensus are on record (consistency effects may be stronger); when the mandate is negotiation; and when the autonomy of agents is low (agents have to represent principals, hence persuasion effects are less likely to be at work, and agents are more likely to transmit the backpatting and opprobrium messages directly back to principals).

But how would one know if social influence had led to pro-norm behavior in international institutions? Ideally, one would look for cases with variation in the following independent variables: institutions where the social environment varied in its conduciveness to social influence; where material costs varied in their effect on relative power; and where there was variation in material side payments/sanctions.

But what might this evidence be? If social influence is at work, one should expect to see the following effects:

• commitments to participate and join power-constraining institutions should take place in the absence of material side payments or threats of sanctions;

- arguments for joining or participating should stress backpatting and image benefits, and opprobrium costs;

- initial bargaining positions, if stuck to, will put the state in a distinct minority, isolating it from the cooperating audience or reference group. Thus, commitments to pro-social behavior will be made only when it is clear that noncommitments will be highly isolating.

THE AGGREGATION PROBLEM

Before I get to the evidence for social influence, I need to be clear about the level of analysis here. The focus on sociological and social psychological microprocesses in international relations compels one to look at individuals or small groups, to examine the effects of social influence on them, and to then trace the effects of these individuals on the policy process. This is a legitimate research process when one starts from a constructivist, complex adaptive systems ontology as I do here. States as unitary actors do not mimic, are not influenced by backpatting and opprobrium, and are not "persuaded."[24]

In particular, the problem comes with observing social influence effects on top-level decision makers. Who in the decision-making system is sensitive to backpatting or opprobrium? How do state "agents" operating inside international institutions transmit international social influence signals back to the "principals," their political leaders? In the China case, why and how would people on the Foreign Affairs Leading Small Group or on the Standing Committee of the Politburo—two places where major foreign policy decisions are made—be sensitive to backpatting and opprobrium directed at China writ large or at the Chinese delegation in some international treaty negotiations?

I do not think there is an especially good theoretical or empirical answer to these sorts of questions. But an answer may lie in the anthropomorphization of the state in international politics. Anthropomorphization is a key feature of religion and nationalism. It is a common response to use human-like metaphors to describe ambiguous nonhuman phenomena (Guthrie 1980; Verdery 1993:40). It enables people to attribute agency to phenomena that are, in reality, collections of agents. There is evidence that political leaders tend to anthropomorphize the state themselves. Indeed, the language of the state and its diplomacy has always been highly

---

[24] Thomas notes that to speak of states as susceptible to status pressure, as much of the literature on opprobrium/shaming does, is to argue metaphorically, not causally, since states are not psychological beings (Thomas 2001:23–24).

anthropomorphic, e.g., fatherlands, motherlands, prestige, dignity, honor, unitary national interests (Wendt 1999:195, 219). As O'Neill shows, much of the description and analysis of international diplomacy by leaders, pundits, and citizens alike relies on a "country-as-person" metaphor (sometimes a "country-as-specific-person," sometimes a "country-as-unspecified-person," sometimes as "country-as-its-leader") to describe interstate relations as social relationships (O'Neill 1999:11–16). This allows complex intergroup relations at the international level (where each group or state is in reality itself a function of complex intragroup relations) to be simplified, understood, and emotionally identified with. As Wendt puts it pithily, for most people most of the time "[s]tates are people too" (Wendt 1999:215).

It should not be surprising, then, that leaders and their attentive publics tend to isomorphize criticism or praise of the state with criticisms and praise of the national in-group, and of each individual in the in-group.[25] Consistent with O'Neill's analysis, in my interviews with governmental and non-governmental intellectuals and analysts in China, many of whom were critics of the regime's repressiveness, a common argument was that leaders and the state are isomorphized especially when Chinese leaders interact with the external world. How China's top handful of leaders are personally treated, for instance, is seen as an indicator of how China the collective is treated.[26] Public opinion polls of Beijing residents also seem to support this isomorphization hypothesis. The Beijing Area Study has found that there is little differentiation between the Chinese state and the Chinese people when it comes to basic identity traits (e.g., perceived level of peacefulness, modesty, civilization).[27] When asked to describe the Chinese people and the Chinese state on a scale of bipolar opposite adjectives, respondents saw virtually no difference in where on this scale the people and state ought to be positioned. In contrast, respondents saw greater difference between the traits of people and state when it came to Americans and the United States, and Japanese and Japan (see fig. 3.6). There is no reason to believe that decision makers themselves do not engage in this type of isomorphization and anthropomorphization.

[25] On the question of aggregation, see Finnemore and Sikkink 1998:904.

[26] This effect could be reinforced by the relationship between self-esteem and perceived esteem bestowed on the social group, a relationship at the heart of social identity theory. See Druckman 1994:48–49.

[27] The Beijing Area Study is an annual randomly sampled survey of Beijing residents. From 2000 to 2004 the survey included questions asking respondents to place the Chinese people, Americans, Japanese, the Chinese state, the United States, and Japan on semantic differential scales. Respondents were asked to place self and other on a 1–7 scale anchored by bipolar opposite adjectives, e.g., peaceful–warlike, modest–arrogant. The difference between perceptions of people and state on these scales (mean state score minus mean people score) runs from −6 to 6.

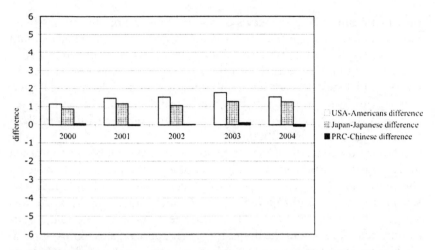

Figure 3.6. Beijing residents' perceived difference between identity traits of a people and their state. Source: Beijing Area Study, 2000–2004.

The process might go in the other direction as well: criticism of the collective is personalized by decision makers. To give one example from environmental diplomacy, Qu Geping, at the time the head of China's State Environmental Protection Agency, argued in internal discussions in the State Council that China would have to participate in efforts to protect endangered species because otherwise China would be criticized as "stupid, backward and savage," harming the "Chinese people's image." He expressed personal frustration with the "pressure" he felt whenever he attended international conferences because of the stories about Chinese eating wild animals (Qu 1990:195).[28]

There is a growing sense among Chinese specialists of Chinese foreign policy that the current, post-Deng leadership in particular has been much more sensitive both to China's international image and, with lines between the two blurred, their own. Jiang Zemin, in particular, was viewed as being especially sensitive to how China was portrayed, and to the implications of this both for his own personal image and for his domestic legitimacy. The fact that Jiang allowed himself to enter a very public debate with Clinton over human rights during both the US and China summits in 1997 and 1998 was seen as a sign of his strength, confidence, and international stature: he could debate the president of the United States

[28] Moravcsik notes that international stigmatization may cue domestic opprobrium that may then raise political and electoral costs for political leaders. This probably helps explain how status concerns operate in liberal democracies, but it still leaves sensitivity to international and domestic opprobrium in some authoritarian systems unexplained. On this criticism of the liberal argument, see Thomas 2001:21–22.

on equal terms and, in the views of many Chinese, hold his own.[29] Jiang emphasized that one of the key themes of Chinese foreign policy should be precisely the promotion of China's image as a responsible major power.[30] In addition, research on the role of ethical and normative discourses in Chinese foreign relations suggests that one element of leadership legitimacy in the eyes of relevant publics in China has been the degree to which the leadership appears to uphold and bolster China's international image (Cummings 2000:62).

Thus, image concerns at the top probably derive from both a top-down and a bottom-up anthropomorphization of leaders and national image on the international stage. The top-down process plays on individual leaders' sensitivities to an anthropomorphized China's status markers. At this stage, psychological variables—the desire for a positive self-image, self-esteem, self-efficacy, and the desire for social approval and liking—probably kick in. The bottom-up process plays on individual leaders' sensitivities to domestic legitimacy derived, in part, from status markers valued by relevant publics. The precise mix will depend on the issue, and the degree to which the relevant publics consider the issue salient.[31] In the cases I examine next, public attention is relatively limited. The issues—a comprehensive nuclear test ban treaty and technical protocols governing landmines, among some other multilateral issues—were generally not high-

---

[29] Chinese foreign policy specialist, conversation with the author, October 1998.

[30] This is based on conversations with scholars from the Foreign Affairs College, and the Institute of World Economics and Politics at the Chinese Academy of Social Sciences, October 1998.

[31] As a general hypothesis, then, paradoxically the foreign policy of dictatorships is more likely to express sensitivity to international image, ceterus paribus, than that of democracies. Individual leaders in dictatorships are more likely to have a direct effect on the foreign policy process. Thus, their own personal sensitivities are more likely to come into play in the policy process. One quick test of this is to see whether dictatorships are more likely than democracies to try to avoid being in a small minority of opponents to a large yes vote in a high-profile international institution such as the UN. One might expect that those states reflecting a high sensitivity to a negative image will be more likely to abstain when the UNGA yes coalition is a supermajority (two-thirds of the vote) than when it is a bare majority (one-half of the vote). These states can hide from opprobrium to some extent in a large group of no voters. The larger the difference in abstentions between these two situations might be a good proxy for the degree of sensitivity of the state (and its leaders) to social isolation. As it turns out, there is a fairly strong negative correlation between the Polity IV scores of countries in the UNGA (averaged between 1989 and 1999 to take into account major political transformations) and the average size of this difference between abstention rates in the face of small majorities versus large majorities across 1989–1999. The lower the state's Polity IV score, the higher the difference in abstention rates between two-thirds majority yes votes and one-half majority yes votes (Pearson's $r = -.402$ $p = 0.000$. N of states = 124 [Polity IV scores were not available for all states]). See pp. 135–37 for more details about these data.

profile features of Chinese diplomacy inside China. They were highly technical and, because they were related to security questions, generally out of bounds for even limited public or intelligentsia debate and criticism. Thus, the top-down anthropomorphization and Chinese leadership concepts of international status markers were likely the most important factors linking status to policy choices.

EMPIRICAL IMPLICATIONS: THE COMPREHENSIVE TEST BAN NEGOTIATIONS

The CTBT negotiations, conducted inside the UN Conference on Disarmament, ran from January 1994 through August 1996. The goal of the negotiations was, essentially, to ban the testing of nuclear weapons by the explosion of nuclear devices. Proposals for a CTBT had floated around for decades but had, essentially, run into opposition from one or more of the P-5 at different times. The original goal was to prevent states without nuclear weapons from acquiring them and to limit the modernization of those states with extant weapons programs. The argument was that without an ability to test, states could not be confident in the reliability of their weapons designs, reducing the value of nuclear weapons as a tool in states' arsenals. Over time the constraining effect of test bans on new and extant programs declined with advances in computer simulation, the proliferation of nuclear power technology, and manufacturing skills. Nonetheless, certain kinds of advanced nuclear weapons designs could still be severely limited by an inability to test through underground explosions. The CTBT had also long been considered by developing states as an important pillar in the global non-proliferation regime because, in principle, it would restrain the P-5's ability to proliferate vertically. A CTBT would also make it more difficult to develop and deploy directed energy weapons, such as the nuclear-explosion-pumped X-ray laser, enhanced electromagnetic pulse (EMP) weapons, microwave weapons, and enhanced radiation weapons. Until the United States and Russia agreed to support negotiations on the CD agenda in 1993, however, there had been no credible multilateral movement toward a CTB.

Right from the start, Chinese officials signaled their unhappiness with a CTBT. When it first entered the CD in 1980, China had taken the position that nuclear test bans were a waste of time unless accompanied by a general program for disarmament. As a Chinese working paper submitted to the CD in 1981 put it, "The prohibition of nuclear tests by itself cannot bring about nuclear disarmament. It can be conducive to the lessening and elimination of nuclear threat only when it is combined with various other measures of nuclear disarmament"(China 1981:2). For its first four years in the CD, China opposed even setting up an ad hoc working group on nuclear test bans. In 1985, under verbal pressure from other states to alter its position, it supported setting up an ad hoc working group and then agreed to participate (Johnston 1986:47).

When the Clinton administration began to push for a CTBT treaty to be negotiated in the CD, Chinese arms control specialists and government officials let it be known that they considered the value of a treaty to cap vertical and horizontal proliferation to be quite secondary to things such as NFU declarations and negative security assurances. This argument was unchanged from the early 1980s. Indeed, Chinese nuclear weapons scientists informally proposed that a CTBT ought to allow for an annual limited quota of tests so as to restrain new weapons design while improving the reliability and safety of existing designs (Wu 1994:11–12; Liu Gongliang 1993; Chen 1993). Although there was a security logic to the argument—NFUs and unconditional security assurances (e.g., assurances that non-nuclear weapons states would not be threatened or attacked with nuclear weapons under any circumstances) would reduce the value of nuclear weapons, thereby placing downward pressure on proliferation—the more pressing concern for these nuclear weapons experts was that China's nuclear capabilities might be frozen into perpetual inferiority vis-á-vis the two major nuclear states. As one weapons designer put it in an interview in an internal circulation publication in 1994, if China were to be prevented from testing before it had developed a lighter, second-generation warhead, it would have to scrap plans to develop second-generation missile capabilities (e.g., MIRVing, or road and rail mobile missiles). "If China abides by the international demands to stop testing nuclear weapons, then China must eliminate its ballistic missile plans, and not continue to research the second generation of missiles. . . . What can we do? This implies China must give up everything, and only possess old-type missiles, which have no survivability whatsoever" (Nuclear Science and Technology Information Research Institute 1994:1). Another internal circulation discussion of the CTBT noted that as of 1994 any moratorium on testing was a "serious challenge" to China because the technical level of Chinese nuclear weapons was relatively low, and because it did not have the capability to undertake simulated nuclear experiments (Fu 1994:7). Another internal circulation publication, summarizing the state of play in the CTBT in the spring of 1996, strongly implied that Chinese leaders might have a preference to catch up qualitatively. Through a combination of superpower reductions and measured Chinese increases, the PRC could reach a state of rough parity with the nuclear weapons stockpiles of the other four declared nuclear powers. If so, the author concluded, China needed to continue to test (Wu Zheng 1996:10). One member of China's CTBT delegation noted in a postmortem of the process that the CTBT negotiations "caught China in the middle of its nuclear weapons program, whereas the United States, Russia, and Britain had completed several development cycles" (Zou 1998:12). In other words, right from the start, authoritative Chinese had indicated that they believed a CTBT might disadvantageously constrain China's relative military capabilities.[32]

This concern was probably all the more pressing for many in the nuclear weapons technical community and within the PLA who had serious doubts about the credibility of China's second strike capability. Indeed, for many the negative implications of a freeze in nuclear asymmetries were probably accentuated, given the prominence of limited nuclear war–fighting arguments circulating in the military. There is considerable evidence that beginning in the 1980s, many nuclear strategists in China began to express a preference that China develop a limited ability to control escalation in the event of a conventional and/or nuclear crisis. This would require a more flexible operational capacity that might include, among other requirements, MIRVing, theater and tactical nuclear weapons, a capacity to penetrate space-, air-, and ground-based ballistic missile defenses, and an ability to hit hardened military targets. Most of these requirements involve smaller weight-to-yield ratios, and hence new warhead designs.[33]

The first puzzle, then, is why China joined the negotiations in the first place. I will come back to this in a moment.

[32] Jeffrey Lewis makes a strong argument that from 1986 on, the Chinese nuclear weapons testing community and China's top leaders had anticipated test ban negotiations and had designed their testing series and policy responses with this in mind. The implication is that the testing community and Chinese leaders were perfectly prepared to accept a CTBT before negotiations began (Lewis 2004:135). Specifically, two important figures in the nuclear weapons program recommended to the top leadership that China step up the pace of its testing program to make sure that it had sufficient information before any test ban was in place. It is unclear to me, however, that this advice was followed or that it reflected predominant views in the testing community. First, although this is what the testers recommended (Song 2001:63–64), it does not mean this is what the PRC actually did, nor that it did it successfully. In fact, the annual frequency of tests after 1986 was lower (1.3/year) than before 1986 (1.4/year). More crucially, Lewis's argument also misses a great deal of the evidence from interviews and open and internal circulation material, cited earlier, that many in the testing community were genuinely worried that the CTBT was not in China's interest. Clearly, many scientists were not convinced by 1994 that China had tested enough. Nor does Lewis's one piece of evidence logically lead to the conclusion that the Chinese government welcomed such a test ban, or that China was not sensitive to international social influence during the negotiations.

[33] See Johnston 1995/6 for details on the concept of limited deterrence. Adding to the uncertainty as to the effects of a test ban on China's deterrence was that, apparently, there had been little discussion inside China over how many penetrated warheads against what targets was enough to constitute a deterrent (interview with arms control specialist from the nuclear technical community, October 15, 1999).

Given this pessimistic assessment of the impact of a CTBT on Chinese security, it is not surprising that once treaty talks got under way, Chinese negotiators began to present bargaining positions that most observers believed were designed to slow down the negotiation process at least until China had completed a test series on its second-generation warhead. Initially, negotiations proceeded under the assumption that a treaty would be ready for submission to the General Assembly (as is required before a CD-negotiated treaty becomes open for signature) by September 1996. The Chinese indicated that they hoped a treaty would be complete by the end of 1996. It is likely that given, roughly speaking, a spring and fall testing schedule, with two tests per year (probably four to six tests would have been needed for a new design), China would need at least until the fall of 1996 before its scientists were confident that new designs were reliable. Thus, when negotiations began in 1994, it is safe to assume that China's weapons testing community (articulating its preferences through the China Academy of Engineering Physics [CAEP] and the Institute of Applied Physics and Computational Mathematics [IAPCM] in the interagency process) argued that delaying tactics might be needed for at least two years. This was a high-risk strategy, since there was no guarantee that the testing series would be successful, or successful enough for a robust design.

China's delegation led off in 1994 with two strongly articulated positions. The first was a demand that the CTBT include an article (later reduced to preambular language) that committed nuclear states to no first use and security assurances for non-nuclear states (NFU/SA) (China 1994b, 1994c). The second was a demand that the scope of the treaty ban all nuclear weapons test explosions that released nuclear energy (a zero yield that would ban, presumably, in-lab hydro-nuclear and subcritical tests). The proposal would have allowed for peaceful nuclear explosions (PNEs), however, as these were not nuclear *weapons* test explosions.[34]

These proposals were nonstarters for some or all of the other P-5. US nuclear doctrine was adamantly opposed to NFU: extended deterrence commitments and an expanding role for nuclear weapons in the post–cold war era in deterring chemical and biological weapons required first use and prohibited unconditional security assurances.[35] PNEs were opposed by the United States, the United Kingdom, and France, the non-nuclear developed states (e.g., the Western Group), and most of the G-21 (the developing states group in the CD). The arguments were twofold: PNEs were an inordinately expensive and unreliable tool for large-scale

[34] CD/PV.676 (March 24, 1994) pp. 20–21. See also China 1994d.
[35] On the expanding role of nuclear weapons in the deterrence of non-nuclear weapons, see Kristensen 1999.

public works projects and had been rejected as such by most of the scientific community in the West; moreover, it was too difficult to differentiate between a PNE and a test explosion for military purposes, making verification of a CTBT impossible.

Why the Chinese proposed PNEs is unclear. Members of the Chinese arms control scientific community developed a range of arguments: some made a general claim that the CTBT should not ban a technology that someday might have some nonmilitary value, even if this value were not obvious today;[36] others argued that PNEs could be useful in breaking down geological barriers between oil deposits, thus reducing the costs of extraction;[37] some argued that PNEs could help develop warheads that might be needed to destroy threatening asteroids (Zhu 1995:135–38; Liu 1995:139–42); some argued that PNEs would justify retaining some of China's nuclear testing infrastructure, meaning jobs and livelihood for scientists in Beijing and in the city of Malan in Xinjiang near China's main test site; and some argued it was a delaying tactic. It is possible as well that PNEs could be used to mask certain tests useful for the modernization of warhead designs. Except for the job creation argument, observers at the CD mainly considered the Chinese position to be a delaying tactic and/or a bargaining chip.

Another position taken by the Chinese delegation that, to many, seemed to be a delaying tactic was the proposal for an extensive international satellite monitoring system for verification purposes (China 1994a:10–11). Many delegations considered the proposal frivolous, redundant, and excessively expensive. One Canadian technical expert on satellite monitoring argued that existing commercial systems could adequately monitor and deter potential violators.[38]

These three positions constituted the core of China's bargaining in the CTBT for 1994 and the first two sessions of the CD in 1995 (there are

[36] This argument was also made by General Qian Shaojun, the primary decision maker in COSTIND on nuclear weapons and arms control policy, when he attended the negotiations in January 1996. See Johnson 1996a.

[37] Zou remarks that in the early 1980s, the Ministry of Petroleum Industry had approached nuclear weapons scientists to see about the feasibility of using PNEs for oil recovery. Around the time of the CTBT negotiations, Zou reports that Russian specialists from its Ministry of Atomic Energy were "providing extensive data which purported to back China's claim that PNEs would be safe and economically viable for a developing country" (Zou 1998:22).

[38] It is possible that the Chinese saw this position as strengthening a case against national technical means (e.g., nationally controlled spy satellites). Since China did not have NTM that matched US or Russian capabilities, an international satellite system would even the playing field by providing NTM-like capabilities to all states. The problem with this explanation is that China's NTM position did not really emerge until a year or so after the satellite system proposal.

three annual negotiation periods in the CD). The NFU/SA and PNE positions were considered treaty killers—that is, were the Chinese to insist on these to the end, it was likely that one or more of the other P-5 would not sign a CTBT. By the late summer 1995, however, two additional positions emerged, both having to do with verification. One concerned national technical means (NTM—information gathered from spy satellite and other technical means of espionage) as a source of information for triggering on-site inspection (OSI) of a suspected CTBT violator. China, and other states such as Pakistan, insisted that given the asymmetries in NTM capabilities around the world, under no circumstances could NTM be used to trigger on-site inspection.[39] The other concerned the decision rules leading to on-site inspection. Essentially the Chinese supported a "green light" system; that is, OSI would not start automatically when a state requested OSI of a suspected violator. Rather it would start after a decision by the treaty's Executive Council had given a green light to inspections. The Chinese proposed a voting rule of two-thirds. Western states wanted a "red light" system wherein OSI was automatic unless stopped by a decision of the Executive Council.

As negotiations entered the first period in January 1996, China continued to stick with its treaty-killing positions on NFU and PNEs, as well as its positions on NTM and OSI. Observers and members of other delegations were unsure whether, with these stances, China would even sign a treaty.[40] Many delegates thought that the reason for China sticking with these positions for so long was to use them as bargaining chips or "placeholders" to be dropped either when China's testing was finished or for some other, as yet unclear, goal in the negotiations. Thus, China did not come under much pressure on PNEs until early 1996 (Johnson 1996c). This pressure increased substantially in March 1996 when, due to China's insistence, in a working paper structured as a draft treaty presented by the chair, Jaap Ramaker from the Netherlands, the option of conducting PNEs remained in the text.[41] A number of states, by one estimate as many as twenty non-nuclear countries, were unhappy that the Chinese language remained in the rolling text. Canada, for instance, indicated to Ramaker that this was unacceptable.[42] Canada's ambassador to the negotiations, Mark Moher, communicated these objections to the chief Chinese negoti-

---

[39] See comments by Sha Zukang in CD/PV.717 (September 5, 1995), p. 6.

[40] I interviewed a member of the US delegation in the fall of 1995, and he was not at all certain that China would sign.

[41] Interview with a senior Canadian diplomat to the CTBT negotiations, July 3, 2001; Johnson 1996b.

[42] Interview with a senior Canadian diplomat to the CTBT negotiations, July 3, 2001; Johnson 1996c.

ator, Sha Zukang. Thereafter, Moher drafted new compromise language that would allow PNEs in the future if in ten years after the treaty's entry into force, a Conference of the Parties unanimously agreed.[43] Since this outcome was highly unlikely, and since the formula gave a veto to any signatory, the Canadians considered this a way of making PNEs for all practical purposes a dead letter even though it left PNE language in the treaty for China's benefit. Sha agreed with the compromise language quickly and, apparently, without consulting Beijing (indicating that by this time he had a mandate to push for PNE language but not to push so hard as to kill the treaty). The formula was accepted by a wide range of states and presented to Ramaker. In late May he issued a "clean" chair's draft treaty incorporating the PNE compromise, while leaving out the Chinese language on both PNE and NFU.[44] This was, in a sense, a face-saving way of dropping these two positions: it required only that China agree to use the clean draft as the basis of negotiations instead of having to publicly retreat from its NFU and PNE positions.[45] Sha Zukang announced China's flexibility on PNEs after he returned from Beijing in early May. This suggests that it was during the break between the first and second negotiating periods (in other words, in April) that the Chinese interagency process approved Sha's deal to accept the diluted and virtually worthless PNE language. The reason, apparently, was that China did not want to be seen as the major obstacle to the treaty.[46]

The Chinese position on OSI and NTM did not change with the introduction of the clean draft, however. The draft treaty accepted a green light system for OSI, but proposed a simple majority rule for triggering inspections rather than China's preferred two-thirds.[47] It also allowed for some use of NTM data as a source of evidence for requesting OSI. And there was another issue that emerged as a key Chinese demand (shared by the United Kingdom and Russia), namely, that all five nuclear weapons

[43] See article VIII of the CTBT for this language on PNEs.

[44] Interview with senior Canadian diplomat, July 3, 2001; and Johnson 1996e. Up until this point, delegates were negotiating a rolling text with as many as twelve hundred brackets, indicating disagreements over wording, grammar, and punctuation. The "clean" text was presented as a flexible fait accompli for more focused negotiation. The presentation of the clean text, and its acceptance as a basis for bargaining, signaled the endgame of negotiations.

[45] The cover for China's concession on PNEs was "an assurance that such explosions could be reviewed at periodic review conferences, although Chinese officials acknowledged that such reviews were unlikely to lead to revisions of the prohibitions" (Zou 1998:38).

[46] This is implied by Zou's summary that "[w]hen people gradually came to the conclusion that PNE was one of the obstacles to signing the treaty, China finally made a major move on this issue in early June 1996" (Zou 1998:23).

[47] This position had been established in a Chinese working paper in June 1994. See China 1994a:11–12.

states and the three threshold states (Israel, India, and Pakistan) had to sign the treaty before it could enter into force (EIF). The UK position was that a CTBT would be ineffective unless those states most obviously in a position to benefit from testing were constrained. It is unclear whether this was the Chinese calculus. One hypothesis is that the insistence on India's signature (when India was signaling that it might not sign the treaty) might have been designed to reduce the likelihood of EIF, and thus leave China legally unconstrained from testing. I will come back to this in a moment, but the short answer is that this calculation does not appear to have been driving China's endgame diplomacy.

Thus, there were only two obstacles to China's signature—the use of NTM, and OSI based on a simple majority decision rule in the treaty's Executive Council. China's tough line on OSI was not a case of obstructing the treaty in the face of overwhelming opposition in the CD. Indeed, on this issue China had the support of many G-21 states and of the US ally, Israel (Johnson 1996d).

Both these issues were resolved after intensive bilateral negotiations with the United States by early August, just after China's last nuclear test. The United States, intent on getting a treaty before the UNGA opened in September 1996[48] was willing to compromise with China on OSI: the two sides settled on a three-fifths voting rule for triggering OSI, a compromise between the US preference for a simple majority and the Chinese preference for a two-thirds supermajority.[49] On the NTM issue, the Chinese essentially caved, as most states (except Pakistan) were supportive of some role for NTM.[50] The treaty therefore allows NTM information to

---

[48] The UNGA had passed a resolution in late 1995 setting a deadline for a CTBT of late summer 1996 so that the treaty could be officially presented to the UNGA for a vote (turning it into a legal treaty) in September 1996. These dates, and the fixed dates for the three annual CD negotiating sessions in Geneva, became rather powerful focal points in the endgame.

[49] As noted, the United States initially preferred a red light system, where OSI was automatic unless stopped by the Executive Council. When it finally accepted a green light system, it wanted the triggering of OSI to be as easy as possible, hence its preference for a simple majority. China, determined to minimize the intrusiveness of the verification system, initially wanted OSI to be as difficult as possible. For a fascinating description of negotiations on this question see Zou 1998:31–35. Ultimately, the insistence on OSI appears to have been a political image calculation. Sha, and the Chinese decision makers, were determined to prevent OSI being used to put a political spotlight on a state through the reckless use of OSI demands. The Yin He incident in 1993—whereby the United States charged that a Chinese ship was taking CW precursors to a country in the Middle East and where these charges were followed up by a fruitless boarding and search—was a precedent they did not want to see repeated. The image of a state suffers even if innocent when it is charged with violating a treaty and subject to intrusive inspections. Interview with senior Chinese diplomat, October 20, 1999; and interview with senior Canadian diplomat, July 3, 2001.

[50] Sha Zukang had actually signaled a willingness to consider highly, but vaguely, circumscribed use of NTM in the treaty in early June.

be used as a basis for requesting OSI as long as it is used in a manner consistent with international law and with respect for the sovereignty of states (article 4, para. 5). With these compromises made, China signed the treaty, abandoning at the last moment its long-standing position that it would stop testing with entry into force (which, without India's signature, would be a long way off).[51]

How precisely did China get to this point when it had initially considered the treaty to be potentially detrimental to China's relative power capabilities? Let me address the alternatives to a backpatting/opprobrium explanation first. The simplest explanation—drawing from standard realist premises—is that the treaty was, in the end, costless. This argument could be made in two forms. The first is that China had, by July 1996, finished its testing series for a second-generation warhead design; the testing and weapons communities were essentially satisfied with the information gathered from the tests. The testing and weapons community played an instrumental role in the interagency process, writing some of the bargaining positions (e.g., on PNEs). Had these specialists concluded the tests were unsuccessful, China would have sought ways to avoid signing.

This argument has at least three problems, however. First, the testing and weapons communities expressed dissatisfaction with the treaty well after China signed. Often they termed the treaty a "sacrifice" for China. Concretely, the sacrifice may have come in two areas. First, while it is possible that sufficient information came from the last series of tests to design a newer, lighter, and smaller warhead and to increase confidence in the safety of warheads, it is not clear that the weapons designers believed this did much to reduce the technical asymmetries (e.g., relative power capabilities gaps) between China's nuclear weapons and those of the superpowers. Nor could China later test for the reliability and safety of any design tested in 1996. In particular, since the probable intended delivery vehicle for the smaller warhead was the DF-31 mobile ICBM, the fact that the DF-31 had not been test flown by 1996 suggests that the Chinese were not able to test the final weaponized bomb design.[52]

Second, the moratorium on testing created difficulties for the Chinese on the issue of stockpile aging. There were continuing complaints from the Chinese side that US simulation technology and China's lack of such technology meant the United States could develop new generations of weapons designs while China was essentially frozen with its second-gener-

---

[51] China declared a unilateral moratorium on testing on July 30, just after its latest nuclear test. This came a few days prior to the compromise with the United States, suggesting that China anticipated an agreement with the United States that would result in China signing the treaty.

[52] Communication with US specialist on Chinese nuclear weapons, 1998.

ation warheads. In other words, the CTBT could worsen China's relative capabilities. Zou Yunhua, one of COSTIND's representatives on the CTBT delegation, put it directly: "A CTB would impose severe limitations on any further modernization of the Chinese nuclear arsenal. For China, it would be better to have at least a few more tests to acquire the adequate experience required for better ensuring the reliability and safety of its nuclear weapons. Judging from a purely technical angle, China does need to conduct more tests. Under the CTBT, the technical gap between China and other nuclear powers is forever frozen" (Zou 1998:43–44). This conclusion was later echoed by some in the military. In a book on nuclear weapons and warfare, two PLA authors argued that given the US lead in simulation technology, the CTBT was designed to enhance US nuclear superiority and to limit the ability of other countries to develop their nuclear power (Li and Zhou 1997:241–42).[53]

Second, there is some evidence that China's leaders essentially decided to sign the treaty in late 1995, prior to the negotiation session in January 1996, and prior to the end of the testing sequence in July of that year. A comparison of the composition of China's CTBT delegation over time is revealing on this score.[54] It was not until the January session that China sent the most senior official in charge of the nuclear weapons and nuclear arms control policy in COSTIND, General Qian Shaojun. Qian's presence probably indicated that the Chinese believed negotiations had entered the endgame, that a treaty was inevitable, and that now the task was to ensure the provisions that really mattered to China were in the treaty. Given the quickened pace of negotiations in an endgame, Qian's presence also reduced the amount of time it would take for China's nuclear weapons community to respond to changes in the treaty. Qian was also, roughly speaking, the military's equivalent to Sha Zukang, the head of the delegation and the chief decision maker on arms control in the MOFA. This meant that decisions on how to respond to negotiations could be made more quickly and between relative equals, both probably with a mandate to decide on China's final bargaining positions. To have this mandate, however, they would have to have had instructions basically approving China's signature in the first place. Thus, the likelihood is that the basic decision to sign was made by China's top political leaders in late 1995.[55]

---

[53] Also interviews with analysts in the IAPCM, CAEP, PLA, and US Department of Defense and Department of Energy, 1996–1998. For a critique of the CTBT for its irrelevance in reducing incentives to proliferate, see Chen and Wang 1996.

[54] See CD/INF.37 (1995) and CD/INF.38 (1996).

[55] One of the Department of Defense members of the US CTBT delegation also speculated that this timeline is probably correct. Interview, January 1998. The January 1996 Chinese delegation also included a deputy director and arms control expert from the IAPCM. This too would suggest that the issue for China by January 1996 was not whether or not to sign, but which specific provisions at the margins in the treaty that might affect the nuclear weap-

Indeed, according to one senior PRC diplomat, it was in late 1995 and early 1996 that Jiang Zemin began to focus personally on the treaty.[56]

Thus, the decision to join almost certainly came prior to at least the last two nuclear tests, both conducted in 1996. This would suggest that the decision came before there was conclusive information about the success of the second-generation warhead design. It is possible, of course, that had China's weapons designers designated the design series a failure after the July 1996 tests, Beijing might not have signed. But as prudent worst- or "bad"-case analysts, Beijing's leaders would have had to have made the decision to sign with a great deal of uncertainty about the impact on China's future nuclear capabilities. The timing of China's positions on OSI and NTM would roughly fit a decision to sign in 1995. From the third negotiation session in late summer of 1995 through the first negotiation session of 1996, China focused its bargaining on verification and dropped the "treaty killing" provisions on PNEs and NFU. This would be consistent with a basic resignation that a treaty was likely, and that, given a sensitivity to sovereignty and transparency, China should try to reduce the intrusiveness of the treaty as much as possible.

Third, there is some evidence that China decided to adhere to the informal P-5 moratorium on testing in April 1996, four months prior to officially announcing adherence and four months before the end of the testing series. According to one interviewee, Li Peng returned from a trip to France in early April and announced internally that China would stop testing upon its signing of the treaty. This was contrary to China's public position that it would stop testing on entry into force; the MOFA initially thought Li might have been unclear about China's diplomatic position on this score. It turns out, however, that he was well aware of the public position, but articulated a new position to be revealed at an appropriate time in the negotiations.[57] Such a decision would have been taken against a fair degree of uncertainty about the success of the test series. This would suggest as well that when Chinese leaders decided when to sign the treaty and when to stop testing, they did so without necessarily knowing exactly how constraining the treaty might be.

A second generally realist explanation for why the treaty was probably costless relates to India's refusal to sign unless the CTBT explicitly included a time-bound commitment from the P-5 for nuclear disarmament.

---

ons community were acceptable and which were not. My argument here was essentially confirmed by a senior Chinese arms control diplomat during an interview in November 2000, and by comments by a senior Canadian diplomat at the CTBT negotiations who personally met with Sha and Qian in early 1996 (interview, July 3, 2001).

[56] Interview with senior Chinese arms control diplomat, November 2000.

[57] Conversation with MOFA official, July 1996.

India's refusal meant that the treaty would not enter into force (a condition that China had supported), and thus China would not be legally restricted from testing as long as India was outside the treaty. This argument has some problems, too. Although the timing is unclear, if China did indeed decide to sign in 1995, this came well before India began to link its signature to a timetable for disarmament, that is, before China could have known that India's position would prevent EIF. The Indians had been hinting in the CD at such linkages from January 1996 on,[58] especially leading up to, and after, the elections in May when the BJP formed a coalition government. Through May, however, most delegations believed that in the end the Indians would "blink" and sign the treaty.[59] It was not until June that India stated firmly that it would not sign unless there was a time-bound commitment to disarmament.[60] Since this was opposed by the P-5 (China was silent on this, but a MOFA source told me the PLA opposed this kind of a commitment), it was not until June that it was clear there would be no short-run EIF. China had insisted on India's inclusion in the treaty as a condition for EIF, but this insistence had come well before India came out in stiff opposition to the treaty (Zou 1998:36).

But even in the unlikely event that, unlike almost every other delegation, the Chinese delegation had anticipated India's refusal to sign, and hence realized there would be no short-term EIF, this does not mean China was therefore not constrained from testing. China's leaders had, after all, decided to abide by a unilateral moratorium, and breaking the moratorium would not be politically costless. Moreover, India's non-signature would not necessarily delay EIF indefinitely. Article 14 of the treaty allowed a Conference of the States (the signatories and ratifiers) (COS) to meet to reconsider the conditions for EIF. If there were consensus to do so (that is, if there were consensus among states that already support the treaty), the COS could drop India's signature as a condition for EIF. China could, of course, oppose consensus on changing EIF requirements, but this would also be politically costly. In general, then, the Indian angle seems not to have played a decisive role in China's signature. China signed

---

[58] The Indian minister of external affairs, Pranab Mijherjee, had called for binding commitments from the P-5 to disarm to be included in the CTBT in September 1995. But evidently the order to CTBT negotiators to make such a linkage was not issued until October 1995, and the position was not articulated in the CD until January 1996. See http://www.nti.org/e_research/profiles/India/Nuclear/2296_2887.html.

[59] Interview with senior Canadian diplomat, July 2001. This diplomat claims, for example, that in a meeting of the Western group in May, he was roundly criticized for warning that including India in the EIF formula would likely provoke an Indian refusal to sign.

[60] This final stance apparently came after a meeting with the BJP prime minister and the chief Indian negotiator at the CTBT in early June. See http://www.nti.org/e_research/profiles/India/Nuclear/2296_2891.html.

the treaty and accepted a moratorium, all with the knowledge that the Indian question did not delay constraints on Chinese testing.[61]

In a sense, the more interesting Chinese decision was to enter the negotiations in the first place back in 1994. At that time, India was in fact a strong supporter of the CTBT. Thus, India's later opposition could not have factored into China's calculations. At the time, though, the British and the French appeared unhappy with the idea of a treaty. China could have probably blocked the treaty before negotiations had started, linking with the other two medium-sized nuclear powers to prevent a P-5 agreement to negotiate a treaty in the CD. It could have done this behind the scenes, with little fear of superpower retribution. Indeed, before the CTBT or any of its major provisions could be brought before the CD, the P-5 in general had to reach a consensus on doing so (Zou 1998:37). Yet China chose to accept the CD's mandate to negotiate a treaty, even though in 1994 Chinese decision makers were even more uncertain than in 1996 about the technical benefits a test series might produce.

In short, the evidence is not very strong that China's decision makers believed the treaty process was relatively inconsequential for China's relative military power capabilities. The decision to join the negotiations and accept the treaty are still puzzles from a standard realist perspective.

In contrast to a realist explanation, contractual institutionalism might look for positive or negative incentives that mediated the military costs of the treaty, e.g., side payments, sanctions, or reputational benefits for immediate exchange relationships. Interestingly enough, the United States concluded early on that side payments might be necessary to ensure Chinese signature. There are reports that around November 1994 the United States discussed the possibility of offering help in developing computer simulation technology that would allow the Chinese to maintain confidence in the safety and reliability of their weapons. According to one highly placed DOD official, the offer came to nothing because the Chinese did not have sufficient data from their tests to use the software effectively. Apparently another approach was made in 1996, but nothing came of it either. There are rumors that the French promised this kind of technology, and the circumstantial evidence might be consistent—Li Peng came back from France in April 1996 apparently prepared to accept a moratorium on testing. French promises of simulation technology would have made this an easier decision, but I have no independent verification of this. Moreover, well after signing the CTBT, the Chinese military continued to float suggestions that the United States provide this kind of technology because China alone among the P-5 did not have it.[62] Some nuclear

---

[61] Chinese arms control specialist involved in the CTBT policy process, May 1998.

[62] The issue came up in my discussions with specialists connected to Chinese military intelligence in January 1998.

warhead designers in the United States also doubted that China could develop sophisticated new warhead designs using simulation technology alone. So, on balance, the Chinese did not appear to have received any useful technological side payments to join.

There were also no threats of sanctions. At no point was there any implicit or explicit threat of economic or technological sanctions should China not join the CTBT negotiations, should it delay, or should it not sign. Indeed, after the election of a large number of conservative Republicans in the 1994 congressional elections, the US Congress was opposed to the treaty.

As for reputational benefits for immediate exchange relationships acquired from cooperation on a CTBT, there is no evidence from interviews with participants in the CTBT negotiations or from China's diplomacy that China's leaders saw cooperation on the CTBT as critical for extracting benefits or concessions in other bilateral exchange relationships. Indeed, precisely because of the influx of a large number of anti-CTBT conservatives in the 1994 midterm elections, there was not much political capital with Congress that China could accrue from signing the treaty.

One possibility is that Chinese leaders believed that signing the treaty was valuable for improving overall relations with the United States. In other words, although there was no specific issue-linkage calculation (e.g., sign the CTBT in return for improvements in economic relations), a general issue linkage could have been a primary concern behind China's cooperation. After all, in broad strategic terms China needed a peaceful international environment for its economic modernization plans. Reasonably stable relations with the United States would be instrumental for constructing and maintaining such an environment. The problem here, however, is that it does not appear that Chinese leaders were thinking strategically along these specific lines, particularly in the last year or so of the CTBT negotiations. Indeed, in July 1995 China had fired some short-range ballistic missiles near Taiwan. Then in December 1995 it initiated large-scale military exercises near the Strait. And in March 1996 the PLA conducted even larger scale live-fire exercises in the Strait and yet again fired missiles very close to two Taiwanese ports, all in an effort to intimidate Taiwan and signal to the United States that the Taiwan issue was a question of war and peace for China. Quite clearly the US administration and the Republican opposition read these actions as provocative and belligerent. It is unlikely that the Chinese leadership believed that supporting the CTBT would buy any countervailing goodwill in the United States.[63]

---

[63] One interviewee, close to the CTBT policy process, did contend that both image concerns and concerns about the overall state of play in the Sino-US relationship were co-equal factors in the Chinese government's calculation (June 2000). In reality, it is unlikely that

Even if China's diplomacy in this period were aimed at improving its reputation with the United States, there were cheaper ways of doing this than signing the CTBT. Some minor movement on human rights issues (e.g., releases of dissidents, allowing Red Cross inspection of prisons, signing the UN Covenant on Civil and Political Rights) would have been low cost (to security) with much higher reputational payoffs precisely because Congress cared more about human rights in China than about the progress of the CTBT. Yet China did not use human rights diplomacy in this fashion, at least not in 1995–1996 prior to signing the CTBT.

The evidence suggests, then, that standard realist and contractual institutionalist-inspired arguments cannot account for China's accession. But what is the positive evidence for social influence effects?

It was clear that the critical discourse within the institution—the CD and the CTBT negotiation process—was very much pointed at China's nuclear testing and the Chinese leadership's wariness of the CTBT treaty. With the exception of the United States and others in the P-5, the condemnations of China's nuclear tests from 1993 to 1996 by most developing states and middle powers stressed a number of themes that had negative resonance with the Chinese leaders' identification of China as a "responsible major power." The discourse tended to stress China's behavior as an affront to the moral norms of a putative international community. China's tests were "deplored" and "condemned" as contributing to a new arms race, undermining or obstructing the completion of the CTBT work, being inconsistent with its previous commitments to the NPT, violating the "moral conscience of the international community,"[64] being irresponsible, being shocking and provocative, offending the feelings of people in the developing world, jeopardizing the NPT regime, and insincere. In short, the language was overwhelmingly moral in content and evocative of a larger community whose norms had been violated. As figure 3.7 indicates, the opprobrium tended to focus on the inconsistency of China's diplomacy with past behavior and with a claim to be supportive of the CTBT.[65] In other words, China was being accused

---

one or the other factor was wholly dominant, but his was not a majority view among my interviewees.

[64] See remarks by the Chilean and Argentinean delegations, CD/1227 (October 13, 1993) and CD/1314.

[65] This is based on an analysis of the thirty-four statements made by states in the CD condemning China's nuclear testing from October 1993 to March 1996 prior to China's indication in June that it would accept a CTBT and a moratorium on testing before September 1996. There were twenty-five separate thematic statements describing the nature of the effect of China's position on nuclear testing. These were then collapsed further into four obvious clusters of themes. The statements are from: CD/1227 (October 13, 1993); CD/1249 (March 17, 1994); CD/PV.675 (March 17, 1994); CD/1262 (June 16, 1994); CD/PV.683 (June 23, 1994); CD/1314 (May 31, 1995); CD/1315 (June 2, 1995); CD/1316 (June 7, 1995); CD/1317 (June 7, 1995); CD/1318 (June 8, 1995); CD/1319 (June 15,

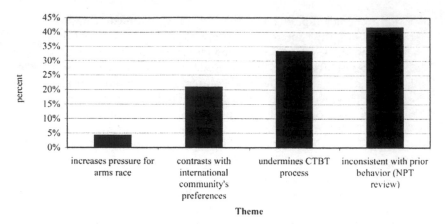

Figure 3.7. Relative portion of themes in states' condemnation of China's nuclear testing and CTBT positions, 1993–1996.

of moral hypocrisy and of behavior inconsistent with its (nascent) identity as a responsible major power.

The NGO community contributed to this moral spotlight on China. Greenpeace, whose China team had behind-the-scenes interaction with the Chinese delegation in Geneva and judged the Chinese delegation to be very sensitive to negative publicity, sent a protest ship toward Shanghai in May 1996 as China was preparing for another nuclear test. The Chinese had implored Greenpeace not to do this, but Greenpeace calculated, correctly, that news coverage of the voyage and the Chinese response would gather a great deal of press attention in Geneva. In one month alone, after announcing the ship's voyage, about three hundred news reports were generated by the story.[66] Environmental NGOs held demonstrations in front of Chinese consulates and embassies around the world. The cross-national state and non-state negative attention on China's diplomacy was, except perhaps for the June 4, 1989, military crackdown, unprecedented for the post-Mao Chinese leadership.

Based on my interviews conducted with a range of people involved in the interagency process and with observers of Chinese bargaining from other countries, I think it was clear that Chinese decision makers were

---

1995); CD/PV.708 (June 15, 1995); CD/PV.709 (June 22, 1995); CD/PV.713 (August 10, 1995); CD/PV.714 (August 17, 1995); CD/1342 (August 24. 1995); CD/1343 (August 28, 1995); CD/1344 (August 28, 1995); CD/1355 (September 20, 1995); CD/PV.723 (February 1, 1996); CD/PV.724 (February 8, 1996); CD/PV.732 (March 26, 1996); CD/PV.733 (March 28, 1996).

[66] Based on LexisNexis search results supplied by Greenpeace. My thanks to Josh Handler for this information.

well aware of this discourse, and of the backpatting benefits and opprobrium costs involved in the CTBT process. The consistent refrain was that China could not stay out of, or in the end sabotage, the CTBT because of the costs to China's international image and because of the image benefits from participating in one of the pillar treaties of the non-proliferation regime. This was, after all, a regime supported by an overwhelming majority of states in the system. Even during the endgame negotiations with the United States over the verification regime, the MOFA and its concern about China's image prevailed over the military and testing communities' demand to hold firm on the two-thirds majority green light system.[67] The language used by Chinese interlocutors to discuss joining and then signing was status oriented. The CTBT was a "great international trend"; China's signing was consistent with it being a responsible world power, and joining the treaty was part of a "global atmosphere," such that China would have been isolated had it ignored this atmosphere; there was a nebulous "psychological pressure" to join once the United States, Russia, the United Kingdom, and France had committed and there was clearly strong support in the G-21.[68] After the fact, one of the members of the Chinese CTBT delegation argued publicly (the first statement of this kind as far as I am aware) that one of the key reasons why China ended up supporting the CTBT was "opinion" among developing states: "Taking into account its historical friendly relations with them, China had to maintain its image in third-world countries. China's image as a responsible major power is reportedly moving to the fore. *The necessity of maintaining its international image* was a reason for China's decision to adjust its position on the CTBT negotiations" (Zou 1998:15; emphasis mine).[69] This is an un-

---

[67] Interview with senior arms control specialist from the MOFA, October 1999.

[68] These arguments come from the following interviews: a senior military officer involved in multilateral arms control policy making, Beijing, July 1996; a senior military officer involved in multilateral arms control negotiations, Beijing, April 1996; an arms control specialist in a nuclear weapons design institute, Beijing, January 1998; an arms control specialist with a intelligence think tank, May 1996; an analyst with a PLA-connected research institute, June 1996; a US DOD official involved in CTBT negotiations, June 1998; a US DOD official involved in non-proliferation policy, June 1998; a senior Canadian official directly involved in the CTBT negotiations, July 2001; and a senior PLA officer with experience in multilateral arms control negotiations and research, Beijing, June 1996 and Cambridge, MA, May 1998 (this official was one of the few to mention a more concrete gain for China, namely that China's signature might make the United States more relaxed about its concerns about China and missile proliferation).

[69] The Chinese were made very aware of the specific pressure from developing states after its May 1995 nuclear test, which took place forty-eight hours after the end of the NPT extension conference. In Zou's words, "The May 15, 1995 test inflicted the most political damage to China.... This test made the Non-Aligned Movement very angry" Zou (1998:13). This is an interesting and exceedingly rare public admission of sharp differences between China and other developing states on nuclear disarmament issues.

usually direct admission of the impact of this form of social pressure from a regime that has traditionally publicly claimed that diplomatic pressure on China is counterproductive.[70] That the Chinese bargained hard over verification issues—in particular on-site inspection—even in the face of considerable dismay among delegations does not undermine the argument about social influence. Bargaining to dilute the verification and punishment elements of the treaty in the last months of negotiations was premised on the existence of a basic acceptance of the core distributional features of the treaty.[71]

There is, as one might expect given the nature of the institutional environment in which China was operating, little evidence that normative persuasion affected the decision making behind CTBT accession. In this case, one would look for two arguments in particular that would reflect an internalization of the theory behind the CTBT's value as a treaty. The first would be arguments in the policy process to the effect that the CTBT would have a critical stabilizing effect on vertical and horizontal proliferation. This was, after all, the primary argument made in favor of test bans well back in the 1950s. Even though technological change through to the 1990s meant that non-testing would not have as dramatic a constraint on the development of some new weapons designs (particularly for the United States with its advanced simulation technologies), the general argument behind the CTBT still held—a ban on testing would reduce the reliability of, hence the value of, nuclear weapons, putting some constraints on vertical and horizontal proliferation. One did not find this argument in the Chinese policy process. Indeed, Chinese arms controllers

---

[70] In some cases, when I followed up with questions specifically on the role of image concerns, my interlocutors would quickly downplay what they had just said, since this implied that China was indeed susceptible to external pressure. Alternatively, they would admit that image concerns were a factor in explaining changes in Chinese positions, but would only allow that China was sensitive to this pressure if it came from developing states, not from developed states (interview with MOFA official, November 2000). For an effort (though quite equivocal in the end) to downplay the role of image in Chinese decisions to cooperate in arms control, see the piece from a CICIR analyst, Wu Yun (1996:605 n. 34). For analyses that argue that image and prestige are secondary in China's arms control behavior, see Malik 1995:22 and Lewis 2004 (on the CTBT).

[71] This suggests that in the China case, at least, the primary issue for its leaders was neither the distributional effects of the treaty (e.g., limits on its ability to modernize its nuclear forces relative to the United States, for example), nor concerns about other states cheating. Rather it was the symbolic effect of highly intrusive, sovereignty-constraining verification provisions that raised the greatest resistance. This reaction does not fit easily with traditional cooperation theory (see Fearon 1998:287). It suggests that bargaining is sometimes over identity—deals that allow an actor to claim it has acted consistently with its self-categorization. In this sense, the CTBT reveals the tension between two self-categorizations found in Chinese leaders' worldviews—a responsible major power identity and an identity as a defender of sovereignty in the face of hegemony.

involved in the process continue to express doubts about the value of the CTBT in this regard.

A second argument, somewhat less obvious, and more controversial among the proponents of a CTBT, would be that the CTBT does not undermine the deterrents of the nuclear states because above a certain threshold of capabilities, more weapons are redundant and do not buy security. In other words, for many advocates the CTBT was implicitly premised on the notion of minimum deterrence: once a nuclear power had enough to inflict unacceptable damage, then there should be no need for continued testing. Minimum deterrence would be a transitional strategy toward a non-nuclear world. The question whether Chinese strategists accept the notion of minimum deterrence is controversial. There is considerable evidence that many in the PLA believe minimum deterrence makes a virtue out of necessity and that China needs a somewhat larger, more flexible limited war-fighting capability to control escalation from conventional to nuclear conflicts and to control nuclear escalation itself.[72] Although the evidence as to the impact of these ideas on force posture and operations is unclear, there is no evidence that the concept of minimun deterrence was used in the Chinese policy process to support signing the CTBT. Thus, persuasion—in this case, the internalization of new cause-effect arguments about how to achieve security embodied in the philosophy of a CTBT as an institution—appears not to have been the socialization microprocess at work in this case.

EMPIRICAL IMPLICATIONS: THE REVISED LANDMINE PROTOCOL TO THE CONVENTION ON CERTAIN CONVENTIONAL WEAPONS

The revised Landmines Protocol, also known as Protocol II (hereafter PII), is part of the 1981 Convention on Certain Conventional Weapons. This treaty banned certain weapons systems that were considered "inhumane" and, in particular, sought to protect civilian populations "from the effects of hostilities."[73] The original treaty had a number of protocols

---

[72] Johnston (1995/6). See also the distinction made between minimum, limited, and maximum deterrence in teaching materials for the National Defense University, Wang 1999:359–61. See also the discussion of deterrence in the influential study on strategy by Academy of Military Sciences scholars, AMS 2001:239, 332. According to one PLA expert on Chinese nuclear forces, even though China can only target US cities, "as the performance of the nuclear weapons of China continues to improve, some important military targets of the enemy will also become the emphasis of the nuclear counterattack of China" Anon. (n.d. ~ 1997:13).

[73] This brief history of the PII draws mainly from the "Summary of Negotiations Leading to the Conclusion of the Convention on Prohibitions or Restrictions on the Use of Certain Conventional Weapon Which May Be Deemed to Be Excessively Injurious or to Have Indiscriminate Effects and of Subsequent Developments Related to the Convention" CCW/CONF.I/GE/5 (May 6, 1994) and from Final Report of the Review Conference, 1996.

covering particular kinds of weapons. Protocol I prohibited the use of weapons "the primary effect of which is to injure by fragments which in the human body escape detection by X-rays."[74] Protocol II prohibited the use of landmines solely against civilian populations. Protocol III placed certain prohibitions on the use of incendiary weapons against civilians.

In May 1996 the signatories to the original treaty concluded an amended Protocol II, which basically stated that certain types of landmines be self-deactivating and more easily discoverable using metal detectors. The Protocol also limited the transfers of mines that did not meet these technical requirements.

The PII case is not as striking an example as the CTBT of the impact of public image concerns on Chinese arms control behavior. Nonetheless, the causal process that led the PRC to accept the amended PII in May was similar. In essence, by accepting the PII restrictions, China was accepting limits on its capacity to produce and export landmines. These limits were initially opposed by the Chinese military for reasons of cost and military efficacy. There were no credible offers of side payments—such as preferential transfers of technology that could reduce the costs of adherence to the PII—nor were any material sanctions threatened for avoiding or obstructing the amendment of the PII. The operative factor in leading to China's concessions was the damage to Beijing's image from resisting a growing and palpable international sentiment in favor of strict controls on so-called dumb mines, if not an outright ban on all anti-personnel landmines.

The original PII prohibited the use of landmines and booby traps solely against civilian populations and nonmilitary targets, and prohibited disguising these weapons in forms that could be mistaken for everyday items (toys, kitchen utensils, pieces of art, etc.). The original PII also required that combatants carefully record the locations of deployed mines. The information was to be made readily available once hostilities ceased. The PII harkened back to the Hague conventions (number VIII in particular) that banned certain kinds of unanchored, automatic contact underwater mines, limited the areas in which submarine mines could be deployed (e.g., not in commercial sea-lanes near ports), and required states to keep records of mine deployments, among other provisions. The point was to limit the ability of states to indiscriminately endanger peaceful economic and human activity.[75] The original PII also drew on principles, as embodied in the Geneva conventions of 1949, that "the right of the parties to an armed conflict to choose methods or means of warfare is not unlim-

---

[74] CCCW Protocol I "Protocol on Non-Detectable Fragments."
[75] See Hague Convention (VIII) "Relative to the Laying of Automatic Submarine Contact Mines" (October 18, 1907).

ited." In particular, those methods that caused "superfluous injury or unnecessary suffering" were to be restricted.[76]

The Conventional Weapons Convention emerged out of a growing normative concern about the indiscriminate use of weapons. The Vietnam War in particular had raised questions about the legitimacy of the US use of napalm and indiscriminate attacks on civilian populations. In 1973 the UNGA adopted a resolution basically requesting that the Diplomatic Conference on the Reaffirmation and Development of International Humanitarian Law Applicable in Armed Conflicts consider napalm, incendiary devices, and the problem of the indiscriminate use of and unnecessary suffering caused by such weapons. In 1974 the Diplomatic Conference then set up an ad hoc committee to look at conventional weapons. Out of the meetings of the ad hoc committee came a proposal, embodied in a UNGA resolution, to convene a UN conference in 1979 to negotiate agreements prohibiting or restricting certain kinds of conventional weapons.[77] Landmines were added to this list as a result of a study by the ICRC in 1975, which pointed out that incendiary weapons were not the only objectionable weapons systems. The UNGA then set up a Preparatory Committee (Prepcom) for the 1979 conference. In August 1978 the Prepcom met and considered draft articles on regulating landmines.[78] A UNGA resolution endorsed the Prepcom's recommendation for a September 1979 UN Conference on Prohibitions or Restrictions of Use of Certain Conventional Weapons Which May be Deemed to Be Excessively Injurious or to Have Indiscriminate Effects.[79]

The conference convened in Geneva. It held a number of plenary sessions through 1979 and 1980 and set up a working group on landmines and booby traps to draft articles for a protocol on landmines. The working group's report included a draft text for protocols.[80] The draft proposed that the treaty "totally prohibit the use of the weapons in question either in offence, defense, or by way of reprisal against civilians. The indiscriminate use of these weapons would also be prohibited and States parties would take all feasible precautions to protect civilians from their effects." The draft also called for states to record and publish the "location of minefields, mines and booby-traps."

The draft had two major sticking points. The first was whether information about the location of mines should be provided to aggressors occu-

[76] See the preamble to the CCCW, 1981.
[77] A/RES/32/152, December 19, 1977.
[78] These were drafted by a group consisting mostly of developed states. See A/CONF.95/ PREP.CONF/L.9 and Add. 1.
[79] A/RES/33/70.
[80] A/CONF.95/8 September 1979.

pying some other state's territory. The other issue was how to handle remotely delivered mines. The draft said these could be used if their location could be recorded or if the mines were self-destructing or self-neutralizing.[81] At the time, a small number of states supported a complete ban on remotely delivered mines.

By the October 1980 plenary session of the conference, the working group on landmines had come to consensus on everything except these two hard issues. As a result, these were left out of the draft protocol. The conference took the reports of this and other working groups and adopted the CCCW treaty instrument that included Protocol II. A UNGA resolution in December 1980 endorsed the treaty, and noted that future conferences could be convened to address amendments to the protocols (namely, the two problem issues).[82] The treaty was open for signature in April 1981 and entered into force in December 1983.

China signed the CCCW in 1981, though it was not particularly active in the negotiations leading up to the treaty. The PRC did not attend the 1978 Prepcom, and during the 1979 conference it only submitted a working paper concerning preambular language.[83] At that time China had only just entered the UN arms control institutions and was only beginning to develop positions and expertise on the global arms control agenda. But it did issue a reservation to the CCCW. It objected to the fact that the treaty language did not discriminate between aggressors and victims. Victims, the Chinese argued, ought to have more flexibility to adopt the military measures necessary for resisting aggression, and aggressors ought to be even more strictly restrained from using landmines in occupied territories. China expressed another concern at the time as well. The CCCW established that if a state wanted out of the treaty, it had to give prior notification one year in advance of its withdrawal. However, if the state was still involved in an armed conflict with another state when the year for withdrawal came up, the treaty would continue to apply until the cessation of hostility.[84]

For the first few years after the CCCW entered into force in 1983, most of the attention on the treaty was aimed at encouraging more states to join. UNGA resolutions each year from 1983 through 1990 continued to urge states to sign on so as to expand the treaty's universality. By 1990, however, attention began to shift toward the content of the treaty and to

[81] From CCW/CONF.I/GE/5, p. 14.

[82] A/RES/35/153.

[83] A/CONF.95/WG/L.8.

[84] For these concerns, see Chen and Zhang 1997:346. The authors, both researchers at the PLA's Academy of Military Sciences, refer to the absence of this principle of aggressors versus victims as "regrettable."

whether it was sufficient in addressing the problems it was supposed to help alleviate. During discussions over the UNGA resolution in 1990 calling for more states to sign, Sweden noted that ten years had passed since the UNGA had endorsed the treaty and that it was time to reopen some of the issues, to expand the scope and perhaps tighten the restrictions. Sweden then proposed a review conference. UNGA resolutions in 1991 and 1992 reiterated this call for a review conference. There were a number of reasons for this growing interest in a review. For one thing, with the end of the cold war, a number of societies, especially in Southeast Asia, were trying to rebuild their local economies. The material and human damage from landmines was a critical obstacle to this goal. For another, as the frequency of UN PKO increased in the post–cold war era, the problem of dealing with landmines' threats to PKO became more salient.[85]

An increasingly active ICRC also encouraged this focus on the humanitarian and economic costs of landmines. It organized a major conference on APLs in April 1993, where NGOs played a key role in underscoring the humanitarian angle of the issue. In February 1993, France formally requested that the secretary general convene a review conference with special focus on Protocol II.

In his 1993 report, the secretary general stressed that "of all tasks involved in setting a nation on a new road to peace and prosperity, perhaps none has the immediate urgency of mine clearance." Around this time the Swiss held an international conference on the protection of war veterans to underscore the need to strengthen law governing indiscriminate use of mines.

Then later in 1993 the United States got in on the act.[86] It introduced a UNGA resolution calling for a moratorium on the export of APLs (the United States had adopted a unilateral moratorium in 1992). The resolution was adopted without a vote by the UNGA in December 1993. The resolution simply called for a moratorium on export of APLs that "pose grave dangers to civilian populations."[87] The preambular language of the resolution underscored the humanitarian normative basis of the issue, namely the dangers that landmines posed to unarmed civilians, to economic development, and to the repatriation of refugees.

In preparation for a review conference, the secretary general set up a Group of Governmental Experts. Following from the US resolution on a moratorium on exports, one of the major new issues looked at by the Group of Experts was whether to include restrictions on the transfer and/ or export of APLs in a new, revised PII. The agenda and principles were

[85] Interview with Chinese Ministry of Foreign Affairs official, November 2000.
[86] For a good summary of US diplomacy, see Sigal 2006.
[87] See A/RES/48/75K (December 16, 1993).

established by a coalition of adversely affected developing states (Afghanistan and Cambodia) and a number of concerned developed states active on the APLs question in a number of draft statements concerning what at the time was to be a new article 6 on transfers. These drafts stressed four basic principles: no transfers to non-state entities; no transfers to states not bound to the PII; no transfers of mines prohibited under all circumstances to other PII signatories; and states that do transfer non-prohibited mines to other signatory states must ensure that the recipient state complies with international humanitarian law.[88]

Another new issue that had not been on the agenda for the original PII was the question of smart mines. Technological advances made it possible to program mines to self-destruct or self-neutralize after certain periods of time. Moreover, if mines included sufficient metal content, they would be easier, safer, and faster to remove. A number of states were proposing that a new PII include requirements for the self-neutralization of landmines after a certain period of time to reduce the likelihood of continued menace to civilians.

With the questions of transfers and dumb/smart mines on the table, the formal review conference ran from September through October 1995 in Vienna. It moved relatively smoothly toward the adoption of a new protocol to prohibit outright the use of laser weapons to blind in combat (Protocol IV). But the conference was unable to come to a consensus about a revised PII. So it decided to hold additional negotiation sessions in Geneva on January 15–19, 1996 and April 22 through May 3, 1996, with the aim of having a revised PII by May. These sessions were tough slogging. In order to streamline the negotiation process, the president of the conference managed to task a group called "Friends of the Chair" to carry out most of the work on the PII and its technical annex. By the end of the May 1996 session, a consensus emerged on a revised PII. The main revisions would focus on technical innovations designed to make the detection and removal of landmines easier and to reduce the likelihood of harming civilians well after conflicts ended. To this end, the protocol prohibited anti-handling devices on landmines. It required a certain metal content in landmines. It banned APLs that did not have a highly reliable self-destruct or self-deactivation capacity. And it banned mines and means of delivery that were clearly not aimed at military targets.

In addition, the new PII restricted the transfer of mines prohibited by the protocol. That is, only mines with the self-neutralization capabilities

[88] See the proposed draft Article 6 CCW/CONF.I/GE/CRP.38/Rev.1 (January 19, 1995); the working paper submitted by a number of developed countries, CCW/CONF.I/MCII/WP.5 (October 4, 1995), and the chairman's draft, CCW/CONF.1/MCII/WP.4/4/Add.1/Rev.2.

and detectability established in the protocols could be transferred to other signatory states. All other transfers were banned. It also included an article on technical assistance to speed up the transfer of de-mining technology. Though the article does not say it directly, the purpose was also to allow technology-poor states to shift to smart-mine production (the article refers to assistance in the "implementation of the Protocol," in addition to assistance in mine clearing).

Finally, the new PII had much more detailed requirements for keeping and publicizing records about the placement of landmines. It included, for instance, provisions in the annex for the exact measurements of mine warning signs.

What was China's approach to the revision of the PII? As with the CTBT, the Chinese entered the negotiations with a number of concerns about the proposed revisions.

At the most abstract level, Chinese decision makers were worried that humanitarian norms were driving the process forward at the expense of the legitimate military needs of states (Li 1995). Here the calculation went beyond simple military security interests. There was an uneasiness that NGOs were driving the agenda, establishing the standards for state behavior, and in some instances actually participating in national delegations. This, in the Chinese view, introduced unpredictability into what should have remained state-to-state negotiations. It was also clear that the NGO strategy was precisely to delegitimate military and "defensive" considerations.

A second worry was that by extending the coverage of the PII to non-international conflicts (internal or state versus non-state actor conflicts), this would somehow attribute an aura of sovereignty to the non-state actor. China insisted, therefore, that the application of the PII to non-interstate conflicts did not mean that the legal status of the parties changed.

A third position was that any standardization, recording, or marking of minefields should not undermine the legitimate military needs of a state party. Thus, in one opening gambit that would have dramatically weakened the entire PII, the Chinese delegation maintained that "a State party should have the right not to make public the records of mines placed within its territory for the purpose of self-defense" (Li 1995).

A fourth major position was that the PII should include assistance not only for mine clearing but also "for helping State parties with less advanced technical capabilities to fulfill their obligations" (Li 1995).[89] This

---

[89] The PRC had teamed up with Cuba, Pakistan, and Iran early on in the Prepcom work for the review conference to propose that this assistance be "free of cost." See CCW/CONF.I/GE/CRP.31 (August 16, 1994) and CCW/CONF.I/GE/CRP.33 (August 17, 1994).

was a less-than-veiled request for assistance in changing over production lines from dumb to smart mines.

A fifth concern was verification. The Chinese led off with a vague position that advocated transparency rather than intrusive verification mechanisms. It was unclear what transparency measures might be incorporated other than voluntary ones.

Finally, the Chinese stressed that since the PII fell under rules governing conduct of war, restrictions on the transfer of mines ought not be part of the agreement. However, perhaps realizing the overwhelming push among the parties for some action on transfers, the Chinese did not object to provisions governing transfers.

Negotiations in Vienna bogged down over many of these issues, according to observers, largely because of objections from China, India, Russia, and Pakistan, among others.[90] The Chinese negotiators were tenacious and tough, often taking the lead among recalcitrant states in opposing any movement on technical limits on landmines and transfers.[91] When negotiations resumed in January 1996, some headway had been made in bringing Russia on board with most of the provisions about smart mines.

As negotiations moved on, Chinese concerns boiled down to four: one was verification. The original chair's rolling draft in 1994 and the compilation of proposals for verification included a Verification Commission that, by majority vote, could conduct an inquiry into any accusations of noncompliance; the inquiry could include on-site inspections.[92] The rolling draft also included some provisions for collective punishment of violators. China joined with Cuba, Pakistan, Iran, and India to submit proposals on verification that would remove the most intrusive measures from the rolling draft. The justification was that less focus on intrusiveness would enhance the universality of the treaty by making it easier for states to join. Instead, the proposals called only for unilateral transparency measures to be reported to the UN on a regular basis (e.g., reports about relevant domestic legislation, de-mining, and any civilian casualties due to mines, among other measures).[93]

---

[90] *CCW News* No. 9 (April 9, 1996), p. 3.

[91] It is possible that the Chinese representatives, two somewhat more junior officials (Sha Zukang was not in attendance), had no mandate from Beijing to explore compromises. This accords with a perception among other delegations that the Chinese entered the Vienna talks having drastically underestimated the public attention to the issue and the growing media and NGO humanitarian interest in tighter restrictions on landmines. Interview with senior Canadian diplomat who attended the PII talks, July 3, 2001. For NGO assessments of Chinese obstructionism in the Vienna round of negotiations, see *CCW News* No. 5 (October 11, 1995), p. 2.

[92] See CCW/CONF.I/GE/CRP.2/Rev.1 (June 28, 1994), pp. 43–45.

[93] CCW/CONF.I/GE/CRP.32 (August 16, 1994) and CCW/CONF.I/GE/CRP.32 (January 17, 1995).

A second issue had to do with the military operational value of land-mines. With twenty-two thousand kilometers of land borders, the PLA border defense forces (represented by the Border Defense Office [*bianfang ju*] inside the GSD Operations Department) believed landmines were a crucial means of defending sparsely manned areas.[94]

Third, there were economic costs involved in shifting production lines from dumb mines to smart or smarter mines.[95] The PLA had a consider-able market for its plastic, and undetectable, mines.[96] The PLA had a large stock of dumb mines that would not meet the PII requirements. Shifting to smart mines therefore involved potential market losses as well as the cost of changing production lines. The PLA was therefore unhappy with proposals in the PII negotiations for self-neutralizing and detectable mines for deployment. It complained to the Foreign Ministry—in charge of ne-gotiating the protocol—that the economic and military costs for an early shift in product lines were too high. The Foreign Ministry had no way of independently confirming these costs, and some in the ministry doubted the PLA's figures. Nonetheless, the bargaining position taken to Vienna and to Geneva did reflect PLA concerns. China initially opposed any re-quirements for detectability delegation and therefore proposed that these two technical requirements—self-neutralization and detectability—should be separated out. Mines could be either self-neutralizing or detect-able, but need not be both.[97]

Moreover, the Chinese demanded that both the transition period *and* the reliability of self-neutralization mechanisms be less stringent than that recommended by developed and some developing countries. Again, the argument was mainly because this would require substantial technologi-

[94] One PLA study of limited war argued that 70 percent of China's land borders faced some level of external threat. See Wang, Wang, and Huang 1990:82.

[95] The following paragraph draws from interviews with a Canadian diplomat, May 1996, two Chinese diplomats, April 1996 and November 2001, and a PLA officer, May 2001.

[96] Although much of China's military production was handled at the time by military industries that were institutionally separate from the PLA proper, there is some evidence that the PLA had a limited landmine production capability. Moreover, sales of landmines may also have come out of the PLA's existing stocks. Other actors with a financial interest against a revised PII were mine producers in the military industrial sector that came under the supervision of the Commission on Science, Technology, and Industry for National De-fense. One authoritative PLA interlocutor claims, however, that COSTIND did not play a too important role in the policy process (interview, May 2001). This leads me to believe that the main economic interests at stake concerned factories and businesses operating under the PLA's General Staff Department. My thanks to Harlan Jencks for pushing me to develop the empirics on this question further.

[97] On China's initial opposition to the shift to detectable mines in the CCW negotiations, see *CCW News* No. 5 (October 11, 1995), p. 2. On the Chinese delegation's technical proposal, see *CCW News* No. 9 (April 9, 1996), p. 4.

cal upgrades for Chinese mines.[98] For instance, in the January 1996 session, the United States, United Kingdom, and Russia proposed that all APLs not inside marked minefields should self-deactivate with a 95 percent reliability rate within 30 days, reaching a 99.9 percent reliability rate within 120 days. Proposals for the length of the transition period for retooling production lines ranged from three to seventeen years, with a compromise figure of eight years. The Chinese delegation instead called for a 90 percent reliability rate in self-deactivation, but it was unclear about over what time period this should occur. As for a transition period for switching over production, China initially proposed twenty-five years, later reducing it to twelve.[99] Most states wanted eight or less. In addition, China proposed that all these requirements for self-neutralization could be suspended if remotely delivered mines were used in areas that were military objectives.[100] In effect, this loophole would have allowed unlimited use of remotely delivered mines in areas designated (unilaterally, one assumes) as military objectives.

Fourth, ultimately the Chinese also appeared to be worried about restrictions on transfers. Here again, the PLA's preferences shaped China's bargaining position. Landmine exports were reasonably lucrative for the PLA (most probably for factories that come under the auspices of the Engineering Corp Department [Gongcheng bing bu] within the GSD, or for companies that sold mines out of extant PLA stockpiles). The cost and time needed to change product lines might lead to some loss of market share.

Given all these objections to revising the PII, it was not surprising, then, that in the 1995 Vienna sessions of the review convention, the PRC only stated that it followed a responsible transfer policy. It was not until late April 1996 that the PRC announced it would accept a moratorium on exports, to the surprise of many.

The PII was not a disaster from the Chinese perspective. The Chinese delegation either managed to get some of their preferred outcomes written into the PII, or it supported others in their efforts to draft a treaty that met Chinese requirements. For example, the Chinese appeared to get preambular language that blunted, if only symbolically, some of the potential intrusiveness of the PII. The new PII article 1 on the scope of the prohibitions excluded "internal disturbances . . . such as riots, isolated and sporadic acts of violence and other acts of a similar nature, as not being

---

[98] The ICBL reportedly overheard the Chinese delegation complaining to American delegates in the hallway that the United States was using the PII negotiations to impose its mine technology standards on other states. *CCW News* No. 5 (October 11, 1995), p. 5.

[99] *CCW News* No. 9 (April 9, 1996), p. 4.

[100] CCW/CONF.I/WP.3 "Compilation of Proposals" (October 13, 1995).

armed conflicts."[101] A state could, in principle, use landmines to put down this kind of civil unrest. Article 1 also stressed that the PII did not affect the sovereignty of states to defend territorial integrity through legitimate means. It also noted that even though the PII applies to conflicts with non-state parties, this does not mean that the legal status of non-state parties changes during the conflict. They are still non-state (hence not sovereign) parties. This would mean, for instance, that a China-Taiwan conflict would be covered by the PII, but Taiwan would not, therefore, be considered legally an equal sovereign entity.

As for verification, the final PII was considerably watered down from some of the initial drafts. As I noted earlier, the 1994 chair's rolling draft PII was much more intrusive than the final version (the final version eliminated the idea of a Verification Commission and left it up to individual states to sanction violators from their nation or on their national territory).

On the technical question of self-deactivation, the PII endorsed a position on reliability rates preferred by the PRC (90 percent) but endorsed the shortest time period (thirty days).

Despite these provisions, however, the new PII did not reflect all the preferences brought to the table by the Chinese delegation. China did not get its way on the question of the transition period from dumb to smart mines or on transfers and exports of APLs. The PRC proposal that all the technical restrictions on remotely delivered mines could be suspended in areas that were military objectives was also rejected in the final version of the PII.

The PII required that after January 1, 1997, all APLs had to have a certain amount of detectable metal (eight grams) and had to meet the 90 percent over 30 days–99.9 percent over 120 days self-deactivation requirements. If a state was unable to meet these technical requirements by January 1, 1997, it had nine years to do so, that is, until 2006.[102] It is hard to determine how onerous a burden this transitioning was viewed by the PLA. Even outside advocates of tight restrictions on landmines recognized that the basic technical restrictions of the PII favored developed states, since the treaty essentially banned dumb mines while sanctioning smart ones. This put countries with more primitive mine technology at a disadvantage (Dolan and Hunt 1999:401). But in the Chinese case, this does not seem to have been an insurmountable problem.

The more important concern for the Chinese delegation was transfers. Initially, the Chinese had indicated that they would accept a moratorium on exports of banned landmines once the PII entered into effect (six months after the twentieth ratification of the amended protocol). During

[101] CCCW PII article 1.2.
[102] CCCW Technical Annex paragraphs 2, 3.

the October–November 1995 session of the review conference, the PRC representative gave lukewarm support for a ban on transfers and did not commit China to a moratorium prior to EIF, let alone at the conclusion of the review process. Li Changhe, the Chinese lead negotiator in Vienna, argued, "[S]ince the Convention and its Protocols fall largely within the framework of the laws of war and humanitarian laws, they should, strictly speaking, deal only with the use of weapons, and not with their transfer." However, in the interests of reducing the threat to civilians, his delegation could agree to the inclusion of provisions banning the transfer of mines the use of which was prohibited by the Protocol.[103]

On April 22, however, just before the final sessions of the PII review conference were to begin, the Chinese delegation issued a statement announcing an immediate moratorium on exports of APLs that did not meet the PII requirements pending entry into force of the amended protocol. The PRC MOFA estimated that EIF could be as long as two to three years.[104] Since China had evidently not yet switched production lines, and judging from China's bargaining position in the review process wanted as long as possible to do so, this implied a willingness to lose two to three years of exports and to accept the costs of retooling product lines.[105]

Why the compromise, especially when the cost—the loss of markets and the costs of transitioning border defenses—would be borne by the PLA and/or military industries? As in the CTBT case, there were no offers of material side payments or threats of material sanctions aimed at China. There were no offers to transfer smart-mine technology to China to make signing the PII less costly. There were no threats of economic sanctions were China not to sign the protocol. There were also more efficient ways of gaining the goodwill of the US Congress in order to exploit gains from reputation than signing the PII.

The best realism-derived hypothesis based on the imperative to preserve relative power would be that Chinese decision makers read the tea leaves and foresaw a bandwagoning effect toward more comprehensive prohibitions happening even as the review conference proceeded. Beijing might have decided that the PII as proposed was better than an emerging APL ban movement (sometimes called the "Ottawa process"), and thus support for the PII was a cheaper alternative (economically and militarily).

But it is unlikely that this was the calculation. While there *was* an emerging sentiment to outright ban APLs *and*, as a consequence, a further

[103] CCW/CONF.I/SR.4 (October 3, 1995).

[104] Interview with MOFA official, April 1996. In the final version of the amended Protocol II, EIF would be triggered six months after twenty states had ratified.

[105] "Moratorium on the Export of Anti-Personnel Land-Mines," CCW/CONF.I/12, (April 22, 1996).

delegitimization of the military and commercial frame at the PII, China announced its moratorium on mine exports in April 1996, before the Ottawa process had really gotten off the ground. There was certainly no hint of a tipping point in ban sentiment at the January 1996 session, where the Chinese delegation evidently decided that the public relations pressure was getting excessive. Indeed, as of April and May 1996, there were still divisions between the Canadian foreign ministry and the Department of National Defense over whether to pursue a total ban on APLs.[106] Moreover, Canada had only just decided in March 1996 an action plan to invite pro-ban states to Ottawa in September. This action plan was then the basis for the approach to PII delegates in April about a meeting of like-minded pro-ban states (Tomlin 1999:194–95). And on April 29 when it hosted a preliminary meeting at the Geneva review conference to prepare for the Ottawa conference, only twelve states showed up, even though by that time there were around thirty pro-ban states.[107] So at the time China decided to accept the revised PII, there was simply no way the Chinese delegation could have anticipated where the Ottawa process was headed, or where it might end up; the Canadians themselves were not sure. Heading this process off, then, was probably not part of the Chinese calculus.

Rather, the emerging pro-ban group produced a more subtle effect on Chinese diplomacy. During the PII negotiations, one saw the development of a critical mass of states—some acting as norm entrepreneurs, some bandwagoning—that began to press for an outright ban on APLs. When the review conference opened in September 1995, fourteen states supported an outright ban. Even the pro-ban NGOs admitted at the time that the dominant frame defining discussions was a military not a humanitarian one (Williams 1995:5; Woodmansey 1995:4). However, by the time the PII was agreed to in May 1996, forty-one states supported the ban (Williams and Goose 1999:33). This, then, was an important feature of the social influence effects—the rise of a ban movement *inside* the PII negotiations. Canada had announced on January 17 that it would declare a moratorium on the production, transfer, and operational use of land-mines (Warmington and Tuttle 1999:54). By April 9, just before the review session opened, twenty-six states had announced support for a comprehensive ban of APLs. By April 22, there were thirty. And by the April 26 plenary session there were thirty-four.[108] These states helped elevate the humanitarian norms frame in the PII, making military and especially commercial cost frames less credible, or more suspect.

---

[106] Interview with senior Canadian diplomat, July 3, 2001.
[107] *CCW News* No. 11 (April 30, 1996), p. 7.
[108] *CCW News* Nos. 9, 10, and 11 (April 9, 22, 30, 1996).

This reframing was assisted by an exceptionally active NGO presence. Some NGOs were actually represented on state delegations (e.g., Mines Action Canada was represented on the Canadian delegation) (Warmington and Tuttle 1999:55; Sigal 2006:76). This exposed the entire negotiation process to a public scrutiny that this kind of arms control process had not experienced in the 1980s. According to Price (1998), there were about 70 different NGOs from twenty countries, totaling over one hundred people at the beginning of the review conference. According to the ICBL, by the final session of the CCW review in May, there were about 150 NGO representatives. Most were organized under the ICBL umbrella. The ICBL engaged in high-profile lobbying. At the 1995 negotiation session in Vienna, mine victims delivered petitions with 1.7 million signatures from people around the world; a million signatures were delivered by the April 1996 session in Geneva. Six tons of shoes were delivered to the Austrian parliament to signify lost limbs.[109] The NGOs called for more than the PII—they called for an outright ban on all APLs. For its part, the ICBL launched an international campaign to ban the production, use, stockpiling, and transfer of landmines in November 1995 after the CCW review session appeared to make little progress on revising the PII.

By May 1996, the ICBL comprised six hundred NGOs (Price 1998:620–21). The ICBL claimed that their pressure led to the emergence of a ban sentiment among a sufficient number of states to help stalemate the negotiations in October 1995 (Williams and Goose 1999:32). The ICBL also claimed that it was instrumental in increasing pro-ban sentiment by actually hosting on-site meetings of pro-ban and other interested countries in January, April, and May 1996.

The effect of this emerging pro-ban bandwagon was to delegitimize the military and commercial frame that China and other mine states had used to balance against purely humanitarian arguments. As sentiment in the PII sessions shifted steadily toward a full ban, China was left in a shrinking group of opponents of a ban. By the April 1996 session, a majority of states at the CCW review were in favor of an outright ban. But consensus decision making at the conference prevented them from ensuring that the CCW reflected their preferences.[110] Indeed, this was one of the reasons why the Canadians decided to develop the Ottawa process of like-minded states. Consensus decision making gave obstructionist states the opportunity to dilute the goals of negotiations. So even though the consensus process gave China and like-minded states an ability to block some of the

[109] See Williams and Goose (1999:32); Sigal (2006:78); CCW News No. 11 (April 30, 1996, p. 2).

[110] See CCW News No. 10 (April 25, 1996), p. 7.

more restrictive elements of certain PII proposals, as the pro-ban majority grew, the anti-ban minority became more and more visibly obstructionist. As one negotiator put it, when the Chinese looked around the room, there was such momentum to restrict landmines that it had no credible allies with which to oppose the PII.[111] In essence, this is the downside for those who fear social pressure in high-profile consensus institutions.

Thus, the primary consideration for Chinese decision makers was image; China was increasingly isolated in the PII negotiations as states either pushed for tougher restrictions on landmines or pushed for an outright ban, deciding, even, to go outside the UN process if necessary.[112] The origins of China's moratorium proposal are consistent with this hypothesis. The proposal evidently came from China's delegation in Geneva after the January 1996 review session. The delegation believed that China was needlessly damaging its image by taking a hard line on the PII. It sent a cable to Beijing recommending the initiative. The PLA, evidently, was reluctant to endorse the moratorium proposal. But the MOFA argued that joining the PII, like other arms control regimes, was a trend that China, as an important part of the world community, could not neglect.[113] Eventually the proposal was endorsed by the top levels of the ministry. The idea was to take a more high-profile, cooperative initiative in the upcoming April meetings in order to reduce the degree of opprobrium China faced at the time.[114] The timing of the moratorium proposal, then, was to facilitate a PII agreement and thus to enhance China's status. After some debate, and with evidence that the top leaders in the MOFA were behind the proposal, the PLA agreed to the moratorium.[115]

[111] Interview with senior Canadian diplomat, July 3, 2001.

[112] The following paragraphs are based mainly on interviews with MOFA officials in April 1996, October 1999, and November 2000.

[113] In an effort, apparently, to make the image argument even more convincing, the PRC Foreign Ministry tried to argue as well that the material costs of the PII were small for the PLA. However, a senior PLA officer noted that the moratorium policy was not so much a function of the PLA giving in on the issue of economic losses as it was China's leaders considering the implications for China's international image (interview with PLA officer, May 2001).

[114] Interview with MOFA official, April 1996.

[115] Sigal cites the chief US PII negotiator to the effect that the Chinese were unresponsive to opprobrium and only agreed to the PII after they were convinced by the United States that technically Chinese landmines could meet the PII criteria for detectability. See Sigal 2006:83–84. The evidence in this paragraph about policy process and interviews with other participants in the negotiations suggest, however, that the US official underestimated the effect of social influence. Moreover, the deputy US negotiator claimed that the Chinese in fact were responsive to the possibility of being viewed as a "holdout" on the question of self-destruction duration (see Sigal 2006:65).

What kind of social opprobrium were Chinese decision makers reacting to?[116] Some Chinese diplomats were privately quite dismissive of the NGOs.[117] Indeed, the initial reaction was that these were mere tools of Western states that were pushing a humanitarian frame for power political purposes.[118] The Chinese delegation in Geneva eventually came to see the NGOs as independent actors motivated by humanitarian concerns, however. These humanitarian arguments were not persuasive ones—Sha was privately particularly dismissive of the NGO frame—but they did help direct unwanted scrutiny toward China's obstructionism in the earlier periods of the negotiations. For instance, the main NGO group monitoring the negotiations, the ICBL issued a special edition of its newsletter specifically criticizing China for marketing blinding laser weapons when a growing number of states in the CCW negotiations were supporting a protocol banning such weapons.[119]

But the most obvious source of social pressure was the direct criticism of China's positions during the negotiations, particularly during the Vienna meetings in late 1995 and the Geneva meetings in January 1996. Chinese statements would often be followed by interventions from other delegations asking China to justify what appeared to be hard-to-justify positions. Chinese diplomats and decision makers back in Beijing decided that image was more important than the economic and limited military costs to signing the PII.

ADDITIONAL EMPIRICAL IMPLICATIONS

As I noted in the discussion of the research design in chapter 1, the CTBT and landmine protocols cases are important cases theoretically. Because

---

[116] The following paragraph draws from an interview with a senior Canadian diplomat, July 2001, and comments by a former Chinese diplomat, July 2001.

[117] See the assessment of Chinese views of the NGOs in the CCW review conference process from a US diplomat and an NGO leader cited in Sigal (2006:68).

[118] In fact, there was some coordination between government delegations and NGOs. The US delegation to the review conference shared talking points and inside information with NGOs specifically for the purpose of more effective lobbying of the Chinese delegation (see Sigal 2006:76).

[119] China eventually agreed to the Protocol IV banning blinding laser weapons. Thus, an additional cost to signing the revised CCW was to the military industry's hope to develop a market for combat lasers. The ICBL pointed out during negotiations that the military industrial company NORINCO was trying to sell the "ZM-87 Portable Laser Disturber," advertised as a means to "injure or dizzy the eyes of an enemy combatant, and especially anybody who is sighting and firing at us with an optical instrument" (advertising flyer from China North Industries Corporation, 1995, reproduced in *CCW News* (September 29, 1995) (extra edition).

image considerations seemed to play such an important role in both instances, it means that we have reason to look for their effect in cases in which the variable controls are less pristine and in which social influence might be one of a number of simultaneous interests at stake.[120] There is plenty of evidence that these two cases were not isolated ones.

Right from the start in the mid-1980s, when Chinese officials and analysts began to argue that China needed to become more active in multilateral arms control institutions, a prominent reason was that this was beneficial to China's general image. At the first major cross-institutional conference on arms control, a number of analysts from different institutions, including the PLA, argued that China had to become more proactive and constructive in order to, among other reasons, improve China's peaceful image externally (Huang and Song 1987:6; Pan 1987:25). One of the concerns behind China's decision to reverse years of opposition and sign on to the Non-proliferation Treaty (NPT) in 1992 was the fear of being isolated as the last remaining member of the five major nuclear powers outside the treaty (France had announced its intention to sign in 1991) (Yu 1988). According to diplomats from a Western state active in the NPT review conference in 1995, China eventually endorsed the consensus decision on unconditional extension of the treaty primarily because of concerns about appearing isolated, even though it could have essentially vetoed the decision.[121]

Status and image concerns can be found in the decision-making process in diplomacy in other issue areas as well. Some of the best examples come from China's international environmental policy. For instance, in an internal circulation resolution passed by the State Council's Environmental Protection Committee concerning China's position on global environmental issues, the first on the list of reasons why China should sign the Montreal Protocols (banning CFCs) was "to establish a positive international image, expressing our country's sincere willingness to contribute to the common interests of humankind" (State Council 1992:11). This was consistent with a summary report from China's observer delegation to the first meeting of the parties to the Montreal Protocols in 1989, sent to the State Council; one of the arguments made in recommending that China join was that by remaining outside and demanding excessive conditions for signature, China could lose out in world public opinion (*shijie*

---

[120] See, for instance, Simmons's key finding that in addition to economic benefits, when states consider a commitment to IMF agreements on monetary conduct "something like 'peer pressure'"—in this case, measured by the number of other states in a region that join—is also at work, a factor that seems distinct from material reputational concerns (see Simmons 2000:350).

[121] Interview with Western diplomat involved in arms control policy, May 1996.

yulun) (State Council 1995a:123). In other internal documents from the early 1990s, when China's rates of participation in environmental institutions began to increase, Chinese decision makers made an explicit connection between China's position as a global major power and its responsibility to participate in the "wave of global environmental protection" and become more proactive (State Council 1995b: 359–60). Qu Geping, at the time head of the State Environmental Protection Agency, argued in internal discussions in the State Council that China needed to develop environmental industries, in part to "catch up" to the "world wave" (*shijie langchao*, that is, surging trend) in environmentalism, and to show the world that in global environmental affairs, China occupied a position commensurate with its status as a great power (Qu 1992:449–50).[122]

In another instance, China reversed its opposition to a blanket ban on African ivory under the CITES when it was apparent that NGO pressure would lead to such a ban. China had originally taken the same position as that of the International Union for the Conservation of Nature and had favored a response that varied depending on how particular states handled the ivory trade. When it came to restrictions on trade in tiger and rhino parts, China again considered image as one of the reasons to go along with a growing NGO-inspired international consensus in favor of restricting these materials. In this case, there was a concrete material incentive to comply with the consensus—a threat of possible sanctions that could negatively affect China's traditional medicine industry. But in internal discussions, the top leader in charge of environmental science, Song Jian, and even the MOFA's International Treaties Department, argued that China had to meet its obligations to the "international community," that it was partially a question of "face."[123]

In many of these environmental cases, the concrete material gains from cooperation were greater than those in the CTBT and landmine cases (e.g., preferential access to technology transfers and development funds, for instance, were invariably also stated reasons in internal documents supporting signing on to international environmental treaties). But the importance of image concerns in the CTBT and landmines protocol suggests that when multiple, "overdetermining" reasons are given in the policy process for supporting other international institutions, we should not automatically discount the effects of social influence.

On international financial questions, image concerns also appeared to have played a role in encouraging participation in international financial institutions. As Pearson notes, "It is clear from numerous policy debates

[122] See also Zhao and Ortolano 2003:715–16; and Economy 1994:168.

[123] Interview with participant in the CITES interagency process, May 1996. "Face" in Chinese—*mianzi*—also connotes social status or standing.

surrounding international economic policy, and especially the question of WTO membership, that for an important segment of the policy elite the desire to 'join the club' is of high priority. It is seen as ridiculous and even humiliating that China—a huge trading nation with extensive ties to the market already—is not a member of *the* global trade organization. In other words, engagement fills the power prestige demands of the post-Mao regime" (Pearson 1999b:226).

Image concerns have also encouraged or locked in behavior on international financial issues that did not necessarily serve China's domestic material interests. Observers generally agree, for instance, that China's decision not to devalue the RMB during the Asian financial crisis in 1997 was influenced by the positive feedback from Asian countries and the United States. This was not the sole reason, nor necessarily the initial one. Chinese leaders were concerned that devaluation might contribute to the further slowing of the regional economy. But in 1997 and 1998, most observers believed that China would not be able to resist the pressure to devalue, and doubted Chinese government statements to the contrary. Even so, Chinese leaders were at the time acutely cognizant of the back-patting rewards they were receiving from leaving the RMB alone, even though it would have made short-run business sense to help the competitiveness of Chinese exports as Southeast Asian exports in particular became substantially cheaper as a result of the crisis. The evidence for these positive social signals comes not just from what other countries in the region stated, but also from how the Chinese interpreted what these other countries stated. By far the largest portion of examples of "responsible major power" behavior that the Chinese leaders attributed to their own diplomacy in the late 1990s had to do with not devaluing the RMB during the financial crisis.

In addition to environmental diplomacy, China's sensitivity to global normative trends has also showed up in explanations for the decision to replace execution by bullet with execution by lethal injection. The connection to China's image is not explicit, though the argument for adopting this form of execution was put in role identity terms: the world was moving from public firing squads to nonpublic "euthanasia," and that this international trend represented the evolution from lesser to more civilized forms of behavior.[124] China, being a civilized state, therefore had to conform to this behavioral shift in executions.

This pattern of sensitivity to image shows up in aggregate data about Chinese diplomacy as well. China's voting behavior in UNGA roll call voting is instructive. If social influence is at work, we should expect to

---

[124] See "Death by Lethal Injection: A Court Fosters Change," *People's Daily*, September 28, 2001, at http://www.china.org.cn/english/2001/Sep/19907.htm.

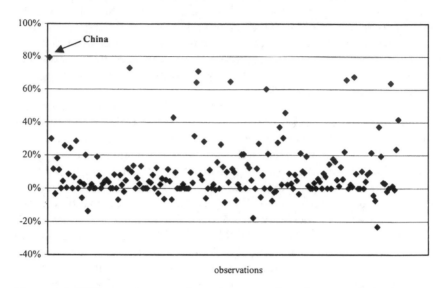

Figure 3.8. Difference between abstention rates when the yes majority is two-thirds of the UNGA and one-half of the UNGA (by country).

see behavior that tries to reduce opprobrium costs when it appears that China might be isolated on a particular issue. In voting, one obvious way of reducing opprobrium costs on a vote when one does not support the resolution is to abstain instead of voting no outright. Thus, one should expect that on resolutions that China does not support, its tendency to abstain should vary directly with the size of the yes majority.

Interestingly enough, the data are consistent with this hypothesis. From 1989 to 2000, in roll call votes that China did not support, if the winning yes majority was about one-half or less of the voting members, China abstained about 20 percent of the time. When the yes majority was two-thirds or larger, China abstained 95 percent of the time. In contrast, for example, the United States abstained 13 percent and 32 percent of the time, respectively. In fact, China was the clear outlier among UNGA members in the magnitude of this shift. Only thirteen other states lay outside two standard deviations above the mean measure for this shift (see fig. 3.8).[125] This pattern cannot be attributed solely to a desire to avoid alie-

---

[125] What explains why these states in particular are outliers is, obviously, an important question. The list includes Cuba, Iran, Libya, Myanmar, Sudan, and Syria, as well as Nigeria, Pakistan, Vietnam, Tanzania, Zimbabwe, Ghana, and Indonesia. It is not the focus of this book. But to hazard a guess, based on social influence theory, a good portion of these states generally share a common feature: they are often seen as outsiders or "rogues" by

nating potential sources of material benefits. One cannot explain the high abstention rate on two-thirds majority votes by reference to the voting pattern, for instance, of the G-7.[126]

In other words, China has tended not to abstain in anticipation of the G-7's support for a resolution. In general, then, it is likely that many of these abstentions were in anticipation of being in the opposing camp per se (as backroom negotiations and unscientific polling of state positions would reveal before a vote which way UNGA opinion was moving), and were an effort to minimize the opprobrium costs from opposing popular resolutions.

CONFOUNDING CASES?

There are two obvious cases in which it would appear that China has ignored opprobrium, and has bucked the massive support for the group's pro-social norms. One is the Ottawa Treaty banning landmines (1997). The other is human rights. The measures on the independent and dependent variables in both these cases appear to undermine the argument about social influence presented in this chapter. In the Ottawa Treaty case, an overwhelming majority of states in the UN system moved quite rapidly to accede to the treaty. China has not yet signed. Likewise on human rights, it appears as though a great deal of international opprobrium has had little effect in improving human rights conditions inside China. Although I am not a believer in "vulgar falsificationism," it nonetheless ought to be worrying for my argument that these important cases exist. A closer look, however, suggests that the social influence argument remains more or less intact.

The Ottawa Treaty to ban landmines was signed in December 1997 after a remarkably swift period of very public diplomacy—led by Canada, some European states, and a well-organized international NGO campaign—triggered a bandwagoning process. In the space of a few months,

---

some key players in the international system. It makes diplomatic sense for the leaders of these states to try to minimize material and/or ideational costs from isolation to the extent possible. Why Chinese leaders (and why in the 1990s) appeared to be more sensitive than many others to social influence is also an important question. There is evidence of cross-cultural variation within and between national populations in the degree of sensitivity to status, image, dignity, and honor (Nisbett and Cohen 1996; Finkel, Harré, Rodriguez Lopez 2001). But to test a social influence theory–based answer would require a full-blown comparative study of the content of identities held by state leaders that exhibit this sensitivity (e.g., China) and those that do not (e.g., the United States and Britain).

[126] The data show that there is essentially no difference in the likelihood that the G-7 is in the yes majority when China abstains, when the yes majority is one-half, and when it is over two-thirds.

an overwhelming majority of states moved to support the ban, even after the UN had just concluded the PII. The Ottawa Treaty process was premised on the "mobilization of shame."[127] Yet China appeared immune to it. Why?

Like the CTBT, the main domestic interests affected by the Ottawa Treaty—the PLA's border defense forces and the military engineering forces—were opposed to the Ottawa Treaty from the start.[128] Their arguments were straightforward and unsurprising.[129] Because the engineering forces were largely responsible for developing and manufacturing mines, they argued that the economic costs of acceding to the Ottawa Treaty were very high in two respects. First, compliance would require removing landmines along China's 20,000+ kilometers of land borders. And second, China would be banned from earning any money at all from mine exports (which were allowed under the Protocol II as long as the exports met the Protocol's technical criteria for deactivation and discovery). The military argument, developed mainly by the border defense forces, was also twofold. First, because China had a very long land border and had territorial disputes with at least some of its neighbors, landmines were a legitimate tool of military defense. Second, as long as other states along China's border were not abandoning mines, it made no sense for China to do so either (as of this writing, no country along China's land borders has signed the Ottawa Treaty). The PLA wanted to retain the flexibility of using mines for military purposes, even though it was de-mining borders with countries such as Vietnam. The legal argument was that the treaty allowed non-signatories to use APL. Thus, the situation could arise where, if China signed on to the treaty, aggressors could use APL on Chinese territory while China was prohibited from using them on its own territory (Chen and Zhang 1997).

This opposition was communicated forcefully to the Ministry of Foreign Affairs. The MOFA evidently did not object too strenuously to the PLA on arms control or image grounds, however. In the interagency pro-

[127] According to Canadian External Affairs minister, Lloyd Axworthy. Cited in Tomlin 1999:201.

[128] The key interlocutors in the interagency process were the MOFA's Arms Control and Disarmament Department; the General Staff Department's Engineering Corp Department (*gongcheng bing bu*) and its Landmine Institute; the GSD's Operations Department (*zuozhan bu*) and its Border Defense Office (*bianfang ju*); and the Academy of Military Sciences, which provided legal and military strategic arguments against the treaty. The PLA's positions were coordinated by the General Staff Department's arms control bureau and approved by the Central Military Commission. On the Engineering Corp and its role in the production of landmines, see the *People's Daily*, December 18, 2000, http://202.84.17.73/mil/htm/20001218/271874.htm.

[129] This discussion draws from interviews with Canadian diplomats, a senior Chinese diplomat, and a senior PLA officer, 1996–2001.

cess the MOFA did point out that non-signatories such as the United States and Russia were wobbly in their opposition, that they might end up joining, leaving China isolated in a small group of more minor states, and that China might have to reconsider its opposition if this occurred. But apparently it never explicitly argued that China ought to join the treaty. Indeed, the MOFA had its own complaints with the Ottawa Treaty, specifically with the Ottawa "process." The treaty was negotiated wholly outside of the traditional UN arms control negotiating process (mainly in the Conference on Disarmament). It was pushed by like-minded states, and eschewed a consensus decision-making process; the process was explicitly designed to prevent opponents such as China from slowing down negotiations. Finally, negotiations involved close interaction between state governments and the anti-mine NGO movement; in the MOFA's view, this polluted a process that should have been wholly in the hands of sovereign state governments.[130]

In its diplomacy the MOFA was torn between strong opposition to the treaty from the Chinese military and by the high-profile international pressure to sign. The MOFA told the Canadians that the Protocol II had been difficult enough to get past the Chinese military, and thus it was a waste of time to try to get the PLA to sign on to the Ottawa Treaty. In part for this reason, according to Canadian diplomats, Sha Zukang was livid that the Ottawa Convention put China in the awkward position of opposing such a popular treaty. Perhaps to minimize any Chinese efforts to make mischief in opposition to the treaty, Canada and China struck a tacit deal—Canada would not put public pressure on China to join Ottawa, while China would not put pressure on Asian states to oppose the treaty.

Thus, China's diplomacy predominantly reflected the preferences of the Chinese military and secondarily the concerns about the nature of the process expressed by the MOFA. Does this dramatically undermine a social influence argument? Not entirely. The fact remains that on the Ottawa Treaty, China and Canada came to a tacit agreement precisely to minimize the opprobrium that could have been targeted on China. Indeed, in stark contrast to the criticisms of China's bargaining on the CTBT and its nuclear testing, there was no public criticism from other states of China's decision not to sign the Ottawa Treaty. For example, when states

---

[130] On these features of the Ottawa process, see Cameron, Lawson, and Tomlin 1999:5, 10. One of the key documents (the 1996 Ottawa Declaration) was not formally negotiated among state delegates to the Ottawa meeting. Perhaps because most participants were "like-minded," they allowed a Chairman's Agenda for Action to be drafted by Canadian diplomats and the ICBL after polling delegates about what kinds of follow-up activities they would like to see. See Tomlin 1999:203; Lawson et al. 1999, and Williams and Goose 1999.

were given the opportunity to comment on their vote on the 1997 resolution in the UN First Committee inviting states to join the Ottawa Treaty, none of the supporters of the resolution condemned any other state, let alone China.[131]

Moreover, China took steps that were obviously taken to minimize its isolation, steps that it otherwise would not have taken. First, it decided to send an observer delegation to the Ottawa meeting in 1997, apparently at the insistence of Sha Zukang, so as to minimize criticisms of China's non-signature.[132] It continued to participate as an observer state in the intersessional work on the implementation of the treaty. Indeed, it appears to have upheld its end of the tacit bargain with Canada. According to Canadian diplomats involved in Ottawa Treaty diplomacy, China chose not to "cause trouble." Specifically, it has not tried to organize any counter-coalitions. Its interventions have been constructive, and have not been designed to slow the work of the parties to the treaty.[133]

Second, along with the United States, the MOFA made a very high-profile offer to contribute money to de-mining activities. Thus, even if the "mobilization of shame" was insufficient to get China to endorse a complete ban, it was sufficient to increase China's public commitment to de-mining activities. Of course, much of this activity has gone on along China's borders (e.g., with Vietnam). This has served as a diplomatic signal of improved relations with Vietnam, and it reduces the dangers for cross-border economic activity. But de-mining commitments elsewhere clearly do not reflect any obvious short-term material interest. These appear to reflect a desire to "do something" to minimize any perceived image damage from remaining outside the Ottawa Treaty.

Finally, China abstained from rather than opposing resolutions in the UN First Committee that called for non-signatories to accede to the Ottawa Convention when it was obvious that these resolutions had overwhelming support.[134]

Moreover, the minimization of opprobrium costs was assisted by the fact that, in Chinese eyes, the Ottawa process was illegitimate. It was clear that from the PRC perspective, the legitimacy of the Ottawa Treaty process was undermined (hence less "persuasive" or socially pressuring)

[131] See resolution as A/C.1/52/L.1 (October 11, 1997). For state comments see A/C.1/52/PV.20 (November 12, 1997), pp. 10–15. China did not take the opportunity to explain its abstention vote on the resolution.

[132] Interview with senior MOFA official, November 2000.

[133] Interviews with Canadian diplomats involved in landmine diplomacy, July 2001.

[134] A/C.1/52/L.1 (October 11, 1997) passed 127-0-19; A/RES/53/77N (December 4, 1998) passed 147-0-21; A/RES/54/54B (December 1, 1999) passed 139-1-20; and A/RES/55/33V (November 20, 2000) passed 143-0-22. In each case China abstained, as did the other major opponents of the Ottawa Treaty, including the United States, Russia, and Korea.

precisely because it was outside of the CD process. This probably helped counteract the influence effects of the large numbers of signatories to the Ottawa Treaty.

Indeed, the irony perhaps was that precisely because the Ottawa process was an unusually direct effort to "mobilize shaming" through the use of NGO–small state partnerships outside of the UN system that, in the Chinese case, this may have had the perverse effect of reducing some of the opprobrium effects.

The Chinese response to the Ottawa Treaty, then, underscores three points about the impact of backpatting and opprobrium on China's cooperation. First, cold, hard military interests determined the main thrust of China's diplomacy, namely non-signature of the treaty. In this sense, the fact of China's relative isolation was not sufficient to fundamentally determine its bottom line, unlike the CTBT. However, it is also clear that opprobrium costs were constrained by the tacit Canadian-Chinese deal on public diplomacy, by the low level of opprobrium generated by supporters of the treaty, by the generally low level of legitimacy the Chinese accorded to the Ottawa process, and by the fact that high-profile opposition to the treaty persisted (e.g., the United States, Russia, India, the ROK, among others). Finally, it is also clear that the Ottawa process generated sufficient opprobrium costs to get China to participate relatively constructively as an observer in the implementation work of the treaty, and to engage in high-profile de-mining actions. The existence of these opprobrium costs means that it is highly likely that should a major opponent of the treaty such as Russia or the United States defect from this coalition of outliers, China will probably have to reconsider its non-signature.[135]

As for the case of human rights and China's response to international opprobrium, this would appear at first glance to be a pretty convincing case against a social influence argument. Shaming, stigmatizing, and embarrassing human rights violators are explicit goals of much of the governmental and non-governmental diplomacy on human rights (Wachman 2001:260–61). Yet, as both Kent (1999) and Wachman (2001) point out, in the 1980–2000 period, shaming appears to have had little effect on China's human rights performance.

The progress that has been made in terms of formal commitments to major human rights regimes and the occasional releases of dissidents ap-

---

[135] Canadian diplomats believe that Chinese decision makers are conscious that the "ground is shifting" on the Ottawa Treaty and that concerns about international image will accentuate the pressures from the growing number of pro-ban states (interviews July 2001). As one Chinese military officer put it somewhat sardonically, China has already done some "thought preparation" (*sixiang zhunbei*) for the possibility of a US or Russian defection, meaning that it has probably thought out a rough diplomatic process for accession.

pears to have been largely motivated by short-term reputation concerns (as opposed to image as an end), or has been a response to direct bilateral diplomatic pressure from the United States. Thus, China's human rights performance from 1980 to 2000 would appear to undermine the social influence argument. As Wachman puts it, China appeared stuck at stage two, or at best stage three, in Risse and Sikkink's ladder of social conformity and the internalization of norms.[136]

Why, then, were opprobrium costs in this instance (or backpatting benefits from joining certain human rights regimes) apparently insufficient to elicit change in China's behavior? This is a complex question. One response would be that there actually was change in Chinese behavior. By 2000 there was far greater freedom in terms of cultural and lifestyle choices, economic activity, access to information, debate on certain public policies (corruption, environment, local official responsiveness, and on occasion even foreign affairs) than at any time since the Communist Party took power in 1949. Moreover, although some of the progress could be attributed to reputational considerations (the desire to maintain good economic relations with the United States, for instance), some of the state's actions were designed to engage, if only to refute, some of the international normative discourse on human rights.[137]

Though there was some progress, clearly the PRC state remained an arbitrary one, ruling often by fiat and force; the public sphere was limited and constrained. So, again, why the ineffectiveness of social influence?

The question, I think, misses the point. It is not so much the ineffectiveness of social influence as much as it is the *absence* of substantial social pressure that explains China's leaders' behavior. The question assumes that on human rights issues, the Chinese leadership was unresponsive to a high level of shaming costs. It is this assumption that is problematic. Two related arguments here underscore why a relatively low level of opprobrium was generated on human rights questions.

First, the international human rights regime comprises more than individual political and civil liberties. The 1993 Vienna Declaration and Pro-

---

[136] At stage two the criticized state engages in a defensive counterattack against norms entrepreneurs, denying that human rights conditions are all that bad. Stage three entails tactical concessions on human rights issues for immediate reputational or material payoffs. See Risse and Sikkink 1999. Kent might put China more firmly at stage three—tactical concessions while working within certain human rights institutions to defend China's position by employing the rules and discursive practices of these institutions. She does appear, however, to be a bit ambivalent as to whether these concessions are responses to immediate reputational or material gains or whether they are designed to garner international "praise" for its own sake (see Kent 1999:240).

[137] For example, China's white papers on human rights and its formal signature on many UN-based human rights regimes.

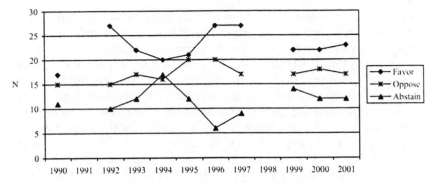

Figure 3.9. Voting in the United Nations Commission on Human Rights on no-action motions on resolutions critical of the PRC. Sources: Kent (1999:60–79); various UN Commission on Human Rights reports, E/1993/23; E/1994/24; E/ 1995/23; E/1996/23; E/1997/23; E/1999/23; E/2000/23; E/CN.4/2001/L.10/ Add.9.

gramme for Action is the most comprehensive international statement on human rights.[138] The declaration reflected a consensus behind the equal status for individual political and civil rights and more collectively held economic and social rights (or right to development).[139] Technically, then, to the extent that regimes are seen to rest on consensus diplomatic documents issued under UN auspices, the international human rights regime recognizes the equal status of both sets of rights. When measuring China's compliance with international human rights, one therefore has to measure it against both sets of rights and their standards. The Chinese leadership believed that its performance on the economic and social rights side was quite good, given the rapid pace of economic development over the last couple of decades.[140] It was often rewarded internationally by many other states when they acknowledged this development.

Second, since Vienna represented a compromise between individual and collective concepts of human rights, it should not be surprising that the "international community" simply was not unified on whether individual political rights should be the sole criteria for judging a state normatively. That is, on human rights issues the opprobrium-generating

[138] On the Vienna conference, see the UNHCR web page on the World Conference on Human Rights, http://www.unhchr.ch/html/menu5/wchr.htm. For the Vienna Declaration and Programme of Action, see A/CONF.157/2312 (July 1993).

[139] See A/CONF.157/23 (July 12, 1993).

[140] It could point to the fact, for example, that the UNDP's annual human development index for China—a net of socioeconomic, educational, and consumption indicators—rose about 28 percent from 1980 to 1999. See UNDP (2001:145).

audience has not necessarily been all that large. Although democracies constitute an increasingly large portion of the state system[141] in the primary forum used to generate shaming costs—the United Nations Commission on Human Rights[142]—in the 1990s China was generally able to assemble a coalition of states to prevent critical resolutions from even being considered for a vote (see figure 3.9).[143] The fact that China worked so hard diplomatically to put together such a coalition to block what would be, after all, a toothless resolution reinforces the social influence argument. The opprobrium costs of losing the symbolic fight in the UNCHR appear to be something to avoid through the expenditure of a lot of diplomatic capital. The opponents of action to criticize China have included influential developing states such as India, a democracy, and Russia, a democratizing state. Abstainers have included Asian democracies such as South Korea.[144]

Thus, unlike the CTBT or the CCCW or being outvoted in the UNGA, on the human rights issue China has not really been confronted by a relatively united and vocal critical inter-state audience. While developing states have been at the core of the community that refuses to signal opprobrium, even some developed states declined to use the UN human rights soapbox to single out China.[145] The most vocal—almost invariably the United States, or American-based human rights NGOs—were dismissed as being motivated by "ulterior" motives—illegitimate power political motives as opposed to normative ones.[146] American criticisms alone,

[141] According to Polity IV data, in 1999 on a democratic policy scale of −10 (autocratic) to 10 (democratic), 64 percent of states had a democratic polity score of 0 or greater and 55 percent had a polity score of 5 or greater.

[142] This is Wachman's characterization (2001:261). See also Kent's description of the UNCHR's role (1999:49–56).

[143] The best description of the diplomacy surrounding the UNCHR resolutions is in Kent (1999, chap. 2). Even Kent admits that some of the tactical concessions on human rights (e.g., signing the International Covenant on Economic, Social, and Cultural Rights and the International Covenant on Civil and Political Rights, the freeing of some high-profile dissidents, the invitation of the UN High Commissioner for Human Rights to China) were designed to undermine support for a UNCHR resolution (Kent 1999:238).

[144] Note that in 1991 and 1998 there were no resolutions critical of the PRC.

[145] Prior to the 1993 Vienna conference, for instance, China was one of the leaders at a conference of Asian developing states that drafted a common position to take into the Vienna meetings. The statement, the Bangkok Declaration, did not reflect all of China's wishes, but it generally endorsed the notion that the collective right to development was as important as individual political and civil liberties. Forty Asian and Pacific countries signed the Bangkok Declaration. On Chinese coalition building with developing states in the face of the UNCHR resolutions, see Kent 1999:64–65. The Bangkok Declaration can be found at http://law.hku.hk/lawgovtsociety/Bangkok%20Declaration.htm.

[146] As Copper and Lee note, even after the crackdown on the democracy movement in 1989, "[C]ontrary to the popular view, China was still not as much under the microscope as many other countries in the world. . . . The United States, and to a lesser extent Western

whether governmental or non-governmental, were almost guaranteed not to generate sufficient opprobrium costs, though they were often signals that concrete material interests were possibly at stake with continued non-compliance with US-defined norms.[147] In other words, for the social influence hypothesis, the measure on the independent variable in the human rights case was low or close to zero, in contrast to the CTBT, PII, and some international environmental cases.

Social influence theory, then, would expect that, to the extent that China's identity as a responsible major power increasingly incorporates elements of compliance with individual political and civil liberties, China's diplomacy will become more sensitive to opprobrium diplomacy from developed and developing states. Already there are hints that, at times, this kind of identity language has crept into the way in which some Chinese discuss the evolution of international human rights norms. Like the "responsible major power" discourse, this identity language paints compliance in terms of the inexorableness of a world trend, where conformity is necessary so as not to be left behind the movement of the "community." As an article in the journal *China Legal Studies* put it just prior to the Vienna conference, "respect for human rights is a demand of *modern times*."[148]

Now, my argument here is not that all the explanatory work in the CTBT and landmines case is being done by social influence. Concerning the CTBT, for instance, one could ask a counterfactual question: had China's 1996 tests been failures, had China's preferences reflected only those of the testing community, or had it wanted to be able to cheat on verification, then it is possible that China would not have signed, regardless of the opprobrium costs or forgone backpatting benefits. So there may have been some threshold of confidence in China's nuclear tests that essentially marginalized the effects of social influence.

European countries, remained China's most vocal critics" (Copper and Lee 1997:157). This is precisely the point, which makes the title of their book somewhat misleading. See also Wachman 2001:268.

[147] In this regard, although I agree with her argument that China's vision of responsible major powerhood is challenged by the emerging discourse on domestic governance as a criteria for responsibility, I believe Rosemary Foot and some analysts of the global human rights movement exaggerate the degree to which there is a clear international social consensus on human rights (Foot 2001). It is not obvious that most major and minor players in the system have endorsed what the Chinese deride as "human rights are superordinate to state sovereignty" (*renquan gao yu zhuquan*). The trend lines may be there, but in crucial fora such as the UNCHR, the votes are not.

[148] Li Ming, "Lianheguo xianzhang zhong de renquan bu ganshe neizheng wenti" [Human rights in the UN charter and the question of noninterference in internal affairs], *Zhongguo faxue*, May 9, 1993, cited in Kent 1999:153. Emphasis mine.

But a different counterfactual is perhaps more insightful: had there been no social influence effects, then, given that this treaty was militarily a bad one for China, China could have avoided the negotiations in the first place, or it could have refused to sign (as India did), or it could have avoided a unilateral moratorium, all with no material costs. This counterfactual underscores the important role that social influence played in *mediating* the military costs of the treaty. China's self-categorization as a responsible major power, its efforts to fit in with what Chinese leaders perceived to be world historical trends in arms control, and to participate in highly legitimate institutions, all meant that status interests became increasingly linked to security interests. This is an interest-based story about optimization, and I do not claim it is anything but. However, interests are not always realpolitik ones, they are not always complementary, and realpolitik interests do not always trump every other kind of interest. Often an actor's own interests are in competition with each other—this is why policy making involves trade-offs. For Chinese leaders, China's emergent identity as "responsible major power" competing in some sense with a traditional Westphalian, realpolitik identity,[149] presented them with a new indifference curve that specified new trade-offs between security and image.[150]

The "responsible major power" discourse emerged in the 1990s, and for a while its precise content was murky. The first mention of the phrase was by Foreign Minister Qian Qichen in a speech to a visiting US delegation in September 1992. Still, for a few years after that the term did not appear in public discourse until 1996, then with much more frequency beginning in 1998 (see figs. 3.10 and 3.11). Apparently at Jiang Zemin's request, there was some research into precisely what roles a responsible major power should play in international relations.[151] Initially, when Qian used the term, it referred simply to China's traditional Five Principles of Peaceful Coexistence and the preservation of friendly bilateral relations.[152] However, over time it began to embody notions of appropriate

[149] For a similar characterization of the tension in Chinese leaders' "worldview," see Gill 2001:29.

[150] China's sensitivity to its international image did not begin with its involvement in status quo international institutions. Arguably, in the days of the Sino-Soviet alliance and later during the period of an independent revolutionary foreign policy of the 1960s, image was also important. The audiences, however, were different, so the nature of the utility or disutility of image was different. During the Maoist period, a certain positive social utility, for instance, came from appearing to be hostile to status quo institutions, and to being a leading radical voice for dramatic reform of the UN system, or of the world trade system, and so on.

[151] Interview with senior specialist in international relations at a government think tank, October 17, 1999.

[152] *People's Daily*, September 24, 1992.

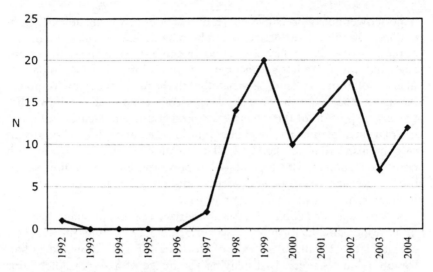

Figure 3.10. Frequency of articles using the term "responsible major power" in the *People's Daily*, 1992–2004. Source: *People's Daily*, on-line full-text version.

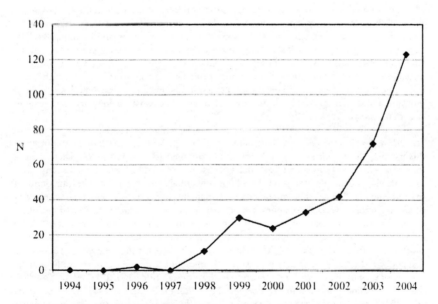

Figure 3.11. Frequency of the term "responsible major power" in academic articles on international relations and foreign policy. Source: China Academic Journals database, China National Knowledge Infrastructure.

major power behavior that would lead to greater involvement in multilateral institutions, a more active role in helping design the rules and norms of these institutions, but a basic acknowledgment that many of the extant rules and norms are not antithetical to China's interests.[153] A simple frequency count of the themes associated with the use of the term "responsible major power" in the *People's Daily* from 1998 to 2001 shows that the largest portion of these themes stressed constructive participation in international institutions, including upholding extant rules and norms inside the institution (see fig. 3.12). The smallest portion had to do with efforts to respond to US "hegemony" or power politics behavior. In short, the "responsible major power" identity discourse has had a distinctively multilateralist and status quo content to it.[154]

An article in the *People's Daily* summarized the predominant meaning of a "responsible major power" when it noted, "Crossing into the 21st century, facing the turbulent wave of world multipolarization and globalization, China is precisely displaying the image of a responsible major power to progressively meld with the world." The concrete manifestations of this responsible major power behavior, the author went on, were

---

[153] For one of the earliest explications of the concept, see Xia 2001:17–25. For more recent discussions that *explicitly* connect this identity with maintaining international norms and institutions, see Meng 2002:4; Qin 2003; Xiao 2003; and Tang and Zhang 2004. The term is now officially part of the language used in the Chinese education system to describe China's foreign policy (Ministry of Education 2004:15). Interestingly, the actual term may have been appropriated from the West. In many of its earliest uses prior to the Asian financial crisis, the phrase was attributed to foreigners: in one instance to an American effort to pull China into international institutions where it would be constrained to act as a "responsible major power" (Yang 1996: 132).

[154] The analysis is based on a keyword search of the term "responsible major power" (*fu zeren de da guo*) in the *People's Daily* net web site (http://www.peopledaily.com.cn/). As of this writing, the *People's Daily* web site does not store articles past 1998. There were a total of seventy-six separate codable articles. These were coded for instances of descriptions, explications, or examples of responsible major power behavior in the sentences surrounding the reference to "responsible major power" or in the paragraph in which the term was situated. Almost invariably the phrase was used as an identity marker to describe China's essential attribute as a state in the international system. A typical phrase would be, "Being a responsible major power, China does X, participates as X, upholds X" (e.g., *Zhongguo zuowei yi ge fu zeren de da guo*). There were ninety-five such valid references. These were first coded inductively into thirty-six distinct themes, and from there reduced to five major clusters of themes. By far the largest portion of these descriptions, mostly appearing in 1998, referred to China's decision not to devalue the renminbi during the 1997 Asian financial crisis (31 percent of the coded references). Typically, reports noted that Asian countries praised China for its responsible behavior in not devaluing even when devaluation could have helped dramatically increase the competitiveness of Chinese exports. If one excludes this very specific and sui generis example of "responsible major power" behavior, as I do in figure 3.10, then the largest portion of references are to participation in and respecting the rules and norms of international institutions.

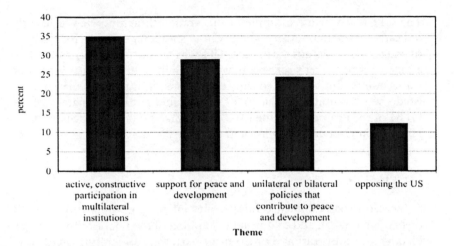

Figure 3.12. Behaviors associated with a "responsible major power" identity. Source: *People's Daily*, 1998–2001.

in places such as the United Nations, APEC, the Asia-Europe Meetings (ASEM), and the Shanghai Cooperative Organization, among other "myriad stages."[155] Note that the article itself implied that the concept of a "responsible major power" is (1) a new and recent feature of Chinese foreign policy, (2) a concept intimately related to an image of appropriate behavior, and (3) a concept represented by participation in and basic conformity with multilateral institutions.

Without this particular emergent identity, the particular trade-off between security and image in multilateral institutions would not exist.[156]

[155] See "The Party Leads China Toward the World," (*Dang lingdao Zhongguo zouxiang shijie*) *People's Daily*, June 30, 2001 (online: http://www.peopledaily.com.cn/GB/guandian/26/20010630/500585.html). See also Foreign Minister Tang Jiaxuan's comments on what constitutes responsible major power behavior in Li and Liu 2000. The MOFA spokesperson used the term to describe China's attitude toward the WTO—maintaining China's obligations once inside would be a hallmark of China's behavior as a responsible major power. Beijing Zhongguo Xinwen She, Foreign Broadcast Information Service, Daily Report—China, FBIS-CHI-2000–0525 (May 25, 2000). More recently, two of China's "new thinkers" have argued that "responsible major power" identity also requires "self-restraint and acceptance of limits" (Tang and Zhang 2004:5).

[156] Explaining the evolution of this particular identity at this particular time in history is, obviously, an important question (Thomas 2001:19). I wish I had a definitive answer rooted in a deductively satisfying model of the historical evolution of great power identities. I do not. The content of this identity is not fixed and has evolved over the 1990s, influenced in part by positive and negative feedback from a range of actors in the "international system" who have more or less converged on an intersubjective agreement that "good" great power behavior means activism in institutions (Chayes and Chayes 1996). Where this particular intersubjective agreement has come from is another puzzle.

The CTBT is a prime example of this trade-off, as interviewees clearly indicated in their comments about China's military sacrifice for the sake of image. This does not mean the CTBT was an all-or-nothing trade-off—a major hit to China's relative power capabilities in exchange for major status points. But had this socially constructed indifference curve not existed, then it is quite possible that China would not be a signatory of the CTBT or the Protocol II of the CCCW, and that it would not be participating at all in Ottawa Treaty–related activities.[157]

CONCLUSION

A focus on social influence raises some interesting implications for IR theory. First, it can add to our understanding of the relationship between identity and cooperation. For the most part, the IR literature on identity has been fairly vague about the theories of action that link identity to behavior. But a careful parsing of the scholarship suggests at least four different arguments about how having an identity can lead to cooperation. The first draws from solidaritist notions of identity. Here the *content* of identity is not as important as the fact that this content is *shared*. Identification generates cooperation because individuals believe they have a linked fate based on affect, particularly if this affect, in turn, is based on the language of kinship (e.g., nationalism).[158]

A second argument draws from social identity theory. In-group cooperation comes from the individual's depersonalization of self, and the taking on of a collective personality. Individuals coalesce around a prototypical member to maximize the valuation of the group (Turner 1987).

A third type of argument is that identity is a source of interest. This claim is associated with a soft rationalist version of role identity theory (Wendt 1994; Kowert and Legro 1996:462; Jepperson, Wendt, and Katzenstein 1996:60–61). Identity provides definitions of material interests that are associated with particular social categories and roles. Actors, however, rationally act to optimize these interests, and their behavior can be analyzed using standard expected utility models.

A fourth argument comes from a more "hard-core" role identity theory where identity provides notions of obligatory or appropriate action—be-

---

[157] In this sense, in contrast to Economy (2001:235), I would include image as one of the core values in Chinese diplomacy rather than a secondary one. That it can be discounted under certain security conditions does not mean it is therefore somehow a consistently less important preference.

[158] On the power of the discourse of kinship in the construction of solidarity, see Horowitz (2000).

havior that is enacted because it is seen as a natural reflection of role. This approach emphasizes that role scripts are followed for reasons of appropriateness, regardless of what might optimize material interests (Knoke 1994:7).

These four sets of arguments all have their value, but they may miss a critical, though perhaps less direct, role that identity, or social category, plays in eliciting cooperation, namely, the link between self-categorization and social rewards/punishments. Given assumptions about status as a motivation for action, identification with a group/role/category creates sensitivity to particular kinds of status markers. The accumulation of these markers becomes a motivation for cooperative behavior. As I noted at the start of this chapter, social influence, therefore, is a function of prior identification *plus* the desire to optimize the social rewards and minimize the social punishments bestowed by the group. A particular identity is a necessary but not sufficient condition—it establishes who the reference group will be, the kind of status markers to be accumulated, and the kinds of behavior that elicit these markers. But action is not purely "appropriate" in a normative sense, nor is it purely optimizing in a materialist instrumental sense. This distinguishes status concerns from "obligation" and from "material interest" as a source of cooperative behavior. It blends the economistic language of optimizing with the sociological language of group processes/social interactions, and thus helps break down the unfortunate dichotomization of (small *r*) "rationalist" versus "sociological" or "constructivist" approaches.[159] Social influence occurs when an actor tries to maximize the accumulation of status markers in the context of a relatively fixed and unquestioned self-categorization.

A second broad theoretical implication of social influence is for collective action. Social influence effects may provide insights into how groups resolve the free-riding problem that hinders resolving collective action problems. That is, traditionally scholars have argued that a critical solution to free riding is to offer material side payments (and sanctions) to make collective action pay for the individual. The conundrum has been, however, that offering side payments is itself a collective action problem. Who will take up the burden of offering side payments, given the resources required to do so? Hegemons and activists are usually part of the answer to this puzzle (though why activists should exist in the first place is hard for collective action theorists to specify a priori). Social rewards

---

[159] Small *r* rationalism refers to the assumption that agents are optimizers or maximizers in the expected utility sense. Big *r* rationalism refers to the ontological and epistemological assumptions of positivism and modernity (that there is an observable and knowable external world independent of the normative preferences of the observer).

and punishments, however, are a particularly interesting kind of incentive to overcome collective inaction. They are relatively cheap to create, but are often infused with a great deal of value. This means that new status markers can be manufactured and distributed without necessarily diminishing their value. In principle, any member of a group therefore can provide social side payments at relatively low cost, indeed at zero cost if the member can also receive these kinds of side payments for providing them to others. This is, after all, what backpatting entails—a mutual, virtuous circle of bestowing and receiving social rewards. Cheap, but social, talk, then, can indeed be cheap to produce but nonetheless still be considered credible precisely because of its social value.[160] Thus, because status markers are so highly valued, it does not take much of a "costly commitment" by providers of these markers to establish the credibility of promises to bestow or threats to retract these markers. All this suggests, then, that one reason why collective action problems are often less frequent and debilitating than theorists expect (Green and Shapiro 1994:72–97) may have to do with the fact that actors are also motivated by the desire to maximize social rewards and that these are relatively easy for groups to produce and distribute.

Following from this argument about collective action, social influence arguments also challenge the conventional wisdom about the optimal size of institutions and groups.

From an institutionalist perspective, ceteris paribus more actors makes cooperation more difficult (collective action problem, problems of monitoring and punishing defection, etc.). Transaction costs increase with more actors. Decentralized institutions are therefore handicapped in dealing with "problems of transaction costs and opportunism" (Abbott and Snidal 1998:15). From a socialization perspective, however, more may be better. Status backpatting and opprobrium effects are likely to be stronger when the "audience" or reference group is larger.

One problem needs to be addressed before I go on—that is, the problem of variation across states. I think the evidence that individual actors are sensitive to social pressure is fairly robust. The difficulty is in explaining variation in this sensitivity across individuals. Some are more sensitive than others. Put differently, k in figures 3.3 and 3.4 is likely to vary across actors, as the UNGA abstention data indicated. As a first cut in modeling social influence, one could start by assuming an equal distribution in sen-

---

[160] This is not dissimilar to Johnson's argument that cheap talk, in the context of persuasion whereby interests and identities converge inside a social relationship, establishes focal points that are necessary to reduce the strategic indeterminacy of bargaining games. See Johnson 1993.

sitivity across actors such that this k is the same for all actors. This would mean, however, a uniform conformity with social norms for each individual identifying with a particular social group, and differences in pro-social behavior across actors would then only be in the values of the group with which it identifies.

This first cut, however, is confounded in practice by the fact that there is variation within groups in the degree of social conformity from individual members, and by the fact that individuals have multiple identities. It seems clear, without having done the requisite comparative work, that there are situations of diplomatic isolation that the current Chinese leadership would avoid that, say, the US leadership would not (e.g., being massively outvoted in the UNGA over a diplomatic relationship with a client state). More obviously, there are situations of relative diplomatic isolation that China's leaders of the past tolerated, indeed touted, but that present leaders would not. Can these variations be deduced a priori? So far we have not been especially successful. Large a priori typologies of social categorization in IR (e.g., major power, minor power, among others) are too blunt and imprecise, particularly because there is variation in how actors understand the appropriate norms and interests associated with these categories. How a self-categorized major power ought to act depends on what the content of major powerhood is and on the distance between desired status as a major power and the status ascribed by others. This content is contested across and within states, though one should be able to isolate and track distributions over time and space in intersubjective views about the content of major powerhood. In principle, however, if there were two actors, both of which adopted the same self-categorizations as a major power of a particular type but that differed in terms of the distance between desired and ascribed status (e.g., one has achieved the status associated with the particular identity, the other has not), then the status-dissatisfied actor will, presumably, be more sensitive to status and image effects from social influence.

There is a tension between Westphalian visions of major powerhood and post–cold war visions within Chinese foreign policy, or between Westphalian visions in US and Chinese self-conceptions, say, and German self-conceptions of major powerhood. This is, of course, Chayes and Chayes's point—the content of identity categories is historically contingent and unevenly distributed spatially and temporally. This has to do with characteristics of the units/actors, in particular the relationship between the historically internalized content of self-categories and the global diffusion of new content (the former present different levels of resistance to the latter). Deducing just how much resistance particular self-categorizations and accompanying content generate may be hard to specify a priori. Even in

Paul Kowert's insightful effort to develop a typology of social categories deduced from dichotomous capability and threat variables (creating four types of self-categorizations and four types of "other" categorizations), it is not obvious what kinds of behavioral expectations flow logically from each category (Kowert 1997). All of this suggests, then, that the macro historical evolution in normative conceptions of major power identity ought to be high on the list of topics for IR theory.

CHAPTER 4

Persuasion

PERSUASION has to do with cognition and the active assessment of the content of a particular message. As a microprocess of socialization, it involves changing minds, opinions, and attitudes about causality and affect (identity) in the absence of overtly material or mental coercion. Or, in Perloff's words, persuasion is an "activity or process in which a communicator attempts to induce a change in the belief, attitude, or behavior of another person or group of persons through the transmission of a message in a context in which the persuadee has some degree of free choice" (Perloff 1993:14).[1] It can lead to common knowledge, or "epistemic conventions" (that may or may not be cooperative), or it can lead to a homogenization of interests. That is, actors can be persuaded that they are indeed in competition with each other, or that they share many cooperative interests. The point is, however, that the gap or distance between actors' basic causal understandings closes as a result of successful persuasion.

Persuasion is a prevalent tool of social influence. Social psychologists have shown, for instance, that in interpersonal relationships people tend to rank changing others' opinions very high in a list of influence strategies, regardless whether the other is considered a friend or an enemy (Rule and Bisanz 1987:192). Some political scientists have called persuasion the "core" of politics, the "central aim of political interaction" (Mutz, Sniderman, and Brody 1996:1). In Gibson's view, politics is all about persuasion: "Real politics involves arguments; it involves people drawing a conclusion, being exposed to countervailing ideas, changing views, drawing new conclusions" (Gibson 1998:821). Communications theorists have argued that all social interaction involves communications that alter people's "perceptions, attitudes, beliefs and motivations" (Berger 1995:1). How persuasion works, therefore, is a focus of a great deal of research in communications theory, social psychology, and sociology, and there is no obvious way of summarizing a disparate and complex literature (see Zimbardo and Leippe 1991: 127–67).[2] But let me try.

---

[1] I would eliminate "or behavior" from this definition, as presumably behavior cannot change in the face of persuasion attempts without a change in some belief or attitude about the validity of the behavior.

[2] Despite the volume of this literature, "[t]o date there is precious little evidence specifying who can be talked out of what beliefs, and under what conditions" (Berger 1995:8).

Essentially, an actor is persuaded in three ways. First, s/he can engage in a high-intensity process of cognition, reflection, and argument about the content of new information (what Bar-Tal and Saxe call cognitive capacity, 1990:122). Also known by some as the "central route" to persuasion, the actor weighs evidence, puzzles through counter-attitudinal arguments, and comes to conclusions different from those he/she began with. That is, the merits of the argument are persuasive, *given* internalized standards for evaluating truth claims. Arguments are more persuasive and more likely to affect behavior when they are considered systematically and, thus, linked to other attitudes and schema in a complex network of causal connections and cognitive cues (Wu and Shaffer 1987:687; Petty, Wegener, and Fabrigar 1997:616; Zimbardo and Leippe 1991:192–97). This process of cognition, linking one set of attitudes to another, is more likely to occur when the environment cues and allows for the actor to consider these connections. That is, it is less likely to be spontaneous than it is promoted. As Gibson has shown with political intolerance among Russian voters, levels of intolerance and tolerance toward political opponents, and the overall balance between these two extremes, will change if counter-attitudinal arguments are presented to respondents that compel them to "think harder" about the implications of their initial attitudes. Thinking harder simply means people are cued, and have the time, to connect the implications of their initial attitude to outcomes that might affect their interests based on different sets of attitudes. Thus, an initially intolerant view might change to a more tolerant one if the respondent is cued to think about the implications of cycles of intolerance for political stability or for opportunities for themselves to present their own political opinions in the face of opposition (Gibson 1998:826–31). Thus, the probability of some change in attitudes through cognition increases in an iterated, cognition-rich environment (where there is lots of new information that cues linkages to other attitudes and interests). As a general rule, then, the probability goes down if the initial attitudes are already linked to a larger, internally consistent "network of supportive beliefs," particularly if these beliefs are about a high-threat group, a "crystallization hypothesis" applied to potential enemies (Sniderman, Brody, and Tetlock 1991:210; Gibson 1998:844).

Second, the actor is persuaded because of her/his affect relationship to the persuader; sometimes called the "peripheral" route, here the persuadee looks for cues about the nature of this relationship to judge the legitimacy of counter-attitudinal arguments. Thus, information from in-groups is more convincing than that from out-groups. Information from culturally recognized authorities (e.g., scientists, doctors, religious leaders) is more convincing than that from less authoritative sources. This will be especially true for novices who have little information about an issue on which to rely for guidance (Zimbardo and Leippe 1991:70).[3] Information from sources that are "liked" is more convincing than that from sources that are disliked. Liking will increase with more exposure, contact, and familiarity. The desire for social proofing means that information accepted through consensus or supermajority in a valued group will be more convincing than if the group were divided about how to interpret the message (Petty, Wegener, and Fabrigar 1997:612, 617, 623, 627, 629; Kuklinski and Hurley 1996:129–31; Napier and Gershenfeld 1987:159; Isen 1987:206, 210–11; Axsom, Yates, and Chaiken 1987:30–31).[4] A favorable endorsement of a candidate or idea in politics by others can lead an actor to adopt a more favorable opinion as well (Bartels, cited in Hirshleifer [1995:201]).[5]

Third, the persuasiveness of a message may be a function of characteristics of the persuadee her/himself. This can refer to a range of variables from cognitive processing abilities, to the strength of existing attitudes (usually these are stronger if developed through personal experience than if based on hearsay or indirect experience, for example), to what appears to be a deeply internalized desire to avoid appearing inconsistent, to the degree of independence an agent might have in relation to a principal. Thus, for example, an attitude associated with an explicit behavioral commitment made earlier will be more resistant to change later because actors experience discomfort at being viewed as hypocritical and inconsistent. Conversely, a new set of attitudes will be more persuasive if associated with a new, high-profile behavioral commitment (Cialdini 1984; Wu and Schaffer 1987:677). Thus, a focus on the characteristics of the persuadee means looking at the individual features that can either retard or propel persuasion. All this means is that actors entering a social interaction bring with them particular prior traits that, interacting with the features of the

---

[3] Or as Gibson puts it, "Especially when people do not have much experience with political institutions and processes, it is easy to imagine that their initial viewpoints are poorly anchored in a highly articulated and constrained belief system, and that considerable potential for effective persuasion exists" (Gibson 1998:821).

[4] Using different language, Habermasian constructivists make a similar point: "[T]rust in the authenticity of a speaker is a precondition for the persuasiveness of a moral argument" (Risse 1997:16; see also Williams 1997:291–92). See also Bourdieu 1991:109–11. Game theorists have come to a similar conclusion, only using different language. Lupia and McCubbins (1998) note that persuasiveness rests basically on the persuadee's belief that she or he shares common interests with the persuader and that the information the persuader is offering benefits both. They do not specify what kind of information leads to the first belief. But it could, in principle, be anything from the list in the previous paragraph.

[5] Crawford (2002:36) suggests that the emotional appeal of an argument adds to its persuasiveness. Arguably, the affective relationship between persuader and persuadee subsumes emotional cueing.

social environment and other actors, lead to variation in the degree of attitudinal change.[6]

Lupia and McCubbins (1998) argue that all of these conditions and characteristics are simply indicators of more basic conditions for persuasion, namely, that the persuadee believes the persuader to be knowledgeable about an issue and that his or her intentions are trustworthy. The more certain the persuadee is about these beliefs, the more likely the persuader will be persuasive. This certainty can be a function of familiarity and extensive interaction that, over time, reveal the persuader's knowledge and trustworthiness. Or it can be a function of "external forces" that make it difficult or costly for the persuader to hide knowledge (or lack thereof) and trustworthiness (e.g., mechanisms for revealing knowledge, penalties for lying, costly actions that reveal the position of the persuader). Any other factors, such as ideology, identity, culture, and so on, are only predictors of persuasion to the extent that they reveal information to the persuadee about the persuader's knowledge and trustworthiness.

Lupia and McCubbins's rigorous formal model of persuasion is probably correct in stripping the process down to these two pieces of perceived information. But they miss the more interesting question about the empirical frequency with which social variables such as perceived ideology, identity, and/or cultural values are in fact the primary cues that people use to determine the degree of knowledge and trustworthiness of a persuader. That is, on average is perceived shared identity between persuadee and persuader more likely to be used by the persuadee as an authoritative measure of a persuader's knowledge and trustworthiness than other kinds of cues? The answer has important implications for how social interactions lead to socialization and how different institutional designs might lead to different socialization paths. Lupia and McCubbins tend to focus, as befits their interest in signaling games, on the role of external forces in clarifying beliefs about knowledge and trustworthiness of persuaders. Since, they argue, social and political environments are rarely ones where persuader and persuadee interact face to face over long periods of time, the familiarity/personal interaction route to beliefs about the persuader's knowledge and trustworthiness tends to be less common.

---

[6] Of course, persuasion in practice is likely to be a combination of all these microprocesses. Jorgensen, Kock, and Rorbech found in a study of televised political debates in Denmark, for example, that the most persuasive debaters were those who used a small number of extended, weighty discussions of specific qualitative examples. The use of these specific, straightforward, and logical examples seemed to accentuate the authoritativeness of the debater and were easier for viewers to assess and adjudicate. See Jorgensen, Kock, and Rorbech 1998.

This may be true at the national level of persuasion (e.g., political messages from politicians aimed at masses of voters), but it is not necessarily true at the level of social interaction in international institutions among diplomats, specialists, and analysts. Here the first route—familiarity and iterated face-to-face social interaction—may be more common. Hence, affect based on identity, culture, and ideology may be more critical for persuasion than external forces and costly signals. Institutions, therefore, that are "lite" in terms of these external forces nonetheless may create conditions conducive to persuasion—and convergence around group norms—even though there are few material incentives for the persuader to deceive and few material costs for the persuadee to defect from the group. I will come back to this at the end of this chapter.

Obviously, persuasion in the end is a combination of all three processes just outlined, and it is hard to run controls that might isolate the effects of any one process. People are more likely to think hard and favorably about a proposition, for instance, when it comes from a high-affect source, in part because affect helps kick in resistances to information from other sources (Mohr 1996:81–82). On the other hand, one can identify ideal combinations that could, in principle, be tested. Given, then, an effort by a persuader to provide information with a view to changing basic principled, causal, or factual understandings, certain kinds of social environments, therefore, ought to be especially conducive to persuasion:[7]

- when the actor is highly cognitively motivated to analyze counterattitudinal information (e.g., a very novel environment);

- when the persuader is a highly authoritative member of a small, intimate, high-affect in-group to which the persuadee also belongs or wants to belong;

[7] For a similar list of hypotheses, see Checkel 2001:222. For a differently worded list that nonetheless can map onto a number of these hypotheses, see Crawford 2002:36. Moravcsik (2001) claims that because one can imagine "rationalist" arguments that make similar predictions, these kinds of "mid-range" theory hypotheses developed by constructivism are somehow subsumed by rationalist approaches, or are at the very least theoretically indistinguishable from so-called rationalist predictions about persuasion. This is debatable on a number of grounds. First, as I note in reference to the only systematic contractualist argument about persuasion (Lupia and McCubbins 1998), even they admit that there may be different, more affect-based reasons for persuasion in face-to-face interactions that are not captured by contractualist or "rationalist" microprocesses. Second, since the microprocesses in social psychological–derived hypotheses are different, the practical implications for the kinds of institutional designs most conducive to persuasion are meaningfully different. Finally, Moravcsik misses the point of critical tests—namely, they are set up precisely because two different sets of theoretical arguments make, in a specific instance, similar predications about behavior. The fact that they do prior to a critical test says nothing about which approach is distinctively superior.

- when the actor has few prior, ingrained attitudes that are inconsistent with the counter-attitudinal message, say, when the actor is a novice or an inductee in a new social environment, or when the perceived threat from counter-attitudinal groups is low;

- when the agent is relatively autonomous from the principal (e.g., when the issue is technical or ignored by the principal);

- when the actor is exposed to counter-attitudinal information repeatedly over time.

In practice, as I will come to in a moment, these conditions are more likely to hold in some kinds of institutions than in other kinds.[8]

The ARF as a Counter-Realpolitik Institution

The first thing to determine is whether or not the ASEAN Way as embodied in the ARF does indeed constitute a counter-realpolitik ideology that is, in some sense, diffusible. Acharya identifies at least four key elements of this ideology: open regionalism, soft regionalism, flexible consensus, and cooperative/common security (Acharya 1997b).[9] The first three refer to the "structure" and form of the ARF, a variable that matters when discussing whether the ARF creates conditions conducive to persuasion (and perhaps social influence). I will come back to these features in a moment. Cooperative security, however, is the normative core of the ARF. First enunciated by the Palme Commission for Europe in the early 1980s, the concept embodies a number of principles: the non-legitimacy of military force for resolving disputes, security through reassurance rather than unilateral military superiority, non-provocative defense, and transparency. Behavior that is reassuring rather than threatening should be the rule, such that the ARF can "develop a more predictable and constructive

---

[8] Kelley (2004) attempts a head-to-head test of "rationalist" (e.g., material conditionality) versus "socialization" arguments (persuasion and social influence), but she does not really examine in any detail whether the conditions under which persuasion and/or social influence are most likely to pertain were present in the cases she examines. Indeed, her findings that the presence of powerful domestic opposition undermines international persuasion attempts does not undermine the argument about scope conditions for persuasion outlined here. One would expect that when domestic opposition forces are powerful, then the agent's autonomy should be relatively low, thus the agent should be less susceptible to persuasion attempts.

[9] Some analysts differentiate between cooperative and common security, but the differences are relatively minor and have to do with the issues that are considered security threatening (cooperative security uses a looser definition of security issues to embrace so-called nontraditional security—environment, social unrest, etc.). See Dewitt (1994).

pattern of relations for the Asia-Pacific region."[10] The security philosophy here implicitly assumes states are essentially status quo (or can be socialized to accept the status quo), and as such it is both normatively and empirically "true" that reassurance behavior is a better route to security than traditional realpolitik strategies. Security is positive sum. As such, traditional axioms like "If you want peace, prepare for war" are outmoded or counterproductive.[11] To this end, the normatively appropriate and empirically effective means for achieving security involve the building of trust through confidence-building measures, and the defusing of security problems through preventive diplomacy and conflict management. This is not to say that all members of the ARF, even the strongest backers of the institution, behave in ways perfectly consistent with the injunctive norms. The point is that these are the articulated and formal, if sometimes implicit, "theories" of security that are supposed to serve as the basis of "habits of cooperation."[12]

For a social environment to have a socializing effect, obviously an actor has to be a participant. The ARF is explicitly designed to be maximally attractive to states. The principles of open regionalism, soft regionalism, and flexible consensus are critical in this regard. Together they reflect the nondiscriminatory goals of the ARF. Although there are evolving rules for participation, the principle of open regionalism means the institution should be as inclusive as possible, combining multilateralist activists and skeptics such that there is no aggrieved actor left out to undermine the efficacy or legitimacy of the institution.[13]

[10] Most of these principles are embodied in the ARF Concept Paper (1995b). See also the comments by the Malaysian defense minister Hajib Tun Rajak cited in Dewitt (1994:12–13) and Lee Kwan-yew's comments about the ARF as a channel for China reassuring Southeast Asia about its status quo intentions in Makabenta (1994).

[11] "*Si pacem, parabellum*" in the Latin. "*Ju an si wei, you bei wu huan*" in the Chinese. These are the security principles of the OSCE as well. The primary difference between OSCE and ARF definitions of security is that the former includes human rights and liberal domestic governance as a component of interstate security. The ARF, sensitive to the postcolonial sovereign-centric ideologies in ASEAN and China, excludes this element.

[12] I do not mean to imply that the ARF was set up to undermine the balance of power ideology and practice, nor that many of its members are not consummate practitioners of realpolitik. My point is that the ARF ideology was not designed to promote balance of power ideology or practice. There are a range of views among ARF actors as to the complementarity between realpolitik and cooperative security. But the logic of the ARF ideology is to restrain the worst features of realpolitik, such as security dilemmas born from uncertainty or conflicts born from revisionist preferences. I thank Ralf Emmers for pressing me on this point. For a thorough discussion of the ARF's ideology, see Katsumata (2006).

[13] In this respect, the ARF reflects what Downs, Rocke, and Barsoom call a transformational regime, precisely the type of design that, they argue, is least conducive to effective multilateral constraints on behavior because it seeks out a lowest common denominator and dilutes the influence of "activists." Their argument holds *if* one assumes that preferences are fixed, that socialization does not occur, and that the ideology of the institution

Moreover, the institution should be as attractive to states as possible (in this case, China). Soft regionalism, therefore, emphasizes the informality and nonintrusiveness of the institution, and explicitly endorses the codes of conduct in the ASEAN Treaty of Amity and Cooperation (TAC), which emphasizes sovereignty-preserving principles such as noninterference in the internal affairs of states, respect for territorial integrity, the right to choose domestic social systems, and so on.[14]

At first glance this would appear to be inconsistent with counter-realpolitik socialization. I do not think there is any easy way of squaring this circle. What this principle does do, however, is send reassurance signals to participants that the institution will not undermine basic interests, that it will not be used by powerful states to exploit less powerful or influential ones. That is, it makes the institution attractive, or at least nonthreatening from the perspective of the most skeptical potential participant.[15]

Flexible consensus ensures both that the institution does not move far ahead of the interests of the most skeptical state *and* that the most skeptical state cannot easily veto its evolution.[16] Consensus decision making is a logical mechanism for reassuring member states that the institution will not threaten sovereignty or national unity. The rule was expressly written into the Chair's Statement summarizing the consensus at the second ARF meeting in Brunei in 1995: "Decision of the ARF shall be made through consensus after careful and extensive consultations among all participants" (ARF 1995a).[17]

---

is also diluted as the membership includes more "skeptics." It is not clear why this should be so, however, if the ideology is relatively stable and legitimate. See Downs, Rocke, and Barsoom 1997.

[14] On the TAC, see Leifer 1996:12–15. As I noted, these stand in contrast to the OSCE definition of common security. It is unclear how long the ASEAN Way discourse about security can resist a turn to the domestic sources of regional insecurity, however. The notion of nontraditional security issues—drugs, crime, refugees, transboundary pollution, and so on—has begun to enter the vocabulary of security specialists there. A number of ASEAN states are unhappy about how Burma's domestic governance performance negatively affects ASEAN's reputation. For a discussion of ASEAN's limited efforts to loosen the norms of noninterference, see Acharya 2004.

[15] These were norms that the Chinese regime, faced in particular with perceived American threats to unity (support for Taiwan) and domestic political order (human rights), wholly endorsed. As one Canadian diplomat noted, the ASEAN Way is a catchphrase for a pace that the PRC is comfortable with. The promise of a slow pace in the ARF is the only reason China came to the table (interview with Canadian embassy officials, Beijing, China, April 1996).

[16] The concept of flexible consensus came from ASEAN practice. See Acharya 2001:69.

[17] This statement, in turn, reflected the ARF Concept Paper, a blueprint for the ARF's institutional and agenda evolution. "The rules of procedure of ARF papers shall be based on prevailing ASEAN norms and practices: Decisions should be made by consensus after careful and extensive consultations. No voting will take place" (ARF 1995b:6).

Consensus decision making might appear to be a suboptimal decision-making rule for a diverse group of actors: although it is more efficient than a unanimity rule, there is always the risk that individual actors can acquire informal veto power.[18] Studies of consensus decision making among political parties in Swiss canton governments suggest, however, that consensus rules are likely to reduce intergroup conflicts in systems with "strong subcultural segmentation" (e.g., diverse subgroups as in the ARF) (Steiner 1974). In addition, as Chigas, McClintock, and Kamp argue in their analysis of consensus rules in the OSCE, consensus means all states have a greater stake in the implementation of decisions because they are collectively identified with a decision in ways that they would not be had they been defeated in an on-the-record vote over a particular course of action. Efforts to buck or shirk consensus decisions will generate more negative "peer pressure" than had clear opposition been registered through a vote (Chigas, McClintock, and Kamp 1996:42–43). Put differently, consensus rules make obstinacy costly in ways that up-and-down voting rules do not: abstinence threatens to undermine the effectiveness of the entire institution because its effectiveness is premised on consensus. It portrays the obstinate actor as one whose behavior is fundamentally at odds with the purposes of the institution. "Principled stands" against efforts to declare consensus are viewed as less principled than had they been expressed in a losing vote. Moreover, a consensus decision reduces the risk of ending up on the losing side. Losing internationally can have domestic political costs. It could be harder to maintain a domestic consensus for an international institution if one appears to lose badly from time to time (Steiner 1974:269–71; Lindell 1988:45).

The ARF's consensus decision rule was an attractive feature for China, even though as the ARF evolved it was hard to use flexible consensus norms for outright veto purposes. Consensus ensured that China would not be on the losing side in any majoritarian voting system. This was probably important for those in the Ministry of Foreign Affairs handling ARF diplomacy: it would have been much harder to sell the benefits of the ARF in the policy process in Beijing if China's leaders had evidence that China was losing in recorded voting procedures.

A subcomponent of consensus decision-making rules in the ARF is a norm of avoiding particularly controversial issues that might end up pre-

[18] The application of consensus rules in international organization varies a great deal. It can take the form of anything from a norm of unanimity in which there is informal vote taking and where one state can veto decisions, to a norm where the chair has such legitimacy and latitude that individual opponents to a declaration of consensus are reluctant to challenge. The ARF tends to operate more closely to the latter than the former. On variations in consensus practices, see Lindell 1988.

venting consensus. This is where Track II activities have been instrumental to the functioning of the ARF, both as a source of ideas and as a channel for defusing potentially volatile issues. These Track II activities come in three forms: ARF-sponsored Track II meetings;[19] activities undertaken parallel to, or in support of, the ARF without the ARF's prior formal endorsement;[20] and the Council on Security Cooperation in the Asia Pacific (CSCAP), an umbrella organization created in 1993 of thirteen national CSCAP committees. Although it is not the only Track II process around, CSCAP is the largest and most organized, with national CSCAP committees collaborating in working groups on topics such as CBMs.[21]

Whether or not by design, the evolving relationship to Track II contributes to the ARF's stability and legitimacy as an institution for states in the region. Issues that are too controversial for Track I can be moved into Track II rather than being discarded entirely. This sustains the momentum behind issues that the ARF might otherwise be compelled to abandon at the Track I level. Given that many Track II participants are government officials who also participate in Track I activities,[22] an issue is never really

[19] For example, in a Paris workshop in November 1996 on preventive diplomacy, the chair's statement recommended that the ARF consider taking a more proactive role in preventive diplomacy through the provision of the ARF chair's "good offices."

[20] For example, Australia convened a workshop on CBMs in November 1994; Canada and Malaysia cohosted a workshop on PKO activities in March 1995; and South Korea hosted a workshop on preventive diplomacy in May 1995. The results of the workshops were acknowledged and commended in the chair's statement at the 1995 ARF. See ARF 1995a:5 and Smith 1997.

[21] The relationship between CSCAP and the ARF has been rather ambiguous. Neither the 1995 nor 1996 ARF chair's statement specifically names CSCAP as the primary forum for ARF Track II activities, although the 1995 Concept Paper does identify it, along with ISIS ASEAN as two potential braintrusts for the ARF. Its absence from the chair's statements reflected, most likely, Chinese objections at that time to handing Track II responsibilities to an organization in which China was not a member. China's membership had been held up as the rest of CSCAP debated how to handle Taiwan's application for membership. The PRC refused to set up a national committee until it was satisfied Taiwan could not participate formally. This decision was made in late 1996; the PRC subsequently put together its national committee and formally applied to join CSCAP. CSCAP emerged as a potential ideas factory for the ARF, somewhat analogous to the non-governmental Pacific Economic Cooperation Council's relationship to APEC (interview 1997 and e-mail correspondence with an Australian government official involved in ARF policy making, February 1997). On the work of CSCAP in providing new ideas and proposals to individual ARF participants and to ARF working groups, see Simon (2001).

[22] For example, in the 1990s about 50 percent of the board of directors of the US national committee of CSCAP had worked in government. The US CSCAP also has a category called observers who are current government officials (US CSCAP 1997). The original Chinese CSCAP national committee was very small and exclusively reserved for senior officials. It included an assistant foreign minister, the senior specialist on American, European, and arms control affairs in the PLA General Staff Department, as well as the Foreign Ministry's senior functional-level officer handling ARF affairs (PRC CSCAP n.d. 1997?). In 2000 the

not within Track I's sphere of attention. This means that states can get more used to an issue being part of their interaction than if it were initially considered illegitimate. Track II can also "filter" or sanitize proposals that would otherwise be deemed more controversial by dint of who made them.[23] *Who* makes a proposal can sometimes be more controversial than the *content* of the proposal itself (Desjardin 1996). But if proposals are depersonalized through the Track II consensus process, and then again through the ARF chair's determination of consensus in the Track I level, much of the controversy can be filtered out. Thus, Track II can help define a Track I agenda that might not have otherwise appeared. As long as this myth of difference is not explicitly challenged, then the destabilizing effect of controversial issues is reduced. Chinese officials have stated openly that CSCAP's unofficial nature was a fiction because of the presence of so many government officials in their "personal capacities." Nonetheless, the Chinese government has played along: in a statement of support for links to Track II, it noted, "Issues not discussed or needing further discussions because of disagreement" can be put into Track II fora.

The form of the ARF, then, exhibits some of the features of an institution that may be likely to create a social environment conducive to persuasion: membership is relatively small (twenty-two states as of this writing) with some consistency over time in the participants at both the senior minister and functional specialists levels; the decision rule is (flexible) consensus; the mandate is deliberative and, partly as a result, this lowers the perception that highly threatening states can control the outcomes of the institution; and initially at least there was a certain amount of autonomy for China's representatives to the extent that the ARF was not central to Beijing's regional diplomacy, and the most likely repository of opponents, the PLA, was not fully involved in policy making.[24]

---

membership was expanded to include younger scholars and think-tank analysts who worked on regional security issues.

[23] "Filter" is Paul Evans's term. I am indebted to him for his insights into Track II. For an insightful discussion of the social psychological theory behind Track II effectiveness, with application to the Middle East, see Kaye 2001. For a discussion of the role of Track II in ASEAN politics, see Acharya 2001:66–67.

[24] The franchise characteristics of the ARF are hard to code. On the one hand, there is no formal recognition of particularly authoritative voices, e.g., there are no scientists' working groups or advisory panels that often define the scientific boundaries of policy discourse in, say, environmental institutions. On the other hand, ASEAN states are clearly authorized to take leadership roles in all ARF activities. All ARF intersessional meetings, for example, must be cohosted by an ASEAN state. The so-called ASEAN Way, therefore, is enshrined as the guiding ideology of the institution. One complicating factor, however, is that often ASEAN states can be quite passive in the promotion of the common security elements of the ASEAN Way, particularly when these conflict with its sovereign-centric elements. Thus, on transparency issues or intrusive confidence-building measures, China is not always the only state pushing for a lowest common denominator solution. On certain multilateral is-

We have, then, two key features of the ARF: a counter-realpolitik ideology and an institutional structure with features conducive to the development of "habits of cooperation" in the absence of material threats and punishments. On top of this, the institution is seen explicitly by many of its participants as a tool for socializing China to accept multilateralism, transparency, and reassurance as a basis for security.[25]

Put differently, some participants in the regional security discourse see the ARF as a tool for increasing China's "comfort level" with multilateralism. Comfort level is another way of saying that an actor's utility level changes positively with changing levels of institutionalization. An actor has a particular distribution of utility associated with particular levels of institutionalization.[26] Different actors may have different distributions of utility. Skeptics of multilateralism would have low values of utility at high levels of institutionalization. Committed multilateral activists would have high values of utility at high levels of institutionalization. Greater willingness to accept institutionalization would be indicated by an increase in an actor's utility whereby it comes to believe that the absence of an institution is less valued than before and the presence of one becomes more valued than before.

The question is, what might cause a shift in this comfort level in this distribution of utility? Mainstream institutionalist theory would probably focus on things such as reassurance (information that underscores fears of even small amounts of institutionalization are exaggerated) or the distributional effects of the institution (leading to change in domestic political balances of power). Socialization arguments would focus on persuasive arguments that more institutionalization is a "good" in and of itself, or on social backpatting and opprobrium effects that link the utility of involvement in the institution to the utility of social status and diffuse image.[27]

---

sues, non-ASEAN activist states take the lead in defining the discourse, e.g., given its experience, in intersessionals on peacekeeping operations Canada has spoken with a more authoritative voice.

[25] I do not want to leave the impression that everyone in ASEAN intended to try to alter Chinese interests. Some were more skeptical about this possibility than others. Even these people, however, did not necessarily have an interest in openly defining the security problem as something akin to a suasion game. The concern was that by focusing on a China threat, the ARF will lose its status as a focal point and ASEAN will lose its leadership status in regional security affairs.

[26] I am subsuming, for the moment, the intrusiveness of the agenda within the level of institutionalization.

[27] I would call this shift in utility distribution a change in preference. I realize some contractual institutionalists would debate this, and consider this a change in strategy. The difference between the two concepts is artificial and depends on the level of ends and means one is examining. For game theorists, the outcome of strategic interaction between two players is the product of a particular strategy pair. States are said to have preferences over outcomes.

Here I want to focus on evidence for persuasion. Recall the required indicators of persuasion: that social environments in the institution are conducive to persuasion; that after exposure to or involvement in a new social environment, attitudes or arguments for participation converge with the normative/causal arguments that predominate in the social environment; that behavior has changed in ways consistent with prior attitudinal change; and that material side payments or threats are not present, nor are they part of the decision to conform to pro-social norms.

Having established that the institutional form of the ARF meets the criteria for an environment conducive to persuasion, the question is whether, then, attitudes or arguments in China converged with the normative/causal arguments at the core of the ARF "ideology." It is quite clear that the public and internal discourse in China on multilateral security dialogues in the Asia Pacific prior to China's entry into the ARF in 1994 was highly skeptical of their value. Indeed, in internal circulation (*neibu*) and open materials alike, the discourse stressed that bilateral relations, particularly among the great powers, were the basis of stability or instability in IR; that there was no urgent need to build multilateral security mechanisms, indeed that multilateralism was unimportant for handling regional problems; that such institutions would be dominated by the United States or Japan while China would be outnumbered; and that sensitive bilateral disputes where China might have an advantage in bargaining power might be internationalized.[28] The skepticism of multilateralism was rooted in even deeper realpolitik assumptions about international relations where structurally (and sometimes ideologically) induced zero-sum competition among sovereign states necessitates unilateral security strategies.[29]

From the mid-1990s on, however, there were some noticeable changes in the discourse. For one thing, China's exposure to regional multilateral institutions led to a dramatic intensification of the discourse about regionalism and multilateralism. As figures 4.1 and 4.2 show, there has been an

---

Yet if an institution is itself a product of a particular strategy pair (or the confluence of more than two strategies in a multilateral institution), then the form and function of the institution itself is a preference. Of course, multilateralism can also be a strategy at a higher level of interaction where the goal is some more abstract good, such as security. But since security is a grand preference of most states, to limit preferences to things as abstract as security, welfare, peace, and so on, means that no outcome below this level can be called a preference. Everything becomes strategy. I think this reduces the utility of the term "preference," and ignores the fact that actors can come to internalize multilateralism, unilateralism, or bilateralism as legitimate, taken-for-granted ends in themselves.

[28] Interview with Chinese intelligence analyst involved in the ARF policy process, Beijing, July 1996; Garrett and Glaser 1994; Yuan 1996; Johnston 1990; Xu 1996:252–53.

[29] On Chinese realpolitik, see Christensen 1996 and Johnston 1998a.

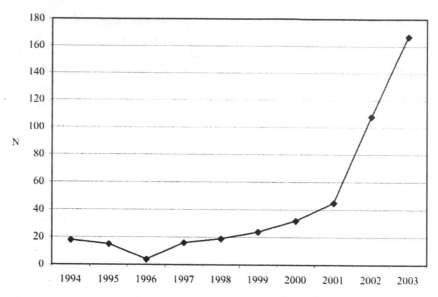

Figure 4.1. Frequency of articles with the term "multilateralism" (*duobianzhuyi*) in Chinese journals on international relations. Source: China Academic Journals database, China National Knowledge Infrastructure.

exponential increase in the discourse about "multilateralism" (*duobian-zhuyi*) in academic and official publications over the past decade. References to the ASEAN Regional Forum have also increased substantially since the organization came into being (figure 4.3). Assuming frequency has some face validity as an indicator of attention paid to an issue, it is clear that interest has increased over time.

In addition to changes in the frequency of the discourse about multilateralism, we can observe a change in its content as well. Initial statements made to the ARF (such as Foreign Minister Qian Qichen's comments at the first ARF in 1994) stressed what can only be seen as traditional "rules of the road" for the management of relations among sovereign, autonomous states. These included the Five Principles of Peaceful Coexistence, economic ties on the basis of equality and mutual benefit, the peaceful settlement of disputes, and adherence to the principle that military power should be used only for defensive purposes (Yuan 1996:11). Terms, concepts, and phrases associated with common or cooperative security were absent.[30]

---

[30] See, for instance, one of the earliest analyses of the ARF by a Chinese think-tank specialist in Asia-Pacific security, Liu 1996.

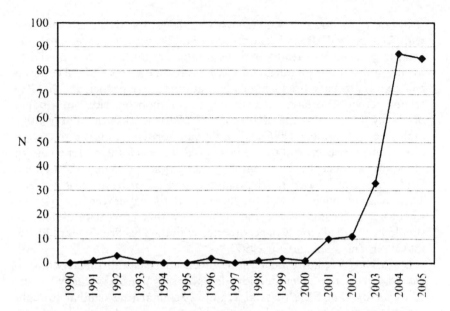

Figure 4.2. Frequency of articles with the term "multilateralism" (*duobianzhuyi*) in the *People's Daily*. Source: *People's Daily*, on-line full-text version.

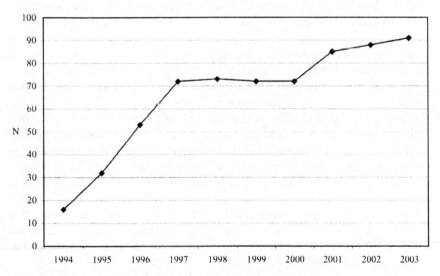

Figure 4.3. Frequency of articles in Chinese journals on international relations with references to the ASEAN Regional Forum (*Dongmeng diqu luntan*). Source: China Academic Journals database, China National Knowledge Infrastructure.

By late 1996, however, Chinese working-level officials directly involved with ARF-related affairs began to articulate concepts that were, to a degree, in tension with traditional realpolitik arguments. Shu Chunlai (a former ambassador to India, and a key figure on China's CSCAP committee) appears to have been China's first authoritative participant in ARF-related activities to have used the term "common security." In a paper originally presented at the ARF-sponsored Paris workshop on preventive diplomacy (November 1996), Shi and coauthor Xu Jian noted that common security was central to the post–cold war need for a "renewal" of old security concepts. This renewal, they argued, entailed abandoning "old" concepts, "based on the dangerous game of balance of power." There was not much more on the subject, and the paper went on to stress, somewhat in tension with common security, that preventive diplomacy should be handled strictly in accordance with the Five Principles of Peaceful Coexistence (Shi and Xu 1997).

By early 1997, however, ARF-involved analysts and officials *unofficially* floated a more well-developed concept of "mutual security" at the first Canada-China Multilateral Training Seminar (the seminar brought together a small number of key officials handling the ARF in the MOFA Asia Department, and a couple of analysts from China's civilian intelligence institution [CICIR] who were also in the ARF "interagency" process). The term meant, according to one Chinese participant, that "for you to be secure, your neighbor has to be secure," a common security concept based on the notion of "win-win." It is possible the Chinese may have felt under pressure to develop an original Chinese contribution to the multilateral security discourse: "common security" was perhaps too closely identified with the CSCE process, and thus might have been too provocative inside the Chinese policy process.

One of the participants in the seminar (a participant in interagency discussions on the ARF, and an analyst in CICIR) also submitted a paper for discussion in which he listed three types of security systems: hegemonic systems, alliance or military-bloc systems, and multilateral systems. The latter he called an "encouraging development" and noted that mutual security, like common security, cooperative security, and comprehensive security, were traditionally unfamiliar concepts in China. But these were now "taking place in the minds of policymakers and scholars and in the actions of Chinese policies," though he did not elaborate beyond this (Chu 1997).

Around the time of the seminar, another analyst involved in ARF-related work in a think tank attached to the State Council wrote a paper on confidence building in the Asia Pacific. The paper provided a sophisticated explanation of Western theories of CBMs, noting, for example, the military reassurance purposes of CBMs. The author also elaborated a bit on "mutual security," noting that the concept was embodied in the April 1996 Five-Power (China, Russia, Kazakhstan, Kyrgyzstan, Tajikistan) Treaty on CBMs (Liu 1997). (One of the Chinese participants at the Canada-China seminar in Toronto had also noted that mutual security had come from the Chinese discourse on the Five-Power Treaty.)

The invocation of the Five-Power Treaty in this common security–influenced discourse on mutual security was important. The treaty comes as close to a CSCE-type CBM agreement as anything in the Asia-Pacific region, with provisions for limits on the size and type of military maneuvers allowed within certain distances of borders, provisions for military observers and military exercises, and so on.[31] In internal Chinese debates over multilateralism, whether or not one believed the principles of the treaty had broader applicability to the region was an indicator of one's skepticism toward multilateralism in general. Those who supported its applicability tended to be stronger supporters of multilateralism.[32] The initial idea for the treaty grew out of bilateral PRC-Soviet negotiations over the border in 1990 and 1991. The Soviets had introduced the idea of a formal CBM agreement, using conventional force reduction CBMs that they had negotiated with Western Europe as a template. Initially, Chinese negotiators were literally unsure of the meaning of the terms the Soviets were bringing over from the European experience. The terminology had to be translated into Chinese with explanation so that MOFA officials understood the implications of certain CBM terminology. Thus, the Five-Power Treaty emerged fairly directly from European CBM experiences tabled by the Soviets.[33] That those articulating the concept of mutual security would do so by invoking the Five-Power Treaty as an example/precedent/exemplar suggests that the term signified an acceptance of more intrusive and formal security institutions. Indeed, the earliest analyses of the ARF tended to explicitly reject the CSCE as a model for the Asia Pacific (Liu 1994:18).

[31] For a systematic comparison of the Five-Power CBM agreement and the CSCE Vienna document of 1994, see Acharya 1997a:16–23.

[32] This was the distinct impression I received when interviewing military and civilian specialists on the ARF. Classic examples were two senior military officers, one a longtime participant in arms control policy, the other in charge of ARF and regional security affairs in the PLA. Both believed that the principles of the Five-Power Treaty had at least some applicability to the rest of the region. This contrasted with other PLA officers with whom I spoke who were doubtful about applicability and about multilateralism in the region. I never met anyone who could be placed in the other two "cells" of this rough 2 × 2: namely, people who believed these principles were applicable and were hostile to multilateralism in the Asia Pacific, or people who believed these principles were not applicable and yet were strong supporters of regional multilateralism.

[33] Interview with Chinese arms control specialist, January 1999.

Interestingly enough, in June 1997 at the first CSCAP General Meeting, when China's national committee participated for the first time, China's representative, Chen Jian (assistant foreign minister, and formally in charge of multilateral security issues at the MOFA), explicitly extolled the Five-Power CBM Treaty as contributing to confidence and security in the region. He did not mention "mutual security," however (nor indeed the term "new security concept") (Chen Jian 1997). This suggested that there was still probably some internal debate about the legitimacy of the concept and whether China should be formally and publicly associated with it. The term had not yet made it into the official policy discourse.

This began to change in the second half of 1997. At an ARF Track II meeting on preventive diplomacy in Singapore in September 1997, Ambassador Shi Chunlai, one of the regular Chinese participants in regional security dialogues, suggested in response to a question that the CBMs China had developed with India and Russia were applicable to Southeast Asia.[34] Then in November 1997, the Chinese paper presented to the ARF Intersessional Support Group on CBMs in Brunei explicitly noted that the Five-Power Treaty embodied the notion of "mutual security" and could be used as a source of ideas for the rest of the Asia Pacific. Mutual security was defined as an environment in which the "security interests of one side should not undermine those of the other side. . . . This kind of security is a win-win rather than zero-sum game" (China 1997:3). We should not underestimate the significance of the incorporation of this loosely game-theoretic terminology into the Chinese discourse (and another, "positive sum"—*zheng he*—used more recently by multilateralists in China)—terms borrowed, one assumes, from interactions with multilateralists in ARF-related activities. The origins are hard to pinpoint, but the term "win-win" does not seem to have been used much prior to 1997 in discussions of regional security; one of its earliest appearances was in comments that some Chinese participants made in the Canada-China seminar in January 1997.[35] The term "win-win," of course, stands in distinct tension with traditional realpolitik notions of security and reflects core assumptions of common security.

Then in December 1997 at the Third CSCAP North Pacific Meeting, Ambassador Shi Chunlai developed the "new security concept" further, linking it to "mutual security" and, by implication, to common security:

[34] Notes on Shi Chunlai's presentation, ARF Track II meeting on preventive diplomacy, September 9–11, 1997, Library of the Institute of Defence and Strategic Studies, Singapore.

[35] The term was first used in a *People's Daily* article in 1993 in reference to China-Taiwan talks in Hong Kong. Its usage, and its spread into other discursive spheres, took off in 1998–1999. The earliest academic article to use the term in reference to East Asia security appears to be Ruan Zongze's analysis of Clinton's East Asia strategy. See Ruan 1996.

the concept, he argued, was "one that is not based on the cold war mentality featuring zero-sum game, but on mutual and equal security." Rather it meant "not creating winners and losers" (Shi 1997:1–2). Both "the new security concept" and its component "mutual security" received the highest-level endorsement when they were included in remarks by China's foreign minister Qian Qichen at the Private Sector's Salute to ASEAN's Thirtieth Anniversary in December 1997. Since then the concept has been incorporated into China's ARF discourse. In the words of one senior diplomat engaged at that time in the ARF diplomacy, the concept comes close to cooperative and common security but stresses trust and confidence building more than institution building.

Over time, official Chinese commentary pushed the discourse further to include rather direct attacks on realpolitik concepts. An analysis broadcast by China Radio International in late December 1998 argued, for instance, that the Five-Power CBM Treaty was a good example for the rest of the Asia Pacific. It had authenticated "a new security concept completely different from the cold war mentality and the traditional security concept, if you desire peace, you must prepare for war. This saying is a vivid description of the traditional security concept." The traditional realpolitik concepts included ideas such as maximizing military force so as to become stronger than one's opponent, a narrow focus on the security of the nation above all else, and the resort to military means in the pursuit of security (China Radio International 1997).[36]

Such talk could be dismissed as rhetorical bandwagoning by state-controlled media. But it reflected an incorporation of language that at least some of its users saw as challenging traditional state practices. More significant, however, was the interest in MOFA's Asia Department in multilateralism. Realizing that it required more sophisticated arguments to bolster and justify the mutual security discourse and policy, the MOFA began to ask some of the key IR thinkers in China, a number of whom one might consider multilateralists and integrationists, how to put more theoretical

[36] The explicit rejection of the parabellum phrase is, in a sense, also a repudiation of a long-standing Chinese equivalent: *Ju an si wei, you bei wu huan* ("When residing in peace, think about danger. With [military] preparations there will be no calamities"). This does not mean that mutual security is a fully developed concept, nor that it wholly replicates cooperative or common security concepts. According to interviewees in October 1998, the terms "mutual security" and "new security concept," although developed by the Asia Department of the Ministry of Foreign Affairs precisely in response to the requirements of participating in multilateral activities in the region, were not fully developed themes in Chinese foreign policy. In 1998 the MOFA tasked specialists in the Chinese Academy of Social Sciences to develop further the theoretical cores of these concepts. Interviews with Chinese think tank analysts involved in the development of the new security concept, October and November 1998; conversation with MOFA official, October 1998.

meat on the conceptual bones.[37] To this end, the MOFA's Policy Research Office, on behalf of the Asia Department, commissioned a study by a respected specialist in regional multilateralism from the Chinese Academy of Social Sciences. The report was entitled "The Concept of Comprehensive Security and Some Theoretical Thoughts about China and Asia-Pacific Security" and was submitted to the MOFA in December 1998. The author, Zhang Yunling, explicitly argued that military power and traditional territorial-based concepts of national security were no longer the most important issues in China's future security in the region. Rather, China faced an increasing array of nontraditional security problems that could not be solved through the augmentation of national military power alone, and thus should focus more energy on developing multilateral cooperative solutions to security problems, including greater activism in the ARF. The report noted—in recognition of security dilemma dynamics— that China's behavior on the ground was one reason why states worried about China's rising power. To deal with this, the report argued, China had to signal that it basically accepted extant rules of international and regional order, while trying to moderate these rules and norms through existing international institutions and procedures. In other words, China's rise was a potentially destabilizing element in international relations because of perceptions of Chinese power in the past, but that China had to credibly signal that it was in essence a status quo power. The report explicitly borrowed arguments and concepts from Western, including Canadian, multilateralists and included an appendix that introduced some of the multilateralist lexicon to its audience (e.g., integration theory, interdepen-

---

[37] Interview with senior MOFA official engaged in ARF work, January 12, 1999. These individuals included Yan Xuetong, Wang Yizhou, and Zhang Yunling, among other well-respected IR specialists. Yan is considered somewhat more realpolitik in his views of multilateralism than Wang or Zhang. Nonetheless, he has argued that the new security concept and mutual security are based on common security and constitute a recognition that security dilemmas are a major source of conflict in the international system (Yan 2005:163). Zhang, an economist, views regional security through the lens of economic integration. Wang is one of China's most influential IR specialists, with a research interest in the process of China's integration into global institutions. His work has been influenced by his exposure to liberal institutionalism and social constructivism. The effort to develop more sophisticated thinking about multilateralism was given a boost in 2001 with China's first conference on the topic, hosted by the Institute of World Economics and Politics at the Chinese Academy of Social Sciences. Admitting that the topic was still very sensitive in China, one of the organizers, Wang Yizhou, wrote that multilateralist theory requires China to rethink its opposition to participation in everything from the G-8 to formal relations with NATO, to participation in ASEAN-US multilateral military exercises. See Wang 2001. Within a short few years, China in fact participated as an observer in the G-8, and broached the question of more formal relations with NATO.

dence theory, democratic peace theory) (Zhang 1998). The arguments in the report were designed in part to assist the Asia Department and other multilateralists to make more sophisticated internal arguments in favor of greater participation in the ARF, that is, to persuade others in the policy process, particularly in the PLA, of the value of multilateral diplomacy.[38]

The discourse on multilateralism in China, then, moved quite some distance over the 1990s, from public skepticism to informal articulations of mutual security and common security to public affirmation of the concepts. The concepts were explicitly linked to real-world institutional exemplars of these principles, such as the Five-Power CBM Treaty. This document was consistent with, indeed modeled in some ways from, CSCE-style institutions. For the protomultilateralists, the Five-Power Treaty was an example of applied mutual security.[39]

Moreover, it appears that those most directly participating in these various regional multilateral security institutions tended to express a higher level of valuation for them than those who had at best an indirect involvement or no involvement at all. As an initial test of this possibility, I analyzed a selection of ARF- and CSCAP-related documents, statements, position papers, and working papers produced by Chinese participants, as well as a collection of articles on regional multilateral security authored mostly by people who are not multilateral security specialists per se nor especially active in these institutions. The latter collection came from two policy journals in Beijing—one published by a Chinese military intelligence unit, the China Institute of International and Strategic Studies (*International Strategic Studies*), and one published by a civilian intelligence unit, the China Institute of Contemporary International Relations (*Contemporary International Relations*). Using a computer-aided content analysis program, I compared the former set of documents with the latter, looking in particular for differences in the valence attached to "multilateralism" and related terms in the texts. The measure of valence was the number of positive words as a percentage of the total number of positive and negative words semantically associated with terms for multilateralism. As it turns out, references to multilateralism were indeed more posi-

---

[38] Interview with Chinese academic specialist on Asia-Pacific multilateralism, January 1999. The report was published about a year later in *Dangdai Ya Tai* (Contemporary Asia-Pacific Studies). See Zhang 2000. Interestingly, even in the post-Kosovo atmosphere in China where more "liberal" voices had to tread with somewhat more caution when discussing international relations, there were essentially no significant changes in the wording or argumentation in the published version of the study.

[39] Interview with senior MOFA diplomat involved in ARF work, January 1999. The diplomat acknowledged that the treaty had been influenced by the OSCE model. The diplomat also acknowledged that the OSCE model was at least partly applicable to the Asia Pacific.

tive in the materials written by active participants in regional security institutions compared with those who were generally outside analysts.[40]

The obvious question is, has all this changing discourse about multilateralism been just cheap talk? A realpolitik actor would have incentives to use such a discourse deceptively: if one believed one was in a prisoners' dilemma environment, then cooperative discourses could encourage others to cooperative, thus creating opportunities to acquire the "temptation" (C,D) payoff. This would, in principle, be especially attractive to an actor in an institution such as the ARF, with little or no monitoring capacity (except for voluntary and nonstandardized "defense white papers") and no ability to punish defection. Some in the US government viewed, and continued to view, the multilateralist and mutual security discourses precisely as that: a deceptive effort to redirect attention from inconsistencies between Chinese security behavior (such as sharp increases in military expenditures and provocative military exercises) and the ideology of genuine multilateralism, while trying to underscore the incompatibility of US bilateral alliance strategies with multilateralism in the region.[41]

[40] The materials from those most active in multilateral institutions were collected in 2003 while I was at the Institute of Defence and Strategic Studies in Singapore. The IDSS has relatively complete records of both ARF and CSCAP meetings starting in 1994. I cannot guarantee I collected the universe of texts, but I believe the number I analyzed ($N = 33$) is fairly representative. The articles from the two think-tank journals were collected according to titles that mentioned Asia-Pacific multilateral security or related topics beginning in 1994. The N for this group was smaller (13). Both sets of documents were entered into the Yoshikoder, a computer-aided text analysis program that allows one to isolate specific terms in the text and then look for positive or negative valenced words within a certain distance of the term of interest. The intuition that generally consistent characterizations and descriptions of a word can be found within a limited distance from the word comes from semantic space analysis (Lowe 2000). In this case, I looked for positive and negative terms within ten words of the term "multilateralism" and related words such as ARF, CSBM, ASEAN, CSCAP, preventive diplomacy, multilateral mechanism, and cooperative security. The dictionaries of positive and negative terms were drawn from the General Inquirer dictionaries. For the ARF- and CSCAP-related texts, the number of positive terms as a portion of the sum of positive and negative terms was 0.91, whereas for the journal articles it was 0.86. A one-tailed t-test shows that the difference is statistically significant at the 0.1 level ($p = 0.06$). I am very grateful to Will Lowe for designing and writing the Yoshikoder program.

[41] The argument is outlined in Garrett and Glaser 1997. See also Finkelstein's contention (1999:43) that much of the Chinese discourse on multilateralism was designed to counter US security bilateralism around the world and particularly in Asia. My own conversations with Pentagon officials involved in Asia policy confirms this particular interpretation. What lent this argument credence was that the mutual security discourse emerged around the same time that the Chinese hosted a rather uncharacteristically contentious (for the ARF) intersessional support group meeting on CBMs in March 1997. The Chinese diplomat chairing the meeting (actually cochairing with the Philippines, though the Philippines played a passive role in the meeting) refused to drop a Chinese agenda item that called for the study of CBMs (military observers, prior notification, etc.) at joint military exercises in the region. Since the United States and its allies conduct joint exercises while the Chinese do not, the

I am not convinced of the pure deceptiveness of this discourse, however. In principle, there is a relatively easy test of this hypothesis. If it were right, then the strongest proponents of the mutual security discourse (and multilateralism in general) and the Five-Power Treaty as an exemplar agreement for the region should have been the strongest opponents of US bilateral alliances in the region. In addition, variations in Chinese efforts to undermine support for US alliances (particularly with Japan) should have tracked directly with variations in the strength and prominence of the mutual security discourse.

On both of these tests, the instrumental or deception hypothesis comes up short. A careful tracking of the discourse, as I have tried to do earlier, suggests that originally the strongest proponents were precisely those who in their private interactions within the Chinese policy process, and with foreign diplomats and observers, indicated a deeper commitment to multilateralism. The proponents included multilateral functional specialists in the MOFA and moderate voices and "new thinkers" in the strategic analysis community. Although these people were generally opposed to the expansion of US-Japanese security cooperation, and wanted to use multilateral diplomacy to pressure the United States to limit the scope of its military cooperation with Japan, they also recognized the alliance was a reality and could indeed constrain Japanese remilitarization. Indeed, Zhang Yunling's MOFA-commissioned report on comprehensive security, mentioned earlier, was explicit in stating that China should not and need not replace US military superiority in the region, and that China need not balance militarily against US power, especially if effective, practical multilateral security institutions could be set up in the region.[42]

The proto-multilateralists have also argued that China's integration in multilateral institutions can help reassure the United States (Tang and Zhang 2004:6).

---

proposal was rightly criticized as being aimed at US military interests. The agenda item, however, was drafted by the PLA. The chief MOFA ARF policy functionary had privately indicated a willingness to drop the issue in discussions with the Canadians a couple of months prior to the meeting. But it is plausible that with the meeting in Beijing, and with a large PLA contingent observing the discussions, the MOFA did not feel free to drop the issue. In any event, the Chinese insistence on maintaining the agenda item in the face of opposition from a range of states prevented consensus on this issue and led to a great deal of concern in the United States about a Chinese offensive against US military alliances in the region. Conversations with Canadian diplomats, May 1997, and a PLA officer involved in the ARF policy process, December 1997.

[42] See Zhang 2000. See also Wang Yizhou's essay (2001) in which he advocates under the banner of multilateralism China's participation in ASEAN-US joint military exercises. See also Tang and Zhang 2004:5 in which they note that China should be able to coexist with the United States as a hegemon, as long as it does not threaten core Chinese interests. All of these authors have advised the MOFA's Asia Department on regional security issues.

In contrast, my sense is that those who were less enamored with the mutual security discourse were found mostly in the military, and it was in the PLA where some of the strongest skeptics of the US-Japan alliance were and are found. One could also imagine that the PLA should have been troubled by the anti-realpolitik content of "mutual security" and its use of a potentially militarily intrusive CBM treaty as a model for the region. Moreover, the Chinese CBM proposals in the ARF that were clearly biased against US military power in the region (e.g., observers at joint military exercises, reductions in military reconnaissance activities aimed at ARF members, etc.) appeared first in 1995–1996, well before the "mutual security" concept emerged, and were promoted by the PLA, not the Ministry of Foreign Affairs.[43] The disconnect is further underscored by the fact that the shrillness of the anti–US-Japan alliance rhetoric died down in the late 1990s, even as the mutual security concept was given higher profile and became more sophisticated in public discourse. This is inconsistent with the deception hypothesis about the origins of the multilateralist and mutual security discourses.

My argument here rests, obviously, on the critical question of whether the mutual security discourse has, to some degree, been internalized among those working most closely in the ARF environment. This appears to have been the case.[44] China's involvement in the ARF and related processes seems to have led to the emergence of a small group of policy makers and analysts with an emerging, if tension-ridden, normative commitment to multilateralism because it is good for Chinese and regional security. One longtime participant observer of multilateral security dialogues in the region, Amitav Acharya, described in a report to the Canadian government in the late 1990s how Chinese participants had developed a more positive evaluation of the role of multilateralism in improving Chinese security. Multilateral institutions such as the ARF helped Chinese leaders understand better how other states in the region perceived Chinese power (an understanding that is the first step in recognizing the potential for security dilemmas). According to one of Acharya's informants, China was "learning a new form of cooperation" (Acharya 1998:4). Another remarked, "Because of the ARF, China is more willing to settle its disputes by peaceful means" (Acharya 1998:5).

---

[43] These proposals came from the Comprehensive Department of the Foreign Affairs Bureau of the General Staff Department, the department that coordinates PLA positions on the ARF.

[44] Interviews with Canadian and Singaporean embassy officials, Beijing, April 1996 and October 1998; Chinese analyst involved in ARF policy, Beijing, July 1996; and Canadian specialist on Track II, January 1997; Smith 1997.

Another keen observer and organizer of some of these dialogues, Susan Shirk, was even more specific about how participation affected two of the leading MOFA supporters of multilateralism in China's Asia policy:

After participating in NEACD [Northeast Asia Cooperation Dialogue] and the official multilateral groups like the ASEAN Regional Forum that were just starting, Fu Ying became an advocate within the bureaucracy for regional multilateral cooperation. As she moved up the career fast track in the Asia Department, China's approach toward regional cooperation became increasingly pro-active. Fu succeeded in bringing Wang Yi (then head of the Asia Department) on board with multilateralism, as I learned when she arranged for me to talk with him after the 1996 NEACD meeting in Beijing. A dashing Japanese speaker, Wang Yi later visited me in San Diego, spent six months at Georgetown University to prepare for future promotions by improving his English, and enrolled as a part-time PhD student at the university attached to the foreign ministry. This bold and bureaucratically nimble duo brought a new spirit of confident cooperation to China's Asian diplomacy. (Shirk 2007:190)

ARF policy in China was initially put in the hands of the Comprehensive Division of the Asia Department of the Foreign Ministry. The division had only about eight to ten overworked officers. Since the Comprehensive Division normally handled a range of functional issues in addition to security issues, only a couple of these officers initially did the preparatory work for ARF meetings and Track II activities. In early ARF activities the Chinese representatives were unaccustomed to the give and take of corridor debate and negotiation. They also came to the discussions with a watchful eye for developments that might impinge on sensitive security or domestic political issues. Over time, however, with experience in informal discussion and familiarity with the ARF norms of interaction, these officers became much more engaged, relaxed, and flexible. Participants from other countries have remarked on the generally sophisticated, nuanced, amicable tone of Chinese interventions in discussions over time. Even Chinese ARF specialists have noted that the institutional culture of the ARF requires them to adjust the tone and tenor of their discourse. Unlike in the UN where vigorous and legalistic defenses of specific positions in negotiations that are often viewed as close to zero-sum are often required, in the ARF there is more give and take, more spontaneous intervention to explain positions, and with some exceptions, an atmosphere that downplays "in your face" defenses of national positions.[45]

[45] Interview with senior MOFA official involved in ARF diplomacy, January 12, 1999; interview with Canadian diplomats involved in ARF work, July 3, 2001.

It is important to note in this regard as well that in some instances, those exposed to multilateral security environments took on positions/ orientations that were distinguishable from others with their own bureaucratic background. It is clear, for instance, that the two PLA officers in the Foreign Affairs Bureau (later Office) who handled the PLA's input into regional security dialogue policy in the 1990s and early 2000s were more favorably disposed to multilateral solutions than the PLA as an institution.[46] Indeed, rare for a PLA officer, at least one of the two agreed that the principles of the Five-Power CBM Treaty of 1995 were applicable to East Asia more broadly.[47] As I noted, one's position on the wider applicability of this treaty was a reasonably good indicator of one's support for security multilateralism in the region.

Most interesting was this protomultilateralist constituency's apparent endorsement, within limits, of multilateralism as being compatible with Chinese security interests. Some foreign diplomats in Beijing who had interactions with these MOFA officers extensively suggested that their agenda was to tie China gradually into regional security institutions so that someday China's leaders would be bound by them. These officers saw involvement in the ARF as a process of educating their own government. Some even remarked that involvement in the ARF had reduced the likelihood of China's resort to force over disputes in the South China Sea because there were now more diplomatic (that is, multilateral) tools at China's disposal.[48] More generally, some Chinese analysts saw the ARF experience as contributing to a greater understanding of the notion of common security. As one article put it, in the context of the ARF's impact on regional politics, "following the growing intimacy of relations among countries in the Asia Pacific, and the increase in international responsibilities after the improvement in China's international position, China also became aware that its own security was not an isolated issue. At the same time as it strengthens its national defense modernization, it must rely on equal dialogues and discussions, and with other countries together discuss issues concerning the establishment of common security" (Liang and Zhao 2001:43).

The main conduit for the infusion of these sorts of ideas into the group of protomultilateralists was experience in Track I and II activities.[49]

---

[46] Interview with senior PLA officer in charge of regional multilateral security policy in the PLA, January 1999; and interview with Canadian diplomats involved in regional multilateralism, July 2001.

[47] Interview with senior PLA officer in charge of regional multilateral security policy in the PLA, January 1999.

[48] Interview with Canadian embassy officials, Beijing, April 1996; interview with Canadian embassy official, Beijing, October 1999; Acharya 1998.

[49] Interview with Chinese intelligence analyst involved in the ARF policy process, Beijing, July 1996.

It seems this group's influence over Chinese ARF policy was helped by further institutional change in China. In January 1998, for instance, the Asia Department set up a separate division just to handle ARF and Track II diplomacy. Interestingly, as one might expect, the creation of this special regional security institution inside the MOFA also led to an emergent organizational interest in ARF diplomacy. As one MOFA interviewee implied, as the ARF agenda moves toward considering more formal arms control like CBMs, the Asia Department has had to defend its prerogatives against the Arms Control and Disarmament Department, which handles most other multilateral security diplomacy for the MOFA.[50]

There is some intriguing evidence of the commitment these individuals had in protecting the policy from domestic political critics—hence, an indication of their growing normative stake in the ARF. A senior Canadian official involved in ARF diplomacy reported that the Chinese delegates to early ARF discussions apparently did not report back to Beijing references by other delegations to the CSCE/OSCE as a possible model for the ARF. The OSCE was not just a symbol of a more intrusive, constraining regime, it was also a regime that dealt with human rights (Smith 1997:18). Downplaying this information, then, was important for preserving support or acquiescence inside China for further institutionalization of the ARF. Canadian and American diplomats also reported that sometimes China's ARF delegates would help other states frame proposals for ARF-related activities in ways that would make these more acceptable in Beijing.[51] When the ARF diplomats were under closer scrutiny from Beijing, they tended to be less conciliatory publicly. During the 1997 ISG on CBMs in Beijing, for instance, Canadian and American diplomats observed that the MOFA diplomats stuck to the proposal for observers at joint military exercises due, possibly, to the large presence of PLA observers in the meetings. The MOFA ARF diplomats had earlier suggested they might drop the position prior to the Beijing ISG due to the opposition of many ARF states, but apparently had decided against this in the face of the PLA firsthand scrutiny of China's ARF diplomacy in Beijing.[52]

The evidence suggests, then, that over time the character of Chinese obstruction or resistance in its ARF diplomacy on the ground shifted from protecting given Chinese "interests" to, in part, protecting Chinese multilateral diplomacy from potential domestic opposition. Tentatively speak-

[50] The interviewee, in response to a question about the ACD Department's interest in Asia-Pacific multilateral security institutions, remarked that the department "had a big appetite" (January 12, 1999).

[51] Interview with senior US diplomat involved in ARF policy, February 2001; and interview with Canadian diplomats involved in ARF work, July 2001.

[52] Interview with Canadian diplomat involved in the ARF policy, May 5, 1997.

ing, one could plausibly see this as diplomacy more empathetic with the institution and less empathetic with other PRC constituencies that may have had different views of the value of multilateralism.

ADDITIONAL EMPIRICAL IMPLICATIONS

Even if the new multilateralism and mutual security discourse was not entirely cheap talk, has it been irrelevant talk in the sense that it has little constraining effect on behavior? This question is central, of course, for showing whether or how socialization matters. But it is not central in showing that socialization occurs. Policy outcomes, like international social structures, should also be seen as products of the interaction of multiple actors in bureaucratic social environments where persuasion, social influence, and mimicking, not to mention strategic behavior, may be at work. This is not the time nor the place to do this kind of analysis, though, of course, it needs to be done in order to show how all the components in figure 1.1 play out. Indeed, one has to have far more information about the highly secretive Chinese foreign policy process than is generally available now.[53] But a couple of points are worth mentioning.

---

[53] There is little doubt that the PLA has played a role in constraining the evolution of China's ARF policy. This is due to at least three factors. First, the military in general is more skeptical of multilateralism, as are militaries in many other nations. The CBM proposals that China has tabled which have raised the most opposition from other states in the ARF · have tended to come from the PLA (e.g., observers at joint exercises; cessation of surveillance activities). This said, however, ARF diplomats have observed that the PLA officers most directly engaged in ARF diplomacy have been somewhat more supportive of multilateralism than other PLA officers (interview with Canadian diplomats involved in ARF diplomacy, July 2001; interview with PLA officer involved in ARF diplomacy, January 1999). Second, in the 1990s at least, policy coordination on the ARF was handled by an interagency process where the PLA appears to have had equal weight to the MOFA. ARF policy was coordinated by an Asia Pacific Security Coordinating Mechanism (*Yatai anquan xietiao* [sometimes *xieshang*] *jizhi*), nominally cochaired by a vice foreign minister and by the vice-chief of general staff in charge of PLA relations with the external world. Third, unlike the MOFA, the PLA did not have a dedicated functional office to handle or coordinate ARF policy. Rather it was handled by the Comprehensive Division of the Foreign Affairs Office of the General Staff Department. A senior officer in this office generally represented the PLA at ARF meetings. This office was understaffed, however, and could not do much original research on proposing or responding to ARF proposals. It therefore had to coordinate with other PLA institutions, such as the AMS Strategy Department, the National Defense University's Strategic Studies Institute, and the Second Department (Military Intelligence) of the General Staff Department. The process was cumbersome, and ad hoc, and other institutions grumbled that the FAO was unwilling to relinquish its control over ARF policy. The effect of these three factors was to give the PLA considerable influence on ARF policy, to slow down the PLA decision-making process on ARF issues, and to encourage a skeptical PLA eye on China's policy. This characterization of the previous role is based on interviews with a senior PLA officer involved in ARF policy, January 1999; with a senior analyst in a govern-

First, even though I am black-boxing part of the policy process (the part where the socialized protomultilateralists then interact with other constituencies and communities and their normative and causal arguments), suppose they had (and have) an influence substantially greater than zero, and suppose that the concept of mutual security had enough normative substance such that policy behavior ought to have reflected some of its elements. There ought, then, to be some empirical implications. First and foremost, one ought to see over time a greater degree of Chinese "comfort" even as the ARF became more institutionalized and developed a somewhat more intrusive agenda. That is, there ought to be things about the ARF that China later accepted that it either opposed (or counterfactually one could plausibly have expected China to oppose) just before it joined in 1994. In fact, the evidence does suggest that Chinese decision makers' changing comfort level allowed the following changes in the ARF institution and agenda.

Institutional Structure

The main innovation in the ARF structure occurred at the Second ARF in 1995. There the ARF agreed to set up two kinds of working groups to undertake intersessional discussions that could not be handled in the annual day-long foreign ministers' meeting. Canada and Australia had floated proposals at the First ARF in 1994 for Track I intersessional work, but these had been rejected at the time, primarily because of Chinese objections (Leifer 1996:32). In 1995 the proposal was put on the ARF agenda again. This time, despite some Chinese grumbling over the terminology and temporal mandate (China objected to the term "working groups" and to an indefinite time frame because both smacked of thicker institutionalization), the ARF created two intersessional meetings (ISM) (peacekeeping operations, and search and rescue) and one intersessional support group (ISG) on CBMs. In practice, these were similar types of activities. Their initial mandate was only to meet once in 1996, and the Third ARF would then decide whether or not to extend their lives, but they have been renewed regularly since then.[54] In 1998, the ARF ISG on CBMs recommended that the ARF convene two meetings of the ISG in 1999, further "regularizing" what is supposed to be

---

ment think tank involved in the ARF policy process, 1996; and with a senior analyst in a government think tank involved in Asia-Pacific security affairs, January 1999.

[54] Much of the previous paragraph came from an interview with a former senior US administration figure involved in Asia policy, Beijing, June 1996, from Smith 1997, and from an e-mail exchange with an Australian government official involved in ARF policy, January 1997.

an ad hoc process (ARF 1998a:8). The ISG and ISMs finally provided the ARF with a process for more detailed and sustained investigation of solutions to security problems in the region. This allowed states with particular expertise and/or interest to influence intersessional work (e.g., Canada and PKO). Most surprising to ARF participants, but consistent with the argument about China's increasing comfort levels, China offered at the 1996 ARF to cochair an ISG on CBMs with the Philippines in March 1997. China became a participant in the intersessional process in a way no one predicted in 1993.

Agenda

Here there have been a number of changes that were either rejected in 1993 and 1994, or were viewed as too controversial. All of these reflect some give by the Chinese. On nuclear testing, for example, despite its sensitivity to criticism on this score, the Chinese did not disrupt consensus when the 1995 and 1996 chair's statements indirectly criticized China (and France) for its nuclear testing programs (ARF 1995a:7, 1996c:3).

On preventive diplomacy (e.g., using the chair's good offices to investigate or mediate disputes, sending ARF special representatives on fact-finding missions, moral suasion, and third-party mediation) Chinese decision makers have traditionally been very uneasy with a more active ARF role because of the potential for the internationalization of core security issues such as Taiwan.[55] Nonetheless, the ARF formally took up the issue at its Track II working group on preventive diplomacy in November 1996 in Paris. Indeed, the explicit mandate of the Paris working group was to propose a list of relevant preventive diplomacy CBMs for the agenda of the ISG cohosted by China in March 1997. At the time, the main concrete recommendation to come out of the meeting was a proposal to expand the role of the ARF chair's "good offices" (ARF 1996c:2). In April 1998 at another ARF Track II working group on PD, the group agreed to recommend to the ARF SOM an "enhanced role for the ARF chair or other third parties in providing good offices in certain circumstances." This was a slight expansion in the list of whose good offices might be called upon for preventive diplomacy. Interestingly enough, China's own experience with border CBMs with the Indians and Russians was suggested as possibly relevant for PD in the rest of the region (ARF 1998b:5). These CBMs

---

[55] China was not alone. South Korea apparently was leery of giving the ARF a preventive diplomacy role if this meant that ASEAN might try to involve itself in Northeast Asian issues. Interview with prominent Canadian academic involved in Track II activities, January 1997.

were, on paper at least, "contractual" CSCE-like agreements placing specific limits on the size and movement of military forces along borders.

The issue moved from Track II to Track I at the Sixth Senior Official Meeting in May 1999, where it was agreed that at the CBM ISGs in 2000, the question of the ARF chair's good offices should be discussed in more detail. A draft paper on preventive diplomacy, prepared by Singapore, was circulated in November 1999 prior to the ISG on CBMs in Singapore in April 2000. The paper outlined the principles and scope of the concept.[56] The Singapore meeting authorized more explicit focus on an enhanced role for the chair and for "Experts/Eminent Persons" (EEP). Papers on these two topics, presented by Japan and Korea, respectively, were tabled later in 2000.[57] This finally initiated a detailed Track I debate in the ARF over PD.

The Chinese position evolved from opposition to PD to a more active, though still wary, diplomacy. The Chinese delegation officially contributed a working paper on PD in February 2000, prior to the Singapore ISG, in which it staked out key principles. These stressed that the ARF was a forum, not a mechanism "for dissolving specific conflicts" (China 2000a:2). Preventive diplomacy should use peaceful diplomatic means (by implication eschewing military operations such as PKO) to prevent armed conflict and only with the consent of all the parties directly involved. Any PD should also be based on mutual respect for sovereignty, territorial integrity and noninterference in internal affairs, and extant international law. On the basis of this paper, the Chinese suggested changes to the Singapore PD paper that would have, by and large, incorporated substantial portions directly from the Chinese working paper.

Some of these suggestions made their way into a revised Singapore paper in April 2000. Some of these changes were minor deletions of language. One, however, enshrined the principles of the UN Charter, the Five Principles of Peaceful Coexistence, and the ASEAN Treaty of Amity and Cooperation in one of the eight principles of PD, thus ensuring that the PD paper placed more emphasis on upholding sovereignty and noninterference in internal affairs. China (and other states) also beat back a Canadian effort to dilute this principle with language on respecting human rights and the rule of law. Not all of the Chinese suggestions were incorporated, in particular a proposal to delete language that, in its view, might

[56] See "ASEAN Regional Forum Concept and Principles of Preventive Diplomacy" (ASEAN Draft, November 6, 1999).

[57] "Enhanced Role of ARF Chair" (discussion of the ARF ISG on CBMs, 2000); "Co-chair's Draft Paper on the Terms of Reference for the ARF Experts/Eminent Persons (EEPs)" (October 2000).

allow PD in cases of bilateral disputes that had the potential of spreading to other states.[58]

The PD issue is, as of this writing, at a stage where states are agreeing to disagree about some of the principles and modalities of the PD. The revised Singapore paper was accepted at an ISG in Kuala Lumpur in April 2001, though as a "snapshot" of the state of discussions on PD and with acknowledgment that substantial differences remained on virtually all of its components. The fact remains, however, that the ARF appears still to be committed to developing a mechanism for more proactive interstate dispute prevention. Indeed, in 2005 it agreed to change the name of its ISG on CBMs to the ISG on CBMS and Preventive Diplomacy (ARF 2005). Chinese diplomacy on PD is no longer aimed at preventing this kind of evolution in the role of the ARF. Rather it has acquiesced to the notion of PD and instead has been essentially aimed at shielding the Taiwan issue and its own bilateral territorial disputes from ARF-based PD, and at strengthening language on sovereignty and noninterference in internal affairs.[59] The fact that the ARF took up these issues and is moving the discussion slowly forward despite China's concerns (and those of some other ASEAN states as well) suggests, again, a changing degree of Chinese comfort with the evolving agenda.[60]

On the South China Sea question, China's leaders' longtime preference has been for bilateral discussions with other claimants. They have worried that in multilateral settings China would be outvoted, its bargaining power diluted, leading to the dilution of China's sovereignty claims or, worse, the carving up of China's claims (Sun 1996:297). They tried assiduously in the past to prevent what they call the "internationalization" of the issue (Shang 1996:288–95). It was considered a conceptual break-

[58] This analysis is based on comparisons of the November 1999 version of the Singapore PD paper, the Chinese comments on this draft (China 2000b), the revised April 2000 version of the Singapore PD paper, and subsequent Chinese responses to this revised draft, submitted in January 2001 (China 2001).

[59] The language on sovereignty and noninterference was already quite strong in the original draft paper. That is to say, China was not an outlier in promoting this kind of language in ARF discourse. The outliers on PD have been the Canadians, who have pressed language that does not subject PD to consensus decision making, that includes respect for human rights, and that allows for military actions such as peacekeeping operations. Canadian diplomats have complained that many Western states have raised very few objections to the issues raised by the Chinese and others and have not been strong supporters of the Canadian position, fearing that the relatively fast-track intrusiveness of the Canadian proposals may undermine support for PD in the end. Interview with Canadian diplomats involved in ARF policy, July 2001.

[60] The MOFA-commissioned report on comprehensive security explicitly advocated strengthening the PD capabilities of the ARF, though there was no immediate concrete manifestation of this argument in China's diplomacy.

through, then, when the SCS was put on the Second ARF agenda in 1995. Even though internal reports indicated continuing fears of multilateral approaches to resolving the issue (Sun 1996:297), the Chinese delegation did not object to the chair's declaration of consensus. Nor was China willing (or able) to prevent the statement from pointedly encouraging all claimants to reaffirm their commitment to ASEAN's 1992 Declaration on the South China Sea—this after China's construction of a small naval post on the disputed Mischief Reef in February 1995. The Third ARF chair's statement in 1996 again touched on the SCS issue—this time welcoming China for its commitment in 1995 to resolve SCS disputes according to international law, but also pointedly commending the Indonesian workshop on the South China Sea for its work on conflict management issues (ARF 1996a:4). The workshop was set up in 1992 and is funded by Canada. The Chinese had been unhappy with this and had tried to pressure the Canadians to stop funding. By the Third ARF, apparently, China did not believe it was necessary to oppose consensus on this issue.

Finally, on CBMs, China was traditionally skeptical about the value of CBMs to the extent these are deemed asymmetrically intrusive. Weak states, like China, it claimed, should rightfully be less transparent than strong states like the United States. In addition, China has criticized the notion that one can transplant CSCE-type CBMs to the Asia Pacific. The First ARF was relatively silent on CBMs. However, by the Second ARF, under Brunei's leadership, the ARF had endorsed the ARF Concept Paper that laid out a timetable for implementing a wide variety of CBMs. These, all voluntary, would be taken from the Annex A list and included the following: statements on security perceptions and defense policies; enhanced military-to-military exchanges; observers at military exercises; promotion of the principles of the ASEAN TAC and the ASEAN Declaration on the South China Sea; exchanges of information on PKO activities, among others. At the ISG on CBMs in January 1996, states presented defense white papers and statements about security perceptions. But no comments on or criticisms of the content were permitted. There were complaints outside the ARF that the Chinese presentation—a white paper on arms control—was not especially detailed or credible. China followed up in 1998 with a more detailed and sophisticated white paper on defense, modeled more or less on the Japanese and British white papers.[61]

---

[61] Evidently the first white paper was called a white paper on "arms control and disarmament," even though it covered topics included in defense white papers, because top Chinese military leaders did not want it to appear that China was bowing to external pressure to produce a white paper on defense per se. Comments by senior National Defense University officer, March 1997. The drafters of the 1998 white paper explicitly examined a range of possible templates, and rejected some Southeast Asian examples for being too slim and nontransparent. Interview with Chinese military officer, 2000.

By the Third ARF, with the results in from the ISG on CBMs, the list of CBMs recommended in the chair's statement lengthened and deepened. Although defense white papers and statements on security policies were still voluntary, there were hints of an emerging template.[62] "Such papers could also cover defense contacts and exchange programmes undertaken by participants" (ARF 1996a:4). The statement also hinted that, unlike in the ISG, the content of these papers would also no longer be off limits to discussion. "Exchanges of views on the information provided in such statements and papers should be encouraged in future ARF dialogues" (ARF 1996a:5). On military observers at exercises and prior notification of military exercises, the statement noted that states were encouraged to exchange information about their ongoing observer and prior notification activities "with a view to discussing the possibilities of such measures in selected exercises" (ARF 1996a:6). The March 1997 ISG on CBMs cochaired by China and the Philippines pushed this further. The agenda for the meeting called for reaching consensus on the invitation of observers to joint military exercises and the prior notification of joint military exercises.[63] Interestingly, although ASEAN and China tend to decry the validity of a CSCE template for the Asia Pacific, the CBMs that are now either on the table in the ARF ISG or endorsed in the ARF Concept Paper Annex B (or embodied in the Five-Power Treaty) are not much different in kind from the first generation of CBMs under the CSCE (Desjardin 1996:7).

By the end of the decade, China had proposed or hosted a number of CBMs ranging from the Fourth APF Meeting of Heads of Defense Colleges, to a seminar on defense conversion cooperation, to exchanges on military law, to military exchanges on environmental protection.[64] The character of these proposals still reflected an impulse toward unilateralism—that is, they were all proposed by China without coordination with other states or without asking other states to cochair or co-organize. Moreover, some proposals were frustratingly vague. For instance,

[62] For which activists were pushing hard. See, for instance, CSCAP Memorandum No. 2, "Asia-Pacific Confidence and Security Building Measures" (n.d. ~ 1995), p. 4.

[63] The agenda focus on joint exercises had been set by China, and it ran into opposition from the United States and its allies, as they are the ones who run joint exercises. China does not. The ISG failed to reach consensus on the issue. Although this was a setback for the CBM process, a range of alternative proposals was floated for implementing other versions of this kind of CBM. The Chinese ran into heavy criticism for this proposal. Subsequently the proposal was dropped. Interview with Canadian diplomat involved in ARF policy, May 5, 1997; interview with PLA officer involved in ARF policy, January 13, 1999.

[64] See the Chairman's Summary, "The Fourth ARF Meeting of Heads of Defense Colleges" (Beijing, September 2000); "The ASEAN Regional Forum Seminar on Defense Conversion Cooperation" (Beijing, September 2000).

China proposed that a maritime information center be set up in Tianjin to provide the region with information about climate and ocean conditions, among other topics. Other delegates had a hard time trying to elicit more specific details about how such a center might be run and how the information might be disseminated (smaller states might be reluctant to rely on information controlled or provided by a great power in the region).[65] In addition, some of the CBM proposals are transparently self-serving, such as the previously discussed CBM on joint military exercises or a proposal for states to cease surveillance operations against each other. But the fact remains that this activity, while limited, was not viewed as particularly duplicitous by most ARF states, and was considered a welcome indication of a growing Chinese sophistication and nuanced commitment to multilateral measures.

Thus, change over time in the ARF was a result, in part, of the social effects of its initial form and function on one of the key actors in the institution. The mutual evolution between social environment and actor interests, understandings, and behavior is precisely what, according to constructivism, we should expect to see.

None of this means that China never got its way. Clearly, despite the changes, the institutionalization and agenda of the ARF did not move, and is not moving, as fast as some countries would like. But often the limits to Chinese comfort levels tended to show up in the language adopted, rather than in the concrete content of discussions. Although preventive diplomacy is on the agenda, the Chinese have been reluctant to support conflict resolution roles for the ARF. The 1995 ARF Concept Paper had divided the timeline for ARF development into three phases: CBM phase, development of preventive diplomacy phase, and a phase for the development of conflict resolution mechanisms. When the Second ARF chair's statement endorsed the Concept Paper, however, "conflict resolution" was changed to "the elaboration of approaches to conflict." The Chinese had objected to "conflict resolution mechanisms" because the term implied giving the ARF a mandate to intervene in conflicts that the Chinese might want to keep bilateral.[66] The slow pace of discussion on preventive diplomacy is, in part, a function of China's worries about its application to bilateral disputes, or conflicts it considers to be internal (e.g., Taiwan, ethnic separatism), though it has to be said that China is not alone in stressing the importance of the principle of sovereignty and independence in the application of PD mechanisms.[67]

[65] Interview with senior US diplomat involved in ARF policy, February 2001; and interview with Canadian diplomats involved in ARF diplomacy, July 2001.

[66] Interview with Singaporean embassy official, Beijing, April 1996; China 1996:3.

[67] Vietnam has been one of the more vocal opponents of efforts by countries such as Canada to dilute the sovereign-centric language or to include military options such as PKO

The second general point is that the multilateralism and mutual security discourse developed through involvement in the ARF and related activities may become even more constraining over time. Borrowing and modifying normative concepts are not cost-free. Alternative normative discourses can affect actor behavior in at least three ways. First, they can underscore a widening gap between discourse and practice.[68] Subjective pressure due to a perceived gap between one's new identity as embodied in the new discourse on the one hand, and identity-violating practices on the other, can lead to practices that are more consistent with the new identity (as consistency theory would suggest). Intersubjective pressure due to opprobrium generated when the new pro-group, pro-social discourse is obviously in tension with behavior can also lead to pro-group practices. In the China case, mutual security (at least its common security elements), the rejection of realpolitik *parabellum* (and incidentally a long-standing legitimate idiom in Chinese), and holding the Five-Power Treaty up as an exemplar of these principles, put China's violation of these principles in starker relief. This can have reputational costs in the contractual institutionalist sense, or legitimacy costs in domestic political processes, or opprobrium costs in terms of self-legitimation, identity consistency, and status.

Second, new normative discourses can positively sanction behavior that otherwise is unallowed or not seriously considered. For example, before China could enter international economic institutions such as the IMF and the World Bank in the early 1980s, it had to revise its long-standing support for Lenin's "inevitability of war" thesis. Early attempts in the late 1970s to do so ran into resistance.[69] Why? Because revisions would mobilize resistance from true believers, opponents of engagement with global capitalist institutions who could invoke Mao as legitimating their arguments. The "inevitability of war" discourse did not mean China was actually preparing for an inevitable global war between socialism and capitalism or within capitalism, nor that Chinese leaders necessarily believed it. But one could not be a Maoist and not believe it. Thus, one

---

in ARF documents on PD. See, for instance, "Vietnam's Views on Singapore's Discussion Paper" (January 2001); interview with Canadian diplomats involved in ARF diplomacy, July 3, 2001. India also stressed the importance of protecting sovereignty, and opposed military PD mechanisms. See its comments on the Singapore PD paper, "Preventive Diplomacy" (mimeograph, n.d.).

[68] See Keck and Sikkink's (1998) discussion of transnational activist and "accountability politics" and Kratochwil's discussion of Durkheim's analysis of morality (1984).

[69] This refers to the CCP's claim in the Maoist years that war between capitalism and communism was inevitable, and was the historical condition for the emergence of world socialism. Conversation with former senior Chinese diplomat and speechwriter for senior officials in the MOFA.

could not reject Maoism in foreign policy without rejecting the discourse. To no longer be a Maoist, to delegitimize Maoism as an obstacle to moving into institutions, required adjustment of the discourse. Revision of the discourse did not determine China's entry into the IMF and World Bank, but it permitted it, allowed action, and delegitimized Maoist opposition. In a similar fashion, mutual security and treating the Five-Power Treaty as an exemplar legitimated common security arguments internally. These also permitted proponents of these ideas to argue and defend their policies in ways that were illegitimate prior to China's entry into the ARF. That is, new discourses can legitimize or empower those who have genuinely internalized these norms to act politically, thus changing interagency balances of power and foreign policy outcomes.

Third, the logics and normative values embodied in discourses can constrain even those who use them instrumentally by narrowing the range of behavioral options that can be proposed or followed. It becomes harder for hyper-realpolitik actors to advocate unilateralist noncooperative security strategies if these fall outside of the range of behaviors acceptable in a cooperative security discourse.[70]

This does not guarantee the discourse will win out over realpolitik discourses and practices, and it does not mean there have not been other considerations behind the ARF policy process—image, rivalry with the United States, the mimicking of unfamiliar but standard diplomatic practices, among others. Nor does it mean there are no multilateral actions designed to enhance China's relative power in some way while diminishing the power of others. But it does suggest that by the late 1990s, there was now one more, legitimate, rival set of arguments that were normatively based on elements of common security and that committed China, perhaps unintended, to support more intrusive multilateral security measures that it would have opposed (indeed did oppose) prior to its entry into the ARF and associated regional security dialogues.

CONCLUSION

My tentative findings about the socialization of at least a portion of those Chinese officials exposed to the ARF have at least four objections. The first is that exogenous material side payments or threats may have been responsible for China's more constructive, comfortable approach to the ARF. This is fairly easy to handle: the ARF has no capacity to put any

---

[70] This is a point made in Evangelista's study of transnational effects on Soviet arms control policy. See Evangelista 1999.

such exogenous sanctions in place. Nor, as far as I am aware, did any other states unilaterally link any such sanctions to China's participation.

The second possibility is that changes in the nature of China's participation in the ARF over the 1990s reflected a deceptive effort to exploit cooperation from other states. One would expect this from a realpolitik actor with prisoners' dilemma preferences. However, if this were all only deception, we would expect that as the ARF handled increasingly intrusive and sensitive issues that could impinge on core interests or relative power issues, the PRC should balk at further change in the institution and agenda. In other words, the comfort level should be negatively related to the level of institutionalization and intrusiveness of the agenda. Yet, change in the ARF and change in comfort levels (at least of those participating in the ARF) were positively related over time. That the ARF moved from having a very innocuous agenda to discussions of more intrusive CBMs and preventive diplomacy mechanisms is evidence of this. Moreover, that eventually there were Chinese protomultilateralists who held up the Five-Power CBM Treaty as a potential model for East Asia suggests that prisoners' dilemma preferences were no longer uniform across the agents in the Chinese policy process.

The third objection is that China's participation and the overall rise in its multilateralist diplomacy in East Asia was and still is mainly aimed at countering US power and influence in the region. As Thomas Christensen argues, China's multilateralism is in part a (smart) reaction to a tougher US policy toward China in the second half of the 1990s (Christensen 2006:117–21). In other words, it is primarily a strategic response to US power, not a product of socialization processes. Or, at best, a tougher US policy was a precondition for the rise of multilateralist arguments inside the policy process. This argument has two problems. The first is, as I noted earlier, that some of the strongest advocates of the multilateralism discourse have tended not to be the same people or institutions as the more hard-line opponents of US military power in the region. Moreover, even if China's top decision makers (and their military advisers) have argued for using the ARF and other institutions as tools for constraining US military power, this does not mean that those exposed to the socialization processes in these institutions developed strategic or instrumental arguments in favor of multilateralism only.[71]

The second problem, however, is that both the shift toward a tough US policy and Chinese perceptions of this kind of shift occurred *after* the

---

[71] Socialization is about explaining how individuals change (or not), not about how the ship of state is reoriented (or not). Obviously, I believe the former is related to the latter, but to return to a point I made at the beginning of the book, the constructivist literature first has to show that the former does occur.

development of protomultilateralist arguments. Despite the 1996 Taiwan crisis, US China policy was even more clearly identified with an accommodationist constructive engagement from 1996 to 1999 than it had been prior. This period saw successful summit meetings between Jiang Zemin and William Clinton in 1997 and 1998. It also included more concrete US statements that US policy welcomed the emergence of a prosperous and stronger China. Finally, it also included much clearer US statements that the United States did not support Taiwan independence (Suettinger 2003:262, 284, 306, 348).

More important than US policy, however, were Chinese perceptions of this policy. In general, contemporaneous and subsequent analyses of US strategy toward China emphasize these positive developments. The turning point was in 1999, with the emergence of severe domestic criticisms of US engagement policy, the US bombing of the Chinese embassy in Belgrade, and increased tensions across the Taiwan Strait, among other events, which led to a serious downturn in the tenor of the relationship. Chinese analysts tend to define 1999 as the start of a more hostile US policy aimed, in their view, at a more vigorous containment of Chinese power in Asia (Li 2003:80–81, 90; Yan 2004:254–55, 257; Wu 2006:112–18; Fang 2003:299–300). There is no doubt that subsequently the proponents of a more proactive Chinese counter-containment strategy viewed multilateral diplomacy as one tool against US power, and particularly against closer US-Japan relations. But the origins of multilateralist ideas and their initial injection into the Chinese policy process preceded this perceived turning point in 1999.

The fourth objection is that China's changing comfort level is, in fact, a function of new information about the benign nature of the ARF. Beliefs about, and hence strategies toward, the ARF have changed, but preferences have not. This argument has a number of related components. The ARF has proven to be largely irrelevant to core security interests; most of the other participants have used the ARF to send assurance signals that it will not become an institution that constrains Chinese relative power; thus, the Chinese have discovered over time that it is relatively costless to participate in the ARF. There has been no real change in China's realpolitik, prisoners' dilemma preferences. At most, therefore, more cooperative behavior inside the ARF might serve short- to medium-term reputational purposes (in Kreps and Keohane's sense of reputation).

This last objection is the most serious and credible one. But I think it, too, has its problems. First, it is unlikely that a short-term concern for reputational benefits applicable to other specific opportunities for exchange was the driving force behind China's participation in the ARF. No other states, particularly those that could provide the most concrete costs or benefits to China—the United States and Japan, for example—were linking ARF participation to other areas of cooperation such as trade. Indeed, the US government and Congress have been somewhat ambivalent about the value of the ARF. If the argument is that a more amorphous, long-term, instrumental notion of reputation mattered—that some material cost may be incurred, or some material benefit may be acquired somewhere in the indeterminate future from some other player(s)—then the reputational argument becomes virtually unfalsifiable.

Second, at the time China joined the ARF, it had not yet developed the overt strategy of improving economic and political relations with ASEAN that emerged in the late 1990s and into the early 2000s. This strategy was not formalized until the Sixteenth Party Congress in 2002, but the principles of such a strategy emerged around 1997 and the Asian financial crisis (Glosny 2007). There was no strong reason to believe that in 1994–1995, had China remained outside of the ARF, its economic relations with ASEAN would have been at risk.[72]

Third, from a theoretical perspective, the "new information" explanation at the heart of material reputational arguments is problematic because it underestimates the uncertain status of "new information." From the constructivist perspective, information is interpreted, and the same information can be interpreted differently in the context of similar institutional rules and structures. Empirically, we know that the same information will be interpreted differently depending on whether it comes from "people like us" (the information is more authoritative and persuasive) or comes from a devalued "other" (Kuklinski and Hurley 1996:127). Economic transactions—for instance, bargaining over price where people exchange information relating to their preferences and their "bottom line"—vary dramatically depending on whether or not the parties are friends (friends offer higher payments and lower prices than strangers) (Halpern 1997:835–68). Social context is an important variable in how well information reduces uncertainty in a transaction, and in which direction this uncertainty is reduced (e.g., clarifying the other as a friend or an adversary).

Thus, if all of China's ARF decision makers were realpolitik opportunists (that is, if they believed they were playing a prisoners' dilemma game in some form in East Asia) and if this basic worldview were fixed, then new information would be interpreted through these lenses. As I noted earlier, there is solid evidence from China's pronouncements and the interpretations of these by other states in the region that China initially looked upon multilateral institutions with a great deal of skepticism, and that its

---

[72] This, of course, does not mean that reputation is irrelevant for explaining the evolution of China's overall strategy toward ASEAN in recent years. See Glosny's (2007) detailed account of this strategy since 1997.

basic preferences were prisoners' dilemma ones. It is probably true that the initial signals provided by an underinstitutionalized and nonintrusive ARF in 1994 could have been interpreted as nonthreatening by realpoliticians.[73] But as the ARF agenda and institution evolved, the signals should have been interpreted with increasing alarm by realpoliticians, since the trend lines were toward issues and procedures that could place some limits on security policy options. Yet, for a small group of China's ARF policy makers, these signals were reinterpreted in less, not more, threatening ways. The fact that this group of policy makers and analysts eventually believed this information *was* reassuring while still expressing concern that others in the policy process (with more realpolitik views of multilateralism) might see this information as less reassuring suggests that the information provided by the ARF was often not unproblematically reassuring. Protomultilateralists did not enter the ARF with this more sanguine interpretation of "new information." Rather, this interpretation of the "new information" came from socialization inside the ARF.

I am the first to admit that the study of persuasion requires much additional fine-tuning of definitions, conditions, hypotheses, and analytical procedures. But if my general argument is plausible, then a focus on institutions as social environments raises important implications for institutional design. Typically, contractual institutions argue that the efficient institutional designs depend on the type of cooperation problem—e.g., a prisoners' dilemma–type problem requires information (monitoring) and sanctions; an assurance problem primarily requires reassurance information (Martin 1993). The flip side is that one can identify inefficient institutional designs for particular cooperation problems as well (e.g., an institution that is designed only to provide assurance information but has no monitoring or sanctioning capacity would be inefficient for resolving prisoners' dilemma–type problems). Additionally, Downs, Rocke, and Barsoom argue that so-called transformational institutions (inclusive institutions that bring genuine cooperators and potential defectors together in an effort to instill norms and obligations in the latter) are less likely to provide efficient solutions than a strategic construction approach. This latter approach to institutional design stresses exclusive memberships of true believers where decisions are made on the basis of supermajority rules. The gradual inclusion of potential defectors under these conditions ensures that the preferences of

---

[73] Though even this is problematic from an institutionalist perspective. As realpoliticians, the Chinese should have been especially suspicious of an institution that activist states such as Canada, Australia, and to some extent the United States supported. The information that their involvement should have supplied, for realpolitician skeptics, was precisely that the ARF was a potentially constraining institution.

the true believers predominate as the institution evolves. Their critique of the transformational approach rests explicitly on skepticism that the preferences of potential defectors can change through social interaction (Downs, Rocke, and Barsoom 1997, 1998).

It is not clear whether this skepticism rests on empirical evidence about the absence of state-level socialization, or simply, as I noted before, on the methodological difficulties of assuming and then trying to observe preference change.[74] In any event, *if* one relaxes the assumption about no preference change (particularly if, as I tried to argue here, this is based on theory and evidence of socialization in institutional environments), then one is forced to revisit the contractual institutionalists' notions of efficient institutional design. An institution that appears inefficient to contractual institutionalists (e.g., assurance institution for a prisoners' dilemma problem) may actually be efficient for the cooperation problem at hand. If, say, a player (or subactors in a policy process) with prisoners' dilemma preferences can be socialized to internalize assurance game preferences through interaction in a social environment with no material sanctioning or side payments, then "assurance" institutions may work in prisoners' dilemma–like cooperation problems. An efficient institution might then be reconceived as the *design* and *process* most likely to produce the most efficient environments for socializing actors in alternative definitions of interest.

---

[74] Indeed, the dependent variable in Downs, Rocke, and Barsoom (1997, 1998) is not the interests, preferences, or behavior of any individual state (say, the potentially worst or most important defector). Thus, it is possible that the (admittedly lower) observed level of cooperation (as they operationalize it) may still be a function of socialization. It is also possible, counterfactually, that the depth of cooperation might have been even shallower had there been no socialization effect in transformational institutions. Too much is blackboxed in their empirical tests, so they are unable to show one way or the other whether there are any socialization effects in either transformational or strategically and sequentially constructed institutions.

Chapter 5

Conclusions

THIS BOOK has made two sets of claims, a direct one and an indirect one. The direct set of claims is as follows: Chinese leaders adopted more cooperative and potentially self-constraining commitments to security institutions between 1980 and 2000 (mainly in the 1990s); much of this took place in an era of unipolarity; it took place in some cases without obvious material side payments and threats of sanctions; and these commitments were undertaken by a leadership that had inherited a hard realpolitik ideology from its Maoist period. Thus, standard structural balancing and contractual institutionalist arguments do not provide especially useful explanations of these examples of cooperation in China's foreign policy.

Rather, a more accurate and precise explanation requires looking at the environments inside security institutions that encouraged either mimicking, persuasion, or social influence (or some mix of all three). These microprocesses can all be subsumed under the concept of socialization whereby pro-group behavior is a function of the social interaction of humans.

In the case of mimicking, it appears that much of the change in the discursive practices of China's small arms control community, beginning in the early 1980s, was in part an effort to mimic the diplomatic language, concepts, and routines of the mainstream international arms control regime. This process encouraged, as well, the gradual development of a more sophisticated and interconnected arms control policy community in China.

As for social influence, it appears that a sensitivity to international image, hence a desire to maximize the normatively accepted markers of a high-status actor, combined with the institutional environment conducive to the attribution of such status, encouraged Chinese leaders to accept limits on their nuclear weapons program by signing on to the CTBT, among other arms control commitments.

In terms of persuasion, the participation of Chinese diplomats, scholars, and analysts in the ASEAN Regional Forum and related Track II security dialogues from the early to mid-1990s on appears to have helped create a constituency of protomultilateralists who internalized a view of security that placed less stress on unilateral security and more on cooperative security strategies.

I have focused on separate processes in separate cases in order to highlight each process individually. But this does not mean these processes cannot interact or be present in the same case. That is, these processes are not incompatible or incommensurate. There is evidence that social influence works to some degree in the ARF (Acharya 2001:182).[1] Mimicking also may be a prerequisite for the other two socialization processes. For example, the actor has to be in the institution and using the same discursive practices as authoritative others before s/he can be persuaded.

Hopefully, these arguments about socialization contribute to a growing body of theoretically informed empirical work that crosses geographical boundaries to look at a long-neglected source of actor motivations and preferences in IR, namely the social context in which agents find themselves when they are supposed to be representing or constructing the interests of a national government. Such arguments about motivation do not replace or even necessarily subsume more mainstream assumptions about motivation—material power preservation or maximization—in IR theory. But they do suggest that explanatory tests that ignore social context and social motivations in political behavior are incomplete. That is, the IR field needs to consider including sociological and social psychological arguments about actor motivation and motivational change in the standard lists of independent variables used for explaining cooperation and conflict. Socialization arguments also underscore the risks of starting one's analysis by assuming fixed preferences. Such an assumption not only rules out plausible alternative motives for human political behavior, but also hinders thinking about motivation, behavior, and social context in an endogenous, interactive fashion.

The indirect claim in the book is that this test of change in security policies provides more evidence that realpolitik preferences and behavior are fundamentally ideational in origins. Since China engaged in more cooperative behavior even as American relative power increased after 1991, it is hard to explain these particular changes from harder to softer realpolitik (or to protomultilateralist) policies as epiphenomenal to material structural conditions. This book was set up as an initial critical test of two basic arguments in IR—that realpolitik preferences and practices are a function of material structural conditions, and that realpolitik preferences and practices are a function of realpolitik norms. If the former

---

[1] Interview with senior US government official involved in ARF meetings, February 2001; interview with Canadian government officials involved in ARF meetings, July 2001.

holds, then one should not have expected to see the effects of socialization that one saw in the cases I have examined here. If the latter holds, then one should expect to see socialization effects in non-realpolitik security and environments. This book (and my previous one) tries to lay out why realpolitik ideology and practice as social facts appear to be empirically divorced from material structures, since the former two variables change in intensity and geographical distribution in ways that are independent of the latter variable.

Obviously, I believe the latter argument has won this particular test. I think the empirical evidence is good enough in the IR field such that theorizing will be unnecessarily handicapped if it does not seriously consider a new research program involving the study of the ideational sources of both realpolitik *and* non-realpolitik practice. The next step is to develop arguments about where realpolitik ideology and practice come from, if not from anarchy, the assumed nature of state interests, or material power distributions. This is not the place to lay out a theory of realpolitik norms (which logically must also account for the emergence of cooperative norms). But I think a good starting point is the notion of identity difference, first systematized in social identity theory. At its simplest, SIT suggests that the degree of perceived difference between the fundamental traits of an in-group and its out-group is a necessary condition for explaining how conflictual or cooperative the in-group will be toward the out-group. The more homogeneous and valued the in-group believes its traits to be, and the greater the perceived difference between these valued traits and the devalued traits of the out-group are, the more primed the in-group is for engaging in conflictual behavior. Thus, the degree of perceived identity difference should be related to the three dimensions of an in-group's strategic culture: the degree to which the external environment is seen as naturally conflictual and dangerous; the degree to which relations with the out-group are seen as zero-sum; and the efficacy of coercive strategies. The greater the perceived identity difference, the more the environment is viewed as conflictual, the more the out-group is viewed as threatening, and the more that realpolitik strategies are considered effective. Conversely, the smaller the perceived identity differences, the more the external environment is seen as cooperative, the less the out-group is perceived as fundamentally threatening, and the more efficacious are cooperative strategies. Most critically, variation in identity difference should be independent of anarchy. This is easy to show if anarchy is a constant and one finds variation in identity differences between an in-group and various other out-groups across time or space. Moreover, variation in identity difference should be independent of variation in material distributions of power.

Considerable experimental evidence, and some empirical evidence from ethnic conflict in the United States, suggests that perceived identity difference can create conflicts of interest where none existed before (that is, SIT trumps real conflict theory);[2] there is far less systematic evidence about how identity difference affects attitudes toward international relations.[3] At the moment, the only evidence comes from a small number of experiments and surveys of populations, rather than of foreign policy elites. Still, this evidence seems compelling. The most sophisticated work on the ideational sources of realpolitik comes from David Rousseau. In some of his early experiments and surveys (2002), for instance, he found that those with harder realpolitik worldviews were more likely to worry about relative gains than those with less realpolitik worldviews. In his most recent book (2006), he traces sources of these worldviews to perceived identity difference. Using a mix of experimental, survey, and agent-based modeling methods, he finds that there is a positive relationship between perceived identity difference, realpolitik values, and sensitivity to relative gains within individuals. This relationship is independent of the distribution of power or other material sources of so-called real conflict. The lower the perceptions of identity difference that individuals hold about another country, the lower the threat perception of that country, even when the balance of power is disadvantageous. Rousseau also takes the first steps to show the domestic political and media priming conditions under which realpolitik norms and practices might diffuse in ways that are independent of material structural variables.

Data from China are consistent with Rousseau's findings. My analysis of the 2000–2004 Beijing Area Study data suggests that, among Chinese respondents, greater perceived identity difference (in this case, with Americans), is related interalia to lower levels of amity toward other

---

[2] On social identity theory, see Tajfel and Turner 2001; Turner 1987; and Turner 1999. On ethnic identity discourse and the construction of conflict, see Romer et al. 1997. Sniderman, Hagendoorn, and Prior (2004) discovered that identity difference (captured in simple questions about national pride and perceived cultural threat from immigrants) is a stronger predictor of harsh anti-immigrant sentiments than perceived or real material (economic) threats from immigrants.

[3] The first to apply SIT to explaining realpolitik practice was Jon Mercer (1995). His use of the theory, however, was to provide a psychological basis—a hardwiring in people and groups—for structural realist assumptions about anarchy and competition. Yet arguably, SIT and structural realism are ontologically incommensurate due to the fundamental materialism of the latter. SIT suggests that perceptions of identity difference vary independently of the material structures within which actors and their groups find themselves. Moreover, Mercer anthropomorphized the state, a problem when applying psychological theories, and a move that cannot account for variation across time and space in the degree of identity difference that in-groups perceive. Still, his was a pioneering examination of how identity difference is related to realpolitik practice via realpolitik worldviews.

countries (in this case, the United States),[4] higher levels of nationalism,[5] support for increasing military spending,[6] and opposition to diverting military spending to social welfare.[7] In some years, those who supported mercantilist definitions of independence also expressed higher levels of identity difference than those who held definitions that stressed mutual vulnerability and mutual gain.[8] The identity difference can even be

[4] As noted in chapter 3, the BAS is an annual stratified random sample survey of Beijing residents' views on socioeconomic issues. It ran from 1995 to 2005. The sample size ranges from around six hundred to seven hundred respondents. In 1998 I was asked by the organizers of the survey if I wished to piggyback various questions about attitudes toward international relations on the main survey. This opportunity was, as they say, a no-brainer, as there had been and still is no non-governmental time series data on Chinese citizens' views of international relations. From 2000 on we added questions that tapped into perceptions of identity difference. These questions asked respondents to place Chinese, American, and Japanese people on a 1–7 scale anchored by bipolar opposite adjectives (a technique called semantic differential analysis) used to describe self and other. These anchoring adjectives included peaceful–warlike, civilized–uncivilized, modest–arrogant, moral–immoral, and sincere–hypocritical. Not all years included all adjectives. The identity difference score was the semantic differential score for Americans minus the score for Chinese. Identity difference ranged from 6 (Americans at the opposite and negative end of the spectrum of traits from Chinese) to –6 (Americans at the opposite and positive end of the spectrum of traits). In general, identity difference is negatively related to levels of amity toward the United States, as measured on a 1–100 feeling thermometer where 1–49 degrees represented cool feelings, 50 neutral feelings, and 51–100 warm feelings. In 2004, for instance, identity difference and amity are negatively correlated (pearson $r = -.25$, $P = 0.01$ two-tailed).

[5] The BAS asked a number of questions to tap into nationalism, including whether the respondent agreed with the statement that people should support their government even if it is wrong, with the statement that China is a better country to live in than most others, and with the statement that they would prefer to be a citizen of the PRC than of any other country. In 2002, 2003, and 2004 the analysis of variance (ANOVA) showed that those who agreed with these questions (with the exception of the 2004 question about PRC citizenship) had significantly higher perceptions of identity difference than those who disagreed.

[6] Respondents were asked whether they believed military spending should be increased, maintained at current rates, or reduced. In 2001, 2002, and 2003 the ANOVA showed that those who supported an increase in military spending perceived a statistically significant greater identity difference between Chinese and Americans than those who did not support an increase.

[7] In BAS 2004 a question was added to get at how respondents thought about the trade-off between military spending and spending on improved social welfare. The ANOVA showed that those who did not support diverting military spending to social welfare perceived a significantly greater degree of identity difference than those who supported such transfers.

[8] From 2000 to 2003 respondents were asked which definition of economic interdependence was closer to their understanding of the term: the struggle with other states over markets and resources increasingly affects a country's economic prosperity (mercantilist definition); countries are increasingly supplying products and services for other countries (a simple exchange definition); and a country's economic prosperity is increasingly dependent on the economic prosperity of other countries (a mutual vulnerability and benefit defini-

implied rather than explicit. Perceptions of China's uniqueness as a major power were also related to tougher foreign policy attitudes.[9] For example, in the 2003 and 2004 BAS, those who supported increasing military spending perceived far greater identity difference between China as a major power and the traits of a typical major power than those who opposed an increase in military spending. In both years, there was also a strong negative relationship between perceived uniqueness and amity toward the United States. The more unique one felt China's identity as a major power to be, the less amity one expressed toward the United States.[10]

In short, the BAS data suggest that identity difference is positively related to realpolitik policy positions. The causal directions of some of these relationships may not be especially clear. Does identity difference predict nationalism or vice versa? Generally, however, the literature (Hurwitz and Peffley 1997) and logic suggest that broader and more abstract attitudes, such as perceived identity difference, undergird more specific policy preferences.

This cross-national evidence means, then, that the dynamics of identity construction and differentiation—a process that cuts across traditional structural, state, and individual levels of analysis (Rousseau 2006:9)—may be critical to understanding why some interstate relationships are

---

tion). In 2000, 2001, and 2002 the Tukey HSD statistic indicated that the difference in level of perceived identity difference for those who gave the mercantilist definition and those who gave the mutual vulnerability definition was statistically significant at or below the 0.1 level. That is, those who supported the first definition expressed the greatest level of identity difference, whereas those who supported the last definition expressed the lowest level.

[9] In addition to asking respondents where they would place Chinese people, Americans, and Japanese along scales anchored by bipolar opposite adjectives, the BAS also asked respondents where they would place China as a major power and typical major powers on similar scales. The degree to which respondents saw China as unique among major powers was simply the difference in scores assigned to major powers in general and those assigned to China.

[10] The fact that in the questions about the identity traits of people vis-à-vis other people and the state vis-à-vis generic major powers the vast majority of respondents positioned Chinese and China at the normatively positive end of these scales has some interesting implications for how identity might affect behavior. The short of it is that there are two basic theories that link identity to action: role theory and social identity theory. The former puts far more weight on the content of identity—the constraining effects of the traits that groups believe they actually have. The latter suggests the actual content of identity may be less relevant than the perceived difference with out-groups. That respondents put China and the Chinese at the peaceful end of the semantic differential scale, for instance, does not seem related to preferences that one might associate with peacefulness. Rather it is the degree to which respondents see Chinese and China as different that is more strongly associated with policy preferences. The BAS data, then, appear more consistent with SIT than with role theory.

more conflictual than others, and why international and regional systems can vary from predominantly realpolitik to predominantly non-realpolitik strategic cultures and basic practices.

Turning from theory, what do these cases have to say about Chinese foreign policy? Here I would like to keep my claims modest (unlike earlier!). First, as I noted at the start, I think this book adds to our growing but still limited understanding of China's involvement in international institutions and normative regimes. Except for a handful of research, most work on Chinese foreign policy has looked at China's relationships with major powers or regional powers. These relationships are critical parts of Chinese foreign policy, but particularly from the 1980s through to the present, these are increasingly limited parts. Samuel Kim was the first to alert the field to the importance of examining China's behavior in international institutions. His work has shown that China's activities inside institutions provide critical insights into Beijing's worldview(s). Moreover, these activities provide evidence about empirical behavior to test hunches about how this worldview(s) may actually affect what China does on the ground.

This study, then, follows on from the work of Samuel Kim, Harold Jacobson and Michael Oksenberg, and others. But unlike these studies, it focuses primarily on the so-called hard case of security institutions, and applies analytical tools from the sociological and social psychological turn in international relations theory. The book highlights two things on which the foreign policy field in China has generally not focused: (1) the processes by which China's foreign policy's ideational base and hence its interests may change (persuasion, for instance); and (2) the interests that are hard to observe but appear critical for Chinese leaders when they calculate trade-offs from cooperation (status and image). As more historical materials about Chinese foreign policy come to light, these processes can be tested on critical changes in Chinese foreign policy in the past. For instance, one could imagine applying the social influence argument to explanations for the revolutionary pro–third world positions taken in Chinese foreign policy in the late 1950s through the 1970s. In this period, given Mao's changing conception of Chinese identity from that of a (junior) partner in a socialist camp to a revolutionary developing country, the new source of status markers would be a community of radical third world states.

Of course, I have looked at only a relatively small part of the totality of change in China's diplomacy in the critical decades of the 1980s and 1990s. Can the cases examined in this book say anything more general about other trends in China's foreign policy history? Is the socially rooted cooperation examined here representative of China's cooperation in other areas?

Obviously, this is a complicated question worthy of another book-length study in itself. But it is worth underscoring precisely how different the official discourses and behavior in Chinese foreign policy today are compared to earlier periods in PRC foreign policy. There have been some obvious changes over time in how Chinese interests are characterized and how international relations are understood. Chinese discourses in the 1950s exhibited a mix of formal sovereign-centric diplomatic principles (particularly in the first half of the 1950s) with the more incendiary language of anti-imperialism and Communist world revolution. The Five Principles of Peaceful Coexistence, developed with India in the early 1950s, stressed norms of interstate relations that, if applied, would minimize conflicts among independent, sovereign states. Although revolutionary rhetoric was always present, in the latter half of the 1950s, this discourse became more prominent as Chinese domestic politics radicalized under Mao and as ideological conflicts with the Soviet Union and the United States sharpened.

The radicalized discourse about world revolution, about the mobilization of an anti-imperialist and anti-Soviet third world, and so on, peaked in the 1960s as China staked out a dual adversary position against the superpowers and as Mao implemented his ideas for internal continuous revolution. China even toyed with the notion of setting up alternative international institutions for radicalized and revolutionary states.

By the mid-1970s, this discourse shifted to more overtly anti-Soviet themes—calling essentially on capitalist states and true socialist and revolutionary states to participate in an anti-Soviet united front. By the late 1970s, Chinese strategists were calling for a quasi alliance with the United States to oppose Soviet expansionism. China denounced international institutions and the diplomatic behavior of individual states, regardless of their ideology, if China's leaders judged that these actors were appeasing Soviet power.

By the mid-1980s as the perceived Soviet threat receded, and as China's own internal development strategy began to embrace market development policies, Chinese diplomacy had all but abandoned Marxist-Leninist, anti-Soviet, and radical third world discourses. Indeed, briefly, in the Zhao Ziyang years, China endorsed developmentalist and multilateralist discourses centering on the importance of promoting international institutions that served the economic development and security interests of the developing world.

In the first few years after the violent suppression of the student and worker movement in 1989, diplomatic discourse stressed even more starkly absolutist concepts of sovereignty. Although this discourse had its reactionary content—it was designed to justify variously the continued repression of political dissent and the maintenance of Han control over ethnic minorities, and to limit intrusive international commitments that might constrain China's relative power—it is also a very conservative rhetoric, designed to defend traditional notions of sovereignty. International relations were characterized again in overtly realpolitik terms—the struggle for power and wealth among national state units in an anarchical system, hardly a call for a revolutionary new type of world politics. Indeed, unlike the 1950s through the early 1980s, Chinese official discourse explicitly calls for noninterference in the internal affairs of virtually all states. It is an ideology of laissez-faire when it comes to how states should organize themselves domestically, in contrast to the call for internal revolution and for the overthrow of the major power–dominated international system in the Maoist era.

From the mid-1990s on, this hyper-sovereigntist discourse has been diluted by a couple of new themes: globalization[11] and multilateralism (see fig. 5.1). Chinese official discourse, reluctantly perhaps, has endorsed the notion that global economic and information integration is to be embraced because of its positive impact on national economic development, even if globalization challenges sovereignty in these select areas. In addition, as noted in the previous chapter, there is a new identity discourse that describes China as a "responsible major power," a key characteristic of which is to participate in and uphold commitments to status quo international economic and security institutions.

In behavioral terms in the 1950s, as a function of shared ideological identity and perceived external threat, the Chinese regime's cooperative interstate relations were centered mainly on states in the Soviet bloc and a small number of non-aligned developing states. Relations with capitalist major powers were severely constrained. As part of its perceived role as a revolutionary actor in international relations, China supported revolutionary movements trying to overthrow established governments and/or colonial regimes throughout the developing world.[12] The main issues in Chinese relations with the Soviet bloc revolved around two issues: the virtually wholesale importation of Soviet forms of economic development, educational, political, and military institutions and ideas; and the question of security cooperation to deter the United States and the KMT from undermining the regime. Trade and economic relationships were to be a new form of non-exploitative managed trade, though in practice the relationship was a hierarchical and dependent one, symbolized by the

[11] See Deng and Moore 2004. On the mellowing of China's hyper-sovereigntist discourse, see Carlson 2005.

[12] Though as Peter Van Ness has shown, in general the decision rule as to whether to support a revolutionary movement was often whether or not the target state supported the foreign policy interests of the Chinese state (Van Ness 1970).

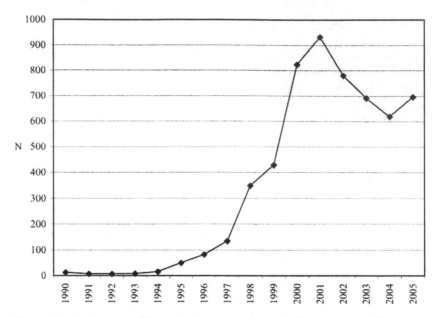

Figure 5.1. Frequency of *People's Daily* articles with the term "globalization" (*quanqiuhua*) in the text. Source: *People's Daily*, on-line full-text version.

secret protocols in the Sino-Soviet alliance of 1950 that gave the USSR extraterritorial economic privileges in China (Goncharov, Lewis, and Xue 1995). In the wake of the disastrous Great Leap Forward, when millions died from economic incompetence, fanaticism, and famine, China experimented with market-style trade relations with a limited number of capitalist states. In the mid-1960s, however, at the height of the Cultural Revolution, China's foreign relations essentially broke down, commandeered for a time by revolutionary diplomats, alienating most of China's few remaining third world friends, and leading to China's almost complete political isolation by the late 1960s.[13] In some ways, this reflected the fact that there was no autonomous foreign policy organization that could sustain policy and decision making. The MOFA bureaucracy was small. There was no international economic policy bureaucracy to speak of. Policy was in the hands of Mao, for the most part. When Mao turned his attention to internal revolution, foreign policy, in essence, ceased to exist.

The anti-Soviet united front diplomacy of the mid- and late 1970s necessitated establishing a new range of diplomatic relationships with capi-

---

[13] During this period, however, China continued its limited foreign trade, and there was no dramatic decline in the value of its foreign trade.

talist countries and reactionary anti-Soviet regimes in the developing world. China's diplomatic space increased dramatically with a spate of diplomatic recognitions with a wide range of states, and with China's entry into the UN in the early 1970s. Nonetheless, the key themes of diplomacy with these states were how to encourage them to take a harder anti-Soviet line. China courted conservative anti-Communist politicians from around the world, encouraging NATO to boost its military spending, supporting anti-Soviet military movements in developing countries even if this meant coordinating with reactionary regimes such as South Africa. In international institutions China took every opportunity to press for anti-Soviet propaganda victories.

By the early 1980s, however, with domestic economic development the key policy problem for the regime, the range and scope of Chinese diplomacy broadened considerably. China entered key international economic institutions such as the World Bank and the IMF. It joined, for the first time, the UN arms control and disarmament negotiation process in the CD in Geneva. The tangible flows of everyday diplomacy—scientific exchanges, cultural and educational exchanges, trade delegations, trade flows, arms control, and security dialogues—all deepened and widened from the 1980s on. As I noted earlier, China's participation rates in international institutions increased dramatically over the 1980s and into the 1990s, reaching levels close to those of major industrial powers. In the 1950s, China fought against the UN and opposed PKO. By the 1990s, China had endorsed the role of UN PKO and had, even if tentatively, begun to participate in PKO in the Middle East and Cambodia (Fravel 1996). In the 1950s through the 1970s, China was an avowed socialist state. Beginning in the early 1980s and culminating with its entry into the World Trade Organization in the early twenty-first century, China joined all the major global capitalist institutions. In addition, largely for economic reasons, the diversity of China's bilateral relations increased over the 1980s and 1990s. China normalized relations with some Southeast Asian states that in the past had been targets of China's assistance to antigovernment revolutionary forces. It normalized relations with Israel—despite China's longtime rhetorical support for Palestine liberation. It normalized relations with hard-line anti-Communist regimes such as Saudi Arabia, South Korea, and Singapore.

In sum, it is not a stretch to characterize Chinese diplomacy since the 1990s as being, in relative terms, more status quo-oriented than at any period since 1949. That is, China has joined most international institutions that regulate interstate behavior; inside the institutions, it generally has not tried to undermine the functioning or purposes of these institutions; and increasingly, Chinese foreign policy accepts that for the foreseeable future it will have to accommodate US hegemony, or when it must be challenged, it will do so mainly inside international institutions.[14]

As I have suggested throughout this book, much of this reorientation in more status quo directions has occurred in the 1990s, a period of material unipolarity when China's relative power vis-à-vis the material hegemon had not obviously improved. It also occurred under a political system—a Marxist-Leninist dictatorship—whose main institutional features had not changed all that dramatically from the pre-1990s periods. This kind of foreign policy reorientation in the absence of major changes in the institutions of domestic power is indeed rare.[15] To a large degree, many of the changes in this orientation were initiated by political leaders who were also leaders (if on and off) in the more autarchic and isolationist periods. And in some crucial cases, it has occurred in the absence of concrete material rewards or punishments. This reorientation, therefore, should be puzzling to mainstream IR theory and practice.

Can one attribute some or all of these macro-historical changes in Chinese foreign policy to the microprocesses that I have outlined in this book? This should be the topic of another book. It is, though, an empirical question. Can one identify the institutions (either international or domestic) that one could hypothesize helped socialize influential individuals and small groups in new definitions of interest and foreign policy tools? Can one identify the policy processes that allowed these new definitions to impact China's external behavior? Can one also identify the institutions (mainly domestic) that one could hypothesize helped socialize agents in attitudes that might be resistant to persuasion and social influence inside institutions? Can one then hypothesize about the kind of hybridity and/or level of resistance that these competing socialization processes produced in the Chinese foreign policy process? These questions, in a sense, constitute a research agenda for testing the "sociological turn" not just on explanations of Chinese foreign policy but also on the policies of any country.

Of course, it is likely that if one looks at all normative regimes in more detail than I have here (free trade, non-proliferation, human rights, environment, etc.), one will find evidence both for changed interests through socialization and for the pursuit of interests that have been un-

[14] Needless to say, assessing whether a state's foreign policy has a predominantly "status quo" versus "revisionist" orientation is a complicated question, one that mainstream IR theorizing has, surprisingly, left more or less untouched. See Johnston 2003 and Chan 2004 for more detailed discussion of the criteria for a "status quo" foreign policy and the degree to which Chinese diplomacy meets these criteria today.

[15] Scholarship is only beginning to investigate these kinds of rare radical reorientations in grand strategy (see Legro 2005).

changed through socialization in international institutions (though are still the products of socialization in domestic institutions and experiences).[16] So it is unlikely that one could claim that all of this macrohistorical change in Chinese foreign policy orientation is due to mimicking, persuasion, and social influence inside international institutions. The drift toward increasingly wide and deep economic marketization over the 1980s and 1990s culminating in China's entry into the WTO, for example, is likely a story, initially, of a political leadership choosing to shore up its legitimacy through rapid economic development instead of through mass mobilization. This was then followed by a process of path-dependent commitments to marketization reinforced by the socialization of economic policy specialists in the ideology of the World Bank, the IMF, and now the WTO. But implementing policies based on this new ideology required a range of tools, some of them the plain old politically coercive kind directed at domestic opponents. Implementation also required tying China's hands through external commitments in order to impress on opponents the international costs of noncompliance with new norms and institutions. But here too, some of the socialization processes that I have identified are present. The legitimacy of opposition to economic and trade reform is undermined if these policies are framed as obligations that China as a "responsible major power" must follow. In other words, identity arguments can be used strategically, though their influence is likely to be, in part, a function of an internalized notion of what is acceptable behavior for China's identity type. In other words, even where strategic, instrumental, and politically coercive strategies are used to implement more "status quo" policies, socialization processes are not necessarily absent. The reformers may be socialized as "true believers." But they may act strategically to implement their beliefs in policy. Even so, a powerful strategic tool is to appeal to identity—to underscore the inappropriateness of opposition to change (in this case trade and economic change) for China's image.

How does one explain those areas of China's foreign policy where the preferences appear to still be revisionist, as most would use the term? Do these cases refute socialization arguments? Not necessarily. The most obviously persistent revisionist preferences in Chinese foreign policy today pertain mostly to territorial disputes. Although most of China's disputes have been resolved over time, through either negotiation or force (Fravel 2003), there remain a handful of outstanding and potentially volatile areas where China's claims and those of others are zero-sum. The

[16] See, for instance, Evan Medeiros's (2006) argument that US political and economic pressure on China was in large measure responsible for China's moves to embrace the global non-proliferation regime.

obvious examples are China's claim to be the sole legitimate government of a country that includes the island of Taiwan, and its desire to prevent other states from controlling atolls and reefs and energy fields in the South China Sea and the East China Sea. Territorial disputes may be especially hard to resolve through the mechanisms of socialization outlined in this book. This is suggested by the puzzle that of all interstate dispute issues, territory ought to be among the most amenable to solution because there is a more or less tangible pie that can be divided, where the piece one receives is often more preferable to the costs of war. Yet more wars are fought around territory than any other issue. The reason often has to do with the symbolic value of territory—if a government cannot control territory, it is awfully hard to establish sovereignty and legitimacy, and hence domestic power and external security for the regime.[17] Moreover, in international relations the need to have territorial integrity is such a powerful social fact that there can be no such thing as a national identity without a claim to geographic space. Thus, one might expect that on territorial integrity issues, a regime or its people will be least susceptible to persuasion and social influence within international fora. Abandoning space means changing identity.

Taiwan is an especially clear example. My argument—or an argument consistent with my argument—would be that in the Taiwan case, there are no institutions of persuasion or social influence that can counteract the powerful domestic forces preventing the leadership from abandoning coercive diplomacy against a democratic Taiwan. The most basic of these forces is a socialization process among the broader population, and probably the party elite as well, that has convinced them that Taiwan is an inalienable part of China's territory. The symbolic value of Taiwan for Chinese nationalism is endogenously related to the dispute with the United States over Taiwan's future. In this ideational context, the party leadership appears to have calculated its more concrete "interests" in retaining power: Anyone who "loses" Taiwan not only will encourage a domestic domino effect among unassimilated minorities in Xinjiang and Tibet, but also will lose power (though no one is specific about the modalities of this—military coup, formal removal from the Politburo, demonstrations in the streets that lead to the overthrow of the entire leadership set). But this fear of the political consequences of "losing" Taiwan rests on the perception that some important portion of the population values the symbol of Taiwan as part of China, regardless of the concrete costs and benefits of this valuation. (Taiwan's de jure independence would have an almost zero effect on the daily lives of the Chinese people.) The Chinese

---

[17] On the question of territory and conflict, see Fearon 1995; Hensel 2000; and Toft 2003.

leadership's steadfast effort to prevent the Taiwan issue from being placed on the agenda of an international institution has helped prevent alternative modes of thinking about Taiwan's symbolic value and about alternative solutions to coercive diplomacy from having much impact on Beijing's choice of strategy toward Taiwan.[18]

This suggests that socialization can have opposite effects on policy, depending on which concept of identity is salient in an issue. The socialization of reform elites in capitalist ideology, often as a result of exposure to international economic institutions in the past, combined with a broader socialization in the notion of China as a major power (which in this era is supposed to practice a "responsible major power" diplomacy of participation in institutions), helps explain the leadership's push for China's integration in the major capitalist institutions today. Socialization in a victimization ideology,[19] particularly among elites and relevant publics, combined with the absence of institutions that might legitimize counter-victimization discourses, helps explain the leadership's continuing sensitivity to the Taiwan issue. In effect, there is a firewall between the Taiwan issue and the discourse of territorial incompleteness and historical victimization on the one hand, and integration into global institutions and the discourse of a responsible major power on the other. This firewall is created by the regime's unwillingness to internationalize the Taiwan issue. As long as it remains uninternationalized, it will remain less susceptible to the kinds of socialization processes I have talked about in this book.

Critics of my argument might respond that all these modifications in Chinese policy toward the ARF, CTBT, and other institutions are possible because the threats just were not big enough, that the US-China relationship was just not bad enough, or that the threat of Taiwan separation was just not dire enough. Thus, ultimately, the pressures produced by anarchy and Chinese weakness were not yet sufficient to prevent minor cooperative adjustments in China's foreign policy. But once these pressures are sufficient, then one can confidently predict there will be no more CTBTs, ARFs, PIIs, and so on, or even, perhaps, no more embrace of market institutions if these are perceived to leave China relatively less well-off than the United States.

There is something tautological to this kind of criticism, since it can never show ex ante just how much of a threat is enough. But I am fairly

---

[18] There is the intriguing counterfactual possibility, however, that Jiang Zemin's CBM proposal, made in late 2002 in private to George Bush, to withdraw some of China's SLBMs from opposite Taiwan in return for constraints on US arms sales to Taiwan would not have been made had Chinese foreign policy makers not been exposed to CBM diplomacy through institutions such as the ARF and other multilateral security dialogues.

[19] See Callahan 2004, 2006, and Gries 2004 on the victimization and humiliation discourse.

confident that in 1989-1991 no self-aware, consistent realist would have predicted these outcomes, precisely because the world was unipolar. This is not to say that a very threatening environment would not provoke reneging or rejecting these institutions in the future. I am not a teleologist. As the Taiwan case amply illustrates, socialization can move in many directions, not always cooperative ones. But in practical terms, in the next few years a threatening environment from the perspective of China's leaders will probably come from a conflict with the United States over Taiwan (or perhaps over a violent collapse of North Korea). Withdrawal from these institutions or a decision to subvert their purposes to fit with an anti-US diplomatic offensive—because they are seen as either too constraining on China or insufficiently constraining on the United States— would not be surprising if a hard realpolitik ideology once again dominates the policy space. But this is not a refutation of the socialization arguments or processes, merely a statement that the PRC and US leaderships' respective valuations of Taiwan—valuations that are in part mutually constitutive—will ensure that hard realpolitik ideology trumps more multilateralist ideologies. The fact that this is likely to happen only when some of the fundamental core values of the political leadership are threatened at least sixteen or more years after structural conditions ought to have led to the further consolidation of this realpolitik ideology suggests two things. First, in the Chinese case at least, standard materialist realism provides few insights into actual thinking and actual behavior. To my mind, this is a problem for arguments about the independent causal impact of material power distributions. Second, realpolitik *ideology* is a powerful norm, in particular when core in-group values are threatened. Socialization arguments tell us something about how Chinese preferences and behavior changed in non-realpolitik directions on certain security questions during the post–cold war unipolar era. But they also tell us that these changes can be reversible.

References

Abbott, Kenneth W., and Duncan Snidal (1998) "Why States Act Through Formal International Organizations" *Journal of Conflict Resolution* 42:1 (February) pp. 3–32.

Abdelal, Rawi, Yoshiko Herrera, Alastair Iain Johnston, and Rose McDermott (2006) "Identity as a Variable" *Perspectives on Politics* 4:4 (December) pp. 695–711.

Academy of Military Sciences (AMS) Strategy Department (2000) *2000–2001 nian zhanlue pinggu* [2000–2001 Strategic Assessments] (Beijing: Military Sciences Press).

Academy of Military Sciences (AMS) (2001) *Zhanluexue* [The Science of Military Strategy] (Beijing: Military Sciences Press).

Acharya, Amitav (1996) "The New Frontier of Multilateralism: Canada and the ASEAN Regional Forum" (paper prepared for the Canadian International Development Agency, November).

Acharya, Amitav (1997a) "The ASEAN Regional Forum" (Department of Foreign Affairs and International Trade, Ottawa, Canada, February).

Acharya, Amitav (1997b) "Ideas, Identity and Institution-Building: From the ASEAN Way to the Asia Pacific Way" *Pacific Review* 10:3, pp. 319–46.

Acharya, Amitav (1998) "The Impact of Multilateralism on Chinese Regional Security Thinking and Behavior: Snapshot of Beijing Views" (unpublished paper).

Acharya, Amitav (2001) *Constructing a Security Community in Southeast Asia: ASEAN and the Problem of Regional Order* (London: Routledge Press).

Acharya, Amitav (2004) "How Ideas Spread: Whose Norms Matter? Norm Localization and Institutional Change in Asian Regionalism" *International Organization* 58:2 (April) pp. 239–75.

Adler, Emanuel (1998) "Seeds of Peaceful Change: The OSCE's Security Community-Building Model" in Emanuel Adler and Michael Barnett, eds., *Security Communities* (Cambridge: Cambridge University Press) pp. 119–60.

Adler, Emanuel, and Michael Barnett (1998) "A Framework for the Study of Security Communities" in Emanuel Adler and Michael Barnett, eds., *Security Communities* (Cambridge: Cambridge University Press) pp. 29–65.

Alker, Hayward (1996) "Beneath Tit for Tat" in Hayward Alker, *Rediscoveries and Reformulations: Humanistic Methodologies for International Studies* (Cambridge: Cambridge University Press) pp. 303–31.

Alter, Karen (1998) "Who Are the 'Masters of the Treaty'? European Governments and the European Court of Justice" *International Organization* 52:1 (Winter) pp. 121–47.

Anon. (n.d. ~ 1997) "The Strategic Use and Development of the Second Artillery in the New Period" (Washington D.C.: US Defense Intelligence Agency, translation, 2002).

Antolik, Michael (1994) "The ASEAN Regional Forum: The Spirit of Constructive Engagement" *Contemporary Southeast Asia* 16:2 (September) pp. 117–36.

ARF (1995a) "Chairman's Statement of the Second ASEAN Regional Forum" (Brunei, August 1).

ARF (1995b) "The ASEAN Regional Forum: A Concept Paper" (mimeo).

ARF (1996a) "Chairman's Statement of the Third ASEAN Regional Forum" (Jakarta, July 23).

ARF (1996b) "Concept Paper of Co-chairs: ARF Intersessional Support Group on Confidence Building Measures" (Jakarta, July 22).

ARF (1996c) "Chairman's Statement" (ARF Working Group on Preventive Diplomacy, Paris, November 8).

ARF (1998a) "Co-chairmen's Summary Report of the Meetings of the ARF Intersessional Support Group on Confidence Building Measures" (Brunei Darussalam, November 4–6, 1997; Sydney, March 4–6, 1998).

ARF (1998b) "Chairman's Statement" (Third ARF Track II Conference on Preventive Diplomacy, London, April 18).

ARF (1999a) "Concept and Principles of Preventive Diplomacy" (ASEAN Draft, November 6).

ARF (2005) "Chairman's Statement" (Twelfth Meeting of the ASEAN Regional Forum, July 29). http://www.aseanregionalforum.org/Default.aspx?tabid=67.

Axelrod, Robert (1976) ed., *The Structure of Decision: The Cognitive Maps of Political Elites* (Princeton, NJ: Princeton University Press).

Axelrod, Robert (1997a) "Promoting Norms: An Evolutionary Approach to Norms" in Robert Axelrod, *The Complexity of Cooperation* (Princeton, NJ: Princeton University Press).

Axelrod, Robert (1997b) "A Model for the Emergence of New Political Actors" in Robert Axelrod, *The Complexity of Cooperation* (Princeton, NJ: Princeton University Press).

Axelrod, Robert (1997c) "The Dissemination of Culture: A Model with Local Convergence and Global Polarization" in Robert Axelrod, *The Complexity of Cooperation* (Princeton, NJ: Princeton University Press).

Axsom, Danny, Suzanne Yates, and Shelley Chaiken (1987) "Audience Response Cues as a Heuristic Cue in Persuasion" *Journal of Personality and Social Psychology* 53:1 (July) pp. 30–40.

Bar-Tal, Daniel, and Leonard Saxe (1990) "Acquisition of Political Knowledge: A Social-Psychological Analysis" in Orit Ichilov, ed., *Political Socialization, Citizenship Education and Democracy* (New York: Teachers College Press).

Barnett, Michael, and Emanuel Adler (1998) "Studying Security Communities in Theory, Comparison, and History" in Emanuel Adler and Michael Barnett, eds., *Security Communities* (Cambridge: Cambridge University Press) pp. 413–41.

Barnum, Christopher (1997) "A Reformulated Social Identity Theory" *Advances in Group Processes*, Vol. 14 (Greenwich, CT: JAI Press).

Batson, C. D. (1987) "Prosocial Motivation: Is It Ever Truly Altruistic?" *Advances in Experimental Social Psychology*, Vol. 20 (New York: Academic Press) pp. 65–122.

Beck, Paul Allen, and M. Kent Jennings (1991) "Family Traditions, Political Periods, and the Development of Partisan Orientations" *Journal of Politics* 53:2 (August) pp. 742–63.

Berger, Charles R. (1995) "Inscrutable Goals, Uncertain Plans and the Production of Communicative Action" in Charles R. Berger and Michael Burgoon, eds., *Communication and Social Influence Processes* (East Lansing: Michigan State University Press).

Berger, Peter L., and Thomas Luckman (1966) *The Social Construction of Reality: A Treatise in the Sociology of Knowledge* (New York: Anchor Books).

Betts, Richard (1993/4) "Wealth, Power, and Instability: East Asia and the United States after the Cold War" *International Security* 18:3 (Winter) pp. 34–77.

Betz, Andrew L., John K. Skowronski, and Thomas M. Ostrom (1996) "Shared Realities: Social Influence and Stimulus Memory" *Social Cognition* 14:2 (Summer) pp. 113–40.

Beyers, Jan, and Caroline Steensels (2001) "An Exploration of Some Social Mechanisms Affecting Domestic Political Actors' Europeanisation: The Belgian Case" (prepared for the IDNET second project workshop, "International Institutions and Socialization in the New Europe," European University Institute, Florence, May 18–19).

Biddle, Bruce J., et al. (1985) "Social Influence, Self-Reference Identity Labels and Behavior" *Sociological Quarterly* 26:2, pp. 159–85.

Booster, Franklin J. (1995) "Commentary on Compliance-Gaining Message Behavior Research" in Charles R. Berger and Michael Burgoon, eds., *Communication and Social Influence Processes* (East Lansing: Michigan State University Press).

Botcheva, L., and L. L. Martin (2001) "Institutional Effects on State Behavior: Convergence and Divergence" *International Studies Quarterly* 45:1 (March) pp. 1–26.

Bourdieu, Pierre (1991) *Language and Symbolic Power*, John B. Thompson, ed., Gino Raymond and Matthew Adamson, trans. (Cambridge, MA: Harvard University Press).

Bowerman, Melissa, and Stephen C. Levinson (2001) Introduction to Melissa Bowerman and Stephen C. Levinson, eds., *Language Acquisition and Conceptual Development* (Cambridge: Cambridge University Press) pp. 1–16.

Brenner, Thomas (1998) "Can Evolutionary Algorithms Describe Learning Processes?" *Journal of Evolutionary Economics* 8:3, pp. 271–83.

Broms, Henri, and Henrik Gahmberg (1983) "Communication to Self in Organizations and Cultures" *Administrative Sciences Quarterly* 28:3 (September) pp. 482–95.

Brown, Rupert (2000) *Group Processes: Dynamics Within and Between Groups*, 2nd ed. (Oxford: Blackwell).

Callahan, William A. (2004) "National Insecurities: Humiliation, Salvation, and Chinese Nationalism" *Alternatives* 29:2 (May) pp. 199–218.

Callahan, William A. (2006) "History, Identity, and Security: Producing and Consuming Nationalism in China" *Critical Asian Studies* 38:2 (June) pp. 179–208.

Cameron, Maxwell A., Robert J. Lawson, and Brian W. Tomlin (1998) "To Walk without Fear" in Maxwell A. Cameron, Robert J. Lawson, and Brian W. Tomlin et al., eds., *To Walk without Fear: The Global Movement to Ban Landmines* (Oxford: Oxford University Press) pp. 1–19.

Campbell, Donald T., and Julian Stanley (1966) *Experimental and Quasi-Experimental Designs for Research* (Chicago: Rand McNally).

Caporaso, James A. (1993) "International Relations Theory and Multilateralism: The Search for Foundations" in John Gerard Ruggie, ed., *Multilateralism Matters: The Theory and Praxis of an Institutional Form* (New York: Columbia University Press) pp. 51–90.

Carlson, Allen (2005) *Unifying China, Integrating the World: Securing Chinese Sovereignty in the Reform Era* (Stanford: Stanford University Press).

CD/PV (1994–1996) Conference on Disarmament, Plenary Sessions.

Cederman, Lars-Eric (1997) *Emergent Actors in World Politics: How States and Nations Develop and Dissolve* (Princeton, NJ: Princeton University Press).

Chafetz, Glenn (1997) "An Empirical Analysis of International Identity Change" (paper presented to the American Political Science Association Annual Meeting, Washington, DC, August 28–31).

Chafetz, Glenn, Hillel Abramson, and Suzette Grillot (1996) "Role Theory and Foreign Policy: Belarussian and Ukrainian Compliance with the Nuclear Nonproliferation Regime" *Political Psychology* 17:4 (December) pp. 727–57.

Chan, Steve (2004) "Realism, Revisionism, and the Great Powers" *Issues and Studies* 40:1 (March) pp. 135–72.

Chayes, Abram, and Antonia Handler Chayes (1996) *The New Sovereignty: Compliance with International Regulatory Agreements* (Cambridge, MA: Harvard University Press).

Checkel, Jeffrey T. (1998) "The Constructivist Turn in International Relations Theory" *World Politics* 50 (January) pp. 324–48.

Checkel, Jeffrey T. (2001) "A Constructivist Research Program in EU Studies?" *European Union Politics* 2:2, pp. 219–49.

Checkel, Jeffrey T. (2003) " 'Going Native' in Europe? Theorizing Social Interaction in European Institutions" *Comparative Political Studies* 36:1/2 (February–March) pp. 209–31.

Chen Jian (1997) "Challenges and Responses in East Asia" (speech to the First CSCAP General Meeting).

Chen Xiaogong, ed. (1997) *Junbei kongzhi yu guoji anquan shouce* [Handbook on Arms Control and International Security] (Beijing: World Knowledge Press).

Chen Xueyin (1992a) "Zhenzheng de quanmian de he caijun" [True Complete Nuclear Disarmament] *Junbei kongzhi yanjiu tongxun* No. 6.

Chen Xueyin (1992b) "Hewuqi de anquan kongzhi yu guanli" [Management and Safe Control of Nuclear Weapons] *Junbei kongzhi yanjiu tongxun* No. 15.

Chen Xueyin (1993) "The Objectives, Definitions, and Related Issues of a Comprehensive Test Ban" (June) JPRS-TND-93-026 (August 10).

Chen Xueyin, and Wang Deli (1996) "The Top Priority of Current Nuclear Arms Control: Some Comments about the CTBT and the Production Cut-Off" (paper prepared for the Fifth ISODARCO-Beijing Seminar on Arms Control, Chengdu, November 11–16).

Chen Zhou, and Zhang Ying'en (1997) "Xianzhi he jinzhi shiyong dilei de guoji gongyue pingjia" [An Assessment of International Treaties Restricting and Prohibiting the Use of Landmines] *Zhongguo guoji fa niankan* [China and International Law Yearbook] (Beijing: China Foreign Translation Publishing) pp. 339–52.

Chigas, Diana, Elizabeth McClintock, and Christophe Kamp (1996) "Preventive Diplomacy and the Organization for Security Cooperation in Europe: Creating Incentives for Dialogue and Cooperation" in Abram Chayes and Antonia Handler Chayes, eds., *Preventing Conflict in the Post-Communist World: Mobilizing International and Regional Organizations*, (Washington, DC: Brookings Institution).

China (1981) "Views on Disarmament and Its Related Questions" Working Paper, CD/206 (August 6).

China (1994a) "Working Paper on CTBT Verification" CD/NTB/WP.78 (June 2).

China (1994b) "Proposed Wording for the CTBT Article on 'Security Assurances for States Parties' " CD/NTB/WP.122 (June 20).

China (1994c) "Proposed Wording for the Preamble to the CTBT" CD/NTB/WP.124 (June 20).

China (1994d) "CTBT Article on 'Peaceful Uses of Nuclear Energy and Peaceful Nuclear Explosions' " CD/NTB/WP.167 (August 23).

China (1996) "Chinese Position on Issues Relating to the Third ARF Meeting" (Beijing, April).

China (1997) "Chinese Paper at the ARF-ISG-CBMs in Brunei" (mimeo, November 3–5).

China (2000a) "China's Position Paper on Preventive Diplomacy in the Asia-Pacific Region" (unpublished document submitted to the ARF, February 1).

China (2000b) "China's Comments on the Draft of the ARF Concept and Principles of Preventive Diplomacy" (unpublished document submitted to the ARF, n.d., February?).

China (2001) "China's Comments on the Draft of the ARF Concept and Principles of Preventive Diplomacy" (unpublished document submitted to the ARF, January 9).

China Radio International (1997) "The Taking Shape of a New Security Concept and Its Practice in China" (December 29), BBC-SWB (January 7, 1998).

Choi Young Back (1993) *Paradigms and Conventions: Uncertainty, Decision Making, and Entrepreneurship* (Ann Arbor: University of Michigan Press).

Christensen, Thomas J. (1996) "Chinese Realpolitik" *Foreign Affairs* 75:5 (September–October) pp. 37–52.

Christensen, Thomas J. (1998) "Parsimony Is No Simple Matter: International Relations Theory, Area Studies, and the Rise of China" (paper presented to the Program on International Politics, Economics, and Security, University of Chicago, February 28).

Christensen, Thomas J. (2006) "Fostering Stability or Creating a Monster: The Rise of China and U.S. Policy Toward East Asia" *International Security* 31:1 (Summer) pp. 81–126.

Chu Shulong (1997) "Concepts, Structures and Strategies of Security Cooperation in Asia-Pacific" (unpublished manuscript, January).

Cialdini, Robert (1984) *Influence: The New Psychology of Modern Persuasion* (New York: Quill Books).

Cialdini, Robert (1987) "Compliance Principles of Compliance Professionals: Psychologists of Necessity" in Mark P. Zanna, James M. Olson, and C. Peter

Herman, eds., *Social Influence: The Ontario Symposium*, Vol. 5 (Hillsdale, NJ: Lawrence Erlbaum Associates).

Cialdini, Robert B., Carl A. Kallgren, and Raymond R. Reno (1991) "A Focus Theory of Normative Conduct" *Advances in Experimental Social Psychology*, vol. 24, (New York: Academic Press) pp. 201–34.

CICIR (China Institute of Contemporary International Relations) ed., (1987), *Guoji caijun douzheng yu Zhongguo* [China and the International Arms Control Struggle] (Beijing: Shishi Publishing House).

CICIR ed. (2000), *Zonghe guoli pinggu xitong: Yanjiu baogao* [System for Estimating Comprehensive National Strength: Research Report] (Beijing: China Institute of Contemporary International Relations).

Cohen, Michael D., and Robert Axelrod (1984) "Coping with Complexity: The Adaptive Value of Changing Utility" *American Economic Review* 74:1 (March) pp. 30–42.

Copper, John F., and Ta-Ling Lee (1997) *Coping with a Bad Global Image: Human Rights in the People's Republic of China, 1993–1994* (Lanham, MD: University Press of America).

Cortell, Andrew P., and James W. Davis, Jr. (1996) "How Do International Institutions Matter? The Domestic Impact of International Rules and Norms" *International Studies Quarterly* 40:4 (December) pp. 451–78.

Crawford, Neta (2002) *Argument and Change in World Politics: Ethnics, Decolonization, and Humanitarian Intervention* (Cambridge: Cambridge University Press).

CSCAP (Council on Security Cooperation in the Asia Pacific) (n.d. ~1995) "Asia-Pacific Confidence and Security Building Measures" (memorandum No. 2).

Cummings, Lucy M. (2000) "PRC Foreign Policy Responsiveness to Domestic Ethical Sentiment: Understanding the Link between Ethics and Regime Legitimacy" (PhD dissertation, Johns Hopkins University).

Dawes, Robyn M., Alphons van der Kragt, and John M. Orbell (1988) "Not Me or Thee but We: The Importance of Group Identity in Eliciting Cooperation in Dilemma Situations: Experimental Manipulations" *Acta Psychologica* 68 (September) pp. 83–97.

Deng Yong (1998) "The Chinese Conception of National Interests in International Relations" *China Quarterly* No. 154 (June) pp. 308–29.

Deng Yong (2001) "Hegemon on the Offensive: Chinese Perspectives on U.S. Global Strategy" *Political Science Quarterly* 116:3 (Fall) pp. 343–65.

Deng Yong, and Thomas G. Moore (2004) "China Views Globalization: Toward a New Great Power Politics?" *Washington Quarterly* 27:3 (Summer) pp. 117–136.

Desch, Michael C. (1998) "Culture Clash: Assessing the Importance of Ideas in Security Studies" *International Security* 23:1 (Summer) pp. 141–70.

Desjardin, Marie-France (1996) "Rethinking Confidence Building Measures: Obstacles to Agreement and the Risk of Overselling the Process" *Adelpi Papers* No. 307.

Dewitt, David (1994) "Common, Comprehensive and Cooperative Security in Asia-Pacific" *CANCAPS Papiers* No. 3 (March).

DiMaggio, Paul J., and Walter W. Powell (1991) Introduction to Paul J. DiMaggio and Walter Powell, eds., *The New Institutionalism in Organizational Analysis* (Chicago: University of Chicago Press).

Dittmer, Lowell, and Samuel S. Kim (1993) *China's Quest for National Identity* (Ithaca, NY: Cornell University Press).

Dolan, Michael, and Chris Hunt (1999) "Negotiating the Ottawa Process" in Maxwell A. Cameron, Robert J. Lawson, and Brian W. Tomlin et al., eds., *To Walk Without Fear: The Global Movement to Ban Landmines* (Oxford: Oxford University Press) pp. 392–423.

Donahue, Ray T., and Michael H. Prosser (1997) *Diplomatic Discourse: International Conflict at the United Nations* (Greenwich, CT: Ablex Publishing).

Downs, George W., David M. Rocke, and Peter N. Barsoom (1997) "Designing Multilaterals: The Architecture and Evolution of Environmental Agreements" (paper presented to the American Political Science Association Annual Conference, Washington, DC, August).

Downs, George W., David M. Rocke, and Peter N. Barsoom (1998) "Managing the Evolution of Multilateralism" *International Organization* 52:2 (Spring) pp. 397–419.

Druckman, Daniel (1994) "Nationalism, Patriotism, and Group Loyalty: A Social-Psychology Perspective" *Mershon International Studies Review* 38:1 (April) pp. 43–68.

Drysdale, Peter, and Ross Garnaut (1993) "The Pacific: An Application of a General Theory of Economic Integration" in C. Fred Bergsten and Marcus Noland, eds., *Pacific Dynamism and the International Economic System* (Washington, DC: Institute for International Economics) pp. 183–224.

Du Xiangwan (1996) *He junbei kongzhi de kexue jishu jichu* [The Scientific and Technical Basis of Nuclear Arms Control] (Beijing: China National Defense Publishing House).

Economy, Elizabeth (1994) "Negotiating the Terrain of Global Climate Change in the Soviet Union and China: Linking International and Domestic Decision Pathways" (PhD dissertation, University of Michigan).

Economy, Elizabeth (2001) "The Impact of International Regimes on Chinese Foreign Policy Making: Broadening Perspectives and Policies . . . But Only to a Point" in David M. Lampton, ed., *The Making of Chinese Foreign and Security Policy* (Stanford: Stanford University Press) pp. 230–53.

Economy, Elizabeth, and Michel Oksenberg (2000) "International Law and Global Environmental Change: The China Case" in Harold Jacobson and Edith Brown Weiss, eds., *Engaging Countries: Strengthening Compliance with International Environmental Accords* (Cambridge, MA: MIT Press).

Einhorn, Robert (2002) "Proliferation Challenges in Asia" (comments at the International Institute of Strategic Studies, Asia Security Conference, Singapore, May 31–June 2).

Elster, Jon (1995) "Strategic Uses of Argument" in Kenneth Arrow et al., eds., *Barriers to Conflict Resolution* (New York: W. W. Norton).

Evangelista, Matthew (1999) *Unarmed Forces: The Transnational Movement to End the Cold War* (Ithaca, NY: Cornell University Press).

Eyre, Dana, and Mark Suchman (1996) "Status, Norms, and the Proliferation of Conventional Weapons: An Institutional Theory Approach" in Peter Katzenstein, ed., *The Culture of National Security* (New York: Columbia University Press).

Fairclough, Norman (2003) "Political Correctness: The Politics of Culture and Language" *Discourse and Society* 14:1 (January) pp. 17–28.

Fang Ning (2003) *Xindiguozhuyi shidai yu Zhongguo zhanlue* [New Imperialism and China's Strategy] (Beijing: Beijing Press).

Far Eastern Economic Review (Hong Kong) (1993–1996).

Farkas, Andrew (1998) *State Learning and International Change* (Ann Arbor: University of Michigan Press).

Fazal, Tanisha M. (2001) "The Origins and Implications of the Territorial Sovereignty Norm" (paper prepared for the American Political Science Association Annual Meeting, San Francisco, August 30–September 2).

Fearon, James (1995) "Rationalist Explanations for War" *International Organization* 49:3 (Summer) pp. 379–414.

Fearon, James (1997) "What Is Identity (As We Now Use the Word)?" (paper provided for the Workshop on Rationalism and Constructivism, Duke University, November).

Fearon, James (1998) "Bargaining, Enforcement, and International Cooperation" *International Organization* 52:2 (Spring) pp. 269–305.

Fierke, Karin M. (2002) "Links across the Abyss: Language and Logic in International Relations" *International Studies Quarterly* 46:3 (September) pp. 331–54.

Finkelstein, David M. (1999) "China's New Security Concept: Reading between the Lines" *Washington Journal of Modern China* 5:1 (Spring) pp. 37–47.

Finkelstein, David M. (2001) "Chinese Perceptions of the Costs of a Conflict" in Andrew Scobell, ed., *The Costs of Conflict: The Impact on China of a Future War* (Carlisle, PA: Army War College, Strategic Studies Institute).

Finkle, Norman, Rom Harré, and José-Luis Rodriguez Lopez (2001) "Commonsense Morality across Cultures: Notions of Fairness, Justice, Honor and Equity" *Discourse Studies* 3:1 (February) pp. 5–27.

Finnemore, Martha (1996a) "Norms, Culture, and World Politics: Insights from Sociology's Institutionalism" *International Organization* 50:2 (Spring) pp. 325–47.

Finnemore, Martha (1996b) *National Interests in International Society* (Ithaca, NY: Cornell University Press).

Finnemore, Martha (1996c) "Constructing Norms of Humanitarian Intervention" in Peter Katzenstein, ed., *The Culture of National Security: Norms and Identities in World Politics* (New York: Columbia University Press).

Finnemore, Martha, and Kathryn Sikkink (1998) "International Norm Dynamics and Political Change" *International Organization* 52:4 (Autumn) pp. 887–917.

Foot, Rosemary (2001) "Chinese Power and the Idea of a Responsible State" *China Journal* No. 45 (January) pp. 1–19.

Foreign Broadcast Information Service (United States): China; Asia Pacific, (1993–1996).

Franck, Thomas M. (1990) *The Power of Legitimacy among Nations* (New York: Oxford University Press).

Frank, Robert (1985) *Choosing the Right Pond: Human Behavior and the Quest for Status* (New York: Oxford University Press).

Frank, Robert (1988) *Passions within Reason: The Strategic Role of the Emotions* (New York: W. W. Norton).

Fravel, M. Taylor (1996) "China's Attitude toward UN Peacekeeping Operations Since 1989" *Asian Survey* 36:11 (November) pp. 1102–21.

Fravel, M. Taylor (2003) "The Long March to Peace: Explaining China's Settlement of Territorial Disputes, 1949–2002" (PhD dissertation, Stanford University).

Freedman P. E., and Anne Freedman (1981) "Political Learning" in Samuel Long, ed., *The Handbook of Political Behavior*, Vol. 1 (New York: Plenum Press).

Freedom House (2001) *Freedom in the World Country Ratings, 1972–3 to 2000–1*. http://www.freedomhouse.org/research/freeworld/FHSCORES.xls.

Friedberg, Aaron (1993/4) "Ripe for Rivalry: Prospects for Peace in a Multipolar Asia" *International Security* 18:3 (Winter) pp. 5–33.

Frieden, Jeffry (1999) "Actors and Preferences in International Relations" in David Lake and Robert Powell, eds., *Strategic Choice in International Relations* (Princeton, NJ: Princeton University Press) pp. 39–76.

Fu Chengli (1994) "Dangdai guoji xingshi zhong de ji ge wenti" [A Few Questions about the Current International Situation] *Shijie xingshi yanjiu* [Research on the International Situation] (Beijing) No. 1 (January 5).

Garrett, Banning, and Bonnie Glaser (1994) "Multilateral Security in the Asia-Pacific Region and Its Impact on Chinese Interests: Views from Beijing" *Contemporary Southeast Asia* 16:1 (June) pp. 14–34.

Garrett, Banning, and Bonnie Glaser (1997) "Does China Want the US Out of Asia?" *PacNet Newsletter* No. 22 (May 30).

General Accounting Office (2002) *World Trade Organization: Observations on China's Rule of Law Reforms* (Washington, DC: GAO-02-812T, June 6).

Gerard, H.B., and R. Orive (1987) "The Dynamics of Opinion Formation" *Advances in Experimental Social Psychology*, vol. 20, (New York: Academic Press) pp. 171–202.

Gheciu, Alexandra (2005) *NATO in the "New Europe": The Politics of International Socialization After the Cold War* (Stanford: Stanford University Press).

Gibson, James L. (1998) "A Sober Second Thought: An Experiment in Persuading Russians to Tolerate" *American Journal of Political Science* 42:3 (July) pp. 819–50.

Gill, Bates (2001) "Discussion of 'China: A Responsible Great Power' " *Journal of Contemporary China* 10:26 (February) pp. 27–32.

Gilpin, Robert (1981) *War and Change in World Politics* (Cambridge: Cambridge University Press).

Glaser, Charles (1994/5) "Realists as Optimists: Cooperation as Self-Help" *International Security* 19:3 (Winter) pp. 50–90.

Glosny, Michael (2007) "Stabilizing the Backyard: Recent Developments in China's Policy towards Southeast Asia" in Joshua Eisenman, Eric Heginbotham, and Derek Mitchell, eds., *China and the Developing World: Beijing's Strategy for the Twenty-first Century* (Armonk, NY: M. E. Sharpe).

Goncharov, Sergei N., John W. Lewis, and Litai Xue (1995) *Uncertain Partners: Stalin, Mao, and the Korean War* (Stanford: Stanford University Press).

Granovetter, Mark (1978) "Threshold Models of Collective Behavior" *American Journal of Sociology* 83 (May) pp. 1420–43.

Green, Donald P., and Ian Shapiro (1994) *Pathologies of Rational Choice Theory: A Critique of Applications in Political Science* (New Haven, CT: Yale University Press).

Gries, Peter Hays (2004) *China's New Nationalism: Pride, Politics, and Diplomacy* (Berkeley: University of California Press).

Guowai hewuqi dongtai [Trends in Foreign Nuclear Weapons] (1994) 12:6 (December).

Guthrie, Stewart (1980) "A Cognitive Theory of Religion" *Current Anthropology* 21:2 (April) pp. 181–203.

Haas, Peter (1998) "Constructing Multilateral Environmental Governance: The Evolution of Multilateral Environmental Governance Since 1972" (paper presented at the Center for International Affairs, Harvard University, April 16).

Halpern, Jennifer J. (1997) "Elements of a Script for Friendship in Transactions" *Journal of Conflict Resolution* 41:6 (December) pp. 835–68.

Hamman, Henry L. (1998) "Remodeling International Relations: New Tools from New Science?" in Vendulka Kubalkova, Nicholas Onuf, and Paul Kowert, eds., *International Relations in a Constructed World* (Armonk, NY: M. E. Sharpe) pp. 173–92.

Hanks, William F. (1996) *Language and Communicative Practices* (Boulder, CO: Westview Press).

Hardin, Russell (1995) *One for All: The Logic of Group Conflict* (Princeton, NJ: Princeton University Press).

Harré, Rom (1979) *Social Being: A Theory for Social Psychology* (Oxford: Blackwell).

Hasenclever, Andreas, Peter Mayer, and Volker Rittberger (1997) *Theories of International Regimes* (Cambridge: Cambridge University Press).

Hatch, Elvin (1989) "Theories of Social Honor" *American Anthropologist* 91:2 (June) pp. 341–53.

Hensel, Paul (2000) "Territory: Theory and Evidence on Geography and Conflict" in John A. Vasquez, ed., *What Do We Know about War?* (Lanham, MD: Rowman and Littlefield) pp. 57–84.

Herrmann, Richard (1988) "The Empirical Challenge of the Cognitive Revolution: A Strategy for Drawing Inferences about Perceptions" *International Studies Quarterly* 32:2 (June) pp. 175–203.

Hirshleifer, David (1995) "The Blind Leading the Blind: Social Influence, Fads, and Informational Cascades" in Mariano Tommasi and Kathryn Ierulli, eds., *The New Economics of Human Behavior* (Cambridge: Cambridge University Press) pp. 188–215.

Holland, John (1995) *Hidden Order: How Adaptation Builds Complexity* (Reading, MA: Addison Wesley).

Hooghe, Liesbet (2002) *The European Commission and the Integration of Europe: Images of Governance* (Cambridge: Cambridge University Press).

Hooghe, Liesbet (2005) "Several Roads Lead to International Norms, but Few via International Socialization: A Case Study of the European Commission" *International Organization* 59:4 (Fall) pp. 861–98.

Hopf, Ted (2002) *Social Origins of International Politics: Identities and the Construction of Foreign Policies at Home* (Ithaca, NY: Cornell University Press).

Horowitz, Donald (2000) *Ethnic Groups in Conflict*, rev. ed. (Berkeley: University of California Press).

Huang Tingwei, and Song Baoxian (1987) "Dangqian guoji caijun douzheng de tedian ji zhengce jianyi" [Special Characteristics of the Current International Disarmament Struggle, and Policy Proposals] in China Institute of Contemporary International Relations, ed., *Guoji caijun douzheng yu Zhongguo* [China and the International Arms Control Struggle] (Beijing: Shishi Publishing House).

Hurwitz, Jon, and Mark Peffley (1997) "How Are Foreign Policy Attitudes Structured? A Hierarchical Model" *American Political Science Review* 81:4 (December) pp. 1099–1120.

Hymans, Jacques (2001) "Why do States Acquire Nuclear Weapons? A Comparison of India and France" in Raju G. C. Thomas and Damodar SarDesai, eds., *Nuclear India in the 21st Century* (New York: Palgrave).

IAPCM (2001) "Introduction—Program on Science and National Security Studies" *Arms Control: Collected Works* (Beijing: Institute of Applied Physics and Computational Mathematics).

Ichilov, Orit (1990) Introduction to Orit Ichilov, ed., *Political Socialization, Citizenship Education and Democracy* (New York: Teachers College Press).

Ikenberry, G. John, and Charles Kupchan (1990) "Socialization and Hegemonic Power" *International Organization* 44:3 (Summer) pp. 283–315.

Isen, Alice M. (1987) "Positive Affect, Cognitive Processes and Social Behavior" *Advances in Experimental Social Psychology*, Vol. 20, (New York: Academic Press) pp. 203–53.

Jacobson, Harold K., and Michel Oksenberg (1990) *China's Participation in the IMF, the World Bank, and GATT* (Ann Arbor: University of Michigan Press).

James, Michael Rabinder (1998) "Communicative Action and the Logics of Group Conflict" (paper prepared for the American Political Science Association Annual Meeting, Boston, September).

Jenks, C. Wilfred (1965) "Unanimity, the Veto, Weighted Voting, Special and Simple Majorities and Consensus as Modes of Decision in International Organisations" in *Cambridge Essays in International Law: Essays in Honour of Lord McNair* (London: Stevens and Sons).

Jepperson, Ronald L., Alexander Wendt, and Peter J. Katzenstein (1996) "Norms, Identity and Culture in National Security" in Peter Katzenstein, ed., *The Culture of National Security* (New York: Columbia University Press).

Jin Xide (2000) "ZhongRi huoban guanxi de queli he weilai fazhan" [The Establishment and Future Development of Sino-Japanese Partnership Relations] in Zhang Yunling, ed., *Huoban haishi duishou: Tiaozheng zhong de Zhong Mei Ri E guanxi* [Partners or Adversaries? Sino-US-Japanese-Russian Relations in Transformation] (Beijing: Social Science Documents Press).

Johnson, James (1993) "Is Talk Really Cheap? Prompting Conversation between Critical Theory and Rational Choice" *American Political Science Review* 87:1 (March) pp. 74–86.

Johnson, Rebecca (1996a) "CTB Negotiations—Geneva Update No. 25" *Disarmament Diplomacy* (January) 1. http://www.acronym.org.uk/dd/dd01/index.htm#T-0013.

Johnson, Rebecca (1996b) "CTB Negotiations—Geneva Update No. 27" *Disarmament Diplomacy* (March) 3. http://www.acronym.org.uk/dd/dd03/index.htm#T-0027.

Johnson, Rebecca (1996c) "Comprehensive Test Ban Treaty: The Endgame" *Acronym* No. 9 (April). http://www.acronym.org.uk/a09comp.htm.

Johnson, Rebecca (1996d) "CTB Negotiations—Geneva Update No. 28" *Disarmament Diplomacy* No. 5 (May). http://www.acronym.org.uk/dd/dd05/index.htm#T-0060/.

Johnson, Rebecca (1996e) "A Comprehensive Test Ban Treaty: Signed but Not Sealed" *Acronym* No. 10 (September). http://www.acronym.org.uk/a10treat.htm.

Johnston, Alastair Iain (1986) "China and Arms Control: Emerging Issues and Interests in the 1980s" *Aurora Papers* No. 3 (Canadian Center for Arms Control and Disarmament, Ottawa).

Johnston, Alastair Iain (1990) "China and Arms Control in the Asia-Pacific Region" in Frank Langdon and Douglas Ross, eds., *Superpower Maritime Strategy in the Pacific* (London: Routledge Press).

Johnston, Alastair Iain (1995) *Cultural Realism: Strategic Culture and Grand Strategy in Chinese History* (Princeton, NJ: Princeton University Press).

Johnston, Alastair Iain (1995/6) "China's New 'Old Thinking': The Concept of Limited Deterrence" *International Security* 20:3 (Winter) pp. 5–42.

Johnston, Alastair Iain (1996a) "Cultural Realism and Strategy in Maoist China" in Peter Katzenstein, ed., *The Culture of National Security* (New York: Columbia University Press).

Johnston, Alastair Iain (1996b) "Learning versus Adaptation: Explaining Change in Chinese Arms Control Policy in the 1980s and 1990s" *China Journal* No. 35 (January) pp. 27–61.

Johnston, Alastair Iain (1998a) "Realism(s) and Chinese Security Policy after the Cold War" in Ethan Kapstein and Michael Mastanduno, eds., *Unipolar Politics: Realism and State Strategies after the Cold War* (New York: Columbia University Press).

Johnston, Alastair Iain (1998b) "International Structures and Chinese Foreign Policy" in Samuel S. Kim, ed., *China and the World*, 4th ed. (Boulder, CO: Westview Press).

Johnston, Alastair Iain (2003) "Is China a Status Quo Power?" *International Security* 27:4 (Spring) pp. 5–56.

Jones, Edward E. (1985) "Major Developments in Social Psychology during the Past Five Decades" in Gardner Lindzey and Elliot Aronson, eds., *Handbook of Social Psychology* (New York: Random House) pp. 47–107.

Jorgensen, Charlotte, Christian Kock, and Lone Rorbech (1998) "Rhetoric That Shifts Votes: An Exploratory Study of Persuasion in Issue-Oriented Public Debates" *Political Communication* 15:3 (June) pp. 283–99.

Jupille, Joseph, James A. Caporaso, and Jeffery T. Checkel (2003) "Integrating Institutions: Rationalism, Constructivism, and the Study of the European Union" *Comparative Political Studies* 36:1/2 (February–March) pp. 7–40.

Karvonen, Lauri, and Bengt Sundelius (1990) "Interdependence and Foreign Policy Management in Sweden and Finland" *International Studies Quarterly* 34:2 (June) pp. 211–27.

Katsumata, Hiro (2006) "Establishment of the ASEAN Regional Forum: Constructing a 'Talking Shop' or a 'Norm Brewery'?" *Pacific Review* 19:2 (June) pp. 181–98.

Kaye, Dalia Dassa (2001) "Norm-Creation in the Middle East: Arguing in Track Two Security Dialogues" (unpublished manuscript).

Keck, Margaret E., and Kathryn Sikkink (1998) *Activists Beyond Borders: Advocacy Networks in International Politics* (Ithaca, NY: Cornell University Press).

Kelley, Judith (2004) "International Actors on the Domestic Scene: Membership Conditionality and Socialization in International Institutions" *International Organization* 58:3 (Summer) pp. 425–58.

Kent, Anne (1999) *China, the United Nations, and Human Rights* (Philadelphia: University of Pennsylvania Press).

Keohane, Robert O. (1983) "The Demand for International Regimes" in Stephen Krasner, ed., *International Regimes* (Ithaca, NY: Cornell University Press).

Keohane, Robert O. (1984) *After Hegemony* (Princeton, NJ: Princeton University Press).

Keohane, Robert O. (1993) "The Analysis of International Regimes: Toward a European-American Research Program" in Volker Rittberger, ed., *Regime Theory and International Relations* (New York: Oxford University Press).

Kier, Elizabeth (1997) *Imagining War: French and British Military Doctrine between the Wars* (Princeton, NJ: Princeton University Press).

Kim, Samuel S. (1999) "China in the United Nations" in Elizabeth Economy and Michel Oksenberg, eds., *China Joins the World: Progress and Prospects* (New York: Council on Foreign Relations) pp. 42–89.

Kinder, Donald R., and Lynn M. Sanders (1996) *Divided By Color: Racial Politics and Democratic Ideals* (Chicago: University of Chicago Press).

Kinder, Donald R., and David O. Sears (1981) "Prejudice and Politics: Symbolic Racism versus Racial Threats to the Good Life" *Journal of Personality and Social Psychology* 40:3 (March) pp. 414–31.

Knoke, David (1994) *Political Networks: The Structural Perspective* (London: Cambridge University Press).

Kocs, Stephen A. (1994) "Explaining the Strategic Behavior of States: International Law as System Structure" *International Studies Quarterly* 38:4 (December) pp. 535–56.

Kojima, Tomoyuki (2001) "To Make China a 'Responsible Major Power'— Japan's ODA Programs for China as Diplomatic Strategy" *Gaiko Forum* (February) pp. 38–45, in Foreign Broadcast Information Service, Daily Report— China, FBIS-CHI-2001–0110 (February 1).

Kowert, Paul (1997) "Place, Politics and National Identity" (American Political Science Association Annual Meeting, Washington, DC, August 28–31).

Kowert, Paul and Jeffery Legro (1996) "Norms, Identity, and Their Limits: A Theoretical Reprise" in Peter Katzenstein, ed., *The Culture of National Security* (New York: Columbia University Press).

Krasner, Stephen D. (1983) "Regimes and the Limits of Realism: Regimes as Autonomous Variables" in Stephen Krasner, ed., *International Regimes* (Ithaca, NY: Cornell University Press).

Kratochwil, Friedrich V. (1984) "The Force of Prescriptions" *International Organization* 38:4 (Autumn) pp. 685–708.

Kratochwil, Friedrich V. (1993) "Contract and Regimes" in Volker Rittberger, ed., *Regime Theory and International Relations* (New York: Oxford University Press).

Kratochwil, Friedrich V., and John Gerard Ruggie (1986) "International Organization: A State of the Art on an Art of the State" *International Organization* 40:4 (Autumn) pp. 753–75.

Kreps, David M. (1992) "Corporate Culture and Economic Theory" in James E. Alt and Kenneth A. Shepsle, eds., *Perspectives on Positive Political Economy* (London: Cambridge University Press) pp. 90–143.

Kristensen, Hans (1999) "US Nuclear Strategy Reform in the 1990s" (paper presented to the International Symposium: Denuclearization of Asia and the Role of Japan on Issues of Realizing Nuclear-Free Asia, Tokyo, December 18–19).

Kuklinski, James H., and Norman L. Hurley (1996) "It's a Matter of Interpretation" in Diana C. Mutz, Paul M. Sniderman, and Richard Brody, eds., *Political Persuasion and Attitude Change* (Ann Arbor: University of Michigan Press).

Laffey, Mark, and Jutta Weldes (1997) "Beyond Belief: Ideas and Symbolic Technologies in the Study of International Relations" *European Journal of International Relations* 3:2 (June) pp. 193–237.

Lake, David A., and Robert Powell (1999) "International Relations: A Strategic-Choice Approach" in David Lake and Robert Powell, eds., *Strategic Choice in International Relations* (Princeton, NJ: Princeton University Press).

Lanteigne, Marc (2005) *China and International Institutions: Alternate Paths to Global Power* (London: Routledge Press).

Lardy, Nicholas R. (1999) "China and the International Financial System" in Elizabeth Economy and Michel Oksenberg, eds., *China Joins the World: Progress and Prospects* (New York: Council on Foreign Relations) pp. 206–30.

Lawson, Robert J., Mark Gwozdecky, Jill Sinclair, and Ralph Lysyshyn (1999) "The Ottawa Process and the International Movement to Ban Anti-Personnel Mines" in Maxwell A. Cameron, Robert J. Lawson, and Brian W. Tomlin et al., eds., *To Walk Without Fear: The Global Movement to Ban Landmines* (Oxford: Oxford University Press) pp. 160–84.

Layne, Christopher (1993) "The Unipolar Illusion: Why New Great Powers Will Rise" *International Security* 17:4 (Spring) pp. 5–51.

Legro, Jeffrey W. (1995) *Cooperation under Fire: Anglo-German Restraint During World War II* (Ithaca, NY: Cornell University Press).

Legro, Jeffrey. W. (2005) *Rethinking the World: Great Power Strategies and International Order* (Ithaca, NY: Cornell University Press).

Leifer, Michael (1996) "The ASEAN Regional Forum: Extending ASEAN's Model of Regional Security" *Adelphi Paper* No. 302.

Lemke, Douglas, and William Reed (1998) "Power Is Not Satisfaction" *Journal of Conflict Resolution* 42:4 (August) pp. 511–16.

Levy, Jack (1994) "Learning and Foreign Policy: Sweeping a Conceptual Minefield" *International Organization* 48:2 (Spring) pp. 279–312.

Lewis, Jeffrey Glenn (2004) "The Minimum Means of Reprisal: China's Search for Security in the Nuclear Age" (PhD dissertation, University of Maryland).

Lewis, Jeffrey M. (2001) "Diplomacy in Europe's Polity: Socialization and the EU Permanent Representatives" (prepared for the IDNET second project workshop, "International Institutions and Socialization in the New Europe," European University Institute, Florence, May 18–19).

Lewis, Jeffrey M. (2003) "Institutional Environments and Everyday EU Decision Making: Rationalist or Constructivist?" *Comparative Political Studies* 36:1/2 (February–March) pp. 97–124.

LexisNexis (1993–1996).

Li Changhe (1995) Statement to the CCW Review Conference, September 27. CCW/CONF.I/SR.4 (October 3).

Li Jingjie (2003) "Zhong Mei jianshexing zhanlue huoban guanxi de queli yu qianjing" [The Establishment of and Prospects for Sino-US Constructive Strategic Partnership Relations], in Zhang Yunling, ed., *Huoban haishi duishou: Tiaozheng zhong de Zhong Mei Ri E guanxi* [Partners or Adversaries: Sino-US-Japan-Russian Relations in Transformation] (Beijing: Social Science Documents Press) pp. 80–143.

Li Mingjiang, and Liu Yunfei (2000) "Setting the Diplomatic Pattern for the New Century—Foreign Minister Tang Jiaxuan Discusses Chinese Diplomacy in 2000" Foreign Broadcast Information Service, Daily Report—China, FBIS-CHI-2000-1228 (December 28).

Li Shisheng (1992) "Guanyu guoji xin zhixu ji ge wenti de tan tao" [Discussion of Several Questions Relating to the New International Order] *Shijie jingji yu zhengzhi* [World Economics and Politics] No. 10, pp. 41–46.

Li Yuetang, and Zhou Bisong (1997) *He wuqi yu zhanzheng* [Nuclear Weapons and Warfare] (Beijing: National Defense Industry Press).

Liang Yunxiang, and Zhao Tian (2001) "Dongmeng diqu luntan de gongneng yu zuoyong tanxi" [Explorations of the Function and Role of the ASEAN Regional Forum] *Shijie jingji yu zhengzhi* [World Economics and Politics] No. 1, pp. 41–45.

Lindell, Ulf (1988) *Modern Multilateral Negotiation: The Consensus Rule and Its Implications in International Conferences* (Lund: Studentlitteratur).

Liu Gongliang (IAPCM) (1993) "Comments on the Legislation of the US Congress Nuclear Testing Limits in 1992" (June 3), JPRS-TND-93-024, July 27.

Liu Huaqiu, ed. (2000) *Junbei kongzhi yu caijun shouce* [Handbook of Arms Control and Disarmament] (Beijing: National Defense Industry Press).

Liu Jiangyong (1994) "On the Establishment of Asia-Pacific Multilateral Security Dialogue Mechanisms" *Contemporary International Relations* (Beijing) No. 2.

Liu Jie (2003) Zhongguo canyu guoji jizhi de lilun yu shijian [The Theory and Practice of China's Participation in International Institutions] *Mao Zedong Deng Xiaoping lilun yanjiu* [Studies in Mao Zedong and Deng Xiaoping Theory] No. 4, pp. 80–84.

Liu Min (1995) "Utilizing the Nuclear Warheads In a Peaceful Method" in Program on Science and National Security Studies, ed., *Arms Control: Collected Works* (Beijing: Institute of Applied Physics and Computational Mathematics) pp. 139–42.

Liu Xue Cheng (1997) "Confidence Building Diplomacy in the Asia-Pacific Region" *International Review* (Beijing: China Center of International Studies).

Lott, Bernice, and Alfred J. Lott (1985) "Learning Theory in Contemporary Social Psychology" in Gardner Lindzey and Elliot Aronson, eds., *Handbook of Social Psychology* (New York: Random House) pp. 109–35.

Lovaglia, Michael J. (1995) "Power and Status: Exchange, Attribution, and Expectation States" *Small Group Research* 26:3 (August) pp. 400–26.

Lowe, Will (2000) "Topographic Maps of Semantic Space" (PhD dissertation, Institute for Adaptive and Neural Computation, Division of Informatics, University of Edinburgh).

Lu Song (1997) "Guoji fa zai guoji guanxi zhong de zuoyong" [The Effect of International Law in International Relations] *Waijiao xueyuan xuebao* [Foreign Affairs College Journal] No. 1, pp. 5–14.

Luke, Timothy W. (1989) " 'What's Wrong with Deterrence?' A Semiotic Interpretation of National Security Policy" in James Der Derian and Michael Shapiro, eds., *Intertextual/International Relations: Postmodern and Poststructural Readings of World Politics*, (Lexington, MA: Lexington Books) pp. 207–29.

Lumsdaine, David (1993) *Moral Vision in International Politics: The Foreign Aid Regime, 1949–1989* (Princeton, NJ: Princeton University Press).

Lupia, Arthur, and Matthew D. McCubbins (1998) *The Democratic Dilemma: Can Citizens Learn What They Need to Know?* (Cambridge: Cambridge University Press).

MacLaren, Robert (1980) *Civil Servants and Public Policy: A Comparative Study of International Secretariats* (Waterloo, ON: Wilfred Laurier University Press).

Macy, Michael W. (1993) "Social Learning and the Structure of Collective Action" in *Advances in Group Processes*, Vol. 10 (Greenwich, CT: JAI Press).

Makabenta, Leah (1994) "ASEAN: China Looms Large at Security Meet" *Interpress Service*, July 22.

Malik, J. Mohan (1995) "China's Policy Towards Nuclear Arms Control in the Post-Cold War Era" *Contemporary Security Policy* 16:2 (August) pp. 1–43.

Martin, Lisa L. (1993) "The Rational Choice State of Multilateralism" in John Gerard Ruggie, ed., *Multilateralism Matters: The Theory and Praxis of an Institutional Form* (New York: Columbia University Press).

Martin, Lisa L. (1999) "An Institutionalist View: International Institutions and State Strategies" in T. V. Paul and John A. Hall, eds., *International Order and the Future of World Politics* (Cambridge: Cambridge University Press) pp. 78–98.

Martin, Lisa L., and Beth A. Simmons (1998) "Theories and Empirical Studies of International Institutions" *International Organization* 52:4 (Autumn) pp. 729–57.

Mearsheimer, John (2001) *The Tragedy of Great Power Politics* (New York: W. W. Norton).

Medeiros, Evan (2006) *Shaping China's Foreign Policy: The Evolution of Chinese Policies on WMD Nonproliferation* (Stanford: Stanford University Press).

Medeiros, Evan, and Bates Gill (2000) *Chinese Arms Exports: Policy, Players and Process* (Carlisle, PA: Strategic Studies Institute).

Meng Xiangqing (2002) "Lun Zhongguo de guoji juese zhuanghuan yu dui wai anquan zhanlue de jiben dingwei" [On the Transformation in China's International Role and the Basic Orientation of Foreign Security Strategy] *Shijie jingji yu zhengzhi* [World Economics and Politics] No. 7, pp. 1–7.

Mercer, Jonathan (1995) "Anarchy and Identity" *International Organization* 49:2 (Spring) pp. 229–52.

Meyer, John W. et al. (1997) "The Structuring of a World Environmental Regime, 1870–1990" *International Organization* 51:4 (Autumn) pp. 623–51.

Ministry of Education (2004) "Sixiang zhengzhi kecheng biaozhun" [Course Standards for Ideology and Politics] (Beijing: People's Education Publishing House).

Modelski, George (1974) *World Power Concentrations: Typology, Data, Explanatory Framework* (Princeton, NJ: Princeton University Press).

Mohr, Lawrence B. (1996) *The Causes of Human Behavior: Implications for Theory and Methods in the Social Sciences* (Ann Arbor: University of Michigan Press).

Moore, Thomas G., and Dixia Yang (2001) "Empowered and Restrained: Chinese Foreign Policy in the Age of Economic Interdependence" in David M. Lampton, ed., *The Making of Chinese Foreign and Security Policy* (Stanford: Stanford University Press) pp. 191–229.

Moravcsik, Andrew (1995) "Explaining International Human Rights Regimes: Liberal Theory and Western Europe" *European Journal of International Relations* 1:2 (June) pp. 157–89.

Moravcsik, Andrew (1997) "Taking Preferences Seriously: A Liberal Theory of International Politics" *International Organization* 51:4 (Autumn) pp. 513–53.

Moravcsik, Andrew (2001) "A Constructivist Research Programme in EU Studies?" *European Union Politics* 2:2, pp. 226–40.

Morgenthau, Hans (1978) *Politics Among Nations: The Struggle for Power and Peace* (New York: Knopf).

Morrow, James D. (1994) *Game Theory for Political Scientists* (Princeton, NJ: Princeton University Press).

Mouritzen, Hans (1990) *The International Civil Service: A Study of Bureaucracy: International Organizations* (Brookfield, VT: Dartmouth).

Muldoon, Jr., James P. (1998) Introduction to James P. Muldoon, Jr. et al. eds., *Multilateral Diplomacy and the United Nations Today* (Boulder, CO: Westview Press).

Muller, Harald (1993) "The Internalization of Principles, Norms, and Rules by Governments: The Case of Security Regimes" in Volker Rittenberger, ed., *Regime Theory and International Relations* (Oxford: Clarendon Press) pp. 361–88.

Mutz, Diana C., Paul M. Sniderman, and Richard A. Brody (1996) "Political Persuasion: The Birth of a Field of Study" in Diana C. Mutz et al., eds., *Political Persuasion and Attitude Change* (Ann Arbor: University of Michigan Press).

Nadelmann, Ethan A. (1990) "Global Prohibition Regimes: The Evolution of Norms in International Society" *International Organization* 44:4 (Autumn) pp. 479–526.

Napier, Rodney W., and Matti K. Gershenfeld (1987) *Groups: Theory and Experience*, 4th ed. (Boston: Houghton Mifflin).

Nathan, Andrew, and Robert S. Ross (1997) *The Great Wall and the Empty Fortress: China's Search for Security* (New York: W. W. Norton).

Nemeth, Charles J. (1987) "Influence Processes, Problem Solving and Creativity" in Mark P. Zanna, James M. Olson, and C. Peter Herman, eds., *Social Influence: The Ontario Symposium*, Vol. 5 (Hillsdale, NJ: Lawrence Erlbaum Associates).

Ness, Gayl D., and Steven R. Brechin (1988) "Bridging the Gap: International Organizations as Organizations" *International Organization* 42:2 (Spring) pp. 245–73.

Nisbett, Richard E., and Dov Cohen (1996) *Culture of Honor: The Psychology of Violence in the South* (Boulder, CO: Westview Press).

North, Douglass C. (1990) *Institutions, Institutional Change and Economic Performance* (Cambridge: Cambridge University Press).

Nuclear Science and Technology Information Research Institute (1994) "Guowai dui women he shiyan de fanying" [Foreign Reaction to Our Tests] in *Guowai hewuqi dongtai* [Trends in Foreign Nuclear Weapons] 12: 6 (December) p. 1.

Nuclear Science and Technology Information Research Institute (1995a) *Fandui junbei jingsai weihu shijie heping* [Oppose Arms Races, Preserve World Peace] CNIC-NMC-045 (Beijing, November).

Nuclear Science and Technology Information Research Institute (1995b) *Fandui junbei jingsai weihu shijie heping* [Oppose Arms Races, Preserve World Peace] CNIC-NMC-046 (Beijing, December).

Nuclear Science and Technology Information Research Institute (1996) *Fandui junbei jingsai weihu shijie heping* [Oppose Arms Races, Preserve World Peace] CNIC-NMC-061 (Beijing, December).

Ochs, Elinor (1986) Introduction to Bambi B. Schieffelin and Elinor Ochs, eds., *Language Socialization across Cultures* (Cambridge: Cambridge University Press).

Oksenberg, Michel, and Elizabeth Economy (1998) "China's Accession to and Implementation of International Environmental Accords 1978–95" in Edith Brown Weiss and Harold K. Jacobson, eds., *Engaging Countries: Strengthening Compliance with International Environmental Accords* (Cambridge, MA: The MIT Press).

Oneal, John R., Indra de Soysa, and Yong-Hee Park (1998) "But Power and Wealth Are Satisfying" *Journal of Conflict Resolution* 42:2 (August) pp. 517–20.

O'Neill, Barry (1999) *Honor, Symbols and War* (Ann Arbor: University of Michigan Press).

Onuf, Nicholas (1998) "Constructivism: A User's Manual" in Vendulka Kubalkova, Nicholas Onuf, and Paul Kowert, eds., *International Relations in a Constructed World* (Armonk, NY: M. E. Sharpe) pp. 58–78.

Organski, A.F.K., and Jacek Kugler (1980) *The War Ledger* (Chicago: University of Chicago Press).

Ostrom, Elinor (1998) "A Behavioral Approach to the Rational Choice Theory of Collective Action" *American Political Science Review* 92:1 (March) pp. 1–22.

Owen, John M. IV (1997) *Liberal Peace, Liberal War: American Politics and International Security* (Ithaca, NY: Cornell University Press).

PacNet (1996) "Chairman's Statement" and "Commentary" No. 47 (November 22).

Pan Zhenqiang (1987) "Dangqian guoji caijun douzheng xingshi yu wo guo de diwei he zuoyong" [The Current International Disarmament Struggle and Our Country's Position and Effect] in China Institute of Contemporary International Relations, ed., *Guoji caijun douzheng yu Zhongguo* [China and the International Arms Control Struggle] (Beijing: Shishi Publishing House).

Pearson, Margaret M. (1999a) "China's Integration into the International Trade and Investment Regime" in Elizabeth Economy and Michel Oksenberg, eds., *China Joins the World: Progress and Prospects* (New York: Council on Foreign Relations) pp. 161–205.

Pearson, Margaret M. (1999b) "The Major Multilateral Economic Institutions Engage China" in Alastair Iain Johnston and Robert S. Ross, eds., *Engaging China: The Management of a Rising Power* (London: Routledge Press) pp. 207–34.

Pearson, Margaret M. (2006) "China in Geneva: Lessons from China's Early Years in the World Trade Organization" in Alastair Iain Johnston and Robert S. Ross, eds., *New Directions in the Study of China's Foreign Policy* (Stanford: Stanford University Press) pp. 242–75.

Perloff, Richard M. (1993) *The Dynamics of Persuasion* (Hillsdale, NJ: Lawrence Erlbaum Associates).

Petty, Richard E., Duane T. Wegener, and Leandre R. Fabrigar (1997) "Attitudes and Attitude Change" *Annual Review of Psychology* 48, pp. 609–47.

Pierson, Paul (2000) "Path Dependence, Increasing Returns, and the Study of Politics" *American Political Science Review* 94: 2 (June) pp. 251–67.

Powell, Colin (2002). Remarks at the Asia Society Annual Dinner, New York, June 10. http://www.state.gov/secretary/rm/2002/10983.htm.

PRC CSCAP (n.d., 1997?) "Preliminary List of Members of CSCAP China Committee."

Price, Richard (1998) "Reversing the Gun Sights: Transnational Civil Society Targets Landmines" *International Organization* 52:3 (Summer) pp. 613–44.

Price, Richard, and Nina Tannenwald (1996) "Norms and Deterrence: The Nuclear and Chemical Weapons Taboos" in Peter Katzenstein, ed., *The Culture of National Security: Norms and Identity in World Politics* (New York: Columbia University Press).

Program on Science and National Security Studies (1994) *Junbei kongzhi yanjiu lunwen ji* [Collected Research Essays on Arms Control] (Beijing: PSNSS).

Qin Yaqing (2003) "Guojia shenfen, zhanlue wenhua he anquan liyi" [National Identity, Strategic Culture, and Security Interests] *Shijie jingji yu zhengzhi* [World Economics and Politics] No. 1, pp. 10–15.

Qing Wenhui, and Sun Hui (2001) "Hou lengzhan shidai de Zhongguo guojia anquan" [China's National Security in the Post–Cold War Era] *Zhanlue yu guanli* [Strategy and Management] No. 1, pp. 1–9.

Qu Geping (1990) "Guowuyuan huanjing baohu weihuanhui fu zhuren, guojia huanjing baohu ju juzhang Qu Geping zai guowuyuan huanjing baohu weiyuanhui di shi jiu ci huiyi shang de jianghua" [State Council Environmental Protection Committee Deputy Director, State Environmental Protection Agency Director, Qu Geping's Speech to the 19th Meeting of the State Council Environmental Protection Committee] (December 18) in State Council Environmental Protection Committee Secretariat, eds., *Guowuyuan huanjing baohu weiyuanhui wenjian huibian* [Collected Documents of the State Council Environmental Protection Committee], Vol. 2 (Beijing).

Qu Geping (1992) "Fazhan wo guo huanjing baohu chanye shi zai bixing" [The Development of Our Country's Environmental Protection Industrial Power Is Necessary] (April 19) in State Council Environmental Protection Committee Secretariat, eds., *Guowuyuan huanjing baohu weiyuanhui wenjian huibian* [Collected Documents of the State Council Environmental Protection Committee], Vol. 2 (Beijing).

Reiter, Dan (1996) *Crucible of Beliefs: Learning, Alliances, and World Wars* (Ithaca, NY: Cornell University Press).

Resende-Santos, Joao (1996) "Anarchy and the Emulation of Military Systems: Military Organization and Technology in South America, 1870–1930" *Security Studies* 5:3 (Spring) pp. 193–260.

Reus-Smit, Christian (1997) "The Constitutional Structure of International Society and the Nature of Fundamental Institutions" *International Organization* 51:4 (Autumn) pp. 555–89.

Ridgeway, Cecilia L., Elizabeth Heger Boyle, Kathy J. Kuipers, and Dawn T. Robinson (1998) "How Do Status Beliefs Develop? The Role of Resources and Interactional Experience" *American Sociological Review* 68 (June) pp. 331–50.

Risse, Thomas (1997) "Let's Talk" (paper presented to the American Political Science Association Annual Conference, Washington, DC, August 28–31).

Risse, Thomas (2000) "Let's Argue: Communicative Action in World Politics" *International Organization* 54:1 (Winter) pp. 1–39.

Risse, Thomas, and Katherine Sikkink (1999) "The Socialization of International Human Rights Norms into Domestic Practices: Introduction" in Thomas Risse and Katherine Sikkink, eds., *The Power of Human Rights: International Norms and Domestic Change* (Cambridge: Cambridge University Press) pp. 1–38.

Roberts, Brad (1995) "Revised Task Force Report No. 2: The Asia-Pacific and the Global Treaty Regime: The Agenda after NPT Expansion" (US CSCAP, April 23).

Rogowski, Ronald (1999) "Institutions as Constraints on Strategic Choice" in David A. Lake and Robert Powell, eds., *Strategic Choice in International Relations* (Princeton, NJ: Princeton University Press).

Romer, Daniel, Kathleen H. Jamieson, Catherine Riegner, Mika Emori, and Brigette Rouson (1997) "Blame Discourse versus Realistic Conflict as Explanations of Ethnic Tension in Urban Neighborhoods" *Political Communication* 14: 3 (July) pp. 273–91.

Rose, Gideon (1997) "Neoclassical Realism and Theories of Foreign Policy" (paper prepared for the American Political Science Association Annual Meeting, Washington, DC, August 28–31).

Rousseau, David L. (2002) "Motivations for Choice: The Salience of Relative Gains in International Politics" *Journal of Conflict Resolution* 46:3 (June) pp. 394–426.

Rousseau, David L. (2006) *Identifying Threats and Threatening Identities: The Social Construction of Realism and Liberalism* (Stanford: Stanford University Press).

Ruan Zongze (1996) "Lengzhan hou Meiguo DongYa anquan zhanlue zouxiang" [The Direction of US East Asia Security Strategy after the Cold War] *Heping yu fazhan* [Peace and Development] No. 2, pp. 49–52.

Ruggie, John Gerard (1993) "Multilateralism: The Anatomy of an Institution" in John Gerard Ruggie, ed., *Multilateralism Matters: The Theory and Praxis of an Institutional Form* (New York: Columbia University Press).

Ruggie, John Gerard (1998) *Constructing the World Polity: Essays on International Institutionalization* (London: Routledge Press).

Rule, Brendon Gail, and Gay L. Bisanz (1987) "Goals and Strategies of Persuasion: A Cognitive Schema for Understanding Social Events" in Mark P. Zanna, James M. Olson, and C. Peter Herman, eds., *Social Influence: The Ontario Symposium*, Vol. 5 (Hillsdale, NJ: Lawrence Erlbaum Associates).

Schelling, Thomas (1960) *The Strategy of Conflict* (Cambridge, MA: Harvard University Press).

Schieffelin, Bambi B., and Elinor Ochs, eds. (1986) *Language Socialization Across Cultures* (Cambridge: Cambridge University Press).

Schimmelfennig, Frank (2002) "Introduction: The Impact of International Organizations on the Central and Eastern European States—Conceptual and Theoretical Issues" in Ronald H. Linden, ed., *Norms and Nannies: The Impact of International Organizations on the Central and Eastern European States* (Lanham, MD: Rowman and Littlefield) pp. 1–32.

Schroeder, Paul W. (1994) "Historical Reality vs. Neorealist Theory" *International Security* 19:1 (Summer) pp. 108–48.

Schwarz, Norbert, Herbert Bless, and Gerd Bohner (1991) *Advances in Experimental Social Psychology*, Vol. 24 (New York: Academic Press) pp. 161–201.

Schweller, Randall (1994) "Bandwagoning for Profit: Bringing the Revisionist State Back In" *International Security* 19:1 (Summer) pp. 72–107.

Schweller, Randall (1996) "Neorealism's Status-Quo Bias: What Security Dilemma?" *Security Studies* 5:3 (Spring) pp. 225–58.

Schweller, Randall (1999) "Managing the Rise of Great Powers: History and Theory" in Alastair Iain Johnston and Robert S. Ross, eds., *Engaging China: The Management of a Rising Power* (London: Routledge Press) pp. 1–31.

Searle, John (1992) *The Social Construction of Reality* (Cambridge, MA: MIT Press).

Sears, David O., and Carolyn Funk (1991) "The Role of Self-Interest in Social and Political Attitudes" in *Advances in Experimental Social Psychology*, Vol. 24 (New York: Academic Press) pp. 2–92.

Sellers, Robert M., Mia A. Smith, J. Nicole Shelton, Stephanie A. J. Rowley, and Tabbye M. Chavous (1998) "Multidimensional Model of Racial Identity: A Reconceptualization of African American Racial Identity" *Personality and Social Psychology Review* 2:1, pp. 18–39.

Shambaugh, George E. (1997) "Constructivism, Entrepreneurship and the Power to Socialize Rogue States" (paper presented to the American Political Science Association Annual Meeting, Washington, DC, August 28–31).

Shang Guozhen (1996) "Lue lun Nansha wenti guojihua qushi ji women de duice" [An Outline Discussion of the Internationalization Trends on the Nansha Question and Our Countermeasures] *Nansha wenti yanjiu ziliao* [Research Materials on the Nansha Question] (Beijing: Chinese Academy of Social Sciences, Asia-Pacific Research Center) pp. 288–95.

Shelly, Robert K., and Murray Webster, Jr. (1997) "How Formal Status, Liking, and Ability Status Structure Interaction" *Sociological Perspectives* 40:1, pp. 81–107.

Shepsle, Kenneth A., and Mark S. Bonchek (1997) *Analyzing Politics: Rationality, Behavior, and Institutions* (New York: W. W. Norton).

Shi Chunlai (1997) "Border CBMs in Asia" (presentation at the 3rd CSCAP North Pacific Meeting, December 15).

Shi Chunlai, and Xu Jian (1997) "Preventive Diplomacy Pertinent to the Asia-Pacific" *International Review* (China Center for International Studies) No. 4 (July).

Shirk, Susan (2007) *China: Fragile Superpower: How China's Internal Politics Could Derail Its Peaceful Rise* (New York: Oxford University Press).

Sigal, Leon V. (2006) *Negotiating Minefields: The Landmines Ban in American Politics* (New York: Routledge Press).

Simmons, Beth S. (2000) "Money and Law: Why Comply with the Public International Law on Money?" *Yale Journal of International Law* 25:2 (Summer) pp. 323–62.

Simon, Sheldon W. (2001) "Evaluating TRACK II Approaches to Security Diplomacy in the Asia Pacific: The CSCAP Experience" (paper presented to the American Political Science Association Annual Meeting, San Francisco, August 30–September 2).

Smith, Gary (1997) "Multilateralism and Regional Security in Asia: The ASEAN Regional Forum and APEC's Geopolitical Value" Working Paper No. 97–2 (Center for International Affairs, Harvard University, February).

Sniderman, Paul M., Richard A. Brody, and Philip E. Tetlock (1991) *Reasoning and Choice: Explorations in Political Psychology* (New York: Cambridge University Press).

Sniderman, Paul M., Louk Hagendoorn, and Markus Prior (2004) "Predisposing Factors and Situational Triggers: Exclusionary Reactions to Immigrant Minorities" *American Political Science Review* 98:1 (February) pp. 35–49.

Song Jian, ed. (2001) *Liang dan yi xing: Yun xun zhuan* [Biographies of the Founding Fathers of the Nuclear, Missile, and Satellite Programs] Vol. 1 (Beijing: Qinghua University Press).

State Council (1992) Environmental Protection Committee Secretariat, *Wo guo guanyu quanqiu huanjing wenti de yuanze lichang* [Our Country's Principles and Positions Regarding Global Environmental Issues] (Beijing).

State Council (1995a) Delegation to Helsinki Meeting on Ozone Layer Protection, "Guanyu canjia baohu chouyang ceng He'erxinji guoji huiyi de zongjie baogao" [Summary Report Concerning Participation in the Helsinki International Conference on Protection of the Ozone Layer] (May 8, 1989) in State Council Environmental Protection Committee Secretariat, ed., *Guowuyuan huanjing baohu weiyuanhui wenjian huibian* [Collected Documents of the State Council Environmental Protection Committee] Vol. 2 (Beijing).

State Council (1995b) "Chuxi lianheguo huanjing guihua shu zhixing lishihui di shi liu jie huiyi de zongjie baogao" [Summary Report of the Delegation to the Sixteenth UNEP Implementation Board Meeting] (May 31, 1991) in State Council Environmental Protection Committee Secretariat, ed., *Guowuyuan huanjing baohu weiyuanhui wenjian huibian* [Collected Documents of the State Council Environmental Protection Committee] Vol. 2 (Beijing).

Steiner, Jurg (1974) *Amicable Agreement versus Majority Rule: Conflict Resolution in Switzerland* (Chapel Hill: University of North Carolina Press).

Sterling-Folker, Jennifer (1997) "Realist Environment, Liberal Process, and Domestic-Level Variables" *International Studies Quarterly* 41:1 (March) pp. 1–26.

Straits Times (Singapore) (1993–1996).

Stryker, Sheldon, and Anne Statham (1985) "Symbolic Interaction and Role Theory" in Gardner Lindzey and Elliot Aronson, eds., *Handbook of Social Psychology*, Vol. 1, *Theory and Method* (New York: Random House).

Suettinger, Robert L. (2003) *Beyond Tiananmen: The Politics of US-China Relations, 1989–2000* (Washington, DC: Brookings Institution).

Sun Xiaoying (1996) "Zhongguo ying bu ying rang chu Nansha qundao?" [Should China Give Way on the Nansha Islands?] *Nansha wenti yanjiu ziliao* [Research Materials on the Nansha Question] (Beijing: Chinese Academy of Social Sciences, Asia-Pacific Research Center) pp. 295–302.

Susskind, Lawrence (1994) *Environmental Diplomacy: Negotiating More Effective Global Agreements* (London: Oxford University Press).

Tajfel, Henri, and John C. Turner (2001) "An Integrative Theory of Intergroup Conflict" in W. G. Austin and S. Worchel, eds., *The Social Psychology of Intergroup Relations* (Monterey, CA: Brooks-Cole, 1979); reprinted in Michael A. Hogg and Dominic Abrams, eds., *Intergroup Relations: Essential Readings* (Philadelphia, PA: Psychology Press) pp. 94–109.

Tang Shiping (2001) "Zailun Zhongguo de da zhanlue" [Once Again on China's Grand Strategy] *Zhanlue yu guanli* [Strategy and Management] No. 4, pp. 29–37.

Tang Shiping, and Zhang Yunling (2004) "Zhongguo de diqu zhanlue" [China's Regional Strategy] *Shijie jingji yu zhengzhi* [World Economics and Politics] No. 6, pp. 1–11.

Tang Shiping, and Zhou Xiaobing (2001) "Dongmeng, Zhongguo, Riben de hezuo ji DongYa de weilai" [ASEAN—China—Japan Cooperation and the Future of East Asia] *Guoji jingji pinglun* [Commentary on International Economics] No. 6, pp. 19–24.

Thies, Cameron (2001) "State Socialization and Structural Realism" (paper prepared for the International Studies Association Annual Meeting, Chicago, February).

Thomas, Ward (2001) "Ethical Stigma and State Compliance with Arms Control Agreements" (paper prepared for the American Political Science Association Annual Meeting, San Francisco, August 30–September 2).

Thompson, William (1988) *On Global War* (Columbia: University of South Carolina Press).

Toft, Monica (2003) *The Geography of Ethnic Violence: Identity, Interests, and Territory* (Princeton, NJ: Princeton University Press).

Tomlin, Brian (1999) "On a Fast Track to a Ban: The Canadian Policy Process" in Maxwell A. Cameron, Robert J. Lawson, and Brian W. Tomlin et al., eds., *To Walk Without Fear: The Global Movement to Ban Landmines* (Oxford: Oxford University Press) pp. 185–211.

Trondal, Jarle (2001) "Why Europeanization Happens: The Transformative Power of EU Committees" (prepared for the IDNET second project workshop, "International Institutions and Socialization in the New Europe," European University Institute, Florence, May 18–19).

Turner, John C. (1987) *Rediscovering the Social Group: A Self-Categorization Theory* (Oxford: Basil Blackwell).

Turner, John C. (1999) "Some Current Issues in Research on Social Identity and Self-Categorization Theory" in Naomi Ellemers, Russell Spears, and Bertjan Doosje, eds., *Social Identity: Context, Commitment, Content* (Malden, MA: Blackwell) pp. 6–34.

Turner, Jonathan (1988) *A Theory of Social Interaction* (Stanford: Stanford University Press).

UNDP (2001) *Human Development Report 2001* (New York: United Nations Development Programme).

Union of International Associations (2000/2001) *Yearbook of International Organizations,* 37th ed. (Brussels: Union of International Associations).

US CSCAP (1997) "USCSCAP Board of Directors."

Valley, Kathleen L., Joseph Moag, and Max H. Bazerman (1998) " 'A Matter of Trust': Effects of Communication on the Efficiency and Distribution of Outcomes" *Journal of Economic Behavior and Organization* 34:2, pp. 211–38.

Van Ness, Peter (1970) *Revolution and Chinese Foreign Policy: Peking's Support for Wars of National Liberation* (Berkeley: University of California Press).

Vasquez, John A. (1993) *The War Puzzle* (Cambridge: Cambridge University Press).

Verdery, Katherine (1993) "Whither 'Nation' and 'Nationalism'?" *Daedalus* 122:3 (Summer) pp. 37–46.

Vertzberger, Yaacov (1990) *The World in Their Minds: Information Processing, Cognition, and Perception in Foreign Policy Decision-Making* (Stanford: Stanford University Press).

Wachman, Alan (2001) "Does the Diplomacy of Shame Promote Human Rights in China?" *Third World Quarterly* 22:2 (April) pp. 257–81.

Waever, Ole (1990) "The Language of Foreign Policy" *Journal of Peace Research* 27:3, pp. 335–43.

Waldron, Arthur (2001) "News: China Agrees to Free US Plane Crew" *Daily Telegraph* (April 12).

Wallander, Celeste (1999) *Mortal Friends, Best Enemies: German-Russian Cooperation after the Cold War* (Ithaca, NY: Cornell University Press).

Waltz, Kenneth (1979) *Theory of International Politics* (New York: Random House).

Waltz, Kenneth (1997) "Evaluating Theories" *American Political Science Review* 91:4 (December) pp. 913–18.

Wang Houqing, Wang Chaotian, and Huang Dafu (1990), *Jubu zhanzhengzhong de zhanyi* [Campaigns in Limited Wars] (Beijing: National Defense University Press).

Wang Shuzhong (1987) "Caijun douzheng yu ji ge renshi wenti" [Disarmament Struggle and a Few Questions of Understanding] in China Institute of Contemporary International Relations, ed., *Guoji caijun douzheng yu Zhongguo* [China and the International Arms Control Struggle] (Beijing: Shishi Publishing House).

Wang Wenrong (1999) *Zhanlue xue* [Strategy Studies] (Beijing: National Defense University Press).

Wang Yizhou (2001) "Xin shiji de Zhongguo yu duobian waijiao" [The New Century China and Multilateral Diplomacy] (paper presented to a research conference on "Theory of Multilateralism and Multilateral Diplomacy," Beijing).

Warmington, Valeri, and Cecilia Tuttle (1999) "The Canadian Campaign" in Maxwell A. Cameron, Robert J. Lawson, and Brian W. Tomlin et al., eds., *To Walk Without Fear: The Global Movement to Ban Landmines* (Oxford: Oxford University Press) pp. 48–59.

Webster, Murray, Jr., and Stuart J. Hysom (1998) "Creating Status Characteristics" *American Sociological Review* 63:3 (June) pp. 351–78.

Weiner, Jonathan (1994) *The Beak of the Finch: A Story of Evolution in Our Time* (New York: Vintage Books).

Wendt, Alexander (1992) "Anarchy Is What States Make of It: The Social Construction of Power Politcs" *International Organization* 46:2 (Spring) pp. 391–425.

Wendt, Alexander (1994) "Collective Identity Formation and the International State" *American Political Science Review* 88:2 (June) pp. 384–96.

Wendt, Alexander (1999) *Social Theory of International Relations* (Cambridge: Cambridge University Press).

Westin, Susan S. (2002) Government Accounting Office Managing Director for International Affairs and Trade, Testimony Before the Congressional-Executive Commission on China, June 6. http://www.cecc.gov/pages/hearings/060602/westinTestimony.pdf.

Wetherell, Margaret (1987) "Social Identity and Group Polarization" in John C. Turner, *Rediscovering the Social Group* (Oxford: Basil Blackwell).

Whorf, Benjamin Lee (1956) *Language, Thought and Reality* (Cambridge, MA: MIT Press).

Williams, Jodie (1995) "Conference Prospects" *CCW News* (September 27).

Williams, Jodie, and Stephen Goose (1999) in Maxwell A. Cameron, Robert J. Lawson, and Brian W. Tomlin et al. eds., *To Walk Without Fear: The Global Movement to Ban Landmines* (Oxford: Oxford University Press) pp. 20–47.

Williams, Michael C. (1997) "The Institutions of Security" *Cooperation and Conflict* 32:3, pp. 287–307.

Wittgenstein, Ludwig (1958) *Philosophical Investigations* (Oxford: Basil Blackwell).

Woodmansey, Ian (1995) "Perspectives: Military, Yes; Humanitarian, No." *CCW News* (October 4).

Wu Chenghuan, and David R. Shaffer (1987) "Susceptibility to Persuasive Appeals as a Function of Source Credibility and Prior Experience with Attitudinal Object" *Journal of Personality and Social Psychology* 52:4 (April) pp. 677–88.

Wu Xinbo (2006) *Taipingyang shang bu tai ping: Hou lengzhan shidai de Meiguo YaTai anquan zhanlue* [Turbulent War: US Asia-Pacific Security Strategy in the Post–Cold War Era] (Shanghai: Fudan University Press).

Wu Yun (1996) "China's Policies Towards Arms Control and Disarmament: From Passive Responding to Active Leading" *Pacific Review* 9:4, pp. 577–606.

Wu Zhan (1994) "Some Thoughts on Nuclear Arms Control" (conference on South Asia Arms Control, Shanghai, March).

Wu Zheng (1996) "Quanmian jinzhi he shiyan tiaoyue tanpan jinzhan qingkuang" [The State of Development of the Negotiations on the Comprehensive Nuclear Test Ban Treaty] in *Guowai he wuqi dongtai* [Trends in Foreign Nuclear Weapons] No. 3 (May 8) pp. 9–10.

Xia Liping (2001) "China: A Responsible Great Power" *Journal of Contemporary China* 10:26 (February) pp. 17–25.

Xiao Yingrong (2003) "Zhongguo de daguo zeren yu diquzhuyi zhanlue" [China's Major Power Responsibilities and Strategy Toward Regionalism] *Shijie jingji yu zhengzhi* [World Economics and Politics] No. 1 pp. 46–51.

Xu Weidi (1996) "Ya-Tai diqu anquan huanjing fenxi" [Analysis of the Security Environment in the Asia-Pacific Region] *Neibu canyue* [Internal Reference Readings] (Beijing: Central Committee Documents Publishing House) pp. 251–54.

Yan Shengyi (2004) *Dangdai Zhongguo waijiao* [Contemporary Chinese Foreign Policy] (Shanghai: Fudan University Press).

Yan Xuetong (1997) *Zhongguo guojia liyi fenxi* [Analysis of China's National Interest] (Tianjin: People's Publishing House).

Yan Xuetong (2005) *Guoji zhengzhi yu Zhongguo* [International Politics and China] (Beijing: Peking University Press).

Yang Bojiang (1999) "Riben lengzhanhou de anquan zhanlue" in Yan Xuetong, ed., *Zhongguo yu YaTai anquan* [China and Asia-Pacific Security] (Beijing: Shishi Publishing House).

Yang Jiemian (1996) "Meiguo daxuan he Kelindun zhengfu tiaozheng dui Hua zhengce" [The US Election and Adjustment in the Clinton Administration China Policy] *Meiguo yanjiu* [American Studies] No. 4 pp. 128–34.

Yang Yiyong, ed. (1997) *Gongping yu xiaolu: Dangdai Zhongguo de shouru fenpei wenti* [Fairness and Efficiency: Problems in Income Distribution in Contemporary China] (Beijing: Today's China Publishing House).

Yee, Albert S. (1996) "The Causal Effects of Ideas on Policies" *International Organization* 50:1 (Winter) pp. 69–108.

Young, Oran (1992) "The Effectiveness of International Institutions: Hard Cases and Critical Variables" in James Rosenau and Ernst-Otto Czempiel, eds., *Governance without Government: Order and Change in World Politics* (Cambridge: Cambridge University Press).

Yu Zhiyong (1988) "Guanyu he bu kuosan tiaoyue ruogan wenti de zai renshi" [Additional Thoughts on Several Questions Relating to the Non-proliferation Treaty] *Shijie jingji yu zhengzhi* [World Economics and Politics] No. 6, pp. 38–39.

Yuan Jing-dong (1996) "Conditional Multilateralism: Chinese Views on Order and Regional Security" *CANCAPS Papiers* No. 9 (March).

Zhang Biwu (2002) "China's Perception of the United States: An Exploration of China's Foreign Policy Motivations" (PhD dissertation, Ohio State University, Department of Political Science).

Zhang Yunling (1998) "Zonghe anquan guan ji dui wo guo anquan de sikao" [The Concept of Comprehensive Security and Reflections on China's Security] (unpublished research report, Beijing).

Zhang Yunling (2000) "Zonghe anquan guan ji dui wo guo anquan de sikao" [The Concept of Comprehensive Security and Reflections on China's Security] *Dangdai Ya Tai* [Contemporary Asia-Pacific Studies] No. 1, pp. 1–16.

Zhao, Jimin, and Leonard Ortolano (2003) "The Chinese Government's Role in Implementing Multilateral Environmental Agreements: The Case of the Montreal Protocol" *China Quarterly* No. 175 (September) pp. 708–25.

Zhao Zijin (1998) "ZhongMei guanxi zhong de Riben yinsu" [The Japan Element in Sino-U.S. Relations] in Zhu Chenghu, ed., *ZhongMei guanxi de fazhan bianhua ji qi qushi* [Changes in the Development of Sino-US Relations and Future Trends] (Nanjing: Jiangsu People's Press) pp. 347–71.

Zhu Jianshi (1995) "Nuclear Explosion for Preventing Collision between the Earth and Celestial Bodies" in Program on Science and National Security Studies, ed., *Arms Control: Collected Works* (Beijing: Institute of Applied Physics and Computational Mathematics) pp. 135–38.

Zhuang Qubing (1984) "Meiguo 'xingqiu da zhan' jihua pouxi" [Preliminary Analysis of the US 'Star Wars' Plan] *Guoji wenti yanjiu* [Research on International Problems] No. 4 (October) pp. 24–31.

Zimbardo, Philip G., and Michael R. Leippe (1991) *The Psychology of Attitude Change and Social Influence* (New York: McGraw-Hill).

Zou Yunhua (1998) "China and the CTBT Negotiations" (draft paper, Stanford Center for International Security and Cooperation, October).

Zweig, David (2002) *Internationalizing China: Domestic Interests and Global Linkages* (Ithaca, NY: Cornell University Press).

Index

Abbott, Kenneth W., 47
Academy of Military Sciences (AMS; China), 58, 59, 61, 62
Acharya, Amitav, 160, 178
adaptation, xxiv n15, 27
Adler, Emanuel, 17n22
Aerospace Ministry (China), 57, 62
Africa Nuclear Weapons-Free Zone, 36
Alker, Hayward, 9, 10, 43
anarchy, conditions of, xiii, xvii, xix, 2–3, 5, 6; and Chinese foreign policy, 205, 211; in constructivism, 28; in contractual institutionalism, 14; mimicking in, 46; and realpolitik, 29, 30, 43, 78, 199
Antarctic Treaty, 36
appropriateness, 16, 17, 22, 42, 49, 74, 79, 151
arms control: China's participation in treaties on, 34–36, 37; Chinese experts in, 53–54; and Chinese foreign policy, 39, 53, 207; Chinese use of term, 69–70; compliance with, 71, 72; conferences on, 59, 62; and domestic bureaucracy, 48–49, 52–64, 72; domestic organizations required by, 55–58; implementation of, 71–72; international institutions for, 30, 32, 41, 133; and mimicking, 197; publications on, 63–64; research on, 56–66; role of experts in, 53–54, 56–64, 67, 71–72. *See also particular organizations*
Arms Control and Disarmament Agency (ACDA; US), 53
Arms Control and Disarmament Department (China), 55, 61, 181
Arms Control and Disarmament Program (CDSTIC; China), 57, 60, 70
ASEAN (Association of Southeast Asian Nations), xvi, xvii, 187, 194
ASEAN Regional Forum (ARF), xiv, xxvi, 41, 160–82; and China, 162, 163, 164n21, 165, 166, 167; Chinese committment to, 176–82; controversy in, 163–65; evolution of Chinese positions in, 184–91; evolution of structure of, 183–84, 195; inclusivity of, 161–62; in-

stitutional culture of, 179; intersessional meetings (ISM) of, 183–84; intersessional support groups (ISG) of, 183–84, 185, 186, 188; intrusiveness of, 192; and persuasion, 197–98; and regionalism, 160, 161, 162; security in, 160–61, 180, 190; socialization of China in, 179–80; Track II of, 164–65, 172, 179, 180, 181, 184, 185, 197–98; and US, 194
ASEAN Way, the, 160, 162n15, 165n24
Asia Pacific Coordinating Mechanism, 182n53
Asia Pacific Economic Cooperation (APEC), 149, 164n21
Asian financial crisis (1997), 135, 148n154, 194
audience: for Chinese image, 146n150; domestic Chinese, 98–99; and human rights, 144; legitimacy of, 84–85, 86, 93; optimal size of, 152; and social influence, 90–91, 92, 93, 95
Australia, 164n20, 183, 195n73
Axelrod, Robert, 22, 85n14

balancing, structural, 4, 5, 37, 46, 197; against rising power, xiii; against US power, 177, 192–93
bandwagoning, 46, 128, 129, 130, 137, 173
Bangkok Declaration, 144n145
Bar-Tal, Daniel, 156
Barsoom, Peter N., 161n13, 195–96
Beck, Paul Allen, 21, 23
Beijing Area Study (BAS), 96, 97, 200–202
Belgrade embassy bombing, 193
Berger, Peter L., 21
biological weapons, 102
Biological Weapons Convention (BWC), 36, 55
Bonchek, Mark S., 12
Bourdieu, Pierre, 50, 84
Brunei, 187
bureaucracy, Chinese domestic: ambassador for disarmament in, 54, 56, 62; and arms control, 48–49, 52–64, 72; coordi-

PRINCETON STUDIES IN
INTERNATIONAL HISTORY AND POLITICS

Lightning Source UK Ltd.
Milton Keynes UK
UKOW03f0005190913

217447UK00002B/39/P